RELIGION AND POLITICS

Religion and Politics

Islam and Muslim Civilization

Second Edition

JAN-ERIK LANE
The University of the South Pacific, Fiji

HAMADI REDISSI
University of Tunis, Tunisia

with a chapter by RIADH SIDAOUI

Routledge
Taylor & Francis Group
LONDON AND NEW YORK

First published 2009 by Ashgate Publishing

2 Park Square, Milton Park, Abingdon, Oxfordshire OX14 4RN
711 Third Avenue, New York, NY 10017

Routledge is an imprint of the Taylor & Francis Group, an informa business

First issued in paperback 2018

British Library Cataloguing in Publication Data
Lane, Jan-Erik
Religion and politics : Islam and Muslim civilization. -
2nd ed.
1. Islam and politics 2. Religion and politics - Islamic
countries 3. Islamic modernism 4. Islamic fundamentalism
5. Islamic countries - Civilization 6. Islamic countries -
Civilization - Western influences
I. Title II. Redissi, Hamadi
297.2'72

Library of Congress Cataloging-in-Publication Data
Lane, Jan-Erik.
Religion and politics : Islam and Muslim civilization / by Jan-Erik Lane and Hamadi Redissi.
p. cm.
Includes bibliographical references and index.
ISBN 978-0-7546-7418-4 -- ISBN 978-0-7546-9176-1 (ebook) 1. Civilization, Islamic. 2. Islam--History. 3. East and West. I. Redissi, Hamadi. II. Title.

DS35.62.L36 2009
909'.09767--dc22

2008048316

ISBN 13: 978-0-7546-7418-4 (hbk)
ISBN 13: 978-1-138-37651-9 (pbk)

Contents

SECTION II ISLAM AS A WORLD RELIGION

SECTION III THE MUSLIM LEGACY

List of Figures

List of Tables

Preface

The focus of our book, the outcome of close collaboration between the Calvinist University of Geneva and the Muslim modernist University of Tunis on the Muslim civilisation, is the social impact of religion, especially upon politics. Max Weber was correct in underlining the immense social consequences of religious beliefs and values, but this insight can be used to launch a new analysis of Islam, different from Weber's own perspective upon this world religion. Posing the question "Why were the European powers early modernisers whereas the Muslim countries were late modernisers?", or reformulating it as "Why did the high Islamic cultures of the medieval period experience a decline in modern times while the Western European developed in the other direction?", entails a Weberian approach. Weber emphasised the role of religion when accounting for the economic differences between the major civilisations of the world, especially the rise of modern capitalism in the Occidental sphere. Weber launched his thesis in 1904.

How are we to understand the Muslim societies today? They now face late modernisation, hesitance towards post-modernity and the emergence of Islamic fundamentalism. Our work has the purpose of presenting a new analysis of Islam, following Weber's emphasis upon the social consequences of religious beliefs. Broadening the perspective on religion to also include politics in comparison with Weber, we concentrate upon the status of human rights and the *Rule of Law*. The Muslim societies today are struggling under two seminal forces, viz. the need for economic modernisation on the one hand and the drift towards Islamic fundamentalism on the other hand. The balance between these two forces – modernity and religious purity – is struck differently in the various Muslim societies, depending upon the constellation of elite groups as well as historical legacies. However, the tension is most real across all of Arabia, not to mention other Muslim countries, such as Pakistan, Bangladesh, Afghanistan and Indonesia.

No one doubts that Islam is a religion with strong economic, social and political consequences. However, the impact of this world religion upon the Muslim societies cannot be subsumed under Islamic fundamentalism. As shown below, radical Islamism emerged in the twentieth century in the form of a new interpretation of the Koran. All through the history of Islam there have been different interpretations, from a liberal and rational approach to the Koran, as with the great Spanish philosopher Averroes, over the firm legal approach typical of the Sunni legacy, to the charismatic bend of Shiism. Actually, the various doctrines linked with the Koran constitute a most complicated web of schools, including for example the very different forms of Shia approaches such as the moderate Alids or Alawites and radical Iranian Shiism, as well as the Sufi orders.

We wish to claim that there is no fundamental opposition between Islam and modernity or post-modernity. Contrary to Islamic fundamentalism, we will argue that the Koran is reconcilable with both modernity and post-modernity. Although using the same perspective as Weber, namely religion and society, our opinion is that Weber's thesis about the link between Calvinism and rationality has limited relevance for understanding why the Muslim societies have fallen behind since the Renaissance. Weber did not clearly separate Islam as a religion (a set of beliefs and values), on the one hand, from Arab traditionalism, which was early married to Islam. If one makes a clear separation between Islam as a religion and Muslim traditionalism, then the slow process of modernisation in Arabia and elsewhere becomes more understandable.

It has been observed that there is one book missing by Weber, namely a book analysing Islam (Huff and Schluchter, 1999). Weber wrote monographs on the major world religions with the exception of Islam. In his comparative studies of religion Weber analysed Islam as a religion and the Arab tradition interchangeably, which creates the confusion that protecting or promoting Islam implies going back to medieval Arab customs. For instance, Weber writes (1978: 818–822) that the *benefice* of the Islamic *ulemas*, or that of examined aspirants for the offices of the *qadi* (judge) or *mufti* (religious juris-consultant), was often granted for only a short time, in order to facilitate its circulation among the aspirants. This amounts merely to a rational policy of preventing permanent appropriation on the part of the individual, thus not impairing the *esprit de corps*. One should make a sharp distinction between the Koran as a system of religious beliefs and values on the one hand and traditional Arab or Muslim institutions such as the *qadi*, the *mufti* or the imam. If traditionalism has hindered the modernisation of Muslim societies, including the arrival of the market economy and democracy, there is nothing in Islam as a religion that makes Muslim societies more backward than other civilisations adhering to Hinduism, Buddhism, Christianity or Judaism.

The structure of the books is as follows: First, Weber's thesis linking religion and the rise of capitalism is examined, emphasising that Weber omitted another very important link between religion and modernity, namely democracy and human rights. Second, Weber's conception of Islam as a religion is analysed by collecting the analytical pieces spread out in his various works. Third, the separation between Islam and traditions is forcefully made, with an analysis of how historical legacies hindered modernisation in the Muslim countries. Fouth, the political developments in one part of the Arab world, North Africa or the Maghreb, are scrutinised with an emphasis on the sources of political instability in the Muslim civilisation. Finally, we bring up the question of the possibility of reconciling Islam with the requirements of post-modernity.

Weber analysed a culturally and politically homogeneous sphere before the formation of the modern Muslim states. Today Islam encompasses 57 countries belonging to the Organisation of the Islamic Conference (the 22 countries of the Arab League, Iran, five Asian countries, The Maldives and Turkey, the remainder being African countries with Muslim majorities or minorities, such as Senegal,

Togo, Ivory Coast and Mozambique, and several former USSR republics). Islam comprises more than a billion people, who are found mostly in the Third World, have a tradition of 15 centuries of history and speak several major languages such as Arabic, Persian, Bengali and Turkish. There are several Islams according to history, language and culture. One may approach this variety with a search for its cultural core of religious ideas and behaviours, although one should not assume a homogeneous cultural type. In relation to Islam it is possible to speak of several specific subcultures like the Arab countries, the Ottoman legacy and the non-Arab countries.

Weber promoted the discipline of the sociology of religion by showing in numerous studies the strong economic consequences that different kinds of religious beliefs have had in various civilisations. Weber believed that the content of religion mattered very much for the behaviour of both elites and ordinary people. He substantiated his claim that religion matters with full-scale investigations of all the world religions, except Islam. Given the emergence of Islamic fundamentalism in the twentieth century, Weber's omission presents us with a lacuna in our knowledge of religions, society and politics.

Setting out to try to fill this gap in our knowledge about Islam and its consequences for society, economics and politics, we first examine the short analyses of Islam that Max Weber presented in a few key passages. Weber's position was extremely negative towards Islam, which calls for an alternative attempt to reconcile Islam with the requirements of modernity, the market economy and democracy. We sincerely believe that such reconciliation is possible, especially if one draws upon the currents of liberalism within the Arab countries. Many of the negative features of Islam that Weber focused upon stem from Arab legacies, which need not be combined with Islam as a system of beliefs. Thus, we examine these Muslim legacies and spell out their consequences for economic and political retardation.

The division of labour between the authors has seen Hamadi Redissi make an initial version of the manuscript in French, which Jan-Erik Lane has then translated into English, adding parts and pieces while creating a new synthesis. A chapter by Riadh Sidaoui was added to the volume in order to unravel the logic of Islamic fundamentalism through an analysis of the FIS in Algeria. Sidaoui holds a doctorate from the University of Tunis but works in Geneva, Switzerland. Erik Verkoyen, then at Geneva University, was highly instrumental in bringing the parts together into a final first edition. In this second edition, the entire text has been updated, corrected and expanded with three new chapters.

Jan-Erik Lane, Suva, Fiji
Hamadi Redissi, Tunis

SECTION I
The Muslim Civilisation and Modernisation

The Muslim world harbours more than a billion people adhering to the religion of Mohammed and regarding the Koran as *The Book* containing their basic guidelines in life. It consists of the Arab civilisation as well as the huge Muslim countries outside of it, for example Iran, Indonesia, Bangladesh and Pakistan. Furthermore, there is the religiously neutral state of Turkey with its Muslims, as well as the Turkic-speaking populations in the former USSR (Khanates and Caucasia), and the people of Kurdistan. Finally, it comprises sizeable Muslim populations in several African countries, such as Senegal, Mali and Guinea, including religiously divided societies like those in Nigeria, Ivory Coast and Kenya, as well as that in India, and considerable Muslim minorities in many other countries, including Western Europe, such as those in France and Germany.

The Muslim world is as large in terms of population as the Christian world, but it is far less developed. It is bigger than the Buddhist world, but again it is less developed. Whatever measures one applies concerning modernity or post-modernity, it is the case that the Muslim world scores lower than other civilisations, including indicators of affluence and human rights. It is true that the Muslim world is not only of one kind, as it comprises countries that are super-rich as well as countries with a quasi-democratic regime. However, the general trend is that the Muslim world underperforms on modernity or post-modernity. Why is this so?

We may formulate our general question in several ways: is there an irreconcilable conflict between Islam and rationality or can the Muslim societies accommodate the ideals of post-modernity? Developments in and around the Muslim civilisation are very much at the centre of the world's attention after the events of 11 September 2001, 11 March 2004 and 7 July 2005. The emergence of global Islamic terrorism is the most spectacular indication of the challenges that post-modernity and globalisation pose to Muslim societies. How these challenges will be met will have a decisive impact upon world politics. Muslims' responses to post-modernity and globalisation depend critically upon how they reconcile religion and rationality. In the field economics, the concept of Islamic finance has been offered as a solution, but in the field of politics things appear to be more problematic, as it is argued that Muslim societies need a strong or even authoritarian government to control extremist groups.

Chapter 1

Modernity, Post-modernity and the Muslim World

Introduction

The question about religion and modernisation may be designated "Weberian", because Max Weber developed a most coherent approach to the analysis of modernity, focusing on the religious element in the major civilisations of humanity. Around 1900 he started to write about the economic consequences of religion, which theme by the end of his life in 1920 had grown into his general sociology of religion (Weber, 1993). Weber dealt only with one aspect of modernity, namely economic development or affluence. Today the majority of Muslim societies are still underperforming on economic modernisation, although the institutions of the market economy have arrived in the Muslim world. Table 1.1 indicates a negative correlation between affluence and the size of the Muslim population.

Table 1.1 Gross Domestic Product and the Relative Size of the Muslim Population 1970–2000

Correlations		MUSLIM 1970	MUSLIM 1980	MUSLIM 1995	MUSLIM 2000
GDPCPP80	Pearson Correlation	–.142	–.146	–.166	–.185
	Sig. (2-tailed)	.155	.147	.092	.061
	N	102	100	104	103
GDPCPP85	Pearson Correlation	–.217	–.219	–.241	–.247
	Sig. (2-tailed)	.024	.025	.011	.010
	N	107	105	110	109
GDPCPP90	Pearson Correlation	–.265	–.261	–.290	–.285
	Sig. (2-tailed)	.004	.005	.001	.001
	N	117	114	129	128
GDPCPP98	Pearson Correlation	–.269	–.263	–.277	–.272
	Sig. (2-tailed)	.003	.004	.001	.001
	N	122	117	137	136

When examining a large set of countries of the world, whatever measure on affluence is employed, we find that Muslim countries tend to score lower than non-Muslim ones. Moreover, Figure 1.1 shows that most Muslim countries had a low level of affluence in 1980, with a few outstanding exceptions, such as the Arab *rentier* states.

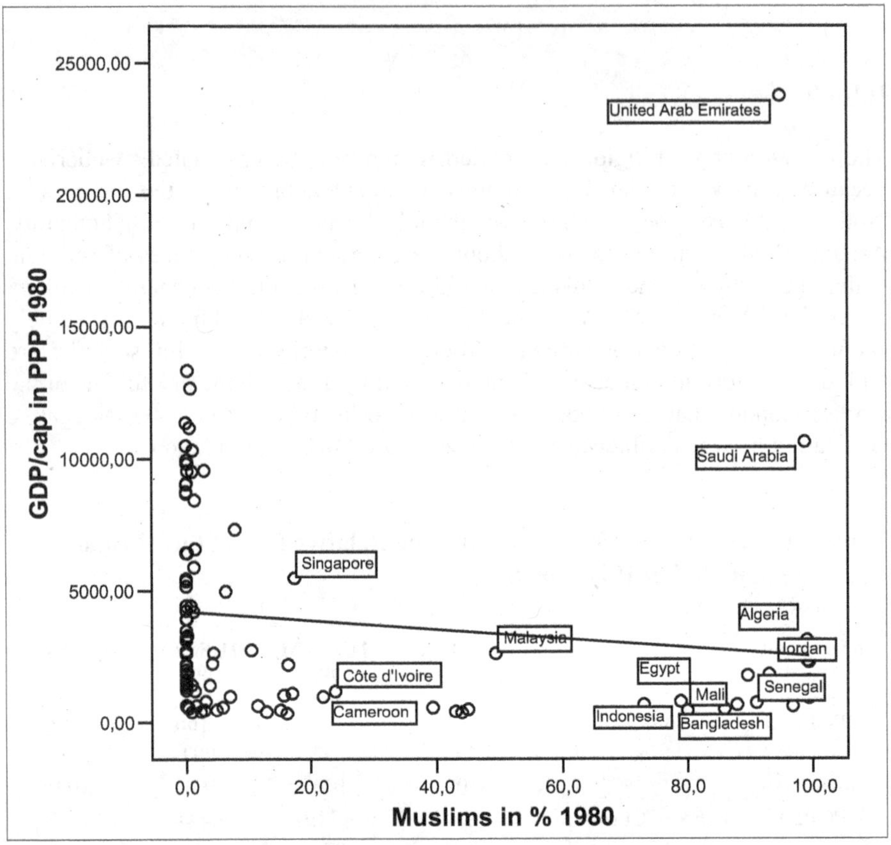

Figure 1.1 Size of Muslim Population and Affluence in 1980

Figure 1.2 shows the interaction between Muslim societies and affluence around 2000. It confirms that the Muslim countries also remained economically backward close to 2000, but there were notable exceptions, such as the UAE, Saudi Arabia and Malaysia. One may also note that very affluent Singapore has an important Muslim minority. Thus, the Weber perspective – religion and affluence – remains relevant today, but it must be broadened to include human rights and democracy. One may wish to enquire into why the Muslim world has great difficulties in accommodating the imperatives of post-modernity, such as individualism, human rights and democracy, and not merely examine the Weber focus, i.e. affluence.

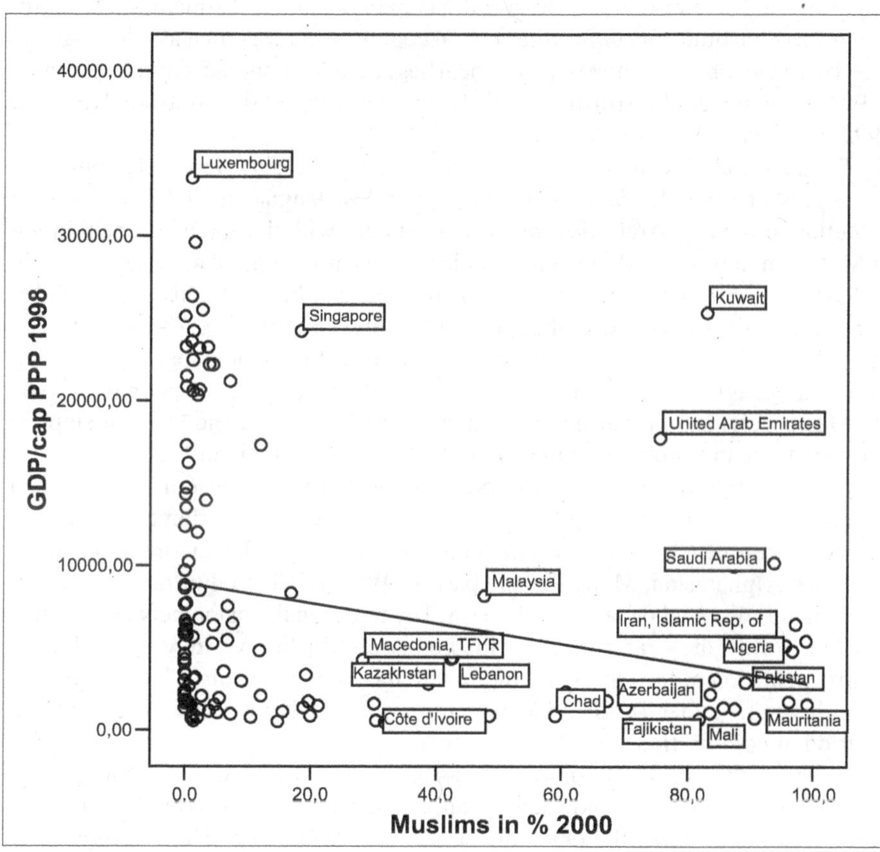

Figure 1.2 Size of Muslim Population and Affluence in 2000

The Two Muslim Worlds

The Muslim civilisation may be divided into two worlds: the Arab world and the non-Arab Muslim world. This distinction is not merely based upon the historical emergence of the Muslim civilisation over time, but it retains its relevance today in view of the ethnic composition of the Muslim population. The Arab world consists of more than 300 million people speaking Arabic and adhering to the Arab culture. It stretches from Morocco in the west to Iraq in the east. Many of its members today live in Western Europe, but there are also Arab minorities in African countries like Sudan, Somalia and Mauritania. The Arab world is the origin of the Muslim civilisation and it has maintained its distinctness within it. The Arabs constitute an *ethnie* with several common features such as one language (the language of the Koran), a historical legacy and a shared culture (Ahmed, 1998; Anderson, 2000; Armstrong, 2001a; Gardet, 1967/2002; Gibb and Kramers, 1995; Lippman, 1982).

The non-Arab Muslim world is larger than the Arab world in terms of population. It consists of several *ethnies* with different pasts, languages and cultures. The evolution of the non-Arab Muslim world coincides with the spread of the religion of Mohammed from the Arab peninsula in various directions. Thus, Iran was early included in the Muslim world, when many Persians became active in Baghdad as the centre of the second of the great caliphates, the Abbasids (750–1258). The Mongol and Turkic (the word is borrowed from a linguistic subgroup covering similar languages from Turkish in the west to Uigur in the east) peoples entered the Muslim civilisation during the medieval period, creating the Mongol empires and the Ottoman Empire with the conquest of Constantinople in 1453.

Although the Muslims (the Moors) were ejected from Western Europe when Granada fell in 1492, the Muslim world during the high medieval period had started a deep penetration into Asia along several routes. Islam strengthened its grip upon Afghanistan, Mongolia and parts of Western China. Furthermore, Islam penetrated India, Malaysia and Indonesia. The traditional tension between the two Muslim worlds, the Arab world and the non-Arab Muslim world, was heightened by the expansion of the Ottoman Empire into the Arab peninsula. Thus, large parts of Arabia came under Turkish rule, which from the Arab point of view constituted a period of colonisation.

Actually, the period of colonialism affected the Muslim world tremendously. The Arab countries were colonised not only by the Turks but also by the European powers, not least when the Ottoman Empire was broken up. Thus, several Arab countries came under European domination. The non-Arab Muslim world was equally affected by colonialism. Mogul India and Malaysia came under British rule, whereas the Dutch governed Indonesia. Moreover, Russia penetrated deep into the Khanates and encountered the British in Afghanistan.

Almost all of the modern Muslim states were created in opposition to Occidental colonialism. Thus, only a few Muslim countries, such as Turkey, Saudi Arabia, Iran and Afghanistan, were never colonised by European powers. Many

Muslim countries had to fight wars of liberation before an independent state could replace various forms of colonial rule. In both the Arab and the non-Arab Muslim world political independence and the erection of a modern state proved highly controversial, resulting in massive political violence where foreign powers were often involved one way or another. The Palestinian issue has remained totally unsettled for decades, as is also now the situation regarding Iraq. In both cases the United States of America is heavily involved. Algeria and Sudan have suffered badly from recent civil wars and Morocco has to face the problem of Polisario in Western Sahara.

The Arab world today consists of a number of independent states that collaborate in the loosely organised League of Arab States, comprising Algeria, Bahrain, Comoros, Djibouti, Egypt, Iraq, Jordan, Kuwait, Lebanon, Libya, Mauritania, Morocco, Oman, Palestine, Qatar, Saudi Arabia, Somalia, Sudan, Syria, Tunisia, United Arab Emirates and Yemen. The Egyptian government proposed the Arab League in 1945 and its charter created a regional organisation of sovereign states that is neither a union nor a federation. The Arab League attempts to promote the interests of member states. It has served as a forum for member states to coordinate their policy positions and deliberate on matters of common concern, settling some Arab disputes and limiting conflicts such as the Lebanese and Palestinian civil wars. The Arab League has promoted economic integration among member states, such as the creation of the Joint Arab Economic Action Charter. It has played a role in preserving the Arab cultural heritage by launching literacy campaigns, reproducing intellectual works and translating modern technical terminology. The Arab League has also fostered cultural exchanges between member states, encouraged youth and sports programmes, helped to advance the role of women in Arab societies and promoted child welfare activities (Mansour, 1992).

In the non-Arab Muslim world, nation-states have been put in place on the basis of different *ethnies*. Iran managed to maintain its independence, but its oil attracted much Western attention and interference until a Shiite regime was established in the wake of the fall of the Shah. After the demise of imperial rule in India, two giant Muslim countries eventually emerged, although it is worth emphasising that India still has a huge Muslim minority. Pakistan (1947), Bangladesh (1971), Malaysia (1957) and Indonesia (1949) became independent after the Second World War. In Saharan Africa we find several Muslim countries, or countries where a majority or large minority of the population is Muslim, e.g. Burkina Faso, Cameroon, Chad and Niger.

To sum up, the Muslim civilisation may be decomposed into the smaller Arab world and the larger non-Arab world. Typical of both is retardation of post-modernity. The Muslim civilisation as a whole is less developed than the other civilisations of the globe, whatever measure one employs: affluence, human rights, gender equality or social development. It is true that the Arab world comprises a few extremely rich countries – the Gulf states. However, their advancement is based upon their being so-called *rentier* states, where governments extract an immense economic rent from selling oil or gas abroad. It is generally true that the

Muslim civilisation is less developed economically and politically than the Western or Buddhist civilisations. Let us look again at the evidence. Table 1.2 shows the correlations between the size of the Muslim population and human rights.

Table 1.2 Correlations between Muslim Population and Human Rights 1981–2000

		Human rights 1981–1985	Human rights 1995–2001
MUSL70	Pearson Correlation	–.374	–.528
	Sig. (2-tailed)	.000	.000
	N	129	135
MUSL80	Pearson Correlation	–.358	–.527
	Sig. (2-tailed)	.000	.000
	N	128	129
MUSL95	Pearson Correlation	–.371	–.550
	Sig. (2-tailed)	.000	.000
	N	130	150
MUSL2000	Pearson Correlation	–.371	–.554
	Sig. (2-tailed)	.000	.000
	N	129	149

As a matter of fact, the correlation between the lack of enforcement of human rights and the size of the Muslim population is even more pronounced than is true of affluence. This basic fact puts immense pressure upon the Muslim civilisation to accommodate post-modernity.

Figure 1.3 shows that no Muslim country scored high on democracy in the 1980s, with only a few countries scoring medium, such as Malaysia, Lebanon, Bangladesh and Senegal. Many Muslim countries are not politically stable and are far from being consolidated democracies.

Figure 1.4 confirms that most Muslim countries score medium or low on human rights today, the only exceptions being Mali and Bangladesh. In fact, there is no country with a sizeable Muslim population that is a highly stable democracy, with the exception of India with its huge Muslim minority.

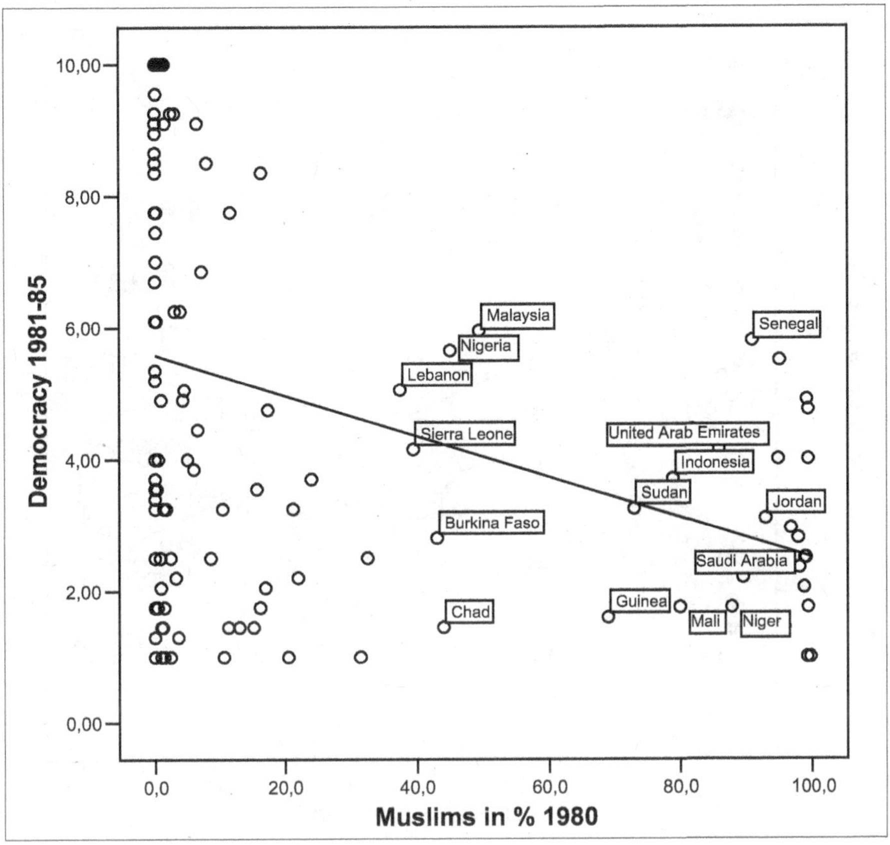

Figure 1.3 Democracy in the Muslim World 1981–1985

Many factors have played a role in Muslim retardation, some of which are peculiar to the Arab world while others are more relevant for the non-Arab world. In this book we focus upon the role of the common elements in the Muslim civilisation, whether Arab or non-Arab. For example, Fish has used six variables to explain authoritarian rule in the Islamic civilisation: Islamic tradition, economic development, sociocultural division, economic performance, British colonialism and communist heritage (Fish, 2002, 4–37). Our enquiry is broader: is Islam the major cause of the confrontation between tradition and post-modernity that is so characteristic of Muslim societies today? This way of framing the question is distinctly Weberian.

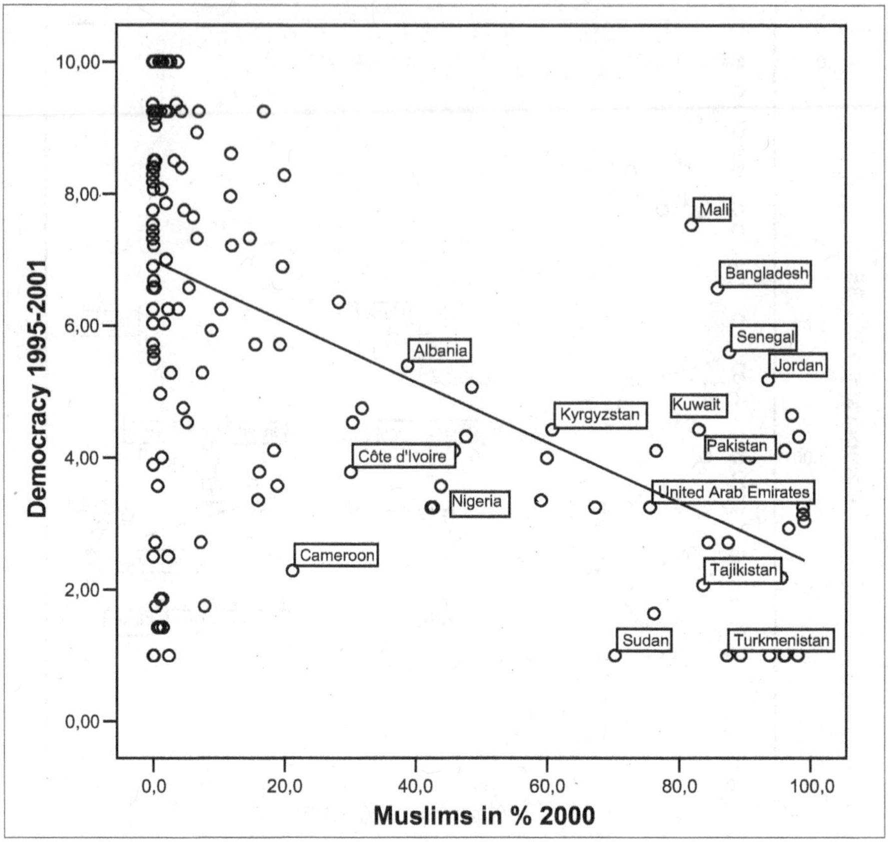

Figure 1.4 Democracy in the Muslim World 1995–2001

Turbulence in the Muslim Civilisation

Today, several Muslim societies are in uproar (Roy, 2004; Kepel, 2004). Where these societies border countries adhering to other civilisations we often find violent confrontations. Why can Muslim societies not settle down and embark upon a slow but steady advancement? These internal and external convulsions occur in several parts of the Muslim civilisation, in the Arab and non-Arab parts. Muslim societies do not have modern advanced economies. Muslim governments do not implement human rights, and Muslim countries do not support the struggle of women for gender equality. On the contrary, Muslim societies tend to be plagued by extensive poverty, by dictatorship and by sharp gender inequalities. Judged by the standards of modernity and post-modernity, Arab societies are less developed than, for instance, many Christian or Buddhist societies (Pryce-Jones, 2002).

In recent years this backwardness has been further underlined by the policy of Islamisation, the most typical feature of which is the reintroduction of Muslim law into the legal orders of Muslim countries. Sharia law is the core of Muslim law and its position in the legal order of the country is an indicator of development. In the most backward Muslim societies Sharia law is the constitution of the state. In other countries Sharia law is applied only in civil law cases. Finally, there are a few Muslim countries where Sharia law has been replaced by modern law, such as Tunisia and Turkey. A few countries that had diminished the role of Sharia law in their efforts towards development and secularisation have recently reintroduced elements of Sharia law or reinforced its position in the entire legal system of the country (Mohammadi and Ahsan, 2002).

Internally, several Muslim countries operate on the edge of anarchy, as political violence results in numerous deaths every year. A few have suffered from civil war over a long period of time, for example Sudan, Algeria and Afghanistan. Others, such as Lebanon and Iraq, have been torn by short but bloody civil wars. Countries like Egypt and Indonesia have also experienced political violence. In border areas, where Moslems live in countries with another civilisation, political violence occurs, for example Kashmir, southern Thailand, Mindanao, Xinjiang and Chechnya.

Regime instability is characteristic of several Muslim countries. In the Arab world traditional authority has a position not experienced in any other civilisation. Thus, several Arab countries are real kingdoms or emirates. Oman has a sultan, as has Brunei in the non-Arab Muslim world. The royal families in Saudi Arabia, Jordan, Morocco, Bahrain, Qatar and the United Arab Emirates are hardly secure and feel the need to strengthen their legitimacy by referring to religion. In the republican Muslim countries, constitutional stability is rare, for example Pakistan is politically as well as constitutionally unstable with numerous coups and deaths from political violence. After independence, all the Muslim republics have changed regime, sometimes several times, like Iraq and Algeria. Two countries that were never colonised, Iran and Afghanistan, have been characterised by much regime instability. Afghanistan remains tribal even today and Iran has opted for an authoritarian religious regime. Among the secular republics in the Muslim world, presidential or parliamentary regimes prevail. It is only Libya that has a constitution with elements from the Soviet model.

Authoritarianism appears in almost all of the Muslim republics, although to varying degrees depending upon the country and the time period. Several of them display a soft form of authoritarianism, such as Tunisia and Egypt. Lebanon, Bangladesh and Malaysia are closer to democracy, whereas Syria and Algeria must be classified as dictatorships. Why do Muslim countries score low on one of the key aspects of modernity and post-modernity – the implementation of civil and political rights?

Given the lack of democracy in the Muslim world, the internal instability characteristic of the Muslim states is not difficult to account for. Why would many citizens and inhabitants in Muslim societies not yearn for human rights in general and political rights in particular? Yet, there are other sources of instability in Muslim societies besides the general lack of rule of law. Where there is religious fragmentation and the Muslim community is large, then political instability is highly likely. The same holds when the country has two large communities of Moslems, Sunnis and Shias. Where Islam collides with other religions, political instability prevails, as for example along the borders of Russia and in the Khanates (derived from Genghis Khan), the seven nations that emerged from the former USSR and referred to as "Central Asia".

A large Muslim population lives in India, where religious confrontations between Muslims, Hindus and Christians occur despite the formal confessional neutrality of the Indian State. Tensions have increased recently, partly because of the rise of Hindu nationalism, provoked perhaps in turn by the appearance of Islamic activism. In many religiously divided societies the split between the Muslim community and other communities results in political violence (Hourani, 1995; Qureishi, 1962; Ro'I, 1995; Van Schendel and Zurcher, 2000; McAmis, 2002; Raymer, 2001; Spencer, 2002). One recent example is the Ivory Coast, which has been split into two parts, the southern Christian part and the northern Muslim part. Nigeria is also politically unstable because of a similar regional tension between the north and the south that resulted in the civil war around Biafra in the late 1960s and early 1970s. In addition, Sudan has been torn apart by the same kind of split.

Appendices 1.1 and 1.2 present an overview of the religious fragmentation of Muslim majorities or minorities in today's nations. They show the expansion of Islam, as relative numbers increased between 1900 and 1995 in many countries, especially in Africa. In China there are two provinces with large Muslim populations, Xinjiang and Ningxia, although they are not numerous on the scale of the Chinese population.

There is yet another source of instability in Muslim societies, namely the tensions among different Islamic groups. Historically, there have been three major groups, the Sunnis, the Shiites and the Karijites, although these groups display several subgroups or sects, especially among the followers of Ali, the Alawites. The split between Sunnis and Shiites is today mainly focused upon the politics of Iran and its relation to other Muslim countries such as Iraq with its Shiite majority, mainly living in the south. India has a sizeable Shiite minority.

Externally, where Muslim countries encounter other civilisations there is often tension and armed conflict. Palestine and Kashmir are perhaps the most spectacular examples of military confrontation between Muslims and non-Muslims. The same tension occurred in the Balkans (Norris, 1993). It also occurs along the southern borders of Russia and in southeast Asia, where Christian East Timor liberated itself from Muslim Indonesia and the Philippines have been affected by a Muslim rebellion on the islands of Mindanao. The Khanates, e.g. Turkmenistan, Kyrgyzstan, Kazakhstan, Tajikistan and Uzbekistan, lie in the zone between the Muslim civilisation and other civilisations. Their populations are mixed both ethnically and religiously. Not only do these countries suffer from internal instability, but they are also in the firing zone between civilisations. The emergence of Islamic fundamentalism has aggravated their situation.

The turbulence, internal and external, surrounding the religion of Mohammed became particularly acute around 1998 with the birth of Islamic terrorism on a global scale in the shape of the al-Qaeda network. Most of the world religions contain fundamentalist movements, but what is unusual about Islamic fundamentalism is that it is a relatively late phenomenon and that it received such strong support in the twentieth century. Islamic fundamentalism presents a major challenge to Muslim societies and states and it fuels conflict with other civilisations. Internally, it has been a major source of political violence, for instance in Algeria and upper Egypt. Externally, it has led to armed conflict between states, for instance the destruction of the Taliban state by the United States and the ongoing terrorism in Iraq. What needs to be emphasised here is that Islamic fundamentalism pushes Muslim civilisation away from the mainstream development in the other civilisations that we subsume under the labels of modernity and post-modernity.

The modernisation of society – changing the social structure from agrarian towards industrial or post-industrial – requires an intellectual atmosphere that is receptive to human rights, research, technology and academic values. All kinds of fundamentalism are at odds with such an atmosphere. If Islamic fundamentalism prevails in Muslim civilisation, then its retardation will only become more pronounced. Although it is difficult to give a concise definition of modernity and post-modernity, these concepts refer to the triumph of science, pure and applied, that is, the search for unbiased knowledge and its application in technology with the consequent immense ramifications for the economy. Can, then, Islam accommodate post-modernity?

Modernity and Post-modernity

It could be said that modernity got its breakthrough with the Great French Revolution and its focus upon liberty, equality and brotherhood among peoples. The values of the French Revolution can be pursued in very different activities and contexts, from the market economy to democracy. When modernity replaced tradition, societies were transformed from agrarian to industrial. The post-modern society is a continuous development along the same path. Weber equated modernity with rationality and found it in both bureaucracy and modern capitalism. The French Revolution ended the legitimacy of traditional rule and put in place the Enlightenment Project that still goes on, increasing the role of science and technology in all kinds of human affairs and inviting all people to share in the fruits of progress on the basis of equality between man and woman.

Characteristic of post-modernity is the emphasis upon affluence, human rights and gender equality. Modernity replaced the traditional society with a society based upon individualism, contract and calculation. Urbanisation and industrialisation created wealth and a class structure conducive to democracy. The post-modern society puts the service sector in the centre of the economy and makes information transmitted globally the essential link. The philosophy of the post-modern society adds a strong dose of scepticism to the modern condition at the same time as it reinforces individualism.

Modernity and post-modernity have spread around the globe and can be found in all countries, although to varying degrees. What is striking is the retarding effect of the Muslim civilisation on the chief expressions of modernity and post-modernity. In both the Arab and the non-Arab Muslim worlds, liberty and equality are not strongly institutionalised. The same is true of rationality and individualism. Why is this? The modernisation of society and culture has been an asset to the Western and Buddhist civilisations, but it constitutes a threat to many in the Muslim civilisation. The adherents of Muslim values sometimes argue that modernisation is a Western phenomenon, meaning it should be rejected *ipso facto*. This constitutes a serious mistake.

The Western domination over the Muslim civilisation has taken other forms, which must be pointed out here. It is stunning that Weber, in his comparative analysis of civilisations, had nothing to say about the effects of Western colonialism. Weber was certainly right in claiming that modernisation was initiated in the Western civilisation and it gave it an undeniable advantage in its interactions with other civilisations, such as the Arab world, the Moguls and Imperial China, as well as the South American Indian civilisations of the Aztecs and the Incas. Understanding what started modernisation in Western Europe was the research project of Weber. However, he failed to enquire into the consequences of Western supremacy for the other civilisations. For instance, the Arab world has still today not understood what caused its civilisation to lose its edge and start a seminal process of degeneration. In the medieval period, the Muslim civilisation was second to none, with Muslim historians speaking of it as the Golden Age.

The Western Grip

Ever since the fall of Granada in 1492, the Muslim civilisation has been under pressure from Western powers. It is true that the Turkish threat against Europe was a real one for almost two centuries, but Ottoman expansion was turned around in the face of continuous Western advances, including those of the Russians against the Ottoman Empire and in Asia. Many Muslim scholars speak of the New Period as the beginning of a long period of Muslim decline or even decadence (Spuler, 1994a, 1994b; Kissling, 1996).

After the First World War, at the height of Western imperialism, the Western grip on Muslim civilisation formed. France dominated the Maghreb, while the British exercised firm control over Egypt and the Fertile Crescent. The dissolution of the Ottoman Empire made new Western inroads possible. Thus, the entire Middle East came under Western influence, which still remains today, albeit in a different from. Muslim rule in Mogul India was overthrown by the British in 1857. When the British left South Asia in 1947, two independent States emerged, one of which was Muslim, later to split itself into Pakistan and the independent Bangladesh, formerly "East Pakistan". The tension between India and Pakistan opened up an opportunity for Western powers, mainly the Russians and the Americans, to play a role. Western presence in southeast Asia is far smaller than in the Middle East, although Singapore, as a rich enclave between giant Muslim countries, has links with both the UK and the United States. Australia is another Western power with interests in southeast Asia, and it intervened in favour of East Timor against Indonesia when the East Timorians were struggling for their independence.

It is thus mainly the Arab world that still remains in the Western grip, at least to some extent. Much has been written about the cultural domination of the West in relation to the Arab world – so-called *orientalism* (Said, 1979). However, here we emphasise the power relations between Western civilisations and the Muslim world. As a matter of fact, it suffices to analyse the immense consequences of Western imperialism in relation to the Muslim worlds, especially the Arab world, to understand the suspicion of many Muslims against so-called Western values. The Western grip upon the Muslim civilisation is still a real one, albeit it is far less extensive than during the twentieth century. Yet, the road ahead for the Muslim civilisation cannot be to deny modernisation. The Buddhist civilisation, covering all the different mixtures of Buddhism with Confucianism, Taoism and Shintoism, did overcome the Western advantage through forced modernisation and some very rapid catch-up processes.

Islamic Fundamentalism

After the events of "9/11", some asked what had gone wrong (Lewis, 2002b). Fundamentalism within the Islamic civilisation, which led to the destruction of the twin towers of the World Trade Center in New York and the loss of many lives, is driven by a new form of religious zeal. It links up with the notion of *jihad*, but pursues this classical idea in Islam on a global scale, where the fight against the domestic tyrant (*taghut*) is replaced by the confrontation with the "world enemy number one", the United States. The events of 9/11 not only constituted a challenge to the United States, whatever the long-run outcomes of the Iraq invasion and the Afghan war may be, but also call for a profound analysis of the place of violence within Islam and the future of the Muslim societies. Let us recall some basic facts about Islamic fundamentalism before we discuss Arab terrorism. The key articles in the development of Islamic fundamentalism are collected in Moaddel and Talattof (eds) (2000).

A search for the roots of Islamic fundamentalism originates in the nineteenth century, starting from the official version of Islam in the Ottoman Empire, Islam being practised in a literary, quiet and aristocratic manner. The first kind of Islamic fundamentalism was an intellectual movement, which called for a return to an idealised Islam but at the same time felt that this new Islam should be purified of its taints from a rigid past. The renewal of Islam would make the Arab countries capable of facing the challenge from the West (Holt, 1958; Lelyveld, 1978; Rizvi, 1982; Metcalf, 1982).

The position taken within the first fundamentalist drive was more reformist (*islah*) in tone, which rejected both blind adherence to the ancients (*salafs*) and servile imitation of the Occident (*taqlid*) (Hourani, 1983: Chapters 3–5; Peters, 1980: 132–145). This first wave of Islamic fundamentalism – the *Nahdha* or renaissance – was carried forward by several currents, all sharing the quest for originality, as with the lay Protestants in Syria and Lebanon (Fontaine, 1996) as well as religious fundamentalists in Egypt. The key question in the search for Islamic and Arab origins was the classical one, put forward in a succinct manner by the emir Shakib Arlan in 1930: "Why are the Arabs underdeveloped whereas the others develop?" (Abu-Rabi', 1996).

In the second kind of Islamic fundamentalism a reinterpretation of tradition transforms *jihad* (Jansen, 1986; Peters, 1996; Ahmed, 1991) from a collective duty into a personal one as a kind of concrete obligation. It used to be the case that there were five individual duties that weighed on each Muslim, the so-called five pillars of faith, but *jihad* as an obligation rested with the entire community of Muslims. This collective duty would be taken care of by a small group of professionals or volunteers while the rest of the community was free from this duty. The social strata that supported this second fundamentalism were for the most part young people in the cities (Ph.D. + beard). They could amass sufficient numbers to present themselves as a challenge to authoritarian regimes.

One may speak of a third kind of fundamentalism, where the focus upon *jihad* is combined with terrorism, or when radicalism is married to criminal or military activity. This third form of fundamentalism belongs to a network of people devoted to the Holy War operating in various countries, often secretly. Among the personalities connected with al-Qaeda one finds at the side of Bin Laden first Aymen al-Zawahiri, who was involved in the killing of Sadat in 1981, and second Suleiman Abu al-Ghaith, who used to be employed by the government of Kuwait as a priest preaching in a mosque. When making the statement to al-Jazira on 13 October 2001, the cassette conveying the message of al-Qaeda contained the phrase: "*Jihad* has become a duty or personal obligation" (*fardh 'ayn*).

Radical Islamic fundamentalism of the third kind has excellent relations with certain Muslim countries such as Palestine and Saudi Arabia and, contrary to the first kind of Islamic fundamentalism, namely reformism, it is not always hunted by the secret police or rejected by society. Radical Islamism does not support itself by means of the private resources of dethroned princes, as was the case for Islamic reformism, nor does it live from collecting money in the street. Instead, new Islamic fundamentalists receive substantial economic support as a windfall gain. They live, in other words, from subventions given to charitable organisations by the Gulf monarchies, which somehow end up with fundamentalist organisations.

Islamic terrorism also benefits from the international economy by employing the various means – legal or otherwise – through which capital can earn income and at the same time avoid control. Bin Laden as the key person in the network(s) has somehow linked various groups together: financial Islam, official Islam, diplomatic Islam, secret Islam and of course radical Islam. Bin Laden comes from a very rich commercial family, is related to one of the wealthiest bankers in Saudi Arabia and is linked with the royal prince Turki al-faycal, who was fired as the head of the secret police a few days before 9/11. He came under the influence of salafism and created al-Qaeda in 1987, during the period in which he fought the Red Army in Afghanistan with the blessing of the Americans (Abrahamovici, 2002: 10–11).

Bin Laden brought many things to Islamic terrorism, such as aristocratic descent, diplomatic ties, the experience of secret information, as well as massive bank guarantees, which have transformed this type of fundamentalism so that it is no longer a movement of the disinherited, the wretched of the earth – the *mustazifin* searching for glory. The network of Islamic terrorists has become an almost global one, as its participants are recruited in a heterogeneous manner. Thus, the terrorists of 9/11 were of different nationalities (although the majority of them were Saudi Arabians or Egyptians) and had various social backgrounds (*Le Courrier International*, 2001: 11–17/10). Islamic terrorists are the new international militia who have transcended both their nationality and the Arab context and found a new home in al-Qaeda. From now on this militia of *Mujahidins* live outside the confines of Humanity, including the House of Reconciliation (*dar solh*) where many Muslims forced to leave their country find a place of comfort in order to express their faith. These warriors abandon the rude appearance of beard and *jellaba* and turn to useful studies in the sciences (aviation, biotechnology). Yet their primary goal is to reach Paradise, as combat supposedly renders eternal life.

Understanding Arab Modernity and Post-modernity

Understanding modernity in the Arab civilisation requires an effort to analyse the roads along which Islamic rationality has orientated itself. The rationalisation of the Occident has proceeded in determined spheres with a special direction involving a methodical conduct of life that incarnates the representations of life within institutions, possessing certain autonomy structurally and functionally. It is this institutional incarnation in the structure of consciousness which "differentiates Weber from the functional theories of modernisation" (Habermas, 1987: vol. 1, 231; 1988: 3). In order to compare historically the processes of modernisation of societies, one must examine empirically which spheres were rationalised, according to what internal or external factors, as well as determining the directions the processes of rationalisation took and the driving forces (Zubaida, 1989: 129–130).

Arab modernisation has accommodated modern capitalism. This could be done without difficulty to the extent that medieval Islam encouraged private appropriation (*kasb*) and the colonisation of the land, which it subsumed under "settlement of land" (*imarat al-ardh*) or countries (*imarat al buldan*). Even usury interest rates (*riba*), which the puritan Islamic ethics forbid, were redirected without bad consequences by the wisdom of legal reason, which multiplied the fictions in order to validate its use within commercial transactions. From the moment that no ethical mortgage weighed upon the capitalisation of the economy, the Arabs could rapidly experience all the good things that they could enjoy from the adoption of modern tools of economic management. Khayr Eddin (1822–1889), Prime Minister of Tunisia (1873–1877), praised the freedom of trade, finance and industry, stating for instance:

> It is this spirit or freedom to initiate activity which in Europe has multiplied all kinds of societies – civil, commercial, financial, industrial, maritime and agricultural. It has also created admirable scientific institutions and institutions of charity as well as the most beautiful establishments of modern industry. Finally it contributed to the exploitation of mines and sandpits, and creation of canals, railroads and the banks, as well as many other enterprises that would not have existed without it. (Khayr Eddin, 1987: 152)

Ahmed Faris Shidyaq (1804–1887), a Syrian intellectual, underlined that work constituted a vocation within Europe which honoured the craft in itself, as "there existed no other source of joy than work". A science without work is "like a tree without fruit and like a river without water" (Shidyaq, 1995: 38–39). Muhammed Ali (1769–1849), the reformer and leader of Egypt, said "activity, the affection for work, the devotion to the national interest, discipline, punctuality – these conditions I favour in order to accomplish our task" (quoted in Fahmy, 1954: 19). The Arabs put themselves to work, as the birth of economic institutions testifies in the nineteenth century. Yet the emergence of capitalism in the Arab countries had to face a number of obstacles that left it exhausted. European penetration had devastating effects upon endogenous modernisation. It destroyed domestic links, wiped out the craft corporations and suffocated the emerging native industries, with the merchants in the *bazar* resisting the influx of foreign goods. Many Arabs believed that one could modernise quickly by imitating the Europeans, especially the tools of their power, namely the army. However, when putting the emphasis upon the role of the mobilising state, the revolutionary governments in the post-independence period discouraged the enterprise spirit and favoured a system of clientilistic social assistance. State involvement, ownership as well as regulation, in the economy has been strong in all Muslim countries. In the monarchies around the Gulf, the economy is based upon the rent from petro-dollars and sponsorship (*kafala*). The economic rent assures nationals of gratis access to various goods and services while the sponsorship allows them to be rightful owners in relation to immigrants, who cannot enter, stay or work without the legal acceptance of the nationals who pay their salaries (Herb, 1999).

The Arab state, as the core of the rational apparatus for the regulation of social modernisation, has adopted certain modalities of formal rationality (Luciano, 1990a). The state upholds the monopoly on material sanctions without having the democratic legitimacy guaranteed by legality. When it decides on taxation, it does so by means of non-negotiated laws. The *rentier* states need no taxation, and thus they offer little in terms of representative institutions. The Arab states have introduced formal bureaucracies, organised in hierarchical order and confronting the population without any form of redress. If there is redress, then the process of complaint and accountability is badly equipped when there is a conflict concerning the rules. Most Arab countries have adopted the primary role of science in society as well as the principle that knowledge offers the mastery of nature. Universities and academies of many kinds were developed from the nineteenth century and continue to be developed at a sustained rate. The contents of the teaching were modernised through the introduction of the learned disciplines, especially the "hard" sciences, with groups of specialised scholars who are relatively autonomous in their function.

However, the rationalisation of culture has been disturbed. First, the propagation of the scientific spirit has been opposed to a certain reading of the Koran that snatches away from it the dignity of science and as a consequence hinders the scientific order from becoming autonomous according to its rules and proper logic. Second, the cultural order is confronted by the theocentric image of the world of traditional culture. Finally, the double movement towards a politicisation of Islam and an Islamisation of politics is translated into the establishment of a state that rationalises religious obedience by inscribing religion into documents of law while at the same time constituting an Islamic theodice. These developments have hindered Arab post-modernity, or the emergence of a modern society with a focus upon the values of liberty, citizenship and the realisation of simple and negotiated objectives.

Conclusion

One may perhaps claim that Muslim civilisation is more active than the other civilisations of the world. It is characterised by high dynamism, both internally and externally. Why all these tremors? They result in immense tensions, both inside and outside Muslim societies. The events of 9/11, shaking the hegemony of the United States, were only the most spectacular expressions of this turbulence within Muslim civilisation.

The tensions and tremors within Muslim civilisation should be seen as reflecting the struggle around post-modernity in today's Muslim world. The Muslim countries tend to score low upon the two main features of modernity: economic affluence and human rights. Figure 1.5 displays the interaction between the two key aspects of all post-modern societies, affluence and democracy, among the countries of the world.

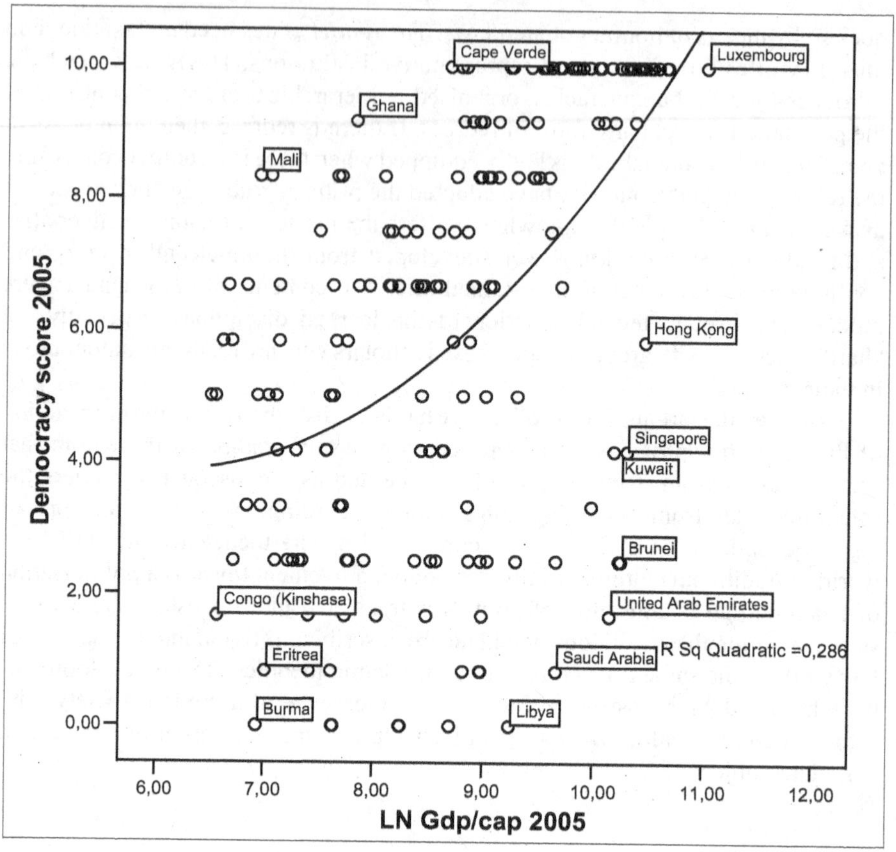

Figure 1.5 Affluence and Human Rights

Muslim civilisation tends to score low on both these dimensions of modernity. When a Muslim country is affluent, then it is still not democratic (see the Gulf States in Figure 1.5). Why is this? First, we have the *internal* explanation: Muslim civilisation has profound difficulty in accommodating to the requirements of modernity and post-modernity. Its core belief system – Islam – refuses to give in to the rationality of modernisation, causing Muslim societies to become retarded. The frustration of lagging behind is the engine behind the turmoil in the Muslim worlds. Second, we have the *external* explanation: Muslim civilisation has never really come to grips with the onslaught of Western colonialism, pushing the early advances of the Muslim conquests back. Although the Muslim states are now independent, they remain under Western pressure, especially in the Middle East. The tremors in the Muslim world are induced from outside through the constant intervention in Muslim affairs by Western powers. This Western interference in its turn fuels salafism, i.e. fundamentalist movements – the internal explanation.

In this book, we will examine the condition of post-modernity in Muslim civilisation. In our view, there is nothing inherently anti-modern in the religion of Mohammed. However, the path of development of Muslim societies has been dominated by tradition to such an extent that one is led to believe wrongly that Islam cannot be practised in a post-modern society.

Chapter 2
Islam and Post-modernity

Introduction

What is modernity? There is no consensus of opinion. Words like "post-modernity" or "modern times" do not have the same deep echo outside Europe as they have in Europe, where they conjure up a whole range of images, from the Renaissance to the twenty-first century. In the European continental tradition, the word "modernity" continues to feed polemics about its origin, its dating, its unity and its limits (Legoff, 1988: 59–104). Even in aesthetics, where the word primarily appeared, the notion is flexible enough to cover modernism and post-modernism. Nor do the social sciences relate to modernity in a similar and coherent definition. Thus, defining Islam as traditional or modern cannot be done clearly and precisely. What, then, does post-modernity entail for Islam? Whether one defines, abstractly and hardly in a crystal clear manner, the founding modernity as the period when being of one's time is a supreme value (Vattimo, 1987: 105, 109) or as the period "drawing its normativity from itself" (Habermas, 1988: 8), we situate modernity in the spirit of the time (*Zeitgeist*), borne by a subject able to make the threefold Kantian distinction (nature, ethics and aesthetics). Thus, modernity has inaugurated a new stage of which the historical threshold "can only be apprehended before being reached or after being passed" (Blumenberg, 1999: 533). The ritual of a certain period of time is always transitory, meaning that there will constantly be a discrepancy between modernity and its definition. Benjamin states the paradox in a clear manner: "when modernity sees its rights recognized, its time has passed. Then it will undergo examination. Once it's dead, we'll see if it's able to become antiquity" (Benjamin, 1979: 117). Today the legitimacy of Modern Times has been shattered. Modernity, which we inherited from the Renaissance to the eighteenth century, is today going through a crisis. Touraine has described its manifestations, from the exhaustion of the initial movement of the Enlightenment (*Lumières*) to the substitution of the society by the market (Touraine, 1992: 111–176). Then Habermas, Manfred Frank and Foucault, as well as the post-structuralists like Derrida, also submitted it to a critical approach, attacking the principle of self-consciousness (*Selbstbewusstsein*). This principle supposed that Descartes's subject builds up its relation to itself, to the other and to the world in full transparency of the founding subjectivity: the "I" ("*Je*"), the underlying *subjectum*, master of what it thinks, says and does (Habermas, 1988; Frank, 1989; Foucault, 1994). It has been demonstrated that the concept of the subject, so much sublimated by the Moderns, is based on the unilateral, dominating and self-referential structure of self-consciousness. Even the post-humanists, who remain attached to the tradition of the argumentation of the *Lumières*, from Kant, Voltaire and Rousseau, admit that we are, in one way or another, disappointed by Modernity (Ferry and Renaut, 1985: 33). Post-modernism entails the unavoidable historicisation of the project of modernity. What about Islam and the Muslim civilisations?

The theory of modernity, holding high its pretensions of a normative evaluation, is especially cultural or philosophical when it assimilates the temporal cut between the European Middle Age and modernity to the spatial difference between the West and the other major non-European cultures. The theory of American modernisation does not give any importance to the philosophical content of modernity, centred on the subject and its self-criticism, which dismisses the self-referential subject, restructures its status or describes the techniques of subjectivisation by which it is constituting itself. It separates modernity and rationality, uproots them from their European background, and unties them on a conceptual pedestal, in order to produce universal requirements, susceptible of being modelled in terms of conditions or functions. In transitional terms it analyses the factors and procedures of transforming from one state into another, from the traditional society into the modern society. When they are used in the research of the social sciences, modernity, modernisation and westernisation are employed without really having their normative content either determined or even questioned (Lewis, 1997a: 114–130). However, more generally, it reserves "Westernisation" for the movement of European influence in the nineteenth century and "modernisation" for the situation of the post-colonial countries (Lerner, 1958: 45). Halpern says that the word has become a "source of distraction"; the modernisation that has taken over is "a native movement", claimed by the Middle Easterners themselves who want to be modern without being English, French or American (Halpern, 1963: 35–36). Sometimes, the logic of modernisation is tempered as if it designates the selective catalogue of modern values: the modern style, the individual freedom, the human rights, science and industry, civic culture and democracy. No doubt is expressed concerning the cultural validity of these monuments of universality; no self-criticism of the reason seems to cross the minds and the defeats inflicted upon modernity in its rich and multi-faceted history are never indicated. One could almost say that, whenever a critical glance is thrown upon Western modernity, it tends to fall into relativism.

In a concrete general formulation, modernisation is the systematic process through which our societies change fundamentally and cross the borders from a rather traditional model to a more or less modern one. It supposes a dichotomy between two types: traditional society and modern society. Conceptual opposites appear, over and over again, one designating tradition and the other modernity: parish culture vs cosmopolitan culture, emotivity vs rationality, collectivity against individual, mechanical solidarity vs organic solidarity, status against contract, primary social relations (parental or tribal) vs secondary ones (classes in competition), traditional against legal authority, community vs society. Since the traditional societies belong to the former type and the modern ones to the latter, the stake of modernisation is the change from one to the other, what is called "the universalization of the community", or what Daniel Lerner – one of the first to study seriously the Middle East – calls "the empathy", in other words the ability of people to project themselves into other positions than those inherited from their daily status. Hence, it puts questions such as: what is changing, at what speed, in which sectors and to what ratio? It focuses our attention on the conditions bringing about modernity distributed onto sectors and sequences: education, urbanisation, communication, the training of the elites (entrepreneurs, bureaucrats and politicians) and political integration. New attitudes and structures emerge and orientate the subject according to principles such as open mindedness, individual independence, meritocratic ambitions, belief in the performance of science, rational accounting and civic participation in affairs and business.

Lerner, defending himself for being ethnocentric, postulated that the model of Western modernisation is global and unquestionable. Thus, "what the West is, the Middle East wants to become": an industrial, urban, literacised/alphabetised and participative society (Lerner, 1958: 47). His model draws our awareness to the tensions between tradition and modernity: village vs city, household economics vs credit economics, resignation vs ambition, reverence vs achievement. It then gets more refined with the psychological notion of empathy, that is, sensitivity to personal mobility, characteristic of the modern society where the individual engages in a large autonomy of movement, going from the countryside into the urban world and its middle-class standards, planning to do things that the traditional population would not even think of, projecting itself into a new life, adopting a new lifestyle and adapting to an ever changing environment. As modernisation consists of spreading the attributes of modernity, it will be enough to collect the signs of transition in the sectors where mobility has a driving force, that is, in the following order: urbanisation, education, media and, finally, political participation.

One of the controversies in the theory of modernity is the following question: "Is the history of Europe unique or is it being repeated in the contemporary underdeveloped countries?" (Przeworski and Limongi, 1997: 155). And the answer that it yields is "yes", in contrast with the thesis of European exclusivism. Modernisation would thus be a universalisable process in any society.

Post-modern Islam

One may ask what has this to do with post-modernity and Islam. Does one celebrate the return of tradition, as a conservative mind or adhere, as a post-modern mind and refined aesthete, to the new spirit of the time: kitsch, pastiche and transgression? Does one defend romantically the tradition of the *Lumières* or refresh one's ideas with its freeing potential against the industrial culture, as with Heidegger? Is there such a thing as a "larger rationality" charging the subject to be tuned in to other people's speech? There are many post-modern types, one being rejecting the perverse effects of modernity with its freeing potential, while celebrating the end of modernity, thus joining what Umberto Eco calls "the new Cartesianism of the irrational".

We find an example of this in Akbar S. Ahmed's thesis, placing side by side, in a dramatic manner, political conservatism and poorly assimilated post-modernism. For him, if modernism were to mean education inside Islam, Westernisation and technophilia, post-modernism would be the return to identity. Thus, Islam contributes to the preoccupations of the post-modern world: the balance between religion and the world, compassion, respect of nature (Ahmed, 1992: 48, 117, 120). He says that the fundamentalist movements are not only modern, in spite of themselves, as we often read it, but are now also "post-modern", because they mix contradictory elements (modernism and traditionalism, pleasure/delight and nostalgia).

A second version of the post-modern is of an aesthetic nature, a movement of literary criticism expanding in the Arab world. It is feeding itself with Heidegger's "destruktion" and with Derrida's "déconstruction" (Derrida, 1996). It wants to scatter the language into a polyphony (moderated or uncompromising) where all languages are spoken (from classical Arabic to the fourth language, English), destroy the monist dogma of a unified culture and undermine the structure articulated around the political and linguistic authority. Hence, the borders are muddled up: "the East is not a movement (dialectical, speculative, culturalist) toward the West anymore. They are, one for each other, the beginning and the end" (Khatibi, 1977: 19; Deeb, 1988: 160–181; Safadi, 1990). This way we would no longer be behind, but in the background, standing back: since the dawn of Islam, we have not stopped declining toward this destiny – the sending that Heidegger calls *Geschick*. It is a contradictory position, which, by positioning the subject outside the world, sends it beyond the world.

The Proto-modern Islam

We call "proto-modern" the primary/initial and typically traditional Islam, without being in a pending, pre-modern state, waiting for its phasis of rupture with its religious background. After all, it is contaminated by modernity as well. It is the will to sacrifice human rights on the altar of an authoritarian economical and social modernisation though. Who could certify that the Iranian way of conservative modernisation, driven from above, will not end up in a field of ruins? In the context of late modernity the only real question is whether the fundamentalist utopia is not an absolutistic neo-conservatism, a decadent speech, a rhetoric of identity, but taking place in a post-modern context, marked by the crisis of access to modernity, the relativist scepticism gnawing the stable foundations of modernity, the search for otherness and the cult of the difference.

The disturbing complicity between fundamentalism and post-modernity is to blame. It would be enough to consider the Islamists' attitude toward corporal punishment (Babès and Oubrou, 2002), women's rights (Afkhami, 1995; L. Ahmed,

1993; Brooks, 1995; Hambley, 1998; Goodwin, 1995; Fahmy, 2002; Mernissi, 2002), the status of religious minorities (Yeor, 2002), their position concerning the West and foreigners in general, their legitimisation of violence and resorting to terrorism. From this standpoint, only the credo of a normative modernity can be opposable to the Islamists. Paraphrasing the watchword of Habermas, "modernity an unachieved project", in Islam modernity is a "pending project". However, to also reject both post-modernism and culturalism is a strong position in contemporary Islam (Azmeh, 1996: 17–40, 59–100; Sharabi, 1988a: Chapter 8, 165–194; Shayegan, 1992: Chapter 7; Tibi, 1998: 47–48).

One of the most common arguments asserts that radicalism deeply wants modernity and, even though it cries its hate of it, vomits the West, spits on its culture and dooms its corrupted civilisation to death, radicalism is modern without knowing it. It collects the positive signs indicating modernity in radical Islamism and, in the opposite case, turns the negative over into positive, following the logic of antinomical thinking. Among the indications normalising the phenomena, the Islamists have attended university, read Shakespeare and Hegel, travelled throughout the world and are sometimes forced to stay in London, New York or Paris. They move in the glorious circles of Islamising orientalists and intellectuals and sometimes pride themselves on knowing Western history better than that of their own countries. They can even claim themselves to be distant from the Islamic traditions that they pretend to renovate, adhering to this "vulgarity, the modernity of the customs and of the passport" that Chateaubriand, as early as 1848, identified with modernity. According to François Burgat's formula, Islamism "is a political project using the inheritance of the West as a foil, but authorizing simultaneously the reappropriation of its principal referents" (Burgat, 1988: 55). Bruno Etienne adds, concerning the "transfer of enthusiasm", that Islamism ensures human rights toward an Islamic revolution which, instead of modernising Islam as non-religious modernists wish, Islamises modernity (Etienne, 1987; 108, 134). Even the new supremacy of jurisconsults in Sunni Islam in Egypt for instance, or the victory of an ecclesiastical hierarchy in Iran, is qualified as "something more western than Islamic" (Pipes, 1995: 20).

Conversely, when radical Islamism denies women's rights, oppresses ethnical minorities and claims an immediate implementation of the Sharia, then it is strongly regretted in the name of the same values of modernity. Yet, most of the time, they are sociologically explained by the redundant inventory of causes: from the urbanism disfiguring the city – refuge of a chaotic exodus – to the numerous symbolic or concrete aggressions that a frustrated population faces, and to its uncontrolled growth. Radical Islamism is not a "reconciliation" (*Versöhnung*) in its Hegelian signification supposing a dialectical exceeding of the negative and the positive into a superior structure: the homogeneous and universal state of human rights. It is not a *nouveauté* either, just waking up, and for which we would be supposed to have the indulgent respect one has for singularities. It is rather neo-conservatism with which we really have to be uncompromising as long as it infringes upon the universal. Of course, Islamism is contemporary with us, but is lacking the reflexive consciousness that could make it an associate for the modern enterprise. To paraphrase Marx, it is our historical contemporary without being our philosophical contemporary.

Yet between, on the one hand, the average Arab's efforts to project himself as a desperately true Muslim, although modern "too", and, on the other hand, the radical Islamist, the normative content of modernity is certainly interposing itself. One has to recognise that Islamism is a form of neo-conservatism and not at all a "movement paradoxically inventing a modernity, a thwarted one". The purpose is not so much a matter of blackmailing the *Aufklärung*, but rather to reverse the question: to see the part of universality in what appears as singular, arbitrary and contingent, and to go toward it as toward a horizon of sense able to yield consensus. From this standpoint, only a normative hypercritique can be opposed to the Islamists. Yes, say it openly: neo-conservatism in general and the Islamists in particular go against the breath of the *Aufklärung*, the Enlightenment, the *illuminismo*, the *Lumières* on which *we* remain – at least some of us – totally dependent, or for some others, only partially dependent, even after the decline/fading of the aura of the *Lumières*. The possibility, even the necessity, of a pacific coexistence with *them* is not a cognitive question, but a political one concerning the invention of the political as a neutral space. It does not concern the commensurability of our languages or the relativisation of our respective views of the world (*Weltanschauungen*).

Modernity in Islam

The double rejection of the post-modern and of the proto-modern would not definitively resolve the problem of the modern in Islam, because they are divided into two sides: some are religiously attached to the *Lumières*, others suspect them of bringing along the plan/mechanism of what Foucault calls the *Disciplines*. The former side opposes to traditional Islam a romanticism of the *Lumières* with a universal reason and a canonised and historicist model of change. Thus, the choice is radical: to be modern or not to be at all. This is a little like Lerner who, in the 1960s, allowed that the Middle Eastern societies face a dilemma: "*Mecca or mechanization*" (Lerner, 1958: 405). This model has been criticised (Eickelman, 2000: 119–135). The latter side is doubly critical: guarded in their attitude toward the modern West, they consider themselves too as "the late fruits" of its understanding/reason, to paraphrase Heidegger, but also toward their own Islamic tradition that they legitimately have it in mind to transform. Such a state of mind is not as tragic as the supporters of a founding modernity – or those who regret the in-between option – make it look.

The discussion concerning rationality and relativism focuses on non-historical, primitive societies, without a written inheritance, marked by a "prelogical" thinking and symbolical, ritualistic and primary forms of social organisation. Islam for good reasons stands outside its object. Islam is not a Nuer tribe, the twins are no birds or lions, and the body of the deceased does not contain any magic/sorcery/witchcraft. It does not have that otherness that has transformed "primitive" societies into a genuine object of knowledge for anthropology (Lévi-Strauss, 1974: 421). And even if it appears to the author of *Tristes Tropiques* that Islam "has remained stiff in its contemplation of a society that was reality seven centuries ago", he has also recognised in Islam the same logical faults that dwell within the modern West, thus explaining the discomfort he has felt at the contact with Islam, the same that formerly made him run away from home: "Islam, it's the West of the East" (Lévi-Strauss, 1955: 485). Islam is a historical, but traditional, society, facing the transitional problems that the two other Western religions have already faced in the past, although, and this is fundamental, in absolutely new conditions and possibilities.

Relativising the world does not mean pleading "against the method", which automatically leads to "anarcho-rationalism" (Feyerabend, 1979; Hacking, 1982; Hollis and Steven, 1982: 48–66). Conversely, all testable distinctions are not simplistic and all grid perspectives of intelligibility are not denying the others. They only become such when they end up in a refusal of "alternative worlds", others' *Weltanschauungen* (Spinoza and Dreyfus, 1996: 735–763 and 1997: 910–932). One of the credible solutions consists of dismissing rival pretentions, both radical relativism and absolutistic rationalism, in order to yield a third and intermediary position: a "weak absolutism" accepting some truths to be absolute (Jarvie, 1983, 44–60); "a secular fundamentalism of the *Lumières*" absolutising only the Kantian process of moral formalism (Gellner, 1992, 5 *et seq.*); a self-surpassing of the reason that would not take the Hegelian form of a synthesis-surpassing (Wellmer, 1988, 159; Ferry, 1990: 317–319); a communicational reason opening onto an intersubjective dialogue in the field of culture, which, on principle, could not comply with the distinction of right and wrong (Habermas, 1987: 96–100).

As Giddens puts it, we are today in a world where the consequences of modernity have become more radical and more universalised than before for everybody: "space and time" have been dissociated, at the same time as "the local and the global" have become connected to each other in ways and manners that no-one could even have thought of in the past (Giddens, 1990: 3–22). We all live, Islam included, in a multi-cultural, multi-lingual, multi-ethnic world; intellectually, we are simultaneously relativists and rationalists, but, inside the big monotheistic tradition, we have hybrid and crossbred identities, and we move around in more than one world, sometimes an incommensurable one. This perspective splendidly breaks the vicious circle of dualism. It sets us free, both from the return of an imperial tradition and from a dialectical irresolute synthesis supposed to transcend the poles that tear the thinking to pieces (Islam and the West, tradition and modernity). The West and Islam are areas with multifarious populations, illegals included! And there are as many traditions as there are modernities, even if the major modernity has been a European project (Eisenstadt, 2000: 1–29).

Jihad

Jihad is promoted by what we have called "proto-Islam" and "neo-conservatism" involved in a post-modern context. Now, what is the relation between the new phenomenon of Islamic terrorism and the classical conception of *jihad*, which is still relevant in other forms of Islam than the fundamentalist version? *Jihad* in its conception among the terrorists has no sense of liberation as used to be the case, either when a country was conquered or an infidel was dethroned. The stakes now do not include pushing away the invaders of Muslim areas or conquering new territory, but they concern global terror, not against the *taghut*, but for the moment against the Americans and their allies. This is what Wright called – before 9/11 – the sacred rage (Wright, 1985) undermining the Islamic world.

The evaluation of the use of violence in combat for faith depends upon the ends that are served. The actions that resulted in the 9/11 events were irrational to the extent that they are pursued against an anonymous enemy without a social project that outlines how society is to be changed in order to promote faith. Since it targets innocents outside the homeland of Islam, especially the Arab countries, this kind of terrorism deviates from the established notions of just war, both within the Occidental mind and within classical Islam. Classical Islam provides legitimacy for the Holy War, but disapproves of what is called *fatk* or the killing by treason or premeditation: "God does not like the unbelieving traitor" (Koran, 32: 38), which is confirmed by the great medieval historian, Tabari, who was advised by the Prophet himself, although Tabari certainly took some liberty in the interpretation of the Koran. It is true that *jihad* sublimates death in combat for faith, but this conception hardly endorses suicide, which is not in conformity with the duty to respect one's life (Koran, 4: 29–30), as the Koran requires that "one is certainly responsible for all: the hearing, the sight and the heart" (Koran, 17: 36). The tradition is thus the following: *jihad* saves those who are not in combat and prohibits the poisoning of the water sources and the use of poisoned meat, which were the arms of biological warfare at the time. Assassination belongs to history with the assassins (Lewis, 2003a; Wasserman, 2001).

Modern Islamic terrorism finds its special intellectual sources within the second type of Islamic fundamentalism, where the standard interpretations of radical Islamism are propagated. Compared with the exegetic works from the nineteenth century, such as *Principles of Exegesis* by Sir Ahmed Khan, *Reconstruction of Religious Thoughts* by Muhammed Iqbal, *Tafsir al-Manar* (the Lighthouse) by Muhammed Abduh, as well as *In the Shadow of the Koran* by Sayyid Qutb (Lee, 1997), the message of Bin Laden – the *fatwa* of 1998 – would be considered ridiculous by Muslims if it had not been followed by concrete application. This message contains an authorisation to kill (Lewis, 1998a: 14–19; Dunn, 1998: 23–28; Wiktorowics and Kaltner, 2003: 76–92), which is essentially a call to eliminate Americans, whether they be civilians or military persons and wherever they may be found. The argument is that they have tarnished the holy soil of Islam, which in this interpretation includes Iraq, Egypt, Sudan and Palestine as well as Arabia.

It may be pointed out that classical Islam only mentions three places as holy, namely Mecca, Medina and one part of Hijaz. On the contrary, the vast areas of Islam called *sawad* in the classical tradition stretch out towards the fertile land of Persia and Maghreb. The five holy consequences linked with the sacred status of Mecca and Medina include the prohibition for non-Muslims against entering, living or being buried in these places. The exception is the corridor with the Hijaz that goes from Medina to Tabuk, where non-Muslims may enter and stay for at most three days. If a non-Muslim does not respect these rules, then he or she will be expelled and punished, but it is not allowed to kill the perpetrator (Mawardi, 1982, Chapter XIV: 333–378).

It seems too simplistic from the point of view of Islam and the Arab societies to employ metaphors such as *jihad* vs McWorld (Barber, 1996) or the coming "clash of civilisations" (Huntington, 1997; see also Ali, 2002, Chapter 4; Gerges, 1999; Collective, 2002; Wedeen, 2003). The thesis of Fukuyama (1992) that the events of 9/11 confirm the end of history, Islam being the only culture that rejects the Occidental values of liberal democracy and the market economy, is hardly more acceptable. Other cultures and civilisations also display hesitance towards the globalisation of Western institutions and culture. It seems a better strategy when interpreting these events of great historical importance to follow the suggestion by Susan Sontag, viz. that each party finds its responsibilities first and foremost on their home yard.

First, the major Western powers have hardly taken radical Islamism seriously. They played both cards – the retardation of the Muslims and Islamic fundamentalism – at the same time until Islamic terrorism exploded in their own country. Second, radical Islamism is often given a favourable interpretation both inside and outside Arab countries, as if Islamic fundamentalism could be combined with liberal institutions somehow, perhaps by means of a *fatwa* that eradicates the core of the message. Finally, Muslims in Arab countries must reflect on why the nationalist struggle against Western colonialism has become transformed into a struggle for or against Islamic fundamentalism. The truth is that Arab nationalism – a second *Nahdha* – did not hesitate to employ *jihad* or the Islamic community when struggling for independence, although the nationalist movement was driven basically by the *bourgeoisie* aiming at the modernisation of the country.

The answer to the question: "Why 9/11?" must be found in an analysis of the Arab countries and their reaction to the various forms of Islamic fundamentalism outlined above. The first reformist kind of Islamic fundamentalism has given place to the second kind of radical Islamism, which now in a third form tends towards terrorism. It is time to go back and ask why reformist Islam failed, searching for the answer mainly within the Arab societies. Instead of blaming the dependence of the Arab countries upon the Western powers, one may ask why these countries were so easily colonised in the nineteenth century. Similarly, one may enquire as to why the struggle for national independence left a large group of people living without much hope, not only in misery but also under dictatorship, creating strongholds for radical Islamism.

Conclusion

Islamic fundamentalism has become a major movement in all Muslim countries, supported by millions of believers in the Koran and practised in the mosques and the religious schools (*madras*). Its political expression varies from one Muslim country to another, from being virtually in power to being suppressed or in jail. With 9/11, Islamic terrorism emerged as a global phenomenon, drawing its key support from Islamic fundamentalism. The exact nature of the links between different terrorist groups and the networks between them is not fully known today (Roy, 2004, 2007, 2008).

Islamic fundamentalism, as well as Islamic terrorism, is very much at odds with the general development towards a post-modern society. Thus, the requirements of post-modernism do not go down well in Muslim civilisation, where Islamic fundamentalism is both cause and effect. It is driven by the backwardness of Muslim societies, but it also further increases this backwardness. Fundamentalism manifests iself not only politically in anti-system movements, attempting to change the political status quo – the FIS in Algeria, Hamas in the Gaza Strip, the Taliban in Afghanistan and to some extent also the Turkish Justice and Development Party (AKP) – but it also shows up in a slow but steady Islamisation of the minor things in society, like dresses, clothes, social interactions, legal practices, the marriage pattern and the ever increasing number of new mosques. Yet, fundamentalism is not Islam, but merely one interpretation of the Koran.

What is the reason, then, for Muslim retardation? Let us examine the Weber thesis about the historical conditions for modernisation and position the Muslim civilisation in relation to these conditions for a modern society.

Chapter 3
The Weber Thesis

Introduction

Religion is *per se* non-social as its beliefs and values typically refer to a metaphysical reality that cannot be validated through the senses. However, religion may, when practised on a large scale by groups of people, have important social consequences. Weber devoted several studies to the analysis of the economic consequences of religious beliefs and practices. Yet in principle nothing prevents one from also examining the political impact of religion. Weber's books on Protestantism, Judaism, Hinduism, Buddhism as well as Confucianism and Taoism have become the standard reference points to which analyses of religion and society refer, either with approval or with criticism. However, there is no similar monograph by Weber dealing with Islam. Weber's argument concerning Islam can, however, be reconstructed by assembling all those bits and pieces at various places where he speaks about Islam, the Muslim civilisation and the religion of Mohammed. All quotations would have to be assembled and examined to determine Weber's fundamental argument concerning Islam. Islam is a tragic religion, Weber said from his Western perspective, meaning that the secular consequences of this religion could not benefit society.

The purpose of this chapter is to reconstruct how Weber analysed Islam and the social impact of Islam. It requires an interpretation effort, but it is worth doing since Weber's argument about Islam recurs with many scholars. Weber's short analysis of Islam and the Arab civilisation contains many of the typical elements of the occidental view of Muslims, called "orientalism" by Said (1979, 1993), albeit the importance of Weber's view of Islam as a "religion of warriors" has been entirely missed among the scholars speaking of orientalism as the "beam in the Western eye" upon Moslems.

Why should we today turn back to Weber and discuss his sociology of religion in relation to Islam? His critics have never exhausted the seduction of his theories (Huff and Schluchter, 1999). Quite to the contrary, there remains "something" in his argument that still invites discussion. Although Weber never took the time to think and reflect conclusively on Islam, his analysis has nonetheless been elevated to the position of a paradigm. Weber took his information from existing German oriental studies, but in orientalism Islam has been approached as a monument that is irrational and inflexible (Said, 1979). There was created a kind of involuntary complicity between Weber and orientalism expressed in a superficial analysis of the historical evolution of Islam from Mohammed to the Ottoman Empire. During the twentieth century one notes a methodological transformation from a eurocentric Weberian methodology to a normative eurocentrism that focuses upon the so-called Islamic mentality, eternal or at least not quite adapted to the demands of modernity. There is yet another thesis that differs from this argument about continuity, namely one that emphasises the difference between medieval Islam and modern Islam. We cannot have an opinion about the validity of these theses without learning what Weber actually said about Islam.

One Monograph Lacking

Although Weber wrote no monograph on the Muslim world or the Arabic culture, one finds several short penetrating analyses in various parts of his major books. One source is his theory of authority, which is to be found in two versions within *Economy and Society* (1978), one shorter and one longer. Two other sources are, on the one hand, his theory of economic institutions, which is stated in *Economy and Society,* and, on the other hand, his perspective upon economic history, contained in his *General Economic History* (1981). One may also speak of a fourth source, namely Weber's comparative analysis of law and legal systems on the one hand and the city on the other. In both these very broad overviews to be found in *Economy and Society*, one concerning the development of jurisprudence and the other concerning the growth of urban settlements, Weber makes comparative assessments of various cultures, including Islam and the Arab World. What one has to do is to put these sources together and interpret them systematically.

Typical of Weber's writings on Islam and the Arab world is that they tend to be very sparse, but on the other hand extremely condensed and yet clear. Thus, he never writes in one place at length about the Muslim world but he throws out a number of points here and there where he makes affirmative and general assessments of the social and economic as well as political consequences of Islam – the religion of Mohammed. Yet, a fifth source, perhaps the most informative, concerning Weber's assessment of Islam is a few comparative pages in his *Sociology of Religion*, aiming at a summary of his various books on religions. It originally constituted a long chapter in *Economy and Society*. One also finds short comments upon Islam in his monographs on the other world religions.

Thus, it is not at all true that Weber did not analyse Islam, but he showed much less interest in Islam than in the other world religions, devoting to some of them a major monograph or essay. Perhaps this fact is in itself an expression of his dislike of the religion of Mohammed, which he calls a "dire" religion. Yet, there are certain very dense sections in various books where Weber enters into lengthy analyses of Islam and the Arab World, as well as the Ottoman Empire. We reconstruct these analyses in order to present Weber's conception of Islam. It is our hope that restating Weber's analysis concisely will help us to understand Islam today.

Weber, for reasons that we will perhaps never know, did not publish a coherent and systematic analysis of Islam. Instead, one finds pieces here and there. What we have done is to collect these pieces together and scrutinise them systematically. We do know that Weber began serious study of Islam in 1910, stemming from his wish to look at other religions and their consequences for economic activity in order to confront his idea about capitalism and Protestantism with other cultures. Between 1911 and 1914 he became well-informed and collected a substantial amount of documentation. As he wished to be exhaustive, he had a tendency – step by step – to collect information about Islam to the same extent as he had done with the other world religions. Thus, upon his death in 1920, he had collected a vast number of appreciations, comments and notes on Islam, although in a fragmentary fashion. According to Marianne Weber's biography, he planned to devote a volume to Islam in the same way that he had written about other world religions (Marianne Weber, 1988; Colliot-Thélène, 1990: 6–30).

Let us thus ask what is the subject of the Weber thesis? Some possible answers could be the cultural uniqueness of the Occident, the exclusiveness of the rationalisation drive or the appearance of phenomena such as modern capitalism that originated in these countries. It would be difficult to derive all the specific characteristics of the occidental civilisation from one unifying factor, for instance the mix of Greek–Roman heritage with Christianity. We will first underline the special nature of the occidental route, before we proceed to look at how Weber examined the Islamic civilisation from this outpost. One may already say that this is not a simple question, as we are facing an arabesque of propositions, which it is necessary to decompose. Here we target the causal link that connects religion and capitalism according to Weber's thesis.

Concepts of the Occident

Weber presents the Occident as a civilisational subject, or as a country variation to be studied comparatively: country-wise or region-wise, according to religion or according to time period. On the one hand, one may claim that there are different kinds of occidentalism in the texts of Weber. On the other hand, the exclusivity of the Occident is all the time assumed. Furthermore, several cultural phenomena that took place in the occidental countries are also found in other cultural spheres. Could they then be universal despite the fact that these trends developed in the occidental world in a determinate direction? The rationalisation of key spheres of existence and their orientation towards a certain kind of rationality (means–end) is underlined by Weber in his words: "*Entzauberung der Welt*", i.e. organising human activities without an idea of divine intervention.

Let us make an overview of the pros and cons stated in relation to the Weber thesis. The critiques hold that Protestantism did not have the force of change that Weber ascribes to it. It did not impact upon all countries, or in the same manner. It had an influence on other spheres than economics, especially politics with the emergence of religious tolerance in England. It had positive effects upon later and other phenomena than those identified by Weber in the sixteenth and seventeenth centuries, namely once the European countries had started to industrialise and once the initial orientations of Protestantism had already worked themselves out. Some argue that Protestantism did not develop a new attitude towards the world. Its economic ethic is even fundamentalist and conservative (Samuelson, 1993). Others say that Protestantism did not play any role in the birth of capitalism (Tawney, 1990). The impact of Protestantism has not been marked, for instance, in France, where capitalism was born thanks to a radical and enlightened bourgeoisie that favoured a separation from religion, as manifested in the 1905 law on the separation between Church and state. Or take the case of Italy, where one had to wait for the Lateran Agreements in 1929 in order to arrive at a definition of the relations between Church and state.

The controversial thesis about structural differences between the ethics of Protestantism and the other world religions is today an anachronism. Weber was interested in the spectacular *birth* of modern capitalism. From this perspective he disqualified all the other religious systems and their ethical norms: the Asian religions and Catholicism, Judaism, Greek Orthodoxy and Islam within the theocentric religions. Weber bypassed the relation between capitalism and democracy, what Barrington Moore Jr called "the road of capitalist democracy" (Moore, 1966). Moreover, the Catholic countries in Western Europe, then Latin America and finally the East European countries were modernised without Protestantism. The Church has shown itself capable of endorsing more or less the institutions of democratic capitalism through the concept of subsidiarity, helping make acceptable the ethics of the *homo economicus*, after the Vatican II Concilium between 1962 and 1965. The Jewish people perhaps emancipated itself in the Diaspora, but it has integrated world capitalism into a democratic state. Israeli religion and politics stand in a relation that Weber had not imagined, as politics is not under the control of religion, neither does it express religion, nor do politics exert a supreme power over religious matters. The cosmocentric religions and philosophies of Asia – Hinduism, Buddhism, Taoism and Confucianism – have adapted themselves to the world. These religions have to such an extent managed to successfully promote capitalist modernity that political elites in Asia have invented a theory about Asian exceptionalism or Asian values meaning ethics. Thus, only Islam seems to stay outside or on the sidelines in relation to democratic capitalism. The Islamic countries are today capitalist, but not democratic. Yet capitalism in Islamic countries did not need the support of Protestantism in order to emerge.

Rationality and Capitalism

A close reading of his text may offer the basis for a discussion of the manner in which Weber pronounces his discourse. One may show how Weber vacillated between various angles, including the occidental countries as a unique civilisation on the one hand and the many socio-cultural phenomena that took place in the

Occident on the other. In the latter perspective, his focus is upon Christianity or one of its modes, namely Protestantism, and finally the relation between Protestantism and modern capitalism. However, one does not always know what time period he is speaking about. Weber refers to different elements explicitly, apparently to historical stages that are far apart, from the ancient period to modernity, ranging over the medieval period and the Renaissance. Here is what he considers to be typical of the occidental countries: a science founded upon mathematics using the method of experiments; a legal doctrine that is rational and systematic; a certain kind of art after the Renaissance; music that is harmonic in a rational manner with instruments, orchestra, opera and a system of notation; the Gothic perspective in art; the development of the press and book-printing; a body of specialised functionaries that became the core of the state and the modern enterprise or big firm; an institutionalised state having a written constitution, an elected Parliament and political parties; finally, modern capitalism or "the most decisive force in our modern life" organising in a large-scale manner the economy on a new foundation.

These elements of the Occident reveal different historical layers. Some have a Greek origin, such as the foundations of mathematics, mechanics, physics and geometry, or a Roman origin like law and jurisprudence. Others have a medieval background such as Canon law, systematic theology, Gothic art and the estate society. Finally, new phenomena emerged in modern times in a wide sense, including the Renaissance with Machiavelli and Leonardo da Vinci: the arts, the laboratory and the scientific technique, the book printers, the specialised functionaries, the free representation in assemblies, political parties and the constitutional state.

This is the field of comparison of civilisations or the comparative analysis of cultures. Weber underlines very much the new economic system, or modern capitalism with the emphasis upon "modern". This is what his investigation into other cultures asks: "Why did not the capitalist interests produce the same effects in China or in India?", a formulation that also covers the Islamic countries. One could believe that capitalism is merely a medallion extra in a long chain of events. However, this is not the case, because the emergence of capitalism in the history of the occidental countries is given such significance that occidental history could almost be reconstructed from the birth of modern capitalism. Weber studied capitalism as an economic–cultural phenomenon according to his general framework comprising two dimensions, structure and culture. He looked at these two elements of every civilisation, searching for the link between them as well as the external and internal conditions of a culture. Unless one imagines that everything goes in the direction of the arrival of modern capitalism, one must allow for the fact that Gothic art or the Renaissance perspective in painting, for instance, had nothing to do with the rationalisation of activities and organisations, as in modern capitalism as Weber theorised it.

Moreover, one must insist upon the fact that this capitalism is the modern version of it, as capitalism is both a historical and a universal phenomenon. It is furthermore true that *modern capitalism* changes its physiognomics, at least in character during modern times. Capitalism in the seventeenth century is the search for economic profit within the framework of a large, rationally set up organisation of free labour within the enterprise and acting on a global scale. From the social point of view, modern capitalism is linked with the emancipation of the bourgeoisie, even if it started earlier in the medieval, agriculturally based economy when trade promoted the emergence of free cities. From the point of view of cultural history, modern capitalism set out simultaneously with the rational practice of ascetic Protestantism; in other words, a religious attitude that propels action in order to rationalise ordinary life. Only in this case, and solely in this case, is the relationship between economics and ethics positively significant – the decisive contribution by Weber. Thus, step by step, a mechanism is put in place that is supported by a number of pillars: the rational firm separated from the owners' domestic management, the profitability criterion, the chances of peaceful gain, the calculability of factors of production, rational accounting, the free work of the working classes receiving a salary. It is the appearance of modern capitalism in time that constitutes the central problem for Weber.

Later on the capitalist system was to become more autonomous from culture. Toward the end of the eighteenth century, Weber maintains, capitalism would have the following seven characteristics:

- a lucrative private enterprise covering daily needs by means of accounts telling gains and losses;
- the freedom of markets;
- a legal system that enhances the ability to plan;
- free labour paid by a salary;
- the commercialisation of agriculture;
- the buying and selling of shares in enterprises;
- speculation on stock markets (Weber, 1978, 1981).

The original question may now be stated more precisely as: which factors explain why other cultures than the Occident did not pursue the route of rationalisation typical of the Occident, although the other civilisations have known capitalism, ancient, colonial, feudal or state? We deal especially with the Islamic civilisation and the Muslim countries.

There is a temptation to state that the occidental countries are special or superior merely because they accomplished a decisive progress toward ultimate rationality that the other civilisations did not, or that they ignored or just took advantage of after its occurrence. Weber's text does not lend itself to such an interpretation. Much work has gone into clarifying his method. First, to Weber the concept of rationality has several ingredients. Rationality and rationalisation – complex and ambiguous concepts – hardly refer to the reason of Enlightenment according to the philosophers of the eighteenth century (Cassirer, 1966). The world can be rational in several different ways in this or that sphere of life. For instance, the mystical contemplation of the world can favour a rational conduct of life, but it can be irrational from a strictly logical point of view. On the contrary, the impersonal nature of commercial relations is rational from the economic point of view, but irrational from the religious point of view as it may lose itself in the immoderate pursuit of gain for its own sake. The rational perspective places the object and the stakes at more than one location. It is a question of polytheism of values, a kind of Nitzschean view on the relativity of values. When he sets out to explain the peculiar occidental rationalisation, Weber establishes this occidental rationalism as the final benchmark of the process of rationalisation of various spheres and praxis as modern rationalism. To believe that this is the highest form of rationality – the means–ends rationality – involves taking a step that is only possible when one takes into account that his thought is enmeshed in the occidental way of thinking – his value bias or the "beam in his eye".

Weber's methodological rationalism is enshrined in a moderate eurocentrism or a heuristic eurocentrism. On the one hand, he refuses the accrediting to modern capitalism of features such as tolerance, individualism, humanism and universalism, for which he admits the plurality of their significant manifestations. In other words, Europe is not the achievement of the spirit as with Hegel or the essence of "infinite teleology of rational ends" that Husserl (1976) speaks of. There are, as we will see, several kinds of Occident. But at the same time Weber displays eurocentrism and partly orientalism, although the latter more in an involuntary manner thanks to his innocence. Weber could not free himself of a certain eurocentric mentality, spreading as we will see value judgements that are incompatible with conduct of neutrality in research.

Weber focuses on two phenomena: the morals of Protestantism and the spirit of modern capitalism involving more than a causal relationship. He emphasises the logical connection between the religious form of Protestantism and the professional ethic of capitalism, or the adequacy, the interior similarity and the congruence between them. He rejects a Marxist interpretation of this connection, where the Protestant spirit is the reflection of, or the most suitable religious complement to, the capitalist relations of production. Weber thus avoids two dangers, first, excessive cultural autonomy as with civilisational philosophers and second the extreme dependency upon the social context as with Marxists.

Yet, one must not overestimate this chosen affinity as the Weberians do, focusing only upon these two entities. Weber examines also the reciprocal influence between the internal and external factors of a culture, which he analyses by means of a distinction between ethos and social forms. Some say that Marx and Weber meet at the end of the day (Wiley, 1987). A close reading of the Weber text shows convincingly that he also employs Marxist concepts like "the decisive factor" or "determinant condition" in such and such configuration or with such and such orientation. We have no ambition to give a complete analysis on how to fully understand Weber. What we wish to concentrate upon is his Islamic studies, or his method when analysing Islam and the Islamic countries.

The Debate After

To talk about Islam today was not what preoccupied Weber, nor to make predictions about its future. His enquiry was confined to the historical path that we have followed. Following the approach of historical sociology, his study focused upon the birth of modern capitalism in all its aspects. Certainly he arrived in some places at an appreciation of contemporary Islam. For example, he examined the status of Mecca in modern times. Looking at the Turkish land code from 1858, he qualified it as a collection of *hanifite* rules. He considered the *waqf* institution as a contemporary obstacle to the modernisation of the system of Islamic property. The same applies to the duality in jurisdiction in Tunisia and in Turkey at the eve of colonisation. But he said nothing about colonisation, which period he lived through – actually nothing at all as his argument basically targeted medieval Islam.

More positively, Weber never did exclude that, outside of the Occident, "other equally favourable circumstances could have opened the road for capitalism", including in the Islamic world (Weber, 1996b). Furthermore, "today all the peoples of the world import this phenomenon as being the most famous product of the Occident", he wrote (Weber, 1978). Weber affirms clearly that in the contemporary period it is not only the case that occidental capitalism has no need for support from Protestantism, but also that other civilisations have the possibility to appropriate for themselves modern capitalism, when it has arrived fully developed economically and technically at the global level (Weber, 1996b). Weber refers to Japan and China without excluding the Muslim world.

In a note concerning the ephemeral resistance in Asia towards colonial capitalism – the geomancy in China and the system of castes in India – Weber remarks that "in the long run no conviction of an ethico-religious kind could stop capitalism from entering from the moment that it was outside the gate ready for battle" (Weber, 1991b: 378, note 1). And if there were obstacles, then one must look for them not in the incapacity of the non-Europeans to appropriate modern capitalism but in the traditions that are solidly anchored in the structures of society. Actually, this is what he did in his research. However, Weber's thesis became paradigmatic, as we have suggested at the beginning of this work. From a thesis concerning the birth of modern capitalism in all its aspects, it has been transformed into a comprehensive theory about various types of religion (Salvatore, 1996; Springborg, 1986). We will survey the criticism of Weber below, after which we turn to the overbids on the Islamic ethos of a Protestant making. We will also discuss the massive influence of Weber upon the sociology of authority, before we conclude with taking a road that is semi-Weberian.

Since the 1930s, there has evolved a literature that contests Weber's contribution of Protestantism to the emergence of capitalism. We may quote the German economic historian Sombart saying: "the puritan spirit has never had one single mine opened or made one single oven burn". Similarly, German sociologist Troeltsch argued that the contribution of Protestantism to the emergence of the modern world concerns "rather or essentially indirect consequences or unconscious ones, i.e. impacts that worked themselves out despite what was intended" (Eisenstadt, 1968: 3–45; 1973: 212–230).

Did Islamic ethics hinder the birth of capitalism? Rodinson was one of the first to refute this. Weber's thesis seemed to him "radically wrong" (Rodinson, 1966: 77). He started from Weber's question: "Why in reality did capitalism triumph in the modern period in Europe and not in the Moslem countries, among others" (Rodinson, 1966: 21). His reply is that no Islamic specificity would have hindered the birth of modern capitalism. The text of the Koran is favourable to private appropriation despite the fact that it forbids the taking of usury rents, due to the multiplication of legal artifices or smart tricks (*hiyal*). Islam is rational to the same extent as the other theocentric, monotheistic and escathological religions, as Islam gives an even larger place to reason than the sacred books of Judaism and Christianity. It condemns magic, the elimination of which according to Weber entails the demystification of the world, which is necessary for the birth of a professional ethics. Finally, Islam accepts the permanent and methodical pursuit of gains. Yet, what is at stake is the practical orientation of rational belief. Rodinson admits that the hindrance to the emancipation of the Islamic bourgeoisie was the "caste of slave soldiers".

Is the Protestant spirit a necessary condition for modern capitalism? Probably it is within the classical age, but certainly not in the twentieth century. Modern capitalism has an autonomy, structurally speaking, which Islam adopted from the nineteenth century partially due to the colonial penetration. Actually, one can argue that Islam is compatible with modernity. Gellner states that Islam as a high culture is characterised by a strict unitarism, an absence of a clergy, a strict adherence to a script, a puritan and sober obedience to the law, as well as individualism. Gellner affirms that this kind of Islam is similar to Protestantism from an ethical point of view and from a sociological point of view, when it is attached to the urban and commercial bourgeoisie. Gellner puts this kind of Islam as "high culture" up against an Islam that is "low culture" meaning non-official, popular, tribal, in revolt, ecstatic and using the mediation of saints (Gellner, 1983: 75–79, 216–219; 1994: 40, 178; 1997: 81–89). In modern times the so-called high elements predominated during the Moslem reformism in the nineteenth century, carried by an urban intellectual movement. This is also the thesis by Rodinson. Similarly Turner, after having considered the Weber thesis on medieval Islam as a reflection of "Oriental prejudices", rehabilitates it by estimating that the reforms in Islam in the nineteenth century were animated by motivations that were "entirely Weberian" (Turner, 1974: 140–144). More recently again, Peters argues in the same direction, stating that Islam knew "the doctrine of predestination, inner-worldly ascetism, rationalism and puritanism" (Peters, 1999: 211). He admits though that Moslem fundamentalism is seeking to transform the world on the basis of tradition, meaning that one can no longer see the similarity with Protestantism. The same thing can be said about Barbara D. Metcalf and Francis Robinson, taking a longer time perspective and analysing Islamic reformism in Asia and elsewhere up until the twentieth century (Metcalf, 1999: 217–219;

Robinson, 1999: 231–245). It would thus be a mistake to contest the basic compatibility of Islam with modernity.

In the nineteenth century the fundamentalists were clearly the reformists who would have liked to renew the tradition within Islam by going back to the sources: the Koran and the *Hadith*. But they hardly associated themselves with modern capitalism. These fundamentalists were rather obsessed by a question that Shekib Arslan (1870–1946) formulated in 1930: "Why were the Moslems late in developing when compared with other civilisations?" As they could not count Islam as being responsible, they regarded the decline as a result of tradition. Yet their answer called for a balanced process of occidentalisation that entailed another question: how to become modern without treason against Islamic authenticity? Today the challenge is a different one as the key issues include political democracy, cultural emancipation of individuals, women and minorities, as well as the social emergence of the middle classes. All these questions actually fall outside of the Weberian paradigm.

The arrival of radical Islamic fundamentalism makes a difference. After the reformist movement there came the new puritans, the Islamic fundamentalists, who, being pious and rejecting the world, wanted to transform it. They believed in predetermination, but they added to it the individual responsibility from an inner-worldly perspective, which may be violent but concerned a millennial perspective. The key in Weber's Calvinism is its outer-worldly destiny (Carré, 1986: 149; Juergensmeyer, 1993: 30–46; Etienne, 1987: 119). All things in the present period move in such a way as to maintain the fervour of the ethical prophecy of yesterday, Islamic sectarianism being in principle revolutionary.

Muslim Traditionalism

Contemporary forms of authority reproduce classical forms in the Moslem countries. Two theses have had success: Arab neo-patrimonialism and neo-patriarchialism. Power within Islam is neo-patrimonial to the extent that it reproduces the personal and arbitrary domination of the ruler, with all his property and his military order, within a context marked by the opposition between tradition and modernity. First, the modern state is favourable to change, but it exerts a political control that is hostile to political participation. Social relations involve an exchange of goods against a conditional loyalty between patrons and clients. This relation is "particularistic and diffuse, unequal and asymmetric" (Eisenstadt, 1984: 48–49). The ambivalent relation that Eisenstadt refers to appears with, for instance, the structure of power in Morocco. The relation between master and disciples in popular Sufism reappears with the sovereign when his sanctity is being acknowledged, as he gives and receives the "*baraka*" and other advantages against allegiance just as in the initial ritual. The relation between the Sufi and the disciple is, however, that of initiation, whereas that between the sovereign and his subjects is that of coercion (Hammoudi, 1997: 81–97, 148–149). Ayman Al-Yassiri points to Ibn Saud, the founder of the Kingdom of Saudi Arabia, who invoked legitimacy based on a combination of charismatic and traditional elements (Al-Yassiri, 1985: 36).

The Arab countries have not been able to reform their patrimonial states, neither the monarchies nor the republics. One finds here several typical features of neo-patrimonial leadership: the personalisation of power with a focus upon the head of state, the closeness of a private circle in the nearness of the palace of the head of state, the informal nature of influence that short-cuts public power – the court, the friends and the family. Moreover the game of conflict is cleverly played out in the centre of power between lower-level elites who are in constant competition with each other, although the relationship between the head of state and his subordinates all the time has a unique meaning, that is, as the setter of an order and the executor of it, the military feat of the head of state who has unified the country or who has accomplished remarkable achievements with arms. Finally, we have the rationalisation of traditional religious obedience which forces the subjects into allegiance with the threat of being accused of stimulating disorder, *fitna* or disunion being the worst of all crimes (Bill and Springborg, 1990: 152–176).

The thesis about neo-patriarchy, which is at the same time an "analytical category, an ideal type, a principle of interpretation and a formal theory" has recently been popularised by Hisham Sharabi (Sharabi, 1988a: 15). The concept of neo-patriarchy articulates two concepts in a union that is contradictory: the medieval patriarchy and the dependence of the Arab bourgeoisie – *compradore* – upon the imperialist centre as outlined in Marxist dependency theories. Sharabi combines the Weberian rationality as modernity with the Marxist notion of the "revolution". Weber though reserves the concept of patriarchy for patterns of Arab domination before the arrival of Islam. The neo-patriarchical system has the following characteristics: an extrovert economy in the service of the global economy, a fragmented culture that is also ritualist, a set of social relations that are dominated by the primary relations of family, clan and *ethnie*, a small bourgeoisie with bureaucratic links to the state and a classical Arabic culture exalting a transcendental revelation that is closed and anti-pluralist.

Traditionalism can take different forms, one of which is the agnatic neo-solidarity – *assabiya* (Carré, 1988: 768–787). Another form is the opposition between two states, the occidental and the Islamic, where the first frees the individual and makes politics autonomous, whereas the other closes itself in a conception of politics based upon unitary monism – the *tawhid* (Badie, 1986: 177). Traditionalism tends to collapse into a kind of essentialist sociology, a sociology that reproduces in its technical code an Islamic essence. It puts up Islam in the form of a *Gestalt* meaning a totality that is affected by the perverse consequences of modernity. A.R. Norton has reacted towards this manner of looking upon contemporary Islam, stating:

> the cultural explanations leave us with a very pessimistic image of the societies that are condemned for despotism due to the effect of schemes that are strongly established by endogamy, patriarchy or patrimonialism, or due to a perverse impact of Islam. (Norton, 1994/1995: vol. I, 6)

Muslim Civilisation and the Oriental Path

The Weber thesis searches for the roots of one aspect of modernity – modern capitalism or the market economy – within religion. To validate his argument, Weber conducted comparative enquiries into religion and economic institutions, from which he learned that other factors also mattered, especially the legal system. In reality, Weber added a number of factors besides the Protestant ethic, which created occidental exceptionalism. Now, how different was the Muslim civilisation? Let us look at how Weber conceived Islam as a religion as well as the Arab societies.

The modernisation of Arab countries raises several problems for historical and social research. One must ask why modernisation arrived late in the Arab countries, especially when taking into account that the Arab-Muslim world was more advanced in several respects than the occidental countries during the medieval period, or at least during an important part of it. One would like to know whether religion played a fundamental role in stopping the rise of a market economy and modern capitalism in the Arab world. We will underline Weber's employment of many criteria as well as his historical approach. What is at stake is to present the differences between occidental rationalism and the rationalism of the other cultures. Weber focuses upon occidental rationality to such an extent that it leads him, willingly or unwillingly, to overestimate the differences to the detriment of the similarities.

The occidental phenomena when transplanted into other civilisations follow a triple logic according to Weber. Either these phenomena did not exist anywhere but in the Occident. Or, when they occurred with other civilisations or other epochs, then they took an incomplete form. Occidental phenomena when transplanted became only embryonic, as they were vague start-ups, unfulfilled beginnings or rudiments. Or, finally, he multiplies the hindrances, which closed the occidental track for the other civilisations. Briefly, compared with the occidental track there is the triple logic of absence, startup and hindrances. However, when in the Occident the internal and external factors supported each other, then these same factors outside the Occident occurred independently or moved out of their track so that their combined development was simply blocked. They could have given the impression that the track had been opened, but the road was to be closed at once. This is Weber's first idea.

His second idea is the law of many criteria. This appears in the respective roles in the Occident and in Islam of the following phenomena: patrimonialism, the Church, sacred and profane law, as well as professional ethics. The point of departure seems to be the same, namely identifying a factor that is advantageous or disadvantageous for modern formal rationality. However, the theory about comparative advantage turns the disadvantage to advantage only for the Occident. Binder regrets this manner of analysing Islam, speaking of a "cluster of absences – the missing middle class, the missing city, the absence of political rights, the absence of revolutions" (Binder, 1988: 225).

Finally, Weber's historical comparison carries the risk of historical telescopy. Islam as analysed by him means the short sequence of the medieval period. On the other hand, the Occident is placed in a long sequence that extends itself from Greece to modernity. In reality, Weber describes the features of rationality in a Europe that is already in its modern stage when the process of rationalisation is once and for all completed, meaning that one could not possibly show the opposite. As a contrast, how can one show that Islam or Asia could have been able to develop or receive modern capitalism, especially as they did not experience it during the time when Weber compared them? This is the criticism of Rodinson, and Crone reiterates the argument: "rationality caused rationality to prevail in Europe whereas traditionalism stops it from emerging elsewhere" (Crone, 1999: 248).

The only way to escape from this vicious circle is an analysis of all the religions on one hand, and Protestantism on the other hand, on the basis of a simultaneous comparison across countries. This is where we touch the core of the historical telescopy: how can one compare the Protestant spirit of the seventeenth century with the Islamic spirit in its origin? And is it adequate to reconstruct the culture of Islam by starting from Protestantism, the blind point of comparison? In order for historical comparisons to have more validity, one would have had to take the precaution of limiting the comparison to the medieval period for both cultures, or extending the comparison to Asia and Islam in modern times. One is not able to explain the ambiguity of the subject of Weber's thesis without putting emphasis upon the historical starting point. Weber builds up cultural history in such a manner that he finds himself placed in a *cul-de-sac*, a fundamental weakness of his methodology.

To summarise, Weber put the emphasis upon the extreme originality of modern rationalist capitalism. Yet as he could not pretend that it was born out of nothing, by means of a miraculous fiat in the heart of Protestantism congruent with the capitalist form, he merely multiplied the factors that would be favourable to the birth of capitalism in the Occident on the one hand. Even the traditional Church institution promoted it. On the other hand, he announced the many hindrances that stopped it from developing in the non-European cultures. However, at the same time, he could not deny that these same cultures had started or had known similar cultural facts, which would imply that the same causes should have the same effects. The obstacles that we are talking about are often the same, in the Occident and the Orient. One recalls that the research strategy of Weber consists of insisting more upon the differences than the similarities. In short, modern capitalism is born in Western Europe with a break in a situation with a favourable set of forces, whereas in the other cultures modern capitalism is hindered by a continuity that is driven by approximately the same forces. The demonstration in the argument fails somewhat.

Weber's Typology

With regard to the ambiguity and imprecision in the research subject, three research lines are open. First, one could place the emphasis upon the opposition between the Occident and Islam. Second, one can focus on the contrast between Christianity and Islam and within Christianity between Protestantism and Islam. Finally, there is the possibility to look at modern capitalism and other economic forms in Islam. The first route targets civilisations whereas the second enquires into comparative religion, and the third focuses upon the economy. We may actually exclude the first route, because nothing is more strange for Weber than a *Kulturphilosophie*, which approaches civilisations as beings animated by a cyclical movement of growth and decadence. The two other routes are plausible and they will be pursued here.

To locate Islam in the Weberian discourse presupposes a definition of Islam. It is a very large religion, a civilisation and a culture – categories that Weber uses almost equivalently. Moreover, he regards Islamic culture as one of the most homogeneous. Yet the basic problem remains: which Islam are we talking about? Islam is sometimes the same as the Orient, but, as he presents his analysis, one should make clear that the "Orient" could refer to oriental Asia or the pre-Islamic Middle East, comprising Babylonia, Mesopotamia, ancient Egypt and Persia. Several times Islam meets with the occidental religions without mixing with them. The Islamic countries are also designated Turkey, Tunisia or Persia. Or he employs concepts from the various types of political regimes such as the caliphate or the Ottoman Empire. In this way Islam takes on a blend of images where several elements mix, which requires all kinds of precisions. Weber leaves the non-Arab Muslim world almost untouched.

It is possible to structure the Weber perspective on Islam by examining pieces here and there in terms of the key themes of his work: the sociology of religion, sociology of authority and economic history. One question is central, namely how to analyse the statute of Mohammed from the point of view of the sociology of religion? He was an ethical prophet with a position as a charismatic leader, which is also a key theme in the sociology of domination. One could take as the basis the three lines of Weber's thought, the cultural line or the motivational line, and the structural or institutional line, as well as the historical evolution of Islam as the guiding factor on the other hand. If these first two lines find discourse legitimacy in the works of Weber, then the analysis of the historical evolution of Islam has almost none. He was often critical against the specialists of the non-European civilisations to whom he addressed himself, hoping to find the essentials. However, the problem is that certain elements relating to the analysis of Islam are, if not wrong, then at least imprecise, as we will have occasion to signal. One may test the Weber analysis by means of a judgement about empirical validity or try to understand the stakes involved in a comparison between religions. We will choose both these options. Thus, from this angle we look at medieval Islam in the way Weber did. However, the extension of the thesis into contemporary Islam and the homology between medieval Islam and present day Islam is absolutely essential.

What makes plausible the historical perspective that we will suggest is exactly its total absence in the texts of Weber. He deals with Islamic history by jumping over whole large segments. Weber moves quickly several times from the origins of Islam to the Ottoman Empire by means of an overview within one phase without any form of explanation of an evolution that is stretched over almost six centuries. The extraordinary homogeneity of the Islamic culture has thus as correspondence the historical discontinuity in its evolution as civilisation. Weber's deliberations about Islam are not only fragmentary, but they are all the time presented within a remarkable lack of historical continuity. It will be necessary to fill in the void to make more precise the historical evolution of Islam.

Behind the many books, chapters and sections by Weber dealing with religion there is a simple scheme or framework of analysis. Thus, he employs two analytical distinctions to arrive at a complete classification of the major religions: (a) inner-worldly–outer-worldly; (b) rational–irrational (Weber, 1988a–c). We have thus the scheme in Table 3.1.

Table 3.1 Weber's Typology

	Inner-worldly	Outer-worldly
Rational	Buddhism	Protestantism
Irrational	Hinduism	Catholicism

The Weber thesis claims that the special drive, combining in one motivation both rationality and an outer-worldly orientation towards salvation, was conducive to a modern capitalist spirit. Yet where then did Protestantism succeed and Islam fail? According to Weber, Islam ignores the features of occidental rationality. Or he admits that Islam sometimes flirts with it, but then he multiplies the obstacles to the development of this rationality. The reader of Weber will have to systematise these, becauseWeber did not find the time necessary to do so. On the basis of the Weber text our argument is much more shaded: we claim that Islam as a religion had the universal features of occidental rationalism, but that the Arab societies could not free themselves of traditionalism. Islam is a theocentric religion in contradistinction to the cosmological religions of Asia. It should in principle push the *virtuosi* (in Weber's terms) to act in this world instead of fleeing it or only adapting to it.

Why, then, did Islam not benefit from a rationalisation similar to that of the Occident? Our answer is that, in relation to the population, political authority moved from charismatic rule to traditional rule, and did not result in the bureaucratic type of rule that is typical of modern or legal authority. With regard to religion, Islam made acquaintance with the Church, but the political authority remained *caesaro-papist*, lacking the fertile tension between Church and state, between Church and the priests with a free spirit. From the point of view of formal law rationalisation, Islamic law was a sacred order animated by material rationality only. It knew in ethics all the routes to salvation except grace with predestination. Or more exactly, it moved away from its initial potential. It knew also a capitalist ethos legitimating the taking of profits, but it rejected the line between capitalist ethics and religious ethics, as the end station and never the point of departure. In this manner, we can better recreate the unique place of Islam within the panorama of the great religions, between the Asian religions and those of the Occident.

Conclusion

There remains a final point to touch upon, namely the recent relevance of the Weber argument that has justified a return to Weber. An examination of post-Weberianism shows that modern research has been more inspired by the dogmatic message dealing with a time that has passed than with a new methodology that could serve as a useful tool for understanding Islam today. Against the opinion even of Weber himself, one has persisted in making contemporary Islam bow to a theoretical framework that is inappropriate, transforming thus the methodological eurocentrism to a comprehensive theory on Islam.

We will employ some of the basic concepts of Weber in his sociology of law as well as his theory of authority to present a different analysis of Islam. It will take into account the developments in modern times, especially the nineteenth and twentieth centuries. The key problem for the Muslim civilisation is not the acceptance of modern capitalism. Rational economic activity can be accommodated within Islam. It is democracy and human rights that create the dilemma within Muslim civilisation today, modernity or traditional. Thus, the difficulty in combining Islam and post-modernity is chiefly political and not of an economic nature.

SECTION II
Islam as a World Religion

One always states that Islam is a universal religion due to its great number of followers. In fact, a religion is universal also because it discusses problems such as the general rules of life, the relation between this world and the next world as well as society. Finally, a religion is universal because it can be studied from a general point of view, methodologically speaking. This approach is little interested in the essence of religions, but looks at conditions, forms, meanings or effects that the religion has for individuals and communities. The religious phenomena are extremely complex, because they are constantly mixed with the regulation of economic life, the social strata that carry a religion, the formation of political authority, the elaboration of holy dogma, the anxiety before the law as well as the ethical attitude in relation to practical incentives in action.

In order to draw the profile of Islam as a religion, two major distinctions help as a guide. The first distinction separates the Asian religions of a cosmological nature on the one hand and the Western monotheistic religions on the other. Let us retain here the key element that expresses the image of the world in the theocentric religions, namely that of God as transcendental, omnipotent and omniscient. A second distinction separates between the ethical prophecy and the exemplary prophecy. The crucial aspect is whether or not the ethical prophet speaks or merely acts in the name of God. These two fundamental distinctions interact and condition each other mutually. We will start with the second distinction due to the fact that in his enquiry into religion Weber integrates the historical developments that a religion has undergone with the roads of rationalisation that a religion has taken. This is his argument: Mohammed is a prophet of an ethical nature within Islam as a monotheistic religion. However, the special nature of Islam stems from the dominant position of the leading class of warriors, in both theory and practice in Islam. Weber noticed this typical feature in history and underlined it as a special characteristic, whatever theme or whichever period in history he referred to. We will conclude with a methodological point that implies an alternative thesis.

Chapter 4
Mohammed – A Political Prophet

Introduction

Bypassing a long tradition of oriental studies that examined whether the prophet of Islam had been sincere or merely a hypocrite, Weber enquired into the teachings of Mohammed in accordance with universalistic criteria. First, there is the ethical prophet, the writer–composer and the preacher. Second, there is the prophet as the builder of a movement, the legislator or judge, behaving in an exemplary manner. Thus, Mohammed is a prophet, legislator, political judge and leader of an army.

A prophet carries personal charisma as he/she announces a doctrine on the basis of a vocation or a mission, which contains, it is believed, divine commands for religious ends. The emphasis is here upon the objective in order to diminish the role of the prophet, the preaching as well as the philosophy, which all vary greatly. The prophet differs from the priest. The latter serves an already established sacred tradition, of which he is a "professional functionary". He is part of an order, the priesthood, although it may happen that he also makes use of a personal charisma, especially if there is a certain magical qualification for the profession, as within Christianity.

The prophet is also different from the magician. Both of them act on the basis of personal gift, but the magician lacks the divine revelation, the personal mission and the ethical doctrine. The magician tries to compensate for these by means of his expertise in the art of good making, which effort can go all the way to the science of the mystic – for example the Indian *gurus* or *yogis*. Finally, the prophet is not a philosopher. It is true that Confucius, in China, Socrates and Plato, as well as other philosophers in Greece, did create schools and had disciples. They influenced governments and had even a social impact, similar to that of prophets. However, what they lacked was the true emotional sermon or the consciousness of an authentic religious ethics, which transplants itself across the sayings and doings of Mohammed, for instance. From this point of view, the relation between the prophet and his disciples is more similar to that of the demagogue or a "political publicist" than to that which unites the master philosopher and his pupils. Mohammed, being a prophet, was neither a magician nor a priest, nor a philosopher. However, the concept of the prophet is sufficiently large not to be limited to monotheistic religions.

The prophet can renew an established religion as did the Indian reformers, or as with Luther and Calvin. Or the prophet can create a new religion, as did the Jewish prophets, Mohammed as well as the founders of the Mormon religion. Weber eliminates the idea that Mohammed could be a renovator of the biblical tradition. He does not take into account the criticism launched by the Arabs of Mecca that the preaching of Mohammed contains "histories told by the ancients" (the Koran 8: 31), which the Arabs knew but which they did not believe in. Nor does he take into account the fact that the Koran is regarded as a sacred book as it is preserved "on the guarded Table" (the Koran 85: 22). If one bypasses this, one cannot understand why Islam invites the Jews and the Christians to believe in the prophecy of Mohammed.

Do the adherents attach themselves to the message or to the prophet? According to Weber, it does not matter whether the disciples attach themselves to the person (Zarathoustra, Jesus, Mohammed) or to the doctrine (Buddha and the Jewish prophets). However, in the case of Mohammed one must moderate this idea making Mohammed more an ethical saviour than an ethical prophet. The attachment to the doctrine is as important as the belief in the prophecy of Mohammed, if not more so. On the one hand, obedience to the prophet goes hand in hand with obedience towards God. A Muslim is a person who obeys both. On the other hand, the Koran is regarded as a supernatural dictation to an inspired prophet; he is a passive messenger of a text in a style that the Koran presents as miraculous and not possible to imitate (the Koran 2: 23). Massignon argued that, if Christianity is basically the acceptance and imitation of Christ, before the acceptance of the Bible, then on the contrary Islam is the acceptaance of the Koran before the imitation of the prophet (http://en.wikipedia.org/wiki/Louis_Massignon, 8 January 2009). At this stage, Mohammed is not the renovator of an established religion but the founder of a new one. Is he, then, a legislator or judge, an ethical prophet or an exemplary?

The prophet as legislator lays down a law that already exists or puts forward a new one, as did the Greek *aysymnetes*, like for instance Solon. Yet, there is a difference, as Mohammed was not a tyrant. It is true that he took power, but he did so in the name of a revelation and for religious ends, not political ones. Moses was similarly a prophet and legislator. Mohammed was also a legislator, except for the fact that his preachings have the peculiarity of presenting themselves as divine revelation, which is different from Greek lawmakers and moral philosophers. The legislator distinguishes himself from the judge in accordance with the Italian model of *podesta*. This latter is external to the social group and he decides or rules impartially in quarrels between the group members. During his exile from Medina (622), the position of Mohammed was similar to that of the Italian *podesta* or that of Calvin in Geneva because he decided in conflicts between the Arabs and the Jews.

Weber argued that the orientation of the prophet was "fundamentally political", meaning that Mohammed was a political prophet to the same extent as the pre-Exodus Jewish prophets. Mohammed exercised three political functions: the judiciary, the administration of the community and especially the fiscal administration, that is, the distribution of the bounty as the leader of the Holy War. Mohammed was both a missionary and a political prophet, but he would be contested as a political leader by Ali Abd el Raziq (1888–1966) in 1926, shortly after the abolition of the Ottoman Califat, on 3 March 1924.

Prophecy

Mohammed is first and foremost an ethical prophet. The ethical prophecy or the mission is underlined by the fact that a holder of religious salvation acts in the name of an abstract or concrete God and by implication calls for obedience as an ethical duty. This is the case with the monotheistic prophets like Mohammed and Zarathustra according to his legend. On the contrary, the exemplary prophet shows by his behaviour the road to follow for those who sense a need to be saved. In no case did Buddha, a prophet of the exemplary type, talk in the name of a divine mission and he did not demand obedience as an ethical duty. Buddha suggested by himself a road to salvation, but without a God. Confucius, who was more a philosopher than prophet, spread an ethics, not only without God, but also without salvation from above.

Many meanings can be attached to salvation or "*Erlösung*". "Salvation" means, depending on the circumstances, merely the need to save one's soul and receive forgiveness for sins committed (*redemption*), either in this world or after – this is true of almost all religions. And it may involve a relation with the world or not, with action or without action. Two things are essential about salvation, the certainty of receiving salvation and its practical effects. In reality, the exemplary prophet offers a model of behaviour that invites contemplation, ecstasy and apathy, as, for instance, with Buddhism and Taoism in the cosmological religions. Yet it also harbours certain universal attitudes in the interior of ethical prophecies or the development of model behaviour as with mysticism, such as Sufism or Gnosticism. On the contrary, the prophecy of a mission is accompanied by demands for action in the world, as with Zarathustra, the Jewish prophets, the Islamic preaching and also naturally Christianity. In this case, Mohammed as an ethical prophet calls for action in this world.

The link between ethics and the motivation to act in the world is a key element in Weber's typology of prophecies. Weber underlines in general the active character of religion, also in relation to Buddhism, despite the fact that the action that it encourages consists of escaping from the Wheel of Time. He compares Buddha and Mohammed, their teaching and social goals (Weber, 1996b: 225). Yet, all depends on the type of action. To act in the world in the name of a transcendental God is not enough. God can guarantee salvation for his believers by demanding that they fulfil the requirements of the ritual, help their fellow human beings, attempt to restrain themselves by an ethics and organise their life methodically. This link manifests itself in the relation between religion and other spheres of existence such as the social strata that support the religion. This link is important in Weber's thought about Islam. In relation to the social strata every prophet counts his followers. These people do not represent social classes or occupational groups, but they are the agents of a religion, which links them with social status. In general, a religion is accompanied by the formation of a community where the members are linked to the prophet by personal fidelity. All religions, Weber claims, find support or their roots in certain social strata of educated laymen, merchants or the nobility. Even the prophet at the outset is a layman. It is in the development of events that the priesthood as a permanent institution is created, which gives grace. By relying upon certain social strata, the prophet supports himself upon social forces. Zarathustra took his base with a mountain people – at least so the myth states. Moses united urban strata and commercial strata whereas Jesus mingled with artisans (Crone, 1987; Crone and Cook, 1977).

With regard to Mohammed, Weber says that his own exceptional line of descendants, including noblemen and princes, supported Mohammed, but in another place he presents Mohammed as a merchant who leads a group of true believers to Mecca. Looking at the historical facts, we find that the first to convert to Islam were recruited from the family of Mohammed and his tribe, *Koreich*, which was a confederation of clan descendents, all of whom had a common ancestor, namely Abdel-Manaf, but they did not belong to "the line of noblemen and princes". If one takes into consideration that the dominating activity in Mecca was commerce, then one can say that they constituted what Weber would call a *petit bourgeoisie*. They went into exile to Medina (622) with Mohammed, where a few from his tribe with a high social and economic position had joined him as an individual venture. The definitive adhesion of the noblemen and the dominant from *Koreich* took place later when Mohammed had triumphed over his adversaries and he reentered peacefully again into Mecca (630). Then the noblemen and the princes declared to him their formal obedience as well as their acceptance of the faith, Arab historiography calling these last converts the *tulaga* meaning those with an amnesty. Mohammed had refused to take vengeance or to apply the laws of war to them, meaning death and the sharing of their spoils.

The nature of the social base (*Träger*) of a religion matters, Weber suggests. One would wish to underline the role that Weber gives to social strata in the historical evolution of a religion. It definitely concerns the status of Islam. If Islam takes support from a class of noblemen, then it joins in with the aristocratic nature of the cosmological religions. If not, then Islam enters the monotheistic religions which find their support with the urban strata, from Judaism to the pietist sects where pietism itself only accentuates this social character. However, neither the trading petit bourgeois pietist nor the noble laymen constitute to Weber the specific social strata for Islam. We are referring to his thesis of Islam as the religion of warriors, or those who combat for faith, meaning that they are at the same time the soldiers and the knights of Islam. This is an absolutely central element in the relationship within Islam between the prophecy and the social strata that supported it, according to Weber. Let us quote Weber:

> If one wishes to characterise succinctly, in a formula so to speak, the types representative of the various strata that were the primary carriers or propagators

> of the so-called world religions, they would be the following: In Confucianism, the world-organising bureaucrat; in Hinduism, the world-ordering magician; in Buddhism, the mendicant monk wandering through the world; in Islam, the warrior seeking to conquer the world; in Judaism, the wandering trader; and in Christianity, the itinerant journeyman. (Weber, 1978: 512)

When Weber separates the prophecy of Mohammed from all the others, then he underlines Islam as belonging to a "politico-military" type. Mohammed is thus the armed prophet. We must raise the question whether this really marks the essence of his religion.

A Monotheist Religion

As we have indicated, religious phenomena are complex. What Islam stands for depends upon the developments after the emergence of the religion and the roads toward rationalisation. Placing Islam between universalism and particularism, we will underline two things: the closeness in terms of doctrines between Islam and the monotheistic religions – especially Judaism; and the traditional elements that weigh heavy in the evolution of Islam – its Arabian heritage. Islam may be characterised as a monotheistic religion, with a simple faith, but its evolution left a strong mark on it. Out of the three monotheistic religions, Islam and Judaism are strictly monotheist, whereas Christianity is so to a lesser extent, due to the idea of salvation through incarnation. The concept of redemption and the Trinity in Christianity may be compared with notions found in Hinduism, Taoism and late Buddhism. In fact Judaism is the avant-garde of universalist monotheism, but also the model of the teachings of Mohammed. Islam is the late offspring of Middle-East monotheism conditioned by the motives of the Old Testament. The connection is often emphasised. The interdiction to take interest payments in Islam and in Christianity (Catholicism) reminds one of the ethics of Judaism, which allows Jews to take interest only from foreigners, or non-Jews. Also, the battle for faith by means of the Holy War may be related to the Jewish idea of a Holy Land and the elevation of the people of Israel above other nations.

Yet, the faith of Judaism and Islam is simple compared with Western Christianity (Goetein, 1968: 200). The belief in the prophecy and a few norms or commandments is enough to constitute the community (*umma*). In Christianity one finds a rationally developed dogmatic system of thought, which had consequences upon the evolution in the Occident, Church and philosophy. Islam limited the multiplication of dogmas, although controversies over doctrines erupted on several questions. This results from the simplicity of faith, but also from the fact that Islam has confidence in the consensus of legal scholars, based upon the principle that the Islamic community cannot make mistakes. However, it is impossible for faith to stay within the limits of its initial simplicity. Everywhere and for different reasons the need to canonise the Holy Scriptures makes itself felt. In the Islamic case, the codification of the Islamic canon – the Koran – made it the sacred book. As it happened, the third caliph, Uthman (644–656), ordered that various texts be united in one book.

Each religion creates its formation of groups supporting it, such as professionals, priests, doctors of law and the theologians, in order to manage the charisma, or gifts of God. Each new religion institutionalises itself and by the same way traditionalises itself. However, these groups enter into competition with laymen, whom they search to exclude or dominate. The evolution of a religion depends upon its level of intellectualisation. Either the clerks take charge of religion in the daily life (in Greece or China for instance), or religion falls into the hands of priests or monks, as with Christianity or Buddhism. The priesthood puts in place its monopoly over metaphysical thinking, dogmas and ethics. Islam could not avoid this, but Islam is a religion of laymen according to the doctrine of Mohammed. Islam harbours a theology, meaning a rationalisation from the intellectual point of view of the religious inspiration. Theology in this sense developed to some extent within Islam, but only occidental Christianity gave it the most finished form of development in history.

The process of intellectualisation was limited in Islam. One reason is that the priesthood was in competition with other social agents, the Sufis, the dervishes or the philosophers who, like Avicenna, Averroes or Ghazali, made religion an intellectual enterprise by means of a combination of rationalisation, mysticism and orthodoxy. Only the isolated heterodox sects had a purely intellectual character. Islam has a Church, but it is a Church of clerks (sheiks, imams). Primitive Christianity was not a religion of letters, but it was to receive a systematic intellectualisation in the form of scholasticism in the Middle Ages. The healing of the soul is an instrument of power of the priesthood in relation to the laymen. The Catholic confession, the pietist pastors, the directors of conscience, the *rabbis* within Judaism, the *gurus* in India and the many dervishes influenced in a continuous and decisive manner the behaviour of laymen and those holding power. Religion conditions those who seek salvation – men or women – but always in relation with particular social concerns. The admission of women on an equal footing with men in the ritual may very well co-exist with a monopoly on the religious function by men, as is the case in most religions, for instance Islam.

A Religion of Warriors

Each religion comprises a typical way of life carried by specific social strata that in their turn render a practical orientation to this conduct. Confucianism was the religion of prebendal literates who propagated a secular form of rationalism. Ancient Hinduism was carried by a hereditary caste of priests – the Brahmans – who offered a ritualistic cure of the spirit for its followers. Buddhism is a contemplative religion, which flees the world supported by commercial groups standing behind the begging monks who wander around. Finally, Christianity is a religion of artisans travelling around (Weber, 1996b: 205–207, 214). Islam was basically to Weber a religion of warriors, an order of knights who continuously moved around to conquer the world. And this military order influences the orientation of its economic ethic. Thus, Islam is a religion of warriors by twofold means, on the one hand socially and on the other hand economically. In other words, if there is one characteristic that weighs heavily on the destiny of Islam, then it is the struggle for the faith, meaning the Holy War or *jihad*.

This insistence by Weber has no doubt marked generations of commentators. We can only deplore it strongly, as one may ask whether Weber was so hostile to Islam that he did not see other things than knights moving around, with the sabre in their hands and the promise of paradise inside their coat. He never denied that the Islamic empires were equally tolerant as the occidental kingdoms, tolerance being a universal phenomenon driven by different forces including political (reasons of state), economic (mercantilism) and religious reasons (pity).

Let us underline two features concerning the economic ethic of *jihad*. First, religion commands Muslims to engage in a Holy War and pushes them towards an organisation with knights based upon clan and motivated by the chase for richness. Islam became very rapidly a religion of masters who disposed of vast domains, where the first to convert became the most affluent. This is especially true as the pietist phase of the prophet was shortened by the move from Mecca to Medina. The establishment of the Umayyad dynasty underlined this further (Wellhausen, 1909/1960: 71–125). Weber emphasised a specific feature that one hardly ever finds in the other religions with regard to fighting for the faith. In Islam the stakes in the combat do not basically concern the defence of the faith or the spread of the faith to new believers as with the other religions mentioned above. In Islam the combat has an essentially pecuniary orientation or fiscal nature (*looting*). It is the appetite for land and the conquest of property that drive the Islamic warriors, from Mohammed and his followers up until the Turkish *spakis*.

To Weber the beginnings of a religion had a considerable influence over how its characteristic features evolved: Islam was a comparatively late product of Near Eastern monotheism, in which Old Testament and Jewish or Christian elements played a very important role. Islam displayed various connections with social groups:

> In the first Meccan period of Islam, the eschatological religion of Mohammed developed in pietistic urban conventicles, which displayed a tendency to withdraw from the world. But in the subsequent developments in Medina and in the evolution of the early Islamic communities, the religion was transformed from its pristine form into a national Arabic warrior religion, and even later into a religion with very strong status emphasis. Those followers whose conversion to Islam made possible the decisive success of the Prophet were consistently members of powerful families. (Weber, 1978: 623–624)

To state the difference comparatively, Islam was different from Buddhism, which emerged from a community of wise ascetics who wanted to free themselves from life. Similarly Islam was different from Judaism, in search of a kingdom devoted to fidelity towards the Law. Islam also differed from Christianity, which sprang out of community that was indifferent to the world while paying homage to the universal Kingdom of God – a brotherhood of souls.

The alliance between the social strata and the economic ethic pushed Islam decisively in the direction of Arab traditionalism, including feudalism. A feudal spirit fundamentally animates Islam with a social organisation according to orders. The predominance of bounty, the acceptance of slavery, as well as of polygamy, are all signs of a traditionalist ethics or a lifestyle that is contrary to a method of life that is ascetic in this world. Islam freezes itself into a patrimonial system of favours (*benefices*). From the moment that the warrior is driven by profit and not strictly by faith, the relationship between external and internal morale is changed. The internal ethic aiming at salvation is thrown into the background as the profit motive advances. Because of this ethical reversal, the promise about paradise made to the warrior who is killed in the Holy War is not a promise of salvation, if one is true to the wording. This was going to have dire consequences for the nature of Islamic predestination, because one could not argue that the promise of Paradise was still valid despite its financial aspects. It is difficult to separate the promise of salvation from the sufferings in the world that it entails, as it is difficult to distinguish rigorously between salvation and the economic and political prestige that religion carries with it. The stakes in relation to predestination focus upon the salvation of the spirit beyond this world. The reason is that, if these dispositions fix the salvation to this world, then predestination becomes predetermination. The Holy War is transformed from a test of true belief to a form of pecuniary reward. *Jihad* brings with it a promise of Paradise for the Islamic Warrior, looking for bounty in this world. However, looting has existed all through the history of mankind. It is not unique for Islam, nor typical of it, except during the period of Arab expansion. The major lootors in Islamic history, the Mongols and the Tartars, did not hesitate to loot their Islamic brothers and sisters.

Conclusion

From the beginning, the destiny of Islam seems to be framed by a double bind, when compared with Calvinism. During the Middle Ages the warrior ethic was feudal and during modern times it is anti-ascetic. However, the strata of warriors disappeared for quite natural reasons. Later, the fight for the faith became weaker because the obligatory military service was abandoned. After the ninth century the Muslims refused combat to such an extent that the caliph had to rely more and more upon mercenaries or slave armies who reinforced the patrimonial features of Islam.

Thus Islam, like all religions, changed hands. The order of knights gave way to other social strata that appeared with time: the legal scholars, the theologians, the Sufis and the brotherhoods from the petit bourgeoisie. In fact, what interested Weber in the relation to economic ethics and social classes is the practical drive to action in the world. It seemed to him that the social strata with a mystical religiosity could better explain this drive to action, especially the drive towards ascetism with the *virtuosi*. Yet, despite these social changes, the ethical orientation of the combat for the faith continued to play a role in Islam. Today, however, it is only Islamic fundamentalism that represents the Weber theory about Islam as a warrior religion. It is vital to identify the core of Islam without the concept of *jihad*, which we will attempt in the next chapter.

Chapter 5

Islam: Faith and Rationality

Introduction

The central question from a Weberian perspective is the following: why did Islam fail to enhance a rationalisation similar to that of the Occident, which brought such advantages? What made Islam close the many roads towards the birth of modern capitalism? This is a proper question, because at the start Islam seemed well equipped. The ethical prophecy of Mohammed placed Islam in the same position as Judaism with Moses and Christianity with Paul. Its strict monotheism seems to better serve Islam than Christianity, which in its primitive and medieval versions propagated an economic ethics, nourished more by divine will than a rationalist ethics. In any case, Mohammed freed Islam from the intermediary of clerical institutions, which retarded the ethics of conviction up until Protestantism proclaimed the fundamental return to the scriptures. The same applies to the religion of the laymen, which is more flexible and less restrictive than a religion of priests or dogmatic theologians. Neither those in power nor the Church will stop the priests of the spirit intervening freely in the prayers. They could thus develop a religiosity that influences the conduct of life in such a way as to push people to organise their lives rather than expecting the clerical organisation to hand over to them the means of salvation, monopolising power and prestige.

To understand rationality in Islam one must include the relations between political power and religious power, including the nature of Islamic law. One must take into account that Islam accepted modern capitalism once it reached the Muslim civilisation. Islam also included an ascetic ethics. It seems to us that Islam displays an open orientation towards all the roads of rationalisation with the exception of the Western road, leading to democracy and the post-modern society. The form that rationality took in Islam was to be different. One trend suggests a road involving the decline of religion or the inevitable sclerosis of religion, given that specific agents take on board religion. Take for instance preaching. It is specific to the prophecy and when one finds it with other persons with charisma, then it is an imitation, as it shows its intensity at the time of great prophetic agitation. Yet, it falls in intensity every time the clergy takes care of that religion on a daily basis. It was only in Protestantism that the preacher replaced the clergy. At the same time, nothing is stranger to prophecy than magic – its elimination is even the condition for a prophecy, or stronger, the demystification of the world. The same applies to aesthetics, which is a human effort in tension with the transcendence of God. Yet in practice religion takes on aesthetic features in the hymns, ceremonies and the rituals. For instance, the cult of the saints weakens the radial monotheism. In relation to factual matters the theme of the religious warriors neglects the relation of Islam to other social strata: the religious and legal scholars, the Sufis, the mysticists, the dervishes, the sects and the artisans.

To put our question explicitly: is there in Islam, or in the Koran, a core body of ideas that makes the accommodation of the principles of the post-modern society impossible or very difficult? Resolving this question leads us to reflect upon the nature of Islam in order to locate where it collides with the principles of postmodernism. It is not in the sphere of economic rationality that we have the major tension between Islam and post-modernity. It is the conception of power that constitutes the major stumbling block.

The Roads to Salvation in Islam

Islam displays a ritual and a set of simple but elaborate cultural ceremonies. The Sufi or the dervish seeks personal perfection (Trimingham, 1971). Faith is starightforward from the outset, as it contains few dogmatic requirements, but only practical commands (the five pillars) guiding the conduct of life, at least until religion was intellectualised by certain doctrines, especially the so-called *mutazilism* (Goldziher, 1981; Gardet and Anawati, 1970: 46–52). From the point of view of salvation, Islam adheres to the logic of a deliverance from sin, whereas for instance Confucianism is to be placed outside of such a framework due to the fact that it does not elaborate dogmas about the good and the bad or the deliverance from evil – redemption.

Following the rituals is one road to salvation. Giving alms is a ritual practice that is universally prescribed for various reasons. On the whole it is for the protection of the weak, the poor, the beggars, women, children and those without resources. It can be extended to the exploited classes without scruples. The prohibition against usury or heavy interest payments forms part of this logic. All religions dislike greed of the heart. In Islam giving alms is even one of the five pillars that constitute the foundations of faith, transforming charity and the prohibition against usury into a ritual. Religion can only adapt to the world. Protestantism, as the exception here, assumes all its distinctiveness:

> One of the most notable economic effects of Calvinism was its destruction of the traditional forms of charity. First it eliminated unsystematic almsgiving. (Weber, 1978: 588)

Calvinism rationalised charity by ending the anarchic forms of well-doing in relation to beggars. The one who asked alms lacked love of his neighbour. Thus, only those who were incapable of working and orphans would be allowed charity. The ethical meaning of charity is either done away with or is transformed into its opposite. Moreover, Protestantism limits the prohibition against the taking of interest to cases where it really expresses an immoral greed. Finally, Calvinism removed the sin of seeking economic gain on behalf of those doing it most rigorously. Thus, in terms of ethics, profit is liberated from prohibition. Unintentionally, Protestantism was conducive to the modern capitalist ethics of investing and amassing capital assets without becoming sybarites.

Another road to salvation is predestination, which is typical within monotheistic religions with eschatology – the *Judgement Day* – because they presuppose a God that is all-powerful. Weber writes:

> The omnipotent creator God must be envisaged as beyond all the ethical claims of his creatures, his counsels impervious to human comprehension. Another facet of this emerging view was that God's absolute power over his creatures is unlimited, and therefore that the criteria of human justice are utterly inapplicable to his behaviour. (Weber, 1978: 522)

This applies to the all mighty Jahve of the Jewish people, the "*deus absinditus*" of the Christian *virtuosi* and Allah for his most passionate followers. Yet this God must manifest his will somehow, such as by giving signs, for instance commands that his followers can put into action in a consistent manner by considering themselves as his instrument and thus render pleasure to God. Perhaps these followers, then, will be those whom God has selected for paradise? The anxiety of religion is being able to predict who will receive redemption.

Thus, the problem now becomes the question of free will. God is not enough to orientate human action in one direction or another, at least not when it is a matter of active ascetic behaviour. The believer not only looks upon himself as instrument of the will of God, but also acts by his own will in a manner to please God, either engaging in mysticism or in a rational conduct of behaviour within this world. Asceticism may take place in the secular world, quite contrary to mysticism, which stretches out of the world by means of contemplation. Judaism did not develop any form of asceticism, which is also true of primitive Islam, whereas within late Islam asceticism occurs with the dervishes as a source of mysticism and ecstasy.

Religious belief may end up in fatalism, as God's will is enigmatic (Armstrong, 1999, 2000). There is, however, predestination when the opposite emerges, as the followers are pushed to act according to God's will in order to make certain that they belong to the aristocracy of God, the ascetics or *virtuosi*. They can do this in various ways, including forgetting themselves in combat or organising their life in a strictly methodical manner. The belief in predestination focuses in its initial purity upon the sovereign will of God or his governance as central, thus de-emphasising the idea of any grace acquired by means of magic intermediation, by institutions as well as finally by the sacraments.

It is in relation to this question of the means of salvation that one may ask whether Islam endorses the idea of predestination or tends towards pre-determination. One would answer this question by arguing that Islam is a religion with predetermination. Weber argued that the potential for predestination within Islam was transformed into an irrational form of fatalism that worked against modern capitalism. Saint Augustin, Mohammed, Calvin and Luther are stated as examples of men who believed in predestination, as they "were motivated by an exuberant need for rational religious power" (Weber, 1978: Section 10), almost being the prey of emotions that they could not handle, except by being sure that they were the instruments of God. The Islamic warrior forgetting about himself in combat for the faith is given as an example of the logical consequence of the belief in predestination to the same extent as the Calvinist puritan. The religious *virtuosi* could have been a conquering order at the time of Mohammed or Omar, or they could be dervishes, Sufis or the Karijites.

Islamic Predestination

First, we have the content of the faith. Second, we have the practical effects. The Islamic form of predestination ignores the double Calvinist form according to which God decides to give some an eternal life, whereas others are given an eternal damnation. One can only understand predestination, or the game between this world and the other world, if the stakes in predestination concern the destiny in the next life and not within this one. It is this element within predestination that could result in a rational ethics.

Islam, however, never did attribute to God the predestination for eternal damnation, even more so as God allows for the distractions of men and women. Predestination concerns in reality less the life after this life than the regulation of cases within this life, like for instance the death of a warrior in the Holy War, which renders him a place in paradise. Islam resembles the *moira* of the Greek. Concerning eternal life, it is positively acquired through the declaration of faith in God and his prophet, adherence to the moral commands in the conduct of behaviour and observation of the rituals. Islam thus also lacks a dramaturgy, as the uncertainty about salvation is calmed down through the knowledge that God forgives the distractions of men and women.

Predestination according to Protestant logic is paradoxical. From the fact that the puritan does not know if he or she is elected or damned in relation to life after death, his or her certainty of being saved – *certitudo salutis* – depends directly upon the confirmation from the conduct of life in this world. The puritan searches for this certainty in the rational asceticism in daily life, which would have positive effects upon economic mentality. This could not happen in relation to a Muslim, who is assured that he or she enjoys eternal happiness by means of the profession of faith and the respect for ritual. In Islam, the practical effects of predestination are neutralised by the absence of asceticism in daily life with the view of transforming the world, Weber writing:

> There was nothing in ancient Islam like an individual quest for salvation, nor was there any mysticism. The religious promises in the earliest period of Islam

> pertained to this world. Wealth, power, and glory were all martial promises, and even the world beyond is pictured in Islam as a soldier's sensual paradise. (Weber, 1978: 625)

And he adds later on that the connection between life in this world and life after was missing in Islam:

> The ruling conception was that predestination determined, not the fate of the individual in the world beyond, but rather the uncommon events of this world, and above all such questions as whether or not the warrior for the faith would fall in battle. The religious fate of the individual in the next world was held, at least according to the older view, to be adequately secured by the individual's belief in Allah and the prophets, so that no demonstration of salvation in the conduct of life is needed. (Weber, 1978: 574)

Thus, by following the simple commandments of Islam, the Muslim is predetermined for eternal life and Paradise.

Islamic Predetermination

The well-known thesis of F. Ulrich (1912) made a complicated distinction between destination (God's kindness) and determination (God's absolute domination) as well as between predestination and predetermination. Weber for his part added the relation between the combat for faith and the confirmation of grace in the world (Weber, 1978: 557–576). What is the relation between predestination and predetermination in Islam? In effect, one should be able to validate the distinction between predetermination and predestination. The Koran contains numerous verses that proclaim predetermination. One single example is enough here: "admire what you have sculptured as God has created You, You and what You have accomplished" (the Koran 37: 95–96). And a counter-example indicates predestination: "anyone wants it, be he believer, and anyone wants it, be a non-believer" (18: 29) (see other verses: Bouamrane, 1978: 105–135; Badawi, 1972: 41–43; Watt, 1946: 131–132; 1985: 15–24). The key concepts mentioned are *jabar* (determination) and *qadar* (predestination). Islamic debate and religious thought have witnessed many clashes over the centuries over whether it is God or man who is the origin of actions, whether pleasure and pain, suffering and wrong have a divine or human origin.

Three doctrines confront each other. The first one is determinist: God is the creator not only of the world but also of the actions of humans. The second, which is rationalist, affirms that everyone is a free judge in the name of reason and divine justice: all acts created by God are good because it is unjust that he does wrong, which is contrary to his essence. Man has on the contrary the power and the capacity to create his actions. A third position may be outlined as moderate determinist: God is the true creator of actions, but men and women attribute actions to themselves and put them onto their shoulders (*kasb*). What, then, is the faith (*iman*), the very act that makes men and women entirely obedient? For some, faith is merely the intimate feeling (*tasdiq*), which alone should condition faith. It is to be understood as an adhesion, obedience to God and his prophet. This conviction amounts to a minimum of faith. For others, faith requires more, for instance the public profession of faith according to the use of language (*qawl*). Finally, the majority position expands the faith to the totality of the five prescribed duties, which constitute by themselves all the acts of obedience (*taat*): the verbal confession, the prayer, the fasting of Ramadan, the legal alms and the pilgrimage to Mecca. Only the Sufis place the faith in their heart as faith becomes the internal correspondent to the external belief created by God (Ash'ari, tenth century, 1980; Mâturidi, ninth to tenth centuries, 1986; http://en.wikipedia.org/wiki/Abu_Mansur_Al_Maturidi, 8 January 2009).

Islam can exist without faith. The hypocrite (*munafiq*) can for instance dissimulate his disobedience by the practice of ritual. On the contrary, faith may exist without Islam, as with the people of the Book, essentially Jews and Christians. Faith and Islam – are they variable? It is in this sense that the pertinent question of the great sinner merits examination. The "great sinner" is a believer who has committed a major sin or wrongdoing. The major sins are those that the Law forbids formally, for instance to kill without cause, or to steal. How is such a person to be described? One would have to reflect over whether one should be intransigent towards the great sinner or display forgiveness. Is he or she a Muslim although a disobedient one, or is he or she clearly an infidel? The double Calvinist decision – the salvation or the damnation as eternal sanction – turned into an obsession to such an extent that a specific form was invented for it: could man or woman be held responsible for that which he or she is not capable of accomplishing? This problem has a technical term in Arabic, *taklif ma la yutaq*, or a duty for which one is responsible before God, but which one is completely incapable of accomplishing (Brunschvig, 1976: 170–220). To say that Islam ignores the idea of predestination is thus wrong.

There are also two kinds of obstacles, structural and cultural, where the first refers to structures of authority but the others are to be found in the "religious attitude". First, the potential for predestination has been turned around in Mahdism. The combat for faith is a phenomenon which exists in all religions that distribute grace. It is the aristocracy of grace that generates this. There is no difference between the person who fights for Islamic faith and the Calvinist or Lutheran pietist. Islam sublimates action in the Holy War, which implies that it devalues ordinary political action, almost as did Cromwell when he opposed action in contradiction to his conscience. Lutheranism as well as Calvinism would fight against the world of sins in a different manner from the just war as with Lutheranism by means of a passive acceptance of authority or even better a passive resistance, while Calvinism sublimates the conduct of rational behaviour. On the contrary, Islam turns away from the idea of an ethics for acting within this world in a professional manner (*Beruf*), which is so typical of Protestantism.

Second, when Islam began to experience the coming of a bourgeoisie, then the potential for predestination was further diminished. However, for Calvinism it was increased by the same influence. More so, the Umayyad caliphate, which suffered from a deficit of legitimacy, used the idea of predestination in a special sense. In principle, predestination concerned only the destiny after this life, being potentially dangerous for all power due to the fact that it is conducive to a special attitude towards all forms of secular power. The Umayyads exploited it in order to say the opposite, namely that God condemns some in the world in order to legitimate a power that is badly received. The Abbasids did not do better, since they went all the way to make the caliphate sacred, qualified as the shadow of God on Earth.

Islamic Fatalism, Asceticism and Salvation

When Islam developed from the prophet and his first followers to the Ottoman Empire, then Islam became fatalist, legalist and ritualist. The initial tension between religion and the world decreased, which handicapped the orientation towards an ethics of conviction focusing upon professionalism. Islamic predestination dissolved itself into either fanaticism or the pursuit of Holy War on the one hand or passive acquiescence – fatalism – on the other hand.

In Islam, predestination acquired fatalist features, which mingled with magical elements, especially within popular religion, as for example *Kismet*, a Turkish word that designates the part attributed to God as destiny. With the exception of Judaism and Protestantism, all religions adapted to the needs of the masses or the social strata that were economically non-privileged such as the petit bourgeoisie, the craftsmen and the women. Popular religions take certain typical forms from the point of view of salvation: the taboo, the sacraments, the fear of demons, illuminated mysticism and magic. The taboo may even create an ethical system, which it validates for the entire community or certain groups. In reality one must realise that it is not respected systematically and it is turned around by fictions. The taboo presents "extremely strong obstacles towards commerce and the development of market communities". An example is the "absolute impurity attributed to those who are exterior to the confession as known by Shiism in Islam" (Weber, 1978). The piety of the dervishes and the rationalist tendencies of the Sufis were favourable to economic activity and profit. In order to understand the tension between Islam and post-modernity it is not enough to concentrate upon the economic consequences of this world religion. Essentially, Islam does not exclude rationality. Yet fatalism is only part of the picture. To it, one must add Arab traditionalism.

From the perspective of religion and economics, where should Islam be located in the panorama of religions? In effect, the relation to the world among the *virtuosi* may take on several forms: he can be enchanted by the world, he can be hopeful in the world or he can contemplate it; he can accept it or he can master it. He lives in the world following a noble or pious existence, or he refuses but takes flight. Or he refuses it but transforms it. Only the negation of the world orientated towards its rational transformation is typical of Protestant asceticism, generated by predestination.

One initial difference is the separation between the cosmological religions of Asia and the occidental religions conditioned by the sovereignty of a God that is distant and omniscient. A second distinction concerns the theoretical contemplation of the world as with the Greeks and the adaptation to the world as in Confucianism and Taoism. A third distinction is that between the negation of the world as with Hinduism and Buddhism on the one hand and the affirmation of the world in the monotheistic religions. Finally, one may distinguish between the eschatological approach as with Zoroasterism and the circular view of time as with the Asian religions approaching life on Earth with the model of the Great Wheel (Glasenapp, 2003).

Articulating the basic attitudes within religions, Weber says that the contemplation of the world, adapting to and acquiescing in it, refusing the world by flight, but never attempting to transform it, enchants the religions of Asia. The occidental religions are dualistic, focusing upon the confrontation between Good and Evil in the hope that salvation will lead to Paradise. Only Protestant asceticism refuses the ordinary world, which is the key entity, in order to transform it. Neither Judaism nor primitive Christianity, despite the debt that Protestantism owes them, develops such a relationship with the existing world.

Rational asceticism changes secular and daily life towards the rationalisation and systematisation of daily activity. It is at this level that the distinction becomes crucial between inner-worldly asceticism orientated towards the transformation of the world and all other forms of salvation–deliverance, which is from a historical point of view decisive from the interior side of redemption religiosity. It is equally basic for the separation between occidental and oriental religions, involving the rejection of the world and the acceptance of the world in two versions: the rejection of the world by means of flight contra transformation, as well as the passive or enchanted acceptance vs the rational and non-magical mastery of the world. Islam contemplates the world and accepts it, masters it and takes flight from it, affirms it and denies it. It even has a potential for initial predestination, but it lacks one single element, namely the rational mastery of the world that originates in dualistic eschatology. It is with regard to this element that the opposition between Islam and Protestantism is decisive. Since we have already made valid the basic adherence of Islam to the monotheistic bloc and shown that Islam knew the roads to salvation–deliverance, we will now place the emphasis upon the limits of active asceticism, which is the ultimate difference.

The first converts, urban strata or pietists from the bourgeoisie, belonged to an eschatological religion, and they rejected the world, states Weber. This happened in Mecca, but in Medina Islam became a "national Arabic warrior religion", as the combat for the faith generated by necessity an aristocracy calling upon man to participate in the dualistic struggle. This aristocracy becomes an active one in Islam, as it tends to dominate the world (Weber, 1993, 1978: 624). The warriors belonged to an ascetic sect. Their "serene happiness in front of the world", being sure that they were going to Paradise, made them constitute an ascetic sect, reinforced especially by the ascetic discipline within the war camps where they lived. Thus, Islam has known ascetic sects (Weber, 1978: 570, 619, 626).

However, Weber denies that asceticism in Islam ever took the same form as asceticism in Protestantism. Certainly it was not the middle-class ascetic systematisation of the conduct of life. Moreover, it was effective only periodically, and even then it tended to merge into fatalism. We have already spoken of the quite different effect, which is engendered in such circumstances by a belief in providence. Islam was diverted completely from any really methodical control of life by the advent of the cult of saints, and finally by magic. On the moral plane, the ethics of warriors is quite distant from that of monks and even more so from the ascetic systematisation of the conduct of life within the bourgeoisie. It remained valid only for definitive periods and it was transformed into fatalism. The warriors were replaced by a feudal aristocracy, which was guided by the idea of the Holy War as well as by the cult of the saints and the reintroduction of magic. Thus, Islam emptied its virtual asceticism.

Moreover, the ascetic character of Islam also appears in relation to the brotherhoods that developed out of sects in medieval times. All of these were made up of the petit bourgeoisie and the craftsmen, but the religious spirit was different when compared with Christianity. The orders of dervishes or the Sufis elaborated a method of salvation each in themselves. It could be of an ascetic nature and it certainly often was. Are they ascetics or contemplative? Sufism may be described either as ascetic-contemplative or, later on, as mystico-contemplative (Weber, 1978: 481). The same applies to the brotherhoods, as they are described as *petit bourgeoisie* living with their religiosity in the world in the manner of the tertiary Christians, that is, the orders created by the Franciscans and the Dominicans, allowing laymen to stay within the world obeying the evangelical model of life.

Conclusion

Islam and post-modernity – where lies the principal difficulty? A post-modern society is an open society where individuals can choose their belief systems on the basis of freedom and reflection, where a multiplicity of viewpoints are in open contest and where reason and argument are employed when different ways of life meet. The political prerequisites of an open society include human rights, democracy and the rule of law. However, Islam never developed these political preconditions of an open society. The political institutions of Islam were always simplistic, focusing upon how the Koran would be inculcated in politics and law. The key political offices – in Islam the caliph, the Emir, the *qadi* and the *mufti* – operated according to a different logic. Truth has been received from above and needs only to be implemented downwards authoritatively. The same logic applies to Shiite Islam where the political role of the Madhi, the imam, the Supreme Spiritual Leader and the *ulemas* is orientated towards the transmission of the truth from above.

The post-modern society reveals the truth from below, through the countless interactions between groups and individuals. It cannot accept the restrictions that Islam imposes upon the search for truth. Islam can be accommodated within the post-modern society, but the politics of Islam must change.

It should be pointed out that Islam as a world religion has included one mystical tradition, despite the koranique rejection of magic. The Sufi movement has attempted to add a sort of internalisation of Islam to the strict outer obedience of the five duties. It may be regarded as both ascetism and mysticism, being practised by teachers and their disciples. Sufism spans continents and cultures, occurring in Arabia, Persia, as well as India and Africa. The Turkish Dervishs constitute a form of Sufism, which is either ascetic or mystical, the latter expressed in the spectacular whirling dances. Medieval philosopher Al Ghazali adhered to sufism, claiming it could be derived from the Koran. Actually, the Sufi movement has adherents among both Sunnis and Shias. However, Sufism is contested among Moslems, as for instance Salafists reject it.

SECTION III
The Muslim Legacy

Since Islam emerged in Arabia, it is hardly a surprise that the Muslim civilisation is a mixture of Islam according to various religious interpretations and numerous traditions from the Arab societies. One would like to try to separate Islam as a universal set of religious beliefs and values from certain of its specific Arabian legacies. We will examine four major Arab traditions: (a) patrimonialism and sultanismus, (b) oriental feudalism; (c) caesaro-papism and (d) Sharia law. We will focus upon the consequences of Arab institutions for Muslim backwardness. Islam could not possibly be an explanation of the strength of the Arab traditions, but the combination of Islam with Arab traditionalism makes political development less probable in the Muslim civilisation (Tibi, 2000, 2009).

Chapter 6
Traditional Domination

Introduction

Islam has known all forms of domination, except the bureaucratic one, which is the legal and rational type of authority that the Occident has employed. One should add modern, because bureaucracy is a much older phenomenon and its historical origins are universal. Islam had not experienced bureaucratic authority until it was exported to the Muslim countries at the end of colonialism. As the system of political domination and the appropriation of opportunities and economic resources are interconnected, bureaucratic authority gives precedence to progress towards a modern capitalist economy, whereas other types of domination hinder it. If one wished to redraw the historical evolution of political authority in Islam, then one could say that before Islam authority was patriarchal, focusing upon the figure of an Arab sheikh. The sheikh represents traditional authority that has had two faces in Islam, namely patrimonial and sultanic power. The first feature is universal, whereas the second is mainly typical of Islam.

This evolution from patriarchalism to patrimonialism and sultanism is what we will describe. We will start with patriarchalism, which is a form of traditional domination, and then move to charismatic rule in order to return after that to traditional rule in its version of patrimonial sultanism, after which we finish with legal authority. This is done in order to emphasise the case that is missing in Islam, namely legal–rational authority. In a second step we will enquire into the relationship between political authority and the economy.

From Patriarchalism to Charismatic Rule

By "authority" is meant the probability that an order will meet with obedience on the part of ordinary people. The various motives behind the motivation to obey matter. In the absence of this obedience, it would only be a question of naked power (*Macht*) and not authority (*Herrschaft*). The latter presupposes an agreement to obey, which tends to be based on a feeling of legitimacy. One speaks about various types of domination as well as legitimacy almost without separating the two. Authority is the perspective of the holder of power while legitimacy is the perspective of the people who obey the servants of the political leaders as well as the population at large. One may enquire into the strategies of creating legitimacy, which comprise as Bourdieu says, making people see, believe and do (Bourdieu 1972; 1980: 104–110; 1982; 2001: 107–108, 306).

In principle, political authority assumes a political community and more precisely an administrative mechanism. However, authority may actually exist without such an administrative apparatus, which is true of Arab patriarchalism. One would be wrong in believing that authority refers to only a political relationship. It may also occur in various other communities like corporations of laymen or religious corporations. These corporations can dispute control over the tools of religious salvation. In the same manner they can share the economic opportunities as well as the appropriation of resources.

Rational authority is based upon belief in the legitimacy of rules, impersonal and objective. Traditional domination holds that tradition is sacred. In this case one obeys the power holder who himself is bound by tradition. In all such cases, one cannot create any law unless it is already part of a sacred tradition or custom. Strictly speaking, this is what opposes it to rationality. Charismatic authority is based either upon a sacred person acting in the name of a revelation, for instance, or on the heroic virtues of a person setting an extraordinary personal example. These three types of authority are universal and have general application. None is pure in reality, as Weber gives examples of all possible combinations. Thus, charismatic authority can be hereditary. Patrimonial authority can tend towards bureaucracy, and legal authority can coexist with charisma.

Patriarchal authority before Islam is a form of the universal traditional authority. Traditional domination sometimes employs an administrative apparatus, but not always. One variety is patriarchal authority where one person only, the master of the house designated according to fixed rules of succession, upholds an absolute authority over the household, property, family and animals. Thus, an economic unit is formed in the household (*oikos*), which is extended to a larger territory, like in ancient Egypt with the pharaos. With regard to the absence of an administrative apparatus, the people in the *oikos* are associated according to their position. The typical example is the manor, but it is also to be found in pre-Islamic Arabia with the Arab sheikh or the Bedouin leader, who levies a contribution upon those who pass by.

The Arab sheikh belongs to an organised clan based upon a family of a particular nature. As *primus inter pares* he is the representative of the group. Weber calls this type "appropriated representation", exercised for example by the sheikh of the tribe, patriarch or the monarch. The sheikh is the oldest of a clan who exercises his authority by his good example and his admonitions. Specialists in the history of the Arabian Peninsula emphasise the existence of a council of elders comprising the nobles of *Koreich* – an oligarchy or domination by *honorationes*. The tribe disappeared in the Occident, but not in the Orient. In order to remove the tribe one must have either a prophet or a bureaucracy. In China, for instance, a bureaucracy replaced it, but in Islam it was the prophetic ethics of Mohammed that undid tribal domination in the form of patriarchical sheikhs.

The charismatic authority of the prophetic kind is distinguished by the fact that it is extraordinary. The charisma is extraordinary when the leader pulls his authority from the attributes of a magician or displays a messianic nature. This type of domination is of a revolutionary import and opposes the rational domination, especially the bureaucratic one, as well as the traditional authority. This is further emphasised when the charisma is carried by a prophet, when the "sanctity of the new revelation contradicts tradition". Its status is also extraordinary. Charisma is always in a precarious situation as it lasts only as long as the carrier of charisma lives and performs. Sooner or later the problem of the succession of the charismatic leader becomes of crucial importance.

Charisma has its origin in the person of the prophet, even if one admits that the infallible character of the prophet is a late theological construction. Mohammed is a typical ethical prophet who assembled a group of pious men that was rapidly transformed into an order consisting of knights who successively conquered a large part of the adjacent areas before he died. At his death the community of faithful, warriors and disciples had a religious interest as well as the resources to make the social relations they had created durable.

The solution in Islam of the succession problem concerning the passage from charismatic rule to the day-to-day administration of the group or religion was decisive for the future developments of the religion. The question of succession had dire consequences in Islam. One cannot even understand the Shiism, the Mahdism, or the notion of the caliphate, without analysing the succession problem. All concepts refer to the way in which Islam resolved the disappearance of the person holding charisma. Weber identified the problem, stating:

> The structure of Islam has been decisively affected by the fact that Mohammed died without male heirs and his followers did not found the caliphate on heredity charisma, and indeed during the Umayyad period developed in an outright antitheocratic manner. (Weber, 1978: 1138)

The succession in general takes place in one of the following ways: (a) finding a new charismatic person; (b) the designation of a successor by the holder of charisma; (c) the designation by a council that has the required qualifications to select a successor; (d) the hereditary succession on the basis of blood or family; (e) the selection of a successor on the basis of charisma inherent in the organisation (Church); and (f) outright election by the community. In effect, the Koran does not pose the problem of succession. One must then *ab initio* exclude the possibility of a new person, such as the Dalai Lama or a double Mohammed, because Mohammed is considered as the last prophet. The same applies to the method of revelation, which is a solution that Islam had refused. There is a wording by the prophet, which has served as the justification *a posteriori* of the rejection in Islam of this solution:

> The prophets governed the sons of Israel. Every time a prophet died, another replaced him. And there will be no more prophets after me. But many will replace me. (Wensinck, 1992, vol. I: 63)

Mohammed did not designate a successor when he lived. The solution that was in place after his death was not in conformity with a hereditary mechanism, at least not immediately after the death of Mohammed, and the transfer from a personal charisma to the charisma of an organisation could not be a valid solution for Islam, which is opposed to hierarchy. There rests the alternative that was most suitable for Islam in its infancy, namely the designation of a successor by a council of qualified men: a caliph. We will examine the outcomes of this procedure. At the death of the prophet a narrow group of people met in an improvised manner. It was composed of the first converts, the adherents, divided into two groups: the people from Mecca belonging to the tribe of Mohammed (*Quraysh*), and the people from Medina, as well as the allied Arabs from these two clans. The first were called the exiled, with reference to the period when Mohammed lived in Medina. The second were referred to as the auxiliaries, and were Arabs recruited in Medina. These two groups then entered into dispute, which was eventually won by the people from Mecca, although not without fighting on the basis of two criteria.

First, there was the early acquaintance with Islam, as the first converts from Mecca included those who were destined to go to Paradise according to the Koran. Second, we have the tribal connection to Mohammed, as his tribe could not accept that any person not belonging to that tribe could direct it. The first successor chosen was Abu Bakr (632–634). On this point Weber was correct. It was not a free choice, but a designation that was strictly correct in accordance with domination by *honorationes*. The second successor was Omar (634–644), who was designated by Abu Bakr himself, which implies the use of another procedure. When Omar died, there was a return to the other procedure involving a council of six persons, composed of his companions who had to choose a successor among themselves. The choice was Uthman (644–656), who was the man responsible for the canonisation of the Koran. He was later to be killed under circumstances that are not fully known and that caused much polemic. The fourth successor Ali (656–661) proclaimed himself caliph after having waited a long time for his chance. Civil war followed immediately, ending with the death of Ali and the victory of Muawiya, who put in place a hereditary dynasty – still another procedure (Djaït 1989: 159–259, Wellhausen, 1909/1960: 47–71). The succession problem resulted in a split between the main divisions in Islam that is still characteristic of Islam, the Sunnis and the Shiites.

From Charisma to Patrimonialism

At this stage the problem of succession had been definitely regulated, but the question of the routinisation of charisma had not been tackled. Once the succession had been assured, the authority pattern changed nature. It received a daily form in order to take care of the concerns of the community on a routine basis. Two possibilities were opened. Either the charismatic authority transformed itself to traditional authority (patrimonialism) or it was made into legal or rational authority. Our basic argument is that patrimonialism was the best option in Islam. At the same time the succession gave birth to two sects that solved the succession problem differently: Shiism and Karijism. What follows below is a list of major chronological events:

Year one of Exile Hijra, 622 A.C., beginning of the Muslim calendar determined by the departure of the first converted towards exile (*hijra*), from Mecca to *Yathreb*, to become *Medina* (city); the Islamisation of the Arabs.

ABU BAKR, 632–634: Chosen *ad hoc* by a conclave regrouping one part of the staff headquarters formed by the banished from Mecca (Muhajirin) and the auxiliaries (*ansar*), Islamised allied at Yathreb (Medina).

OMAR, 634–644: Publicly designated by Abou Bakr, assassinated by an unknown person. No pertinent political incidents.

UTHMAN, 644–656: Chosen by a group of six companions surviving the nine first exiles, designated by Omar before his death on the basis of antecedence in conversion and the companionship of the prophet. Uthman was assassinated by the troops that came from Egypt, cccused of nepotism, injustice and distance with respect to tradition.

ALI, 656–661: Publicly proclaimed successor. The rupture: civil war, arbitration, dynastic event, 656–661: the great discord (*al-fitna al-kobra*) around “Ottoman blood”. Civil war between Ali, having granted refuge to the murderers, and his adherents (*shia*) on one hand, and on the other hand between his enemies, whom Muawiya, the powerful governor of Damas, assembled around Aïsha, the widow of the prophet.

657: Acceptance of an arbitration jury by the principal actors of the civil war, Ali and Muawiya. Split of one party of adherents of Ali who refused the principle of human arbitration. They will later be named “outgoers” (*Karijites*).

661: Assassination of Ali in Kufa by a Karijite (shrine in Najaf). Beginning of the Umayyad Dynasty (661–750) after the name of the Muawiya family, victorious and recognised caliph by “the community” (*jamaa*). He requests public allegiance, in 678, to the profit of his son Yazid – start of the first Arab dynasty with Damas as the capital.

680: Martyrdom of Hussein (tomb in Karbala), son of Ali, assassinated by the Umayyad troops. Fermentation of Shiism through a powerful feeling of mourning, revenge and faithful attachment to Ali’s decimated family. Start of the *Twelvers* in Shiism.

Around 700: Shiism adapts the ideas of occultation and the return of the imam; the idea of transmigration of the saint Spirit into the order of the imams.

750: End of the Umayyad dynasty following revolutions and the beginning of the Abbasid dynasty (750–1258), clan of the prophet's family by the uncles. Caliphate of Cordoba 756–1031.

Baghdad as capital in 762. The empire counts on the non-Arab elements, especially Iranians and Turks.

The Fatimides in Egypt, 909–1171 (Ismaili branch of Shiism; "*seveners*").

1258: End of the Abbasid dynasty. Inside under the control of military chiefs and worn by several shiite and Karijite revolutions; outside exploded into numerous autonomous powers, since the ninth century.

1258–1512: The Mamlouks, military aristocrats of slave origin in Egypt.

1501: The Shah of Iran Ismail imposes shiism as the state religion and creates a clergy.

16–19th centuries: Ottoman Sunnite hegemony of patrimonialism or sultanism in the Muslim world.

1924: End of the caliphate (Garcin, 1988).

Two things have special weight in the logic of routinisation in Islam. The first concerns the articulation between the routinisation of charisma, the lines of descendence and the family. The holder of power is either called "caliph", meaning the successor of the prophet from an etymological aspect, or he could be called an "imam", that is, a guide. His two functions – government and religion – are clearly indicated: he supplies prophetism (where the prophet was the last representative) in order to protect religion and the governance of mundane interests (Mawardi, 1982: 1). He is distinguished by a number of attributes pertaining to charisma: knowledge of religion, piety and competence. From an ethical point of view, he should belong to the tribe of Mohammed: *Quraysh*. Moreover, the first four caliphs were linked to the prophet by marriage, which reinforced their charismatic qualifications.

After his victory over Ali in 661, Muawiya put in place a dynasty. The caliph became at the same time a religious and worldly leader, a *qurayshite* and a monarch. Sunna developed into the tradition that honours above all conflicts the memory of the four first caliphs and maintains community consensus. Sunna presents one solution to the problem of routinisation of charisma, its links with tradition and its foundation upon Arab tribalism (Lewis, 1964; Hodgson, 1974, vol. 1; Crone, 2003). Because of the successive decline in power of the caliphate, authority was diffused onto two caliphates. Warlords divided what remained of the caliphate from the tenth century and onwards after having attacked it from the inside. An attempt to restructure the caliphate took place in Egypt in the thirteenth century. The Ottoman Turks reestablished the caliphate in the Ottoman Emire from the fifteenth century onwards. The symbolic charge in relation to the caliphate was kept, but the tribal link around *qurayshite* had disappeared. Towards the sixteenth century, Iran escaped from Sunnism, as Shiism became the official religion in Iran, assuring religious legitimacy to the political order.

The second important phenomenon is the birth of sects rejected in opposition. They have been numerous. Besides the domination of a group, the stakes included the appropriation of grace – "the principal domain of discussion" according to Weber in Islam as well as in Judaism. Shiism goes back to the procedures for the succession with preference for the lineage originating with Ali, a relative of the prophet (cousin and husband of Fatimah). The possibilities for succession include: (a) election somehow; (b) designation by will of the holder of power; and (c) heritage. In Shiism the imam is heir to the prophet on the basis of grace and not by birth. To accomplish this, Shiism refers to the Koran by reinterpreting a few verses so that they favour the designation of Ali (the Koran, 33: 31–32), pretending that the prophet just before dying designated Ali by means of will (*wassiya*) – a special doctrine of legitimation: "the Koran and the will of the Prophet". In reality, grace is transmitted from one imam to another by means of the hereditary link within the lineage of Ali.

The Sects

The adherents of Shiism were persecuted by the caliphate. The twelfth imam disappeared in mysterious circumstances in 878. Yet the Shia adherents have developed a hermeneutics of the grace that has as its object the messianic waiting of the hidden imam who will reestablish justice upon his return. Weber refers to this under the generic label "Mahdism". The title of Mahdi had been given to Ali (661) and this title was spread with different sects among both Shiites and Sunnis in order to refer to the eschatological drive with a charismatic leader (Laoust 1965: 15 and 350). During the period of waiting for the return of the imam, the Shiites put in place a religious hierarchy (*Wilayat faqih*), contrary to the early spirit of Islam, which does not recognise a Church. Eventually, the charisma moved from the person of the imam to the function of *faqih*.

Thus, the Shias believe that Ali ibn Abi Talib, Mohammed's cousin and husband of his daughter, Fatimah, was the true successor of the prophet, and they accordingly reject the legitimacy of the first three Rashidun caliphs, contary to the beliefs of the Sunnis.

The Shia faith includes many different groups. There are different Shia theological beliefs, schools of jurisprudence, philosophical beliefs and spiritual movements. Shia Islam offers a completely independent system of religious interpretation and political authority in the Muslim world. Shia theology was formulated in the second century and the first Shia governments and societies were established by the end of the third century. Shia Islam is divided into three branches. The Twelver constitutes a majority of the population in Iran, Azerbaijan, Bahrain and Iraq. Other smaller branches include the Ismaili (seven imams) and Zaidi (five imams), who dispute the Twelver lineage of imams. Though there are several subgroupings within the Ismailis, one major group is the Nizari community, who are followers of the Aga Khan. While many of the branches have extremely different exterior practices, spiritual theology has remained largely the same since the days of the faith's early imams. In recent centuries Ismailis have largely been an Indo-Iranian community, but Ismailis are also to be found in India, Pakistan, Syria and Lebanon. In addition, there are the Alawites in Syria, a politically prominent sect of Shiite Islam. *Alawī* is not to be confused with Alevi, a different religious sect based in Turkey, although they share the same etymology. Karijites are today numerous in Oman and the Zaidis are to be found in Yemen.

Karijism places a high value upon communitarian charisma. The Karijites – meaning literally "Those who Went Out" – argued that the government of God is not a matter that can be negotiated politically. This is the accusation that they made against Ali, who accepted an arrangement between him and Muawiya. Later on they in their turn rationalised a communitarian kind of charisma. At the same time being against the tribal spirit of the Sunnis and the family loyalty of the Shiites, the Karijites believe that the religious community holds the hand upon grace. Every Muslim may wish to become a caliph in accordance with the words of the prophet, who has certainly been invoked *a posteriori* saying "listen and obey the leader, even when he is an Ethiopian slave" (Crone 1994, 59–67). At the same time, Karijism invoked a word belonging, one believes, to Omar who, on his death bed and before designating the group of six companions to be charged with choosing among themselves the third caliph, is believed to have said "if Salem (a slave freed by the prophet) were alive, I would not have hesitated to designate him as '*imam*'".

We have thus several mechanisms of an ethnic and political nature that are progressively put in place by various strata in order to hopefully resolve the succession question. On the one hand, the caliphate is at the same time a rationalisation of the prophetic charisma in daily life but also an invitation to create traditional authority by means of dynastic heritage. On the other hand, we observe a semi-rationalisation of charisma, either of a personal nature with the imam in Shiism (lineage), or of the communitarian nature as within Karijism (election). Actually, Karijite theology has been seen as a form of radical extremism, preaching uncompromising observance of the teachings of the Koran in defiance of corrupt authorities. Interestingly, they preached absolute equality of the faithful, in opposition to the aristocracy of the Quraysh that emerged dynastically under the Umayyad caliphate. They propagated a righteous *jihad* (struggle) as the presumed sixth pillar of Islam. On the contrary, the Zaidi beliefs are moderate compared with other Shiite sects. The Zaidis do not believe in the infallibility of the imams, nor that the imams receive divine guidance.

Islam creates a community of believers – the *umma*. How is it to be governed? By the prophet of course. Yes, but after the prophet? Typical of Islam has been the effort to combine political authority and religious leadership in one office: caliph or imam. What has no doubt characterised Islam as a civilisation is the unsuccessful ambition to solve the succession problem by means other than legal–rational authority. The outcome was a dynasty with the Sunnis (emirates, sultanates) but Mahdism with the Shias, neither of which accomplished legal–rational authority.

Sultanismus

Patrimonial authority emerged after the caliph was created as a monarch of tribal origin who divides the grace with others. Compared with pre-Islamic patriarchalism, which was authority without administration, the caliphate operated by means of an administrative mechanism: those "associated" within the primary social relation and within the household became "subjects", taking part in a community handed down by tradition. Omar, the third caliph, had put a core administration in place. He called himself the *Diwan* in charge of the collection and distribution of resources, as well as of scribes and a territorial administration dividing the Islamic countries into provinces with governors. According to Becker (1910), what characterises patrimonialism is the "absolute right" of the holder of power, who appropriates the subjects as objects of patrimony, whereas patriarchal authority rests upon admonishments, example and conciliation. However, patrimonialism varies in Islam. Samir Amin wrote about the "trading warriors" and showed how Islam is politically centralised, economically patrimonial and ideologically religious (Amin, 1970a).

First, the power of the caliphate depends upon the type of recruitment of administrative people. Either the apparatus is recruited on an extra-patrimonial basis thanks to links of confidence and fidelity or by means of free functionaries. European patrimonialisation oriented itself towards this model. Or the administrative apparatus is recruited on the basis of links of respect or veneration among noblemen, the aristocracy. A final possibility is that the administration is composed in a sultanistic manner. In Islam, the agents of the apparatus are either members of the family of the caliph or freed slaves who could even occupy the position of *vizier*, or even domestic functionaries including slaves with among them the guardians of the harem – the *eunuchs*. They could also be colonisers, as Islam experienced an army of mercenaries paid by land, as for example in the late caliphate of the second Abbasid dynasty (750–1258). It was typical of Muslim rulership that the caliph, emir or sultan from time to time became the hostage of his own administration, being in the hands of military orders of former slaves or mercenaries.

The prestigious caliphate became the object of fighting between brothers, because only the members of a family of Arab origin had the right to become a caliph. The political unity of the Arab Empire was lost as the logic of palace politics invaded the caliphate. The Abbasid caliphs founded their claim to the caliphate on their descent from Abbas ibn Abd al-Muttalib (566–662), one of the youngest uncles of Mohammed. The Umayyads were descended from Umayya, a clan separate from Mohammed's in the Quraish tribe. The Abbasid take-over amounted to a coup d'état, eliminating the Umayyads except for one person, who fled to Spain and his decendants later set up the competing caliphate of Cordoba (929–1031). Tthe Abbasids moved the capital from Damascus, in Syria, to Baghdad in Iraq. The position of the *vizier* was established to delegate central authority. In addition, greater authority was delegated to local emirs. The Abbasid caliphs were eventually relegated to a more ceremonial role than that of the Umayyad caliphs, as the *viziers* began to exert greater influence, and the role of the old Arab aristocracy was slowly replaced by a Persian bureaucracy. Yet the turmoil surrounding the recruitment of the caliph weakened the Arab empire. The Abbasids presented an unbroken line of caliphs for over three centuries, consolidating Islamic rule and cultivating great intellectual and cultural developments in the Middle East. However, in the tenth century the power of the Abbasid caliphate was waning as non-Arabs, particularly the Berbers of the Maghreb, the Turks and later the Mamluks in Egypt in the latter half of the thirteenth century, gained influence, sultans and emirs becoming increasingly independent. The religious unity of the caliphate did not prevent the disintegration of purely secular sultanates, a creation of the slave generals, into sub-empires. However, the unity of the well-disciplined slave armies in turn favoured the indivisibility of these sub-empires once they were established; partly for that reason hereditary division never became customary in the Islamic Orient (Weber, 1978: 1053–1054). A division *de facto* was made, as religious matters went to the Arabs, whereas the politico-administrative power fell to the mercenaries. The Umayyad dynasty (661–750), for instance, counted more upon the members of the ruling family than the functionaries of Arab origin (Crone, 1980: 74–81).

The power inherent in all patrimonialism can spread without limits. This becomes a type of Islamic rule raised to an ideal type as sultanistic authority when the power holder stretches out his authority in an unlimited manner. The power holder grabs all of the grace, becomes arbitrary and distributes all kinds of favours to his clients. He frees himself, at least somewhat and apparently, from the tradition to which he is normally linked. Because of this fact, sultanismus tends to become both anti-traditional and anti-rational. Weber writes:

> Patrimonialism and, in the extreme case, sultanism, tend to arise whenever traditional domination develops an administration and a military force which are purely personal instruments of the master. Only then are the group members treated as subjects. (Weber, 1978: 231)

And he goes on to regard sultanism as unlimited patrimonialism. It is basically a form of oriental despotism (Wittfogel, 1964), which one finds also outside of the Muslim civilisation. Weber states:

> Sometimes it appears that sultanism is completely unrestrained by tradition, but this is never in fact the case. The non-traditional element is not, however, rationalised in impersonal terms, but consists only in an extreme development of

> the ruler's discretion. It is this, which distinguishes it from every form of rational authority. (Weber, 1978: 232)

Yet, patrimonial domination in Islam was neither always total nor exclusive. The authority of the sultan is in competition with that of the lord, the religious communities, the legal orders and the functionary. The power of the sultan can be combined with the influence of corporations when the administrative apparatus appropriates powers and especially administrative resources to the benefit of feudal orders: the big landlords disposing of fiefs and the vassals being the master of their equipment are typical examples. Weber refers to the Mamluk Sultanate in Egypt from 1250 to 1517, after the ending of the Abbasid caliphate by the Mongols, but one could certainly also add the warlords of the caliphate who appropriated part of the power of their master and set up emirates, if not dynasties or even a new caliphate, as with the so-called Fatimids.

The Fatimid Caliphate

Interestingly, an Arab Shia dynasty ruled over varyious areas of the Maghreb, Egypt and the Levant from 909 to 1171, constituting the fourth and final Arab caliphate. It was merely based upon invasion of the authority of the Abbasid caliph. This caliphate was ruled by the Fatimids, who established the Egyptian city of Cairo as their capital. The ruling elite belonged to the Ismaili branch of Shiism. The leaders of the dynasty were also Shia Ismaili imams – the only period in which the Shia Imamate and the caliphate were united to any degree, excepting the caliphate of Ali himself. The Fatimids had their origins in Ifriqiya (modern-day Tunisia and eastern Algeria). The dynasty was founded in 909 by Abdullāh al-Mahdī Billah, who legitimised his claim through descent from Mohammed by way of his daughter Fatima as-Zahra and her husband Alī ibn-Abī-Tālib, the first Shia *imam*, hence the name *al-Fātimiyyūn* "Fatimid".

Abdullāh al-Mahdī just extended his territories, as his control soon extended over all of central Maghreb, which he ruled from Mahdia, his newly-built capital in Tunisia. The Fatimids entered Egypt in the late 900s, conquering the Ikhshidid dynasty and founding a new capital at Cairo in 969. Unlike other governments in the area, Fatimid advancement in state offices was based more on merit than on heredity. Members of other branches of Islam, like the Sunnis, were just as likely to be appointed to government posts as Shiites. Tolerance was extended even to non-Muslims such as Christians and Jews, who occupied high levels in government based on ability. There were, however, exceptions to this general attitude of tolerance, most notably Al-Hakim bi-Amr Allah.

In the 1040s, the Zirids, who were governors of North Africa under the Fatimids, declared their independence from the Fatimids. Their conversion to Sunni Islam led to the devastating Banū Hilal invasions. After about 1070, the Fatimid hold on the Levant coast and parts of Syria was challenged first by Turkish invasions, then the Crusades, so that Fatimid territory shrank until it consisted only of Egypt. After the decay of the Fatimid rule in the 1160s, the Zengid ruler, Nūr ad-Dīn, and his general, Shirkuh, seized Egypt in 1169. Shirkuh died two months after taking power, and the rule went to his nephew, Saladin. This began the Kurdish Ayyubid Dynasty. Salah al-Dīn Yusuf ibn Ayyub (1138–1193), better known as the famous Saladin in medieval Europe, was a Sultan of Egypt and Syria – a Kurdish Muslim. At the height of his power, the Ayyubid dynasty he founded ruled over Egypt, Syria, Iraq, Hejaz and Yemen. He led Muslim resistance to the European Crusaders and eventually recaptured Palestine from the Crusader Kingdom of Jerusalem. Although basically a warlord, Saladin is a notable figure in Arab, Kurdish and Muslim culture.

Patrimonial Administration

In Islamic patrimonialism one observes the competition between the prince and the religious order as well as between the prince and the professionals of law. This tended to diminish the radicalism of Sultanism at the same time as it gave coherence to political authority *stricto senso* over the subjects. Thus, traditional domination in Islam did have an administrative apparatus with offices but in a personalised form. There existed the corporations but with limited power or in a military structure, as well as the institutions, but in a form regulated by religion. It is the strictly formal Weberian characteristics of bureaucratic authority that are missing in Islam.

Bureaucracy holds the seed of the modern Western State. Modern capitalism needed bureaucracy by the fact that it required a rational financial administration for handling the financial resources of the country, but the two had different historical origins. Concerning bureaucracy, it originated within the patrimonial state, at least when it is recruited on an extra-patrimonial basis, that is to say in a free manner. Moreover, the bureaucracy is based upon individual functionaries. Another form of administration is the collegial type, which played an important role in the development of constitutional authority as with parliaments or the assemblies in the estates society in the high medieval period.

In Islam, collegiality played a role similar to that in the Occident, as the idea of representation is missing. Yet, the great *viziers* and the *diwan* exercised a collegial authority together with the prince, but without replacing him. However, this collegiality did not result in a body of rational functionaries from the point of view of technical specialisation. Legal–rational domination occurs only in the purest type from a formal point of view, i.e. the bureaucratic authority. It has the ideal-type features that Weber identified: the conformity with rules, the precision, the discipline, the predictability and the permanence, the variety of competencies fixed according to impersonal and objective norms, the stable hierarchy, the free recruitment, the specialised formation, the long-term payment fixed according to contract as well as the impartial protection of the bureaucrat against arbitrariness.

In the Muslim empires bureaucracy was never fully implanted as patrimonial administration remained outside of the Rule of Law framework (Spuler, 1994a, 1994b; Kissling, 1996). Let us continue the analysis of the Arab legacy by examining the nature of its religious power – theocracy – and the special kind of feudalism that went together with patrimonial rule in the Middle East.

Caesaro-papism

Islam developed a type of authority that is typically described as patrimonial or sultanic, but this absolute power was to varying degrees actually shared with the rights of corporations – economic, administrative, religious, secular and juridical. And when power focuses upon religion, then it puts in oscillation the relation between political authority and religious authority. We need to understand how an authority can be at the same time sultanic and caesaro-papist, as the latter type involves a compromise between the religious and political order.

The relation between political power, *stricto senso*, and the institutionalised religious power is a reciprocal one, involving fighting and compromise. It takes widely varying forms and the stakes are multiple, like the monopoly on grace or the access to the resources. Each of the two powers either attempts to make itself autonomous or to increase its influence over the other, or even to dominate the other. This relationship also includes the status of religious charisma. When this charisma is institutionalised, then it becomes a function that is independent of those who have received grace. Everywhere the relation between state and Church impacts upon society, but this universal relation of tension and struggle was to have different outcomes in the Orient and the Occident. In Islam there was caesaro-papism, as the relations between the two powers are of a compromise nature. The outcome was that both forces, secular and religious, closed the road to a rationalisation involving economic and ethical conduct.

On the contrary, the Occident is characterised by autonomy for the two powers and a double logic of tension, which constitutes a specific seed of the occidental culture. On the one hand, the Church stays relatively independent of political power, influences it and organises itself under a rational and bureaucratic mode. On the other hand, there is tension between charisma and governance. The occidental culture was less homogenous than the Muslim, involving splits between religious and political actors and groups. The compromises within the various world cultures prevented them from experiencing an evolution towards a complete separation between secular and religious powers along the lines of the Occident.

Caesaro-papism has been looked upon as one of the sources of the troubled relation between religion and politics in Islam. The fundamental orientalist thesis is that Islam is at the same time "*autorité spirituelle et pouvoir temporel*", religion and politics, spiritual and secular, state and city, society and individual. This argument starts from the unquestionable fact that Mohammed (570–632) took on a purely political task, in both theory and practice. According to a formula invented by Massignon, Islam is a "lay theocracy" (without Church) and "egalitarian" in spirit among its adherents (Massignon, 1975: vol. 1). Being fundamentally lay, Islam lacks a Church, or a sacerdotal hierarchy. Being theocratic, Islam puts the Koran in place as the main legislation. It is lay and theocratic in that it mingles Church and state in one and the same person, the colonel of God or the caliph, as well as egalitarian in the sense that all believers constitute the community of Islam with its own legal order. Carsaro-papism is an inversion of theocracy, in which institutions of the Church are in control of the state, meaning combining the power of secular government with, for instance, the spiritual authority of the Christian Church. In its extreme form, the head of state, notably the Emperor, is also the supreme head of the church.

In caesaro-papism the holder of political power may be anointed with holy oil, or legitimated by the religious power on the ground that he incarnates the divine will or its incarnation (divine rights of kings), but he becomes at the same time the apex of the religious order. In the theocracy, the ruler is himself part of a religious institution, the high priest, and he exercises the political function, which constitutes a kind of a sacerdotal rulership within a secular domain. However, Islam rather belongs to a third type where the spiritual power is placed under the political power, and the spiritual hierarchy under the secular sovereignty. In this last type the sovereign disposes of a supreme power in the religious domain as a proper right. He directs the religious matters as if they adhered to an administrative competence. Caesaro-papism is exemplified best in the authority the Byzantine emperors had over the Eastern Christian Church from the sixth to the tenth centuries. The Byzantine emperor would typically protect the Eastern Church and manage its administration by presiding over councils and appointing patriarchs and setting territorial boundaries for their jurisdiction. The emperor, whose control was so strong that "caesaro-papism" became interchangeable with "Byzantinism", was called "pontifex maximus", meaning chief priest, and the Patriarch of Constantinople could not hold office if he did not have the emperor's approval.

It should be recognised that these three types are not pure. The two polar types are the pure hierocratic authority and total caesaro-papism. It remains the case that political power in Islam is not subordinated under a religious institution. In Islam, religious power instead is subordinate, as political power prevails, and religious authority does not constitute a theocracy. The caliphate and the Turkish and Mongol sultanates all adhere to caesaro-papism. The power of the caliph reinforces itself at the expense of the hierocratic power. This is very apparent within the caliphate. Even if the *sheikh al-Islam* exists as a religious authority besides the authority of the caliph, he remains a layman, nominated by the caliph. The caliph could be compared with a Byzantine *basileus*. Shiism is closer to theocracy, at least in the present Islamic Republic of Iran. The Supreme Leader of Iran is responsible for delineation and supervision of the general policies of the Islamic Republic of Iran. The Supreme Leader is Commander-in-Chief of the armed forces, controls the military intelligence and security operations, and has sole power to declare war or peace. The heads of the judiciary, state radio and television networks, the commanders of the police and military forces and six of the 12 members of the Council of Guardians are appointed by the Supreme Leader. The Assembly of Experts elects and dismisses the Supreme Leader on the basis of qualifications and popular esteem. The Assembly of Experts is responsible for supervising the Supreme Leader in the performance of legal duties. The Assembly of Experts, which meets for one week annually, comprises 86 "virtuous and learned" clerics elected by adult suffrage for eight-year terms. As with the presidential and parliamentary elections, the Council of Guardians determines candidates' eligibility. The Assembly elects the Supreme Leader and has the constitutional authority to remove the Supreme Leader from power at any time. As all of their meetings and notes are strictly confidential, the Assembly has never been publicly known to challenge any of the Supreme Leader's decisions.

Caesaro-papism in Islam dates back to the Abbasid dynasty (Weber, 1978). What happened with the Abbasids is more an accentuation of the holy character of the caliph due to the massive introduction of the literary genre consisting of the Mirror of princes, which has diverse Persian, Hindu and Greek origins. First, we have the Islamisation of the Persian Empire. Second, there is the strong emergence of translations of pre-Islamic works and finally the movement of the empire from Damascus, an Arab city, to Baghdad, a metropolitan and cosmopolitan city. The caliphate freed itself from its ethnic base in order to unite itself with non-Arab elements, especially the Iranian ones.

The literature on the Mirror of Prince (*andaz*, in Persian) seldom raises the question of legitimacy, which is so central for authority. On the contrary, this literature avoids it by stating that power is a natural and eternal phenomenon. Actually, the Mirror of Prince assumes that power is so natural that the only question that it poses is to know how it can be morally supported: "the state is 'given' and there is no attempt at its justification or its control" (Lambton, 1971: 419). The Mirror of Prince Literature in Islam separates itself from the religious ethics, which makes it an obligation towards the scripture to obey authority (the Koran 9: 59). This genre wishes to moralise autocracy by having it obey the household or the regime that is called *tadbir* in Arabic: the art of taking good care of one's body, one's soul, one's family and one's kingdom. However, it played a minor role in the relation between political authority and the religious order due to the fact that it had been developed by lay writers and not by the legal scholars or theologians within the *ulema*.

Mosque and Sect

In Islam the relation between the two forces, political authority and the religious orders, involves a fusion in the caliphate institution. This fusion closes the road to the appearance of asceticism in the world, whereas the tension opens up this possibility. Is there a Church in Islam? The Church is first an institutionalised community involving a corpus of professional priests, scriptures, a system of dogmas and an institutionalised ritual. Moreover, this community aims at autonomy and perhaps universal domination, which goes beyond the family, clans, ethnies or other relations. In addition, the Church has a relation to political power, whereas the sect tends to be an anti-political group. Finally, the Church handles the administration of the means of salvation, certainly offered to everyone, albeit it does so since birth. Moreover, in the Church charisma is exercised by the function linked with the institution (*amt charisma*). This is what distinguishes the church from the sect into which one enters freely and where those associated pull their charisma from their persons and not from the function. In Islam there is a Church to the same extent as in Christianity or Judaism, but it never reaches the autonomy of the Catholoic Church during the medieval period. This is true of Sunnite Islam especially, but equally of Shiism in the more restricted sense given its links nationally and ethnically with Persia. Even Calvinism has a Church from the sociological point of view, meaning that it has a religious institution, although the Calvinist sects erected free religious associations with strong lay participation in contradistinction to the Lutheran state Church in Northern Europe.

It must be emphasised that a hierarchy analogous to that of the Catholic Church hardly exists in Sunnism, except if one were to consider the *ulemas* as the functional equivalent of an organised institution. Sunnism has a strong political element, but this is also true of Shiism and Karijism and other sects as well. The only apolitical sects are the *sufis* and the brotherhoods. The rationalistic *mutazilites* are mainly interested in dogma, but they have had a troubled relation with politics, supporting at the same time Shiism and Sunnism. Islam has nothing similar to the apolitical sects, like Calvinism, or the anti-political sects like the Lutheran ones. If Islam has a Church, then one cannot see how those in power will prevail in religious matters. Perhaps the key element is monasticism. Islam would constitute a Church without monks. The conflict between Church and sect tends to contain the difference between obligatory community and free community, charisma linked with function vs personal charisma, political relations against apolitical or anti-political relations. In fact, Islam is universalist, and admission is free, without reference to any ethnic link or other relation that may condition admission, as with the case of Shiism or Mahdism.

Even if every hierocracy has a tendency to constitute itself as a Church, it does not impose upon its priests a monastic lifestyle. Thus, Judaism, Sunni Islam and Mahdism ignore the monks as a phenomenon. This absence of monks could be a good thing to the extent that it opens the door to a rational ethics that is inner-wordly. However, the monk within the Christian Church is the first man with a vocation or a profession in the sense that he lives methodically according to his rigorous use of time, as well as far from mundane preoccupations such as the enjoyment of the fruits of this world. The monk leaves the monastic cell in order to service the laymen, reinterpret the scriptures and proclaim himself the shepherd of the sheep. He does it within the frame of his function, but in conflict with the institution. Here the tension in the relationship between outer-wordly ascetism on the one hand and hierocracy or clergy on the other hand is conducive to secularisation.

From the point of view of caesaro-papism one may say that, when this form of authority is extreme, it reduces religion to a ritualist technique. It stereotypes inevitably the ethical content of religion and consequently it counteracts the evolution towards a religion of salvation. This occurred within Islam, contrary to the Occident, which was characterised by the relative autonomy of the Church. In Islam, asceticism takes an ecstatic form as for example, within the dervishes' orders, whose religiosity is of an opposite kind to that of the *ulemas*. There is no conflict between ascetic ethics and power when a religion is propagated by means of violence. From the perspective of Islam as a religion of warriors, it is not a religion of salvation. Thus, the question that can be posed is the following: does Islam contain some kind of tension between religious asceticism and political power? More exactly, does a right to religious revolt against tyranny exist? If Islam knew this confrontation, contrary to primitive Christianity and Lutheranism, then it was only among the sects, like for instance the Mahdists. The same is true of Calvinism, but this tension is feeble in Islam.

Caesaro-papism and the Economy

The relationship between hierocracy and political power is indirectly conditioned by the economy. Yet the economy, especially when it is monetised, operates basically according to the logic of appropriation. Each one of the protagonists wishes to master the economic resources made available to the Church. The occidental Church of Catholic faith resisted the caesaro-papist drive, while also handing down victory for the asceticism that it provided for its monks and nuns. In Islam, caesaro-papism found favour due to the absence of monks and the tension between religion and politics. Islam piles up economic privileges for the communities. The hierocracy cut out resources for itself by removing from free circulation land that it got hold of through the special mechanism of the *waqf*. In addition, Islam "married itself with the expansionist ideas of the Arabs", Islam becoming a "communism of warriors". And in Islam one does not even find the rudiments of an economically rational ethics of a professional nature, due to an almost exclusive focus upon wealth appropriation. In short, caesaro-papism supported the feudalism of *benefices*, as did patrimonial domination.

Every hierocracy has negative effects upon the professional ethics in relation to capitalism. In effect, the authority of the institution turns daily management into a stereotype. When a Church is institutionalised, it starts to promote the personal values of the brotherhood, instead of the love of neighbours and charity. It freezes economic life through the unchangeable prescriptions of the Holy Law, like the Tora or the Sharia. Each hierocracy is traditionalist. It is partially anti-rationalist and anti-capitalist, that is, antagonistic towards the two forces that threaten her authority.

Conclusion

The politics of a Muslim country has in a historical view always displayed a strong tendency towards centralisation – harem or palace politics – hindering transition to capitalism (Amin, 1970a; Dobb and Sweesy, 1977; Gran, 1980; Frank and Gills, 1992; Sanderson, 1995; Falah, 1997). After truth had been revealed in the Koran, there basically only remained administrative and legal tasks relating to the implementation of the Message. Thus, the community – *umma* – would be ruled through a caliph or an imam together with the sheikh and the *mufti*. In reality, several groups of people claimed a role in Arab politics beside the dynastic family. Thus, Muslim politics has a strong centralisation heritage from a historical point of view. After the prophet and his charismatic rule, there followed patrimonialism (emirates, sultanates) together with oriental feudalism. As a matter of fact, sultanism was the most typical outcome in both Arab and non-Arab countries. It still exists in many parts of the Muslim civilisation and it expresses caesaro-papism in religious matters.

To Weber, the compromise between the lord and the prince propelled Western feudalism based upon the *fief* towards a constitutional state, whereas the military nature of oriental feudalism (*benefices*) blocked such a development. The compromise between politics and religion had the opposite result, namely it weakened asceticism. Weber's thesis concerning the feudalism of benefices is compatible, at least on the structural level, with the Marxist thesis concerning the transition from feudalism to modern capitalism (Dobb and Sweesy, 1977) and applied to Islam (Amin, 1970a; Gran, 1980; Falah, 1997). This linking is nowadays much discussed and opposes three approaches: first, the protagonists of a classical transition from feudalism to capitalism (Amin); second, the world system theories (Wallerstein, Abu-Lughod, Chaudhuri; http://en.wikipedia.org/wiki/World-systems_approach, 9 January 2009); and third, those who synthetise capitalism as a historical phenomenon and the long-run dynamic of civilisation, making them both coincide (Frank and Gills, 1992; Sanderson, 1995). This last general thesis has been specifically applied to Islam (Voll, 1994: 213–226; Eaton, 1993: 1–36).

Within the rapidly growing discipline of "Islamic economics" or "Islamic finance" there is a body of theories on how capitalism developed in a special way in Muslim countries. Islamic economics and finance represent attempts by Muslim economists to accommodate the market economy with the setting of Islam, involving the evolution of institutions, banking, assurance and conferences (Fahim Khan, 1995; Choudhury, 1997a, 1997b, 2003; Kuran, 2004). It also involves an interpretation of the economic development of Arab and non-Arab Muslim countries in order to understand their specificity. We will emphasise the nature of Islamic law and the *waqf* institution.

Chapter 7

Islamic Law and Arab Legal Institutions

Introduction

Rules play an important role in modernisation, as they may be framed so that they facilitate human interactions, such as economic transactions, when enforced. Law takes on a key position in modern societies, as advanced social structures are only possible when law is secular and autonomous. What about Islamic law? Weber's argument concerning Islamic law is of considerable complexity and refinement. To formulate it briefly, one may say the following: Islamic law ignores formal rational law, or the law of specialised jurists. This argument is based upon two theoretical distinctions.

The first distinction divides law into four types: rational law, irrational law, formal law and material law. The second involves the four stages of the socio-historical evolution of law that in Weber's view constitute the degrees of rationalisation: charismatic law, the law of higher social strata, patrimonial law and formal law with jurisprudence. The Occident has known the four types of law and it has gone through these four stages (Gephart, 1993: 497–522). However, in contrast Islam lacks one type of law: formal rational law. Weber concentrates upon the lack of a formal rational law that is: (1) systematic, (2) analytical, (3) generalisable and (4) concrete. Similarly, Islam lacks one of the four stages or historical periods in the evolution of law, namely the law of the specialised jurisprudence. Thus, Islam has one major lacuna in the form of the absence of formal rational law, which is also that of specialised jurisprudence, both being a feature of the Occident. One arrives at the question of the main development of Islamic law. Does Islamic law orientate itself toward secular and formal rationalisation? In this chapter we will discuss this question and focus upon certain special Arab legal institutions.

Evolution of Law

Following Weber's distinctions, we have on the one hand rational law vs irrational law and on the other hand formal law against material law. Let us combine them and start with law that is irrational, formally and materially. Law may be characterised as irrational from a formal point of view when it employs instruments not controllable by reason, such as magic, oracles, ordeals or prophecies. Law is irrational from the material point of view when it is based upon concrete evaluations from one case to another instead of general rules. Law is rational when it adopts external forms of validity such as the signature, the written form, the introduction of a request, or when it is placed within the internal juridical logic as with the creation through interpretation of abstract concepts applicable to concrete cases. Law may otherwise be created merely by means of casuistry. Formal rationality of law does not have a uniform content and it manifests itself to different degrees. Between the two extremes of casuistry and the purely formal modern law, intermediate forms may develop. Finally, law is rational from the material point of view if the legal rules are based more upon imperatives with an ethical or utilitarian content than if they are discovered by deductive logic.

In the historical perspective, Weber speaks about stages in the evolution of law, constituting ideal types that never totally correspond to reality. The four stages are as follows:

1. The charismatic law of the prophets, the oracles and the magicians.
2. The law of the nobilities who judge from case to case.
3. Patrimonial law, or the governance by religious or secular leaders (for example a prince or a lord).
4. Formal law of specialised jurisprudence having four features: systematic, analytical, generalisable and concrete.

The generalisation of law entails the reduction of the principles guiding the legal prescriptions or norms. Making law concrete is the inverse process by which the general rules are applied to the particular cases. Analytical jurisprudence is the putting into place of relationships between the rules in the form of a coherent structure. This systematisation is the "logically meaningful interpretation" of the rules, aiming at all kinds of imaginable facts, capable of being subsumed under norms. Law in the fourth stage would be a system governed by the continuous creation of new formal rules. These four evolutionary stages emphasise in different ways the basic features of law: rationality against irrationality and formality vs material content.

The development of law and jurisprudence in a civilisation depends upon how the following questions are tackled: what is the statute of subjective and objective rights? Who creates law, in which teaching, and by what techniques? How does jurisprudence go about systematising law? In general, Occidental law is orientated towards secular, abstract and formal law, whereas Islamic law includes religious elements, as well as a case-to-case approach, that is, material rationality. The development towards the formal rationalisation of law helps the privileged classes, especially the bourgeoisie, to emancipate itself, whereas an emphasis upon material law constitutes a hindrance to the free market economy. The Occident took the first road, but Islam stayed with the second. Such an argument requires further clarification, as Islamic law is more complex than Weber suggested.

Islamic Law and the Four Kinds of Law

Islamic law has its origins in an external event, or more specifically the revelations to the prophet. Thus, the free creation of law by means of reason is excluded, at least from this angle, as the law is sacred. The Islamic judge, the *qadi*, or the judicial authority that delivers the consultations, the *mufti*, handle conflicts case by case. They do not consider themselves bound by general rules that are independent of their wishes. Judicial precedents also do not contain general norms that are determinant for cases to follow. In this situation one cannot talk about the "normative character" of the rule, as it depends upon the subjectivity of the creators of law – the Islamic doctors of law. Even sacred law may have a proper rationality, which stabilises itself in some form of jurisprudence as well as in general rules applicable to concrete cases. Sharia law contains general rules that are to be applied *erga omnes* when all conditions are similar. From a material point of view Sharia law obeys ethical and religious goals to be interpreted in civil and penal matters on the basis of justice rendered by the *qadi*.

Is Sharia law rational when the judge employs a system of external validation of juridical claims through the means that Islamic law has developed, such as the witness, the written act, the contract? Islamic jurisprudence or *fiqh* is a creation of the jurists, developing a legal perspective, promoting the logic of jurisprudence that can be applied in Arab countries on the basis of the Koran and *ijtihad*, meaning analogical reasoning (Schacht, 1983). Let us discuss the hindrances that, according to Weber, blocked the development of Islamic law towards formally rational law (Kohler, 1905).

Islamic law developed only three of the four logical stages in the general development of law. First, Islamic law is charismatic law as the prophet pronounced bits and pieces of it. Moreover, it is also the law of nobility represented by the *muftis*, the *qadis* and the doctors of law – the *fiqh*. Besides the fact that they judge case by case, they also engage in juridical prophecy, creating law by means of a procedure of individual reasoning. The *responsa* are made up of consultations in law given orally or in writing to the parties involved, stating what is the law, and are handed down case by case. The *fatwa* constitutes law-like pronunciations. Thus, one can say that it is a matter of decisions enunciated from a subjective point of view.

Islamic law is not entirely lacking in a material rationality, because these so-called *responsa* or *fatwa* are proclaimed in accordance with criteria. The *qadi*, a functionary of the prince, handles law in a rational manner as he avoids any method of proof that is irrational, instead concentrating upon *ijtihad*, or reason by analogy. There is no difference in principle between the *responsa* of *qadi* on the one hand and the justice made in the democratic courts of Athens, the Canon law decisions of Church authorities and the opinions of Jewish rabbis on the other hand. The *responsa* of a Roman lawyer has its analogue in the *fatwa* by the *mufti* in Islamic law. Yet Islamic law is theocratic patrimonial law. State coercion is decisive in guaranteeing a legal order, even if it is a Holy Law. The types of authority articulate themselves in formal qualities of law. Authority is patrimonial when the worldly prince administers law. With Islamic law goes caesaro-papist authority. Caesaro-papism poses the question of asymmetry in the relationship between religious authority and political power, while patrimonial authority concerns the domination between the holder of power and his subjects. Theocracy is expressed in Sharia law, while the *qadi* and the *mufti* display patrimonial authority in the administration of justice. Law and the administration of justice, instead of being in conformity with formal rationality, are animated by political and religious rules.

Thus, one link is missing in the chain towards formal rational law, namely the specialised jurist or autonomous jurisprudence characterised by generalisation, deduction and systematisation. These features are the result of a slow historical maturation, which ends with modern formal law. Thus, Islamic law experienced development towards modern law with one exception, namely formal rational law, which is typical of modern jurisprudence.

The nature of law reflects a number of factors: the creators and holders of rights, the kind of teaching used, the techniques employed in jurisprudence, the administration of justice, the relation to political power and the religious order. The first major difference in the evolution towards formal rational law is sacred law vs secular law. A sacred law does not distinguish rites, ethical norms and purely juridical prescriptions, as all are put in place on an equal footing. This is the case in holy Islamic law. It shares this feature with Mosaic law, the Pharisees, the religion of the Vedas in India, the sacred books of China, and so on. From this stems an ambiguity of norms and silence in the face of new facts. Since the norms are unchangeable, they are mingled in an arbitrary manner with problems and circumstances that surface in an improvised manner. Thus, law becomes unpredictable. However, predictability is a condition for the rationalisation of law. The sacred norms in the Koran blocked the roads to the emergence of a secular law. Sacred law within Islam may be seen as a paradigm of the typical influence of sacred law within a religion based upon a written prophecy (Weber, 1978: 696, 714, 756–57, 758, 790, 815). One can summarise this influence in the role religion played for the jurists who first crystallised the law and later went on to stabilise it in the four classical schools of Islamic law, in order to finally solidify it in redundant compilations towards the fourteenth century. Islamic law according to Sunna is the "stereotypic law of the jurists". Weber states:

> The dominance of law that has been stereotyped by religion constitutes one of the most significant limitations on the rationalisation of the legal order and hence also on the rationalisation of the economy. (Weber, 1978: 577)

The similarity with Jewish law is telling, even more so with Hindu practices, although their law is sacred without being prophetic (Weber, 1978: 816–818: 823–828). However, only in the Occident did secular law emerge, the origin of which was paradoxically to be found in the Canon law of the Catholic Church (Weber, 1978: 828–831; see Berman, 1983).

Sources of Law in Arabia

One must first distinguish between the sources or foundations of law in Islam and the four schools of law. There are four sources: (1) divine – the Koran contains without lacuna "a series of rules with relevance for positive law"; (2) semi-divine – besides the Koran there is the Hadith or Sunna, the sayings or doings of the prophet, the validity of which is said to be guaranteed by a chain of witnesses, going back to the certified entourage of the prophet, in the same sense as the Hinduist *Dharmas* or Jewish law. The third and fourth sources are human ones, but made sacred by tradition. (3) The *ijtihad* or analogue reasoning serves as a deductive basis for judgements about similar cases having the same cause. (4) The fourth source is consensus among the great jurists. This is not the same as custom, in the English sense, but a *tacitus consensus omnium*, which refers to precedents and has a pretension to being sacred.

Neither the Koran nor the Sunna constitutes, however, an immediate source of law. Law is developed by the *fiqh*, which is jurisprudence stemming from the schools of law and their methods. Islamic law is a law of jurisprudence where the great historical jurists become "charismatic prophets of law". The scholars of *fiqh* appeared more than a century after the death of the prophet in 632. They took about two hundred years to fully emerge and even more time to consolidate themselves towards the tenth century in four Sunni law schools referred to by the names of great jurists and the school's founders: Hanifite – Abu-Hanifa (died 767); Malikite – Malik (died 797); Shaffiite – Shafii (died 820); and Hanbalite – Ibn-Hanbali (died 855) (Khadduri, 1961; Coulson, 1964).

If the four schools of Islamic law agree on the four sources, they have different views about technical solutions in the legal field (the five rites, marital status, sanctions of crimes, possessions). Abu Hanifa gives more importance to the *ijtihad*, whereas the Malikites and the Hanbalites are more strict and give more importance to the Sunna of the prophet. Shafii, finally, put into his *Risala* (Letter) the principle of hierarchy of the legal sources and the way of reasoning in order to find the appropriate judgement (first the Koran, the Sunna being complementary; in the case of silence of both sources, elaborate standards, proceeding by analogy of the judicial precedents). Although these schools differ by means of separate articulation of sources, which is without interest from our perspective, they all pose questions of an epistemological nature (Schacht, 1966; Coulson, 1964; Fyzee, 1964). Thus, they asked, for example, in the name of which source? Or by which protocol of validation and by means of which deductive procedure?

Islamic law is certainly not merely sacred law, because there exists at least two essential techniques for secular law. The first one in penal law is called *ta'zir* – a discretionary punishment pronounced by the *qadi* in two ways: either by weakening or replacing a punishment already handed down by sacred law, or by punishing acts that were not foreseen in the Sharia, but suspected to damage a third party or to shake the public order. *Ta'zir* belongs neither to ancient custom law in the Arab peninsula, sometimes ratified by Islam, nor to the Islamic rules that appeared with the Koran and the traditions of the prophet (Schacht, 1983: 35, §7). The second secular technique is to be found in commercial law. It belongs to the *hiyal* – the clever – and it consists of juridical fictions that allow contracting parties to escape or to deviate from sacred law, especially the prohibition against the taking of interest payments. Several methods are available where the parties multiply the complexities: selling with the right to pre-empt, double selling and selling on condition (Schacht, 1926: 211–232).

Islamic law is a historical construction with a complex structure and it is necessary to clarify its doctrines. In reality, the schools crystallised law, as they created jurisprudence that was later compiled towards the fourteenth century, and even more so later on. What is called the "gate of ijtihad" was closed (Hallaq, 1984: 3–41), as there will be no more charismatic prophets in law, but only imitations of the great masters. Does this mean that Islamic law definitively became a stereotype? In Muslim countries one could always reinterpret the sacred law for new situations or needs, but the basic fact is, of course, that "the sacred law can be neither avoided nor applied in a real sense" (Weber, 1978). Thus, Islamic law had to be created in a casuistic manner through the irrational process of *fatwa*, for example, in a different way from one school to another (Hallaq, 1984; Mumisa, 2002; Janin and Kahlmeyer, 2007).

The Four Schools (*Figh*)

The four schools (or *Madh'hab*) of Sunni Islam were named by students of the classical jurist who taught them. The Sunni schools (and where they are commonly found) are:

- *Hanafi* – Turkey, Pakistan, the Balkans, Central Asia, Indian subcontinent, Afghanistan, China and Egypt;
- *Maliki* – North Africa, the Muslim areas of West Africa, and several of the Arab states of the Persian Gulf;
- *Shafi'i* – Arabia, Indonesia, Malaysia, Egypt, Somalia, Eritrea, Yemen and southern parts of India;
- *Hanbali* – Arabia.

Fiqh is Islamic jurisprudence. It is an expansion of the Sharia Islamic law – based directly on the Koran and Sunna – that complements Sharia with evolving rulings/interpretations of Islamic jurists. *Fiqh* deals with the observance of rituals and social legislation. There are four prominent Sunni schools of fiqh (Madh'hab) and two schools for Shia and Karijites.

The variation among these four schools of Islamic jurisprudence is a fascinating area for research. One can study the geographical spread and acceptance of these four schools on the one hand. On the other, one can attempt to categorize them according to the extent of fundamentalist creed in their law interpretations (Vikor, 2005: http://www.upenn.edu/emeritus/IslamicLaw.pdf).

Casuistry

Islamic law is far from being monolithic. From the time when there existed several schools of law, it has lacked unity despite efforts at adaptation. Religious law coexists with a secular law (*qanum*) of a customary origin, applied especially in economic transactions in relation to various professions, places and moral norms, such as loyalty. With a duality of jurisdiction we have all the matters belonging to the principal domain of *fiqh* such as the statute of the person, penal law and personal belongings on the one hand. On the other, lay jurisdictions handle certain matters that have not been ruled upon by religion. Finally, besides this internal lack of unity there is also the absence of external unity: law is confessionally based and is only applied to Muslims in accordance with the personality of the law. Each school in addition has its law, and the other confessions or sects have their specific religious law.

We are confronted by an accumulation of juridical dualisms making the systematic creation of one law for the purpose of internal and external unification impossible. Turkey codified its law in 1869 by unifying a collection of rules from the Hanefit school (Weber, 1978). Schacht states that, contrary to Judaism, both Canon law and Islamic law are dominated by the dualism between religion and state. The difference is that the opposition between state and Church takes a conflictual form in the Occident, whereas in Islam there was merely dissonance due to the lack of a Church (Schacht, 1964: 12). However, in the nineteenth and twentieth centuries a canonical dispute over legal reform occurred in Islam (Fareed, 1995).

Islamic law is not orientated towards a systematic elaboration of principles of law, but rather toward solutions in practical cases. Yet how then could Islam develop a science of the fundamentals of law (*usuls al-fiqh*), a *ratio legis*, which contains deliberative rules concerning the manner of creating law? If it would indeed be difficult for a charismatic prophet to hand down a systematic exposition of law under formal and abstract concepts, then the same probably applies to religiously inspired jurists. This holds for Sunnite Islam and even more so for Shiite Islam. The unpredictability of law in Shiism is further increased due to the fact that it lacks the point of firm support within Sunna, which it replaces with the belief in the infallibility of the imam. There is a peculiarity with Shiite law, namely the priority given to *ijtihad* (consensus) at the expense of *taqlid* (tradition) to such an extent that the title *mujtahid* (interpreter-savant) is given to the great imams who make law. This is the position of *wilayet faqih*, the tutor of the jurists' consultants who create law by means of their excellence in the absence of *Mahdi*.

Religious justice focusing on the *qadi* is the crux of the matter. The *qadi* invents law with fictions and corrections of abuse. In Rome, law and the administration of justice by the group of jurists became secularised. The parties needed to consult the law. The great jurists (*jurisconsuls*) were independent of the lawyers and judges and could organise the legal concepts in an abstract manner to make them applicable to all possible economic situations. In contrast, the *qadi* stayed dependent upon sacred law. Islamic law developed differently from Canon law, because Canon law does not limit itself to collecting opinions, as it delivers decisions, finds sources and creates law by means of a rigorous and logical method as well as a formal technique for codification. This method stemmed from the specificity of the Catholic Church, itself organised under a hierarchical and rational format. When developing a pedagogical and technical activity, it is the only organisation that "provides itself with the organs to create in a rational manner law, which endeavour fails in all the other great religions" (Weber, 1978: 181–182). Thus, the role of the Catholic Church becomes "the decisive factor, relatively speaking" (Weber, 1978: 183).

However, it can be pointed out that the casuistic nature of English law – the common law – did not prevent Great Britain becoming the first capitalist country, Weber states:

> It may thus well stand in the way of the interests of the bourgeois classes and it may indeed be said that England achieved capitalistic supremacy among the nations not because but rather in spite of its judicial system. (Weber, 1978: 814)

In this case, formal rationality is not a necessary condition for the birth of modern capitalism, one would conclude (Crone, 1999: 252–253; 2002; Hallaq, 1984/1985: 79–96). In Western countries law is casuistic or theoretical, secular or sacred, but the outcome is that the formal rationalisation of law is conducive to the emergence of capitalism in its modern version. On the contrary, within Islam law develops by the same track, but the result is the impossibility of a formal rationalisation of law, which is a severe handicap to the evolution of modernisation.

Finally, concerning professionals in law, in relation to the type of legal thought there are two possibilities in the teaching of law. One kind offers practitioners pragmatic teaching conducive to a craft in, for example, church schools, which teach theology and law. Another kind is orientated towards a theoretical teaching in the sense of a jurisprudence dominated by the intellectual ability of the scholars. The formal rationality of the theoretical teaching is pronounced and systematic, whereas the craft-based teaching is rather casuistic, orientated towards the practical needs of people seeking redress or correction of an error. It also tends to be entrusted to theologians who are also jurists. Within Islam, as is also true of India and of Judaism, this kind of teaching is handed over to practitioners, rendering the teaching of law a casuistic enterprise (Weber, 1978: 252–253). In contrast, Western law has separated the two types of teaching, thus avoiding the hybrid form of education. By developing Canon law, the Church helped secular law to become more rational, taking Canon law as its guide. Later on only the professionals of jurisprudence received a specialised theoretical education in the universities, based upon a separation between law and theology (Weber, 1978: 183) stemming from the rediscovery of Roman law.

In short, rational formal justice is the bedrock of modernisation as it shatters patriarchalism (Weber, 1978: 162), making law stable, predictable and to the advantage of the economically powerful groups, who have an interest in the law guaranteeing smooth economic activity. In Islam, however, law is material justice. Law is handled by means of ethnic and religious criteria and it does not decide conflicts by means of formal rules. Justice based upon *qadi* casuistry better suits patrimonial authority than legal–rational authority (Weber, 1978: 167).

Waqf

How was the building and maintenance of all the new mosques financed? Islamic law developed certain peculiar legal institutions, one of which was the religious *waqf*, or trust (http://islamic-world.net/economic/waqf/). It is recorded that the mosque of Quba' in Medina, a city 400 kilometres north of Mecca, was built upon the arrival of the prophet Mohammed in 622. Six months later, Quba' was followed by the mosque of the prophet in the centre of Medina – these would be the first examples of *waqf*. Mosques and real estates for providing revenues to spend on the maintenance and running expenses of mosques fall under the religious institution of *waqf*. The accumulation of *waqf* properties all over Muslim lands and the variety of its objectives concerning widespread religious and philanthropic activities has rendered the *waqf* institution a most important role in the economic–political life of Muslim societies, to which we will return when the modernisation effort is discussed below. The *waqf* revenues were most often spent on mosques. This usually includes the salary of the imam (prayer leader and speaker for Friday's religious ceremony), as well as teacher(s) of Islamic studies. Let us quote from a reliable definition of *waqf*:

> *Waqf* in Arabic language, means hold, confinement or prohibition. The word *waqf* is used in Islam in the meaning of holding certain property and preserving it for the confined benefit of certain philanthropy and prohibiting any use or disposition of it outside that specific objective. (Kahf, 1993)

This definition underlines the perpetuity of the *waqf* institution. It applies to non-perishable property whose benefit can be extracted without consuming the property itself. *Waqf* widely refers to land and buildings, but may comprise books, agricultural machinery, cattle, shares, and stocks and cash money. When a *waqf* is created, then what is required is that the property should be handed over on a permanent basis. Some jurists approve temporary *waqf* only in the case of family *waqf*. Moreover, it is required that the *waqf* founder should be legally fit and able to take such an action, meaning that a child or a person who does not own the property cannot make *waqf* (http://www.islamic-world.net/economic/waqf/waqaf_mainpage.html).

Another type of *waqf* started shortly after the death of the prophet during the reign of Omar (634–644). When Omar decided to document in writing his *waqf*, he invited some of the companions of the prophet to attest this document. What the caliph suggested was a new type of *waqf*, putting as a condition that the fruits and revenues should be first given to their own children and descendants and only the surplus given to the poor. This kind of *waqf* is called a family *waqf*. Therefore, *waqf* in Islamic society may also be for one's own family and descendants.

Yet, the basic objective behind the *waqf* is linked with an act of charity from both the point of view of Sharia and of the founder. Hence *waqf* for the rich alone is not permissible because it is not charity. Finally, beneficiaries – person(s) or purpose(s) – must be alive and legitimate, as *waqf* for the dead is not permissible. Philanthropic *waqf* is the second kind of *waqf*, supporting the poor and consisting of activities that are of interest to people at large, such as libraries, scientific research, education, health services, care of animals and the environment, lending to small businessmen, parks, roads, bridges, dams, and so on. Accumulating wealth for religious purposes broadly speaking may have been the driver behind the *waqf* institutions, but did it also slow the private accumulation of capital that is an engine for economic development? The development of the *waqf* institution has been linked with the slow modernisation of the Muslim civilisation, as it restrained capital accumulation and diverted investments away from wordly productive purposes. Another example of an institutional obstacle to modernisation is the Muslim commercial law. Institutional economists searching for the causes of the slow modernisation of the Muslim civilisation have suggested other answers than the Koranic message when debating the conditions for economic development in Arabia and elsewhere in the Muslim civilisation.

From a legal point of view, the ownership of *waqf* property is not with the person who created the *waqf*. Some Muslim jurists argue that the right of ownership of *waqf* belongs to Allah, but it may also be said to belong to the beneficiaries, although their ownership is not complete as they are not permitted to dispose of the property or use it in a different way from what was decreed by the founder. In this regard, *waqf* differs from a foundation since the management of a foundation is usually able to sell the property, perpetuity thus being stronger in *waqf* than in foundations. Once a property or a real estate is dedicated as *waqf*, it remains *waqf* for ever. The elimination of the *waqf* character of a property is a difficult process, as exchange is needed for another property of equivalent value after approval of the local court. Upon completion of such an exchange, the new property immediately becomes *waqf* for the same purpose.

It should be emphasised that the *waqf* is always based upon an act of benevolence. This entails that the conditions specified by the founder must be fulfilled as long as they do not violate Sharia rulings. The revenues of *waqf* should be used for the objective stipulated by its founder, which may not be changed as long as the objective is compatible with Sharia. When a *waqf* purpose becomes infeasible, the revenue should be spent on the closest purpose available and if not, it goes to the poor and needy. The *waqf* founder determines the management of his *waqf*. The *waqf* manager is usually called *mutawalli* and his responsibility is to administer the *waqf* property to the best interests of the beneficiaries. The first duty of the *mutawalli* is to preserve the property and second to maximise the revenues of the beneficiaries. The *waqf* document usually mentions how the *mutawalli* is compensated for this effort, but if the document does not mention a compensation for the *mutawalli*, then he either volunteers the work or seeks assignment of compensation from the court. The judicial system, or the *qadi*, is the authority with regard to disputes related to *waqf* (http://www.mideastweb.org/Middle-East-Encyclopedia/waqf.htm).

In the early part of the eighth century, a judge in Egypt established a special register and office to record and supervise *waqf* in his area. This led to the establishment of an office for registration and control in Muslim countries. In the early nineteenth century, a special ministry was established for *waqf* in the Ottoman Empire and laws relating to *waqf* were enacted. The most important among them was the Law of *Waqf* of 1863. This law remained in application in several countries (Turkey, Syria, Iraq, Lebanon, Palestine and Saudi Arabia) for many years after the dismemberment of the Ottoman Empire in 1918. Most Muslim countries have either ministries or departments of *waqf* and religious affairs combined together. Muslim communities in non-Muslim countries have organised their *waqf* in accordance with Islamic Sharia, within the limits of prevailing laws and regulations. In India, a *waqf* act was adopted at the federal level in 1954 and the Union Minister of Law was made the supervisory authority on *waqf*. Each state in the Union of India has a *waqf* board.

In the United States and Canada, Muslim communities administer their *waqf* properties in accordance with the foundation acts. The usual practice is that each Muslim community establishes a non-profit organisation that in turn owns the *waqf* property, consisting of the local mosque or Islamic centre. In 1975, the North American Islamic Trust (NAIT) was registered in the state of Indiana, one of main objectives being to promote the *waqf* of Muslims in North America. A few years later a sister organisation under the same name was registered in the state of Ontario in Canada. NAIT and its Canadian counterpart maintain many mosques, Islamic centres and Islamic schools in the United States and Canada.

Information extracted from the registers of *waqf* in Istanbul, Jerusalem and Cairo indicates that such *waqf* lands covered a considerable proportion of the total cultivated area in the past. For instance, in the years 1812 and 1813, a survey of land in Egypt showed that *waqf* consisted of 600,000 *feddan* (1 *feddan* = 0.95 acre) out of a total of 2.5 million *feddan*; in Algeria the number of deeds of *waqf* of the grand mosque in the capital Algiers was 543 in the year 1841; in Turkey about one-third of the land was *waqf*; and finally in Palestine, the number of *waqf* deeds recorded up to the middle of the sixteenth century was 233, containing 890 properties in comparison with 92 deeds of private ownership containing 108 properties. Upon the occupation of Algeria by French troops in 1831, the colonial authority took control of the *waqf* property in order to suppress religious leaders who fought against the occupation.

Since the beginning of Islam in the early seventh century, education has been financed by *waqf* and voluntary contributions. Government financing of education used to take the form of constructing a school and assigning certain property as *waqf* of the school. *Waqf* of the Ayubites (1171–1249) and the Mamalik (1249–1517) in Palestine and Egypt are good examples. According to historical sources, Jerusalem had 64 schools at the beginning of the twentieth century as *waqf* or supported by *waqf* properties in Palestine, Turkey and Syria. Founded in Cairo in 972, the University of Al Azhar was financed by its *waqf* revenues until the government of Mohammed Ali in Egypt took control in 1812. *Waqf* financing of education usually covers libraries, books, salaries of teachers and other staff and stipends to students. This financing helped create a learned class not derived from the rich and ruling classes (Shatzmiller, 2001).

The purposes of the *waqf* include benefits for the poor, needy, orphans, persons in prisons, and so on. Other uses of *waqf* revenues include health services, covering the construction of hospitals and the provision of physicians and training, as well as expenditure on patients. One example of the health *waqf* is the Shishli Children's Hospital in Istanbul that was founded in 1898. There is also *waqf* for the benefit of animals. There are *waqf* for helping people go to Mecca for pilgrimage and for helping girls who are getting married, and for many other philanthropic purposes.

However, the Western system of education introduced by colonial authorities and supported by newly created economic opportunities dealt a blow to the traditional education, financed by an underdeveloped *waqf*. With the independence of most Islamic countries the new leadership took a negative stand towards *waqf*. For instance many *waqf* properties in Syria, Egypt, Turkey, Tunisia and Algeria were added to the public property of the government and were distributed through land reforms. Governments in those countries took over the responsibility for funding mosques and some religious schools, including Al-Azhar University in Cairo. Many Muslim countries established a branch of the government for *waqf* and religious affairs. After being stripped of its developmental content, *waqf* is now mostly used only for mosques. However, a few countries such as Lebanon, Turkey, Jordan and recently Algeria have revived *waqf* properties (www.islamic-world.net/economic/waqf).

Why Did the Mid-East Fall Behind in Trade?

Arab merchants were highly successful capitalists in, for instance, the trade in the Indian Ocean, but they were confined by the Islamic institution of partnership. The Joint Stock Corporation and the modern corporation in Europe evolved as the partnerships expanded and grew in size, posing the question of risk management. Typically, problems had to be resolved by creating new institutions, putting pressure on the legal system to recognise these and enforce them. Partners who wanted to issue and sell their shares needed a financially fungible mechanism, leading to transferable shares and stock exchanges. The legal system responded to the requirement for fungibility. The same thing did not happen in the Islamic world, because the partnerships did not grow. As a matter of fact, Islamic partnerships could not be divided up and sold in pieces. They had to be dismantled entirely if one partner died or wanted to leave. This is the basis of the institutional explanation of Muslim economic decline (Kuran, 2007; Nienhaus, 2007).

However, this difference did not matter for a long time, because the small partnerships were still extremely successful, and most of their trade was with Africa or Asia (Choudhuri, 1991). Not until the eighteenth century when trade with Europe became a big part of Middle Eastern commerce did the difference between the systems become important. Until the late Middle Ages, the Muslim Middle East was at least as economically developed as Europe. With the rise of the great Italian traders in the sixteenth century, Europeans pulled ahead, while the Islamic world gradually declined. By the nineteenth century, European economic clout had translated into political domination of the Middle East. The Islamic world never fully recovered, and that disparity feeds resentment today, although the advent of the petro economy has involved a stunning comeback for at least some Arab countries.

Muslim traders were successful in earlier eras, but only because they remained successful in trade with other regions like India and East Africa. European law institutions, however, had evolved to suit the scale of modern businesses, in which thousands of people may be involved as investors and employees. Christians and Jews using those laws began to prosper in comparison to their Muslim neighbours. Only in the nineteenth century did Middle Eastern governments begin to adopt secular commercial laws that allowed Muslim-owned enterprises to grow.

Partnership and inheritance of Islamic law interacted to keep Middle Eastern enterprises small, never allowing the development of corporate forms (Kuran, 2001). In the Middle Ages, both Islamic and European law required that a partnership dissolve if one partner died or was incapacitated, which tended to limit the size of such arrangements. Typical partnerships would be two financial backers and one trader who brought merchandise to or from a distant locale. The more people were involved, the more likely it was that the partnership would have to dissolve in the middle of a venture. In Europe, the consequences of a partner's death could be limited. Inheritance law often allowed a person to designate heirs, so a particular son might inherit the partnership share. The partnership would still have to dissolve technically, but it could be immediately reconstituted. Even in places where inheritance law was stronger, heirs were generally limited to the nuclear family, limiting the number of claimants and therefore the potential for the disruption of partnerships. As a result, European partnerships were able to expand over time, allowing more ambitious, better-financed ventures.

Under Islamic law, by contrast, inheritance was prescribed in rigid detail, with all sorts of family members – uncles, cousins, siblings, parents, and so on – getting pieces of the estate. There was no way to limit a stake to a single heir.

These prescriptions were rooted in the Koran, which meant they were virtually impossible to alter. The fragmentation produced by inheritance law, combined with the structures of partnership law, kept Middle Eastern enterprises small. Today, Islamic inheritance law poses no problems to large-scale endeavours. The estate simply divides up the securities among the heirs, and the business goes on undisturbed. Secular corporate law lets the religious inheritance law work in a modern economy (Vogel and Hayes, 1998).

Thus, one may say that Christians and Jews in Islamic countries had a business advantage, institutionally speaking. As religious minorities, they chose whether to do business under Islamic law or, with mutual consent, under some other law. Although their own religions also provided laws and courts, they generally relied on Islamic law. When Europeans started dominating Middle Eastern trade, however, they brought European courts with them, which gave Middle Eastern religious minorities a new option – to use European law in economic affairs (Cizakca, 1996).

The Puzzle of Islamic Law

Jurisprudence is basically a practical and a pragmatic science. It adapts to a changing environment, being flexible in relation to social transformation and its implications for human interaction. Thus, law changes all the time as both statute law and case law develop in various ways. Yet, Islamic law is said to be immutable. But is that really possible? And why would it be desirable? Only the history of the emergence of Islamic law can explain this paradox in comparative law. Law in the Koran was mostly a set of moral guidelines for behavior and the settlement of disputes. How were the essential prescripts of Islamic law established, and from what sources?

Some 80 Koranic verses comprise legal pronouncements, introducing significant amelioration of existing tribal customary rules as regards various criminal offences, polygamy and divorce. The standing of women was actually improved in the rights of inheritance, providing women with a formal legal status, although unequal to that of men. Tribal influences on law remained, but were softened and Islamicised, leading to the organisation of Islamic jurisprudence some 200 years after the death of the prophet.

As the Arab empire expanded to cover many new territories and people, there was a need for law and jurisprudence. In the Moslem civilisation, the organisation of law rested upon the judge – *qadi* – and the jurisconsultants – *muftis*. The *qadi* was a representative of a local governor and his main task was to arbitrate disputes. In the course of time, a *qadi*'s official function became that of a judge and he rose in prestige and rank. The *qadi*'s duties diversified as the empire expanded. He oversaw the functions of the *muhtasib*, inspector of the markets, and the *sahib ash-shurta*, the chief of police. Taken together, these three legal offices were at the core of the institutions of the Muslim city, but what law to employ, meaning rules laid down somehow by the caliph or the *qadi*?

It was early recognised that a process of reasoning had to be used, and that it was expected to follow a particular order when solving legal problems. The first recourse was to the Koran, then to reasoning by analogy (*qiyas*), then to independent judgment (*ijtihad*). Because the very notion of human reasoning used in conjunction with the divine word caused considerable argument, it led ultimately to the acceptance of a new fundamental adjunct to classical Islamic legal theory, the doctrine of *ijma'* – the consensus of qualified jurists (*fuqaha*) in a given time and place. Such consensus was believed to be infallible.

The foundation of schools with some jurisprudence – *madhahib* – occurred without design. As the body of legal ideas of a given school crystallised, those doctrines were formulated by individual religious scholars or theologians (*alim*, plural *ulama*), who formulated them and thus gave their name to the particular school. During the time of both the Umayyad and Abbasid dynasties, the practice of *ra'y* (personal reasoning) remained widespread. Those *ulama* who advocated making the Medina period the ground root of legal interpretation came to oppose the practice of *ra'y*. They argued that the only true source of law was, first, the Koran then the words, actions and precedents of the Prophet, that is, his Sunna (habitual practices and actions) and Hadith (traditions/sayings). The Sunna and Hadith of the Prophet are still today regarded as the only genuine source of Islamic law other than the Koran. The advocates of Hadith, in the long course of their doctrinal wrangle with the practitioners of *ra'y*, produced a prodigious number of fabricated Hadith in their effort to make traditionalist dogma the standard jurisprudence throughout the Islamic realm. However, if the Koran was not enough as a source of law, then how could one go about identifying the doings and sayings of the prophet in a reliable manner?

A scholar of Medina named Malik ibn Anas, who died in 796, composed the first compendium of Islamic law, little more than a manual of jurisprudence that contained the known precedents that Malik interpreted using *ra'y* and the traditions of Medina. In Cairo Shafi'i formulated the fundamental paradigm for Islamic law in his seminal treatise composed between the years 815 and 820, the year of his death. The school of law that bore his name became highly influential. He argued that absolute certain knowledge of God's divine law comes exclusively from the divine revelations given to Mohammed directly by God and that these are enshrined in the Koran. Yet, the norms in the Koran were not encompassing enough for the purposes of law, so Shafi'i had recourse to the divinely inspired dictums and prescriptions of the Prophet himself. Only he could stand as the legitimate source of law in all matters not clearly explicated in the Koran. Shafi'i believed that trustworthy reports and traditions of the Prophet and reliable reports of his conduct – the Hadith and the Sunna – were logically imbued with the same aura of divinity as Mohammed and so could be used to explain or clarify the Koran or as its auxiliary as a source of divine law. Yet, which sayings did the prophete actually pronounce? The uncertainty comes back onto Islamic law in whatever way resolution of the incompleteness problem is attempted.

The chain of transmission (*isnad*) of the Hadith determined the authenticity, and thus the quality, of a particular Hadith and that, in turn, relied on the dependability of each individual transmitter or reporter. The authenticity of a given Hadith was determined by how closely it could be traced back to the time of Mohammed or to Mohammed himself. Inevitably, this circumstance generated a vast number of false Hadith – perhaps only about 20 per cent of Hadith are authentic. Many compilations of Hadith appeared, but only a few were considered to be reliable.

There were already two schools of law – the Maliki and Hanafi – when the adherents to Shafi'i's tenets, who were a minority among legal scholars, formed a third school. However, Shafi'i's doctrine of legal unity based on the authority of the Hadith and Sunna inadvertently produced more diversity than uniformity. After the enunciation of his doctrine and creation of his madhhab, two more schools of law came into being. Those schools, one founded by Ahmad ibn Hanbal (died 855) – the Hanbali School – and the other by Dawud ibn Khalaf (died 883) – the Zahiri School – were even more firm in their rejection of any human reasoning whatever, including reasoning by analogy (*qiyas*). They espoused the belief that every legal finding had to be rooted exclusively in the Koran and Sunna, and in their literal and evident meaning (*zahir*). Ibn Hanbal collected 80,000 Hadith in his Musnad (manual). Theorists of the previously established schools, the Maliki and the Hanafi, found ways to compromise with Shafi'i's dogma by a combination of interpretation and the application of legal principles they claimed could override the authority of the Hadith. Those principles were, for the Hanafis, the cogency of "juristic preference" (*istihsan*) and, for the Malikis, the believability of "the consensus of the Medina scholars". Eventually, the Hanbalis accepted the reality that analogy was a jurisprudential necessity, while the Zahiris, refusing any alterations to their system, came to a dead end.

By the end of the tenth century, independent judgment (*ijtihad*) ceased to be accepted practice. The passing of *ijtihad* and the universal implantation of consensus wiped out the bases of Shafi'i's doctrine – traditional customs (*'urf*) and independent judgment or reasoning by individual jurists. The implications of this development were that Islamic law, having come from God, become in theory changeless and sacrosanct, meaning true moral behavior and values would always be the same. However, such rigidity in the application of Sharia was incompatible with the demands of governing the various multi-cultural, politically variegated Islamic empires from Morocco–Spain to India–Indonesia. The caliphs and sultans actually tried to increase by degrees the flexibility of the system of Sharia jurisprudence, often employing tricks like the instrumentality of what might be called creative misinterpretation. The outcome of all this was to render Islamic law somewhat unpredictable and increase to the discretion of the judge – what Weber correctly called "*Qadi-Justiz*".

Conclusion

Material justice according to Weber has its inevitable economic consequences, because it hinders capitalist exploitation of land in a free and rational manner, as well as preventing commercial law from being founded upon only a purely formal validity. However, Islamic law represents a unique phenomenon in the respect that it is based upon a science of law – *fiqh* – and only the scholarly manuals have the force of law (Schacht, 1964: Chapter 26). As a consequence he underestimates the role of the jurisconsultants who by means of their creative imagination not only invent the most complicated arguments for their clients, the merchants, but also reconcile the existing customs with the official justice of the *qadis*.

Islamic law presented a role to both the jurists and the *ulemas*. Some scholars have emphasised the separation between political power and the religious elites. Crone asks whether Muslim failure does not originate in the circumstance that the state, when separated from the *ulemas*, has not been able to convince the educated elites to collaborate with them in their endeavours (Crone, 1980). When legal power is separated from the *ulemas*, then the state distinguishes itself from the community that has its focus upon the religious leaders. If this is the case, then the problem of Islamic law relates more to the comparative status of science than to the overall constellation of domination – political, religious or legal. However, in our view the thesis about the autonomy of the *fiqh* and the *ulemas* is exaggerated. Not only is it the case that the *ulemas* never constituted a fixed order, but their domain of power was never separated from the *fiqh*. The *fiqh* tends to be depoliticised and placed outside of public law, as it never achieves the status of secular jurisprudence.

Islamic law is one of the major legal systems of the world, co-existing with Western law (civil law, common law, Scandinavian law) and Socialist law. Islamic law contains an essential component of sacred law, but it is far more than mere Sharia law. It consists in addition of a large component of jurisprudence, resulting from the four major schools of law in Sunni Islam – *fiqh*. The activity of the jurists and jurisconsultants, the *muftis* and the *qadis* resulted in a body of law that covered most aspects of life in the *umma*, including economic activity. It is true that Islamic law remained to a large extent casuistry, resulting in unpredictability and systematically lacking coherence. However, Muslim backwardness can only be explained by a legal theory if one focuses upon special legal institutions such as the *waqf* or Islamic trust as well as partnership law in commerce. When Muslim countries embarked upon modernisation, then several of them simply adopted whole Western legal codes into their legal orders. In Shia Islam the four schools (*figh*) are not recognized. In stead, jurisprudent Ja'fari Shia employs *Sunnah* as the oral traditions of Muhammad together with their implementation by the Imams, which involves more use of *fatwas* and more discretion than in Sunni Islam.

Chapter 8
Capitalism in Muslim Countries

Introduction

Capitalism is a universal phenomenon and has existed within all the various large cultural spheres, including the Occident and Asia, as well as within the various historical periods: Antiquity, the Middle Ages, the colonial period and the age of globalisation. As the economic documents indicate, one finds within all the civilisations of the world one form of capitalism or another (Weber, 1978, 1981, 1993, 1998, 1996: 113). Within all periods, and in all places, the search for profit has structured both the economy and societies. On this point, there is no difference between Marx and Weber, Schumpeter, Braudel and Wallerstein, who all accepted the existence of capitalism since the ancient times. All acknowledge also that modern capitalism, defined by Marx as the separation between the producers and the means of production or by Braudel and Wallerstein as the world economy, emerged after the Reformation and the Renaissance. Some even consider that Islam and even Asia practised capitalism before the Western world (Abu Lughod, 1989; Chaudhuri, 1991; Inalcik, 1973).

One must start by admitting that Islam has experienced capitalism as a universal phenomenon, but Islam did not have the *bourgeoisie* as a class, nor the city, which are two typical features of modern capitalism. In relation to ethical matters, Islam has also known the road to salvation through grace on the basis of predestination, although to a lesser extent than Calvinism. It is this kind of ethics that is conducive to the ethos that the idea of a vocation or call (*Beruf*) expresses, according to Weber. What is lacking in Islam is thus the transition from the religious ethic to the moderm capitalist spirit, because, contrary to Protestantism, Islam multiplied the obstacles to the rationalisation of the inner-worldly ascetic orientation. This opposition between political economy (Anderson, 1995) and cultural approach (Hudson, 1995) is central in political science (Anderson, 1995 vs Hudson, 1995). Both perspectives may be brought to bear upon the question of economic development in the Moslem civilisation.

Capitalism and Islam

Islam has known various forms of capitalism. With trade, the Muslim civilisation experienced the phenomenon of *commandia*, which is a form of transaction of goods where each party retains a quota of the profits (Weber, 1998). Moreover, Islam is familiar with domestic industry in the form of subcontracting, of which one kind is the *bazar*. In this case, the locations of fabrication and sales are separated from the dwellings of the craftsmen and the location of fabrication is linked with the sales centres (Weber, 1981). We know that this separation between the place of work and the place of living anticipates the separation between private property and the modern capitalist enterprise (Weber, 1978).

At the same time, capitalism may also be orientated towards government. There has existed a capitalism that searches for profits from politics when these economic opportunities result from positions of domination, or when the economic operations are executed to the benefit of those in power. There are many forms of this: tax collection and tax farming, concessions, licences and even colonies. Marxist scholars argue that this kind of political capitalism is linked with enterprise capitalism, sometimes along with the emergence of modern capitalism. One may also wish to consider certain forms of slavery as slave capitalism, especially when slavery is driven to its extreme in huge slave markets as in Antiquity in, for example, Rome, or in modern times in the Deep South of America (Rostovzeff, 1986; Vogel and Engerman, 1995). In addition, there is also feudal capitalism or agricultural capitalism, as for instance with the exploitation of the serfs in the manorial system in Eastern Europe, or the harsh use of share-cropping in countries like India and the southern United States.

Moreover, the sources of modern capitalism are universal. In his polemic with Sombart, on the link between Jewish communities and modern capitalism, Weber states exactly this. When analysing the variety of capitalism, one typically makes a review of the different techniques of capitalism, from borrowing money in the banking system to the huge enterprise emerging from the trading house. Ancient capitalism can be classified as Hellenistic, Byzantine, slave, agricultural, commercial or feudal (Schumpeter, 1989). Typical of modern capitalism are the forms and values of the rational capitalist system where huge enterprises operate on anonymous markets (Weber, 1978).

The Occident has improved and revolutionised certain Arab economic methods, such as calculating techniques coming from the Islamic world. Here, for instance, we also have the fabrication of coloured clothes, carpets and products for luxury in the medieval Occident, made according to the oriental model. The Arabs were pioneers in navigation on the oceans, and they became the founders of astronomic nautics. The notion of brokerage in the occidental world has an oriental inspiration, from occidental merchants in foreign countries. The sequential number system, which was indispensable to modern capitalism as a tool for rational calculus, was passed to the Occident by the Arabs and the Jews of the Greater Middle East. Yet, only the Occident developed an accounting system based upon these numbers.

Thus, Islam did certainly recognise capitalism, but it could not release modern capitalism. In order for modern capitalism to exist there must be acquisitive capital within the context of an economy comprising large-scale firms operating in markets for the free exchange of goods, as well as for the means of production. There are two socio-economic conditions upon which Weber puts emphasis due to their role in the emergence of modern capitalism, the bourgeoisie and the city. These two factors are external to the ethics of capitalism, but constitute crucial social conditions for its spread. Applied to Islam, the Weber thesis implies that modern capitalism distinguishes itself through a set of mixed characteristics that one hardly finds within Islam. Islam did experience capitalism within agriculture, commerce and government, but a feudal economy involving benefices and rents in money or in *natura* cannot bring forth modern capitalism (Weber, 1981, 1998). Regarding the Ancient period, one may only speculate whether it could have experienced evolution towards a modern capitalist economy to an extent that is important from the point of view of history (Rostovzeff, 1988; Adas, 1993). The employment of modern concepts such as the firm, the proletariat and the bourgeoisie is dangerous in economic history. This is indeed the criticism Weber made against Edouard Meyer (Weber, 1922, 1998). Let us examine his argument about the bourgeoisie and the city.

Islam Ignores the Bourgeoisie

As a social category, the bourgeoisie designates the group that is involved in commerce and industry, thus comprising both the small and large bourgeoisie, entrepreneurs, merchants and craftsmen. In a restrictive sense, the bourgeoisie is a social group with high prestige, uniting wealthy entrepreneurs and people with culture. Second, from an economic point of view it is a more or less unified class defined in opposition to the nobility and the proletariat at the same time. It presupposes modern enterprise and the free salary contract. Third, in a political sense, the bourgeoisie refers to citizens, in particular those holding political rights. The existence of a bourgeoisie in Islam in all the three meanings listed above may be questioned.

Politically, the concept of a citizen is unknown in the Islamic world, in India or China. Economically, Islam has not seen a unified class – a bourgeoisie – appearing on its territory. Finally, there is no broad social strata with special prestige either. Weber writes that the bourgeoisie in its social aspect is linked with the city and he argues that this kind of city only exists in the Occident (Weber, 1978). In this case, the link between the city and the bourgeoisie is organic.

Let us begin with the first element, citizenship. In contrast to Antiquity and the medieval West, Islam has never known the concept of citizenship due to the fact that the subjects within Islam traditionally did not have the right to participate in the affairs of the city. The only rights that they had referred to either public allegiance to a prince or a king during prayer, or the right to religious revolt against an infidel prince who was unjust. When the Arabs translated Greek philosophy in the ninth century, the concept of a citizen was considered synonymous with either aristocratic honour (*fadhila*), or inhabitants (*ahl*) or people (*jumhour*), depending on the ircumstances (Walzer, 1970; Badawi, 1968; Lewis, 1988). The Greek word "*polis*" was translated into Arabic by the word "*medina*", designating a neutral place such as the city, the state or the empire. Therefore, the citizen was then an inhabitant or resident of a city, and nothing more.

In reality, the Islamic city was structured around the mosque, which was the Agora of Islam or the place for "religious–political discussion recognised by convention". The mosque is placed close to the palace (*qasr*) of the caliph or the prince. It is in the centre of the world, both in terms of architecture and with regard to social and economic matters (Djaït, 1986: 86). In the mosque, the caliph or his representative conducts the *prayer de jure*, and from the mosque emanate the sects who always bid higher on the use of divine grace. Islam is familiar with a bourgeoisie to the extent that it is understood it as a social stratum having certain economic privileges covering agents linked with a market, close to what we used to call the "petit bourgeoisie": craftsmen, merchants, brokers, artisans and shopkeepers. With regard to Islam, one speaks of the bourgeoisie of Mecca, the bourgeoisie of the religious sects like the dervishes, the bourgeoisie of the domestic industry and the people of the *bazar*, often orientated towards political affairs.

Following Rodinson's analysis, Islam developed a bourgeoisie during the Abbasid caliphate towards the tenth century. An urban civilisation emerged at that time with professional orders and craftsmanship, flourishing commerce and a monetary economy that gave birth to an active bourgeoisie that "was well aware of itself and its interests" to such an extent that Rodinson asks herself why this bourgeoisie did not manage to take any political power. Her answer places the burden on the typical political domination of the group of "slave soldiers" or mercenaries within Islam (Rodinson, 1966: 72). In any case, Rodinson states that the Muslim capitalist sector "was evidently the most extended and the most developed that had ever seen the light of day before the emergence of the global market created by the European bourgeoisie" (Rodinson, 1966: 72).

The Islamic City: A Patrician City

The bourgeoisie belong to an urban environment, but the reverse is not true. Islam experienced the city but not with a bourgeoisie. There are several kinds of urban agglomerations covering different social groups (classes, orders, clans, *ethnies*), according to a certain number of combined criteria defined by economic, political and legal characteristics and the nature of the activities. With regard to Islam, one can say that it has known a certain number of these types, with one exception of the type specific for the Occident: the community, whose influence was important for the development of modern capitalism. An Islamic city without citizens and without a community thus becomes the prototype of an urban environment that is "disorganised, labyrinthine, without face and spontaneous" (Djaït, 1986: 139).

Islam has known the city in the economic sense, i.e. an agglomeration of inhabitants who live from activities linked with industry and commerce and not from agriculture, including crafts and know-how. The same applies to the city in the politico-administrative sense to the extent that it is an urban territory that is organised with a fortress and guarded by a garrison. Combining economics with politics, the Islamic city was at the same time a mixture of citadel and market. In Islamic cities the "*kasbah*, fortified camp of the warriors, is spatially separate from the *bazar*" (Weber, 1978: 1224). This dualism is also adopted with reference to *kasbah* and *bazar* in India (Weber, 1996b: 87), but if the city existed in Islam, then how could it present an obstacle to the spread of modern capitalism? The Islamic city may be compared with the occidental city. The first kind of city adheres to a universal type: the patrician urban agglomeration. Mecca is the most typical example. The second kind expresses a bourgeoisie emerging from the folds of the medieval city. A city is a patrician one when it is directed in fact or according to law by a group of notables called "the urban patricians". Its economic force rests upon commerce, land ownership and slavery and its military power is combined with the order of knights. Conflicts often occurred between the patrician families, opposing each other and the prince. The outcome of these conflicts had an influence upon the destiny of the city. Mecca served as a prototype for Weber when analysing the patrician city (Weber, 1978: 1231–1234).

Acknowledging his intellectual debt to Snouck Hurgronje (1857–1936), Weber employed Mecca as the classical example of the patrician city. In other places he compared Mecca with medieval cities such as Venice or Florence. He did not examine Kufa, the first Islamic city established on a tribal basis, or Baghdad, and he only briefly mentioned Bukhara and Istanbul. Mecca was a patrician conglomeration, where the aristocracy lived, recruited among the emirs and the noble *sherif*, who used to belong to the family of Mohammed, his relative Ali or his tribe. The *sherif* of Mecca was invested in office by the caliph, but in practice he was chosen to become *sherif*. Mecca lived from commerce, the income from pilgrimage as well as from land ownership. Around Mecca there amassed lands (*bilads*) in the hands of various tribes governed by oligarchs originating in the aristocracy.

Serving as a lecturer at the University of Leiden (1880–1889), Hurgronje visited Arabia (1884–1885), including Mecca. His classic work *Mekka*, in two volumes (1888–1889), reconstructed the history of the holy city, penetrating into the origins of Islam, early traditions and practices, and the first Islamic communities. The second volume, translated as *Mekka in the Latter Part of the 19th Century* (1931), contains many details of daily life in Islamic culture and deals with the Indonesian Muslim colony at Mecca.

As a matter of fact, the control of the Muslim city involved open conflicts and punctual alliances within the circle of nobles between the families, their allies and their respective troops on the one hand, as well as between these groups and the central power on the other hand. Often a conflict ended with a new alliance among families that enforced its domination. The groups who lost left the city, but ordinary courtesy demanded that the life and assets of the families and the clients of those exiled would be saved. The conflict between different powers was characteristic for the patrician city and one may find this kind of conflict within the

European city in the competition between the bishop, the lord, the crafts and the judges. Among these groups temporary coalitions were formed in order to handle the conflicts corresponding well to the alliances between the major families in Mecca. Similarly, it occurred, just as in Mecca, that one part of the nobility was banned and exiled from Venice, but contrary to Arab courtesy their assets were confiscated (Weber, 1978: 1268–1272). The same applies to Florence (Weber, 1978: 1302–1307).

The evolution of urban affairs in Islam in modern times is interesting. Mecca fell under the domination of the Ottoman Turks. At that time the city had established authorities such as an administrative collegium (*mejlis*) created by the Turks, a judicial authority shared with four jurisdictions of which each one had an Orthodox ritual and the first judges were designated by the *sherif*, a corporation of nobles directed by the *sherif* as well as corporations of craftsmen (merchants, guilds, traders, artisans, butchers). Istanbul constituted a medieval Islamic city up to the sixteenth century comprising guilds, corporations of merchants, military associations and religious organisations among which were the *ulemas* and the dervishes. We thus see Islamic cities that are close to the European medieval city with its established authorities, its law and its political corporations (nobility), religious corporations (brotherhoods) and economic corporations (crafts) (Lapidus, 1969). What then distinguishes the Islamic city from the European one?

The Weber argument is that the Islamic city remains a patrician one and does not evolve towards a city for the bourgeoisie. Two elements were missing in the Islamic city compared with the occidental one, a juridical one – the community – and a political one, the usurpation of power by the bourgeoisie. With regard to the community, in order for an agglomeration to be a city not only in an economic sense, a mere market, or in a political sense, a fortress, it was necessary for it to have an industrial character and a dominant commercial one. This involved a proper court or a legal system, social relations and an autonomous representation based upon the participation of the citizens. The city would constitute a corporation in the legal sense of the word and would have a patrimony that operated in its name. Thus, the key point is that the community carried the corporative privileges of a legal entity. The Islamic city could well rest upon the medieval orders and it had a legal system, but it did not have the legal status that was typical of the community. It was not a city for citizens, as is true of the Greek and Roman cities, underlining the political rights of *homo politicus*, but at the same time it offered chances of peaceful profit to *homo economicus*, according to medieval convention (Weber, 1978: 1226–1236).

Weber denies the existence of the communal association as a legal corporation in Asia or within Islam. Thus, he claims that Mecca lacked an organisation, which would give it a communal unity constituting a corporation on its own (Weber, 1978: 1241). It did not own its own patrimony. For instance, the conflict that opposed the family of Ali and those in power in the form of the caliph installed in Mecca concerned the so-called "garden of Fadak". The issue at stake was whether the garden of Fadak – the landed property of the prophet – belonged to the Ali family, his nephew, who very well could have inherited from Mohammed, or rather to the "commons" of Mecca. However, Weber informs us that the community that the caliph referred to as the owner of the property in question was the religious community of Islam and not the political community of Mecca, which did not exist at all (Weber, 1978: 1241).

Non-communal cities like Mecca and Istanbul were dependent for their administration upon family groups and upon the participation of professional associations, guilds and corporations of merchants, as the case may be. The business of the cities was in no way handled as a legal entity to which the members of the locality were stakeholders (Weber 1978: 1231–1234). What Islam did know was the institution of a foundation, orientated towards a pious purpose – the *waqf* (Weber, 1978: 7/4) but as a family asset and not a communal one. The concept of an institution as a juristic person is from its purely juridical aspect a construction of modern legal theory (Weber, 1978: 705–729). Islam knew the corporation only in the form of an association of artisans specialised in terms of occupations that were regulated and monopolised. Weber even states that there were a few rare cases of corporatist revolutions, for example in Bukhara (Weber, 1978: 162). During the rule of the Samanids, Bukhara became the intellectual centre of the Islamic world. Bukhara was by far the largest city in Central Asia and it was one of the biggest and most populated cities with a population of over 300,000 in the world along with Córdoba, Cairo and Baghdad. The city was also a centre of Sufi Islam. However, in general Weber claims that Islamic law did not contain the beginnings of a theory of a secular legal corporation like the city (Weber, 1978: 818–822).

The City and the Bourgeoisie

The political element, as underlined, is the usurpation of power by the bourgeoisie in the Occident. Whereas property in the city could freely be sold and made the object of an inheritance, rural property was circumscribed by feudal rules, focusing upon the rights of lords. A unique historical occurrence was when the bourgeoisie managed to have its privileges accepted by the political authority or the lords. When this power was not accepted, then the bourgeoisie often seized it by revolutionary means. Typical examples of this can be found in the Italian city, a reminder of the anarchic situation that prevailed in Mecca. Thus, the occidental city could orientate itself towards the formation of a corporative body founded upon a fraternity based upon law.

Christianity constituted a cultural element conducive to the vitality of cities. Its influence was important for the dissolution of tribal links, magical constraints and taboos due to the weakness or absence of such obstacles in the Christian religion. Christianity helped in the formation of the medieval city and contributed to the process of creating fraternities established by means of law and not on the basis of tradition. For all forms of Christianity within all time periods it holds that "it was and remained a religion especially of an urban character and essentially adhering to the bourgeoisie. The city in the Occident, which is unique in relation to other cities, and the bourgeoisie in the sense that only existed in the Occident, constituted the principal basis of Christianity". (Weber, 1978: 1236–1262). Weber expresses his idea, no doubt, in an exaggerated manner, but the link was for him evident between Christianity and the rationalism of a new class, the *bourgeoisie*. The connection is the city or the special nature of the occidental city.

On the other hand, the oriental city remained enmeshed in magical taboos, the ritual of the ancients and the division into castes. Islam never really overcame the divisiveness of Arab tribal and clan ties, as shown by the history of internal conflicts in the early caliphate; in its early period it remained the religion of a conquering army of tribes and clans. In India, Islam surrendered to the engulfing tendency towards caste formation (Weber, 1996b: 20), although the "so-called Islamic castes are eventually status groups and not castes". Thus, what makes for a large distance between Islam on the one hand and Judaism and Christianity on the other is the fact that the latter are "specifically connected with the bourgeoisie and the city", but Islam ignored the city and focused upon its fortress (Weber, 1978: 1251–1252).

Economic Rationality and Salvation

The argument that only Protestantism among the religions of the world would have known the spirit of capitalism – economic profit – is, of course, wrong. On this point, Weber is more than once explicit, stating that "capitalism" existed among all the world religions, of the same kind and to same extent as in occidental Antiquity and the medieval period (Weber, 1978: 629–630). He adds that human motivation and economic talents are the same among all the peoples of the world. To assume that the Hindu, Chinese or Muslim merchant, trader, artisan or labourer was animated by a weaker "acquisitive drive" than the ascetic Protestant is to fly in the face of the facts. Indeed, the reverse would seem to be true, for what is distinctive of Puritanism is the rational and ethical limitation of the quest for profit. There is no proof whatever that a weaker natural "endowment" for technical economic rationalism was responsible for the actual difference in this respect between the civilisations.

By which roads may the religious *virtuosi* assure himself of the certainty of his salvation – "*Erlösung*"? The issue at stake is not as much the salvation of the spirit as the ethical or practical effect of religion upon the conduct of life. Islam did recognise different ways to salvation, including predestination. However, Islam seems to have given predestination a fatalistic twist that neutralises the impact that is essential for the birth of modern capitalism. This is the thesis by Weber: the universal roads to salvation turn into special roads, whereas the special way of salvation within ascetic Protestantism is transformed into the universal canon from which is judged all the major world religions. Protestantism, thus, becomes the criterion in the last resort for judging all the other religions as well as modern capitalism of all forms of economic systems.

In reality, the religious *virtuosi*, whether he was an isolated individual or belonged to an order (*Stand*), could draw upon recognised prestige, as he searched for his salvation along several roads. Yet, the conduct of life by the *virtuosi* is judged on the basis of the distinction between inner-worldly asceticism, which transforms society, and other forms of salvation. It is this form of inner-worldly asceticism that makes certain the link between the economic rationalism of modern capitalism and religious spirit. Without additional delay, we may identify the main roads to salvation as follows: (a) gain the certainty of salvation by means of ritual, that is, service to God, for instance prayer or making sacrifices; (b) plunge oneself into various social endeavours such as charity or death in combat; (c) look for the perfection of oneself by means of individual accomplishments, such as economic prosperity or scientific research; (d) lift oneself up to a certain belief or metaphysics that is considered an exalted truth; (e) finally, consider that salvation and deliverance are a gift from a distant inaccessible God, for instance according to the theory of predestination that is typical of monotheistic religions. Islam experienced all these roads. Our belief is that Islam is to be placed somewhere between predestination and predetermination, if we follow Weber's analysis. However, it is true that the potential for predestination is compromised in favour of predetermination.

Islam encourages profit (A), but lacks the link between economic rationalism and professional ethos or vocation (B). Some forms of religion endorse the pursuit of profits. In China, richness and longevity of life are given to subjects according to the table of good things in the Confucian texts: these texts are divided into two categories, known as the "King" (Classics), and the "Shuh" (Books). The texts of the "King", which stand first in importance, are commonly reckoned as five, but sometimes as six. Zarathustra expected from his God especially affluence, and in Judaism God compensates Jewish piety with political advantages. Weber contrasts the splendour of Islam with the frugality of the other world religions. The Confucian attitude toward bureaucratic service and humble loyalty is opposed to that feudal enjoyment of lavish expenditure prominent in statements of the prophet in early Islam, which is also compared with the Buddhist rejection of attachment to worldly goods. *Islamic opulence* is confronted with the strictly traditionalist ethic of Hinduism and the Puritan hallowing of inner-worldly ascetic and profitable work in a rationally specialised *vocation*. If, for once, we disregard this fundamental contrast, there are all sorts of particularised affinities to be found between Confucianism and the sober rationalism of Puritanism (Weber, 1968: 161).

As a matter of fact, one finds within Islam texts suggesting an economic ethic. One is secular in nature, where the typical case is a kind of economic ethnic by a certain Dimashqi sometime between the ninth and twelfth centuries (Dimashqî, 1994). He suggests ethical norms in order to make trade a noble activity, obedient to balance, prudence and loyalty. Besides this secular ethics, there existed a second religious ethic, which was the target of manuals like Hisba, that is, the surveillance of the public order from a moral and economic point of view. It was a matter of an ethical duty, although a collective one; in other words, something for the community of faithful to take up as a burden. It is founded upon the credo "inviting all that is good, enjoining what is right, and forbidding what is wrong" (the Koran 3: 104). The Prince in a caesaro-papist manner for this objective designates a public agent called *muhtasib* to survey economics and morals. He inspects the quality of foodstuff, controls the price, surveys the weight and suppresses frauds (Mawardi, 1982: Chapter 20). Whereas the secular ethics is destined for professionals in commerce, manuals of *Hisba* type "are not targeting the merchants but form guides suggested for a functionary kind of the state" (Essid, 1995: 133). However, the secular ethics of a professional has not changed to a formal ethics in the service of the bourgeoisie, nor has the religious ethics addressed to the bureaucrat passed into a collective duty in the sense of an ethics of the interior, the professional duty becoming a moral one (Weber, 1993).

Modern Capitalism and Protestantism

The special affinity between economic rationalism and the type of religious ethic occurs only accidentally outside of the Occident. Thus, the various forms of Protestant asceticism make the acquisition of affluence an indicator of the confirmation of the reception of grace. In relation to ethics religious duty exists within Christianity, especially across the two proverbs of primitive Christianity: "Stay with your vocation" (St Paul, Corinthians 7: 20) and "Give to Caesar what belongs to Caesar" (Luke 10: 25). To Weber these proverbs chiefly express indifference in relation to the state. The professions are of key importance, but they will be considered only when the monastery orders – asceticism – have been founded. When it comes to the acceptance of the profit incentive, then it is not orientation towards the capitalist enterprise spirit that it distrusts. In short, what is lacking in primitive Christianity and within the Catholic Church is the connection that makes capitalist profit the ultimate salvation objective of the ideal ethics, the profession. In Islam, the Koran admonishes the believer in an almost infinite number of verses to concentrate upon the profession, which the Koran describes by words like work, duty or act. However, Islam does not make the observance of profession (vocation) a condition for salvation.

Protestantism initiates a change, not as much stimulating the profit motive as disciplining it. Further, it legitimates it, because it masters it through a rational ethics, whereas the other religions only stimulate or master it through other means than the ethos of a profession. Weber's solution is of such finesse that it is worth examining by means of a small detour. The Protestant believer, a religious *virtuosi* devoted to his religious experience, distances himself from all forms of eudaimonism, or search for pleasure. The reason is that the puritan, estimating that he is the "object of divine election" or "the instrument of divine power", places his salvation in the methodical conduct of life, the accomplishment of a duty, which he conceives of as a vocation or profession (*Beruf*), which is the only way to both express faith and receive confirmation of divine grace (Weber, 2001). Consequently, starting from an irrational ethics of suffering and pain, as well as negation and asceticism, placing the salvation of the puritan with an irrational divine decision, Protestantism, paradoxically, has rational consequences upon the economic practices of modern capitalism. When a person is motivated by ascetic action within the daily world, then this ethic transforms the religious conviction of passive Catholic ritual. In other words, the Protestant mobilises a practical rationalism, which places it at the service of capitalist development. Protestantism, when making economic success a means for the confirmation of salvation and not an end in itself, became a leverage for – and a mighty ally of – modern capitalism, which it helped to formulate its own rational ethos.

When elaborating the Protestant ideal type, which covers all the different sects, Weber compares it with other forms of belief. Catholicism is a religion with an ethical conviction that may develop into the asceticism of monks, though it is weakened by the rites of the sacrament and repentance, whereas the Protestant implements asceticism in the secular sphere, the family and the profession (Weber, 1993). In contrast to Judaism in the Ancient period, where one finds the concept of *Beruf* and the elimination of magic – primary conditions for occidental rationalism – Protestantism supported the organisation of capitalism in its bourgeois form and the spirit of the enterprise, whereas Judaism developed towards a lending form of capitalism (Weber, 1978: 611–615), focusing upon the predicament of the Jewish community as a diaspora or even paria people (Weber, 1978: 493).

While the cosmological religions in Asia were either acquiescent with the world as it is, at the same time appealing to the adept to conduct a noble, refined and wise existence (Confucianism and Taoism), or encouraging contemplation and the flight from the world (Hinduism and Buddhism), the Protestant on his or her part refuses the world which is in need of transformation or improvement. Islam is diametrically opposed to the puritan position due to the role that lawful bounty as well as political enrichment play. The idea of sin in Islam is of a feudal orientation, as it is assimilated with a ritual impurity, a *sacrilegium* and a disobedience in relation to positive prescriptions, or a lack of dignity of the order to which one belongs, or the violation of morals or social conventions. Islam lacks the sentiment of tragedy that is typical of Protestantism (Weber, 1978: 623–627), where sin is linked with lack of salvation (grace). Furthermore, Islam is a sensual religion. It is true that prostitution is infrequent in the Islamic world. It existed before Islam, more specifically in the form of a temporary marriage (Weber, 1981). Weber does not say that this type of marriage is still legitimate for the traveller within Shiism. Even if Mohammed gave prominence to sexual pleasure, he made it obligatory through the Koran to take care of the maximum number of legitimate wives (Weber, 1978: 604). Incidentally, Weber evaluates the institution of polygamy in Ancient Islam negatively, stating as he does about Mohammed:

> Such an effort was even made by Muhammad, although in his personal life and in his religious preachments regarding the world beyond he permitted unlimited sexual freedom to the warrior of the faith. It will be recalled that in one of his *suras* he ordained a special dispensation regarding the maximum number of wives permitted for himself. The various forms of extra-marital love and prostitution, which were legal before the establishment of orthodox Islam, have been proscribed in that religion with a success scarcely duplicated elsewhere. (Weber, 1978: 604)

This is in line with his overall assessment of Islam as "essentially a martial religion" (Weber, 1978: 474) as well as the "military type of prophecy – such as Islam" (Weber, 1978: 489). Weber argues that it is a unique fact for a religion of salvation that Islam is a religion with sensuality. Besides asceticism in the form of fasting, prayer and mortification, it rather exalts the possession of goods, drives the believer to display luxury and praises success with women. Because of this, he says, Islam is hardly a religion of salvation. Weber ignores the concept of redemption in the ethical sense of the word and not as a religious concept (Weber, 1978: 625), but a more grave omission is that Weber omits the anti-sensual rigorism within Islam called the *zuhd*, occurring within practical life and within mysticism. In ordinary life, tradition bans the consumption of alcohol, and it recommends avoiding carrying extravagant clothes, gold or shimmering colours. An exemplary life should be austere, rigorous, pious and sober. The *zuhd* becomes a test of intellectual detachment within mysticism to the point where it has more value than the Gnostic acquaintance with God. When the ascetic recommendations are addressed to all living believers in the world, then the adept searching for mysticism has a tendency to free himself from social obligations in order to conduct a life in retreat, far from the world.

Islamic faith in its primitive core is a road to salvation which rejects outer-worldly asceticism and especially monk-hood (*rahbaniyya*). Inner-worldly asceticism could by devaluating the intermediation between God and man emphasise the evaluation of professional work within the world. In doing so, it resembles both Judaism and Lutheranism. However, the simple faith of primitive Islam, to the same extent as the cult of Yahve, rests upon a relation of faithfulness and compensation between God and man. Thus, God compensates the faithful and punishes the infidel. For faith to become an ethics of profession, it is necessary that it acquire new features such as grace to *Träger*. Lutheranism did not develop its notion of *Beruf* as a condition *sine qua non* for the salvation of the spirit, which Calvinism did. Finally, Lutheranism accommodates the world and it does not search to change it. In the same sense, the Karijites return to the notion of hope (*amal*) and require the confirmation of salvation through good work or a methodical attitude towards life. The hope for salvation through grace is not the same as a duty of *Beruf*, which is the core of Calvinist professional ethics. In order to arrive at this approach, it is necessary that the elected confirm grace by means of a rational organisation of life. Working because of a duty, as within Islam, is not working as expressing duty, as within ascetic Protestantism.

Modern Capitalism

Modern capitalism is different from earlier forms of capitalism in terms of the scope and impact of economic rationality. Weber describes the capitalist firm in the modern market economy in the following way:

> It is only in the modern Western World that rational capitalistic enterprises with fixed capital, free labour, the rational specialisation and combination of functions, and the allocation of productive functions on the basis of capitalistic enterprises, bound together in a market economy, are to be found. (Weber, 1978: 165)

For Weber, modern capitalism or the market economy was the core of modernity. It changed the entire basis of society from tradition to rationality. It brought about massive urbanisation and industrialisation, modernising the agrarian society. In the end, it also changed politics, opening up the possibility of mass politics and democracy. An objection to Weber could be that he narrowly targets capitalism as the only element in modernity. The meaning of "capitalism" is ambiguous and there is wide disagreement about the nature of capitalism and its origins (Schumpeter, 1989; Sayer, 1990). Weber emphasises the distinction between modern capitalism and older forms of capitalism, which he links to the difference between Western capitalism and oriental capitalism. Let us follow his argument as stated succinctly in *Economy and Society* (1978), which is a short summary of his many findings in separate studies in economic history (Weber, 1988d, 1991b, 1997).

Weber speaks sometimes about "modern capitalism" and sometimes about the market economy. To him, a number of elements of economic activity, under the conditions of a market economy, are decisive (Weber, 1978: 110). In varying degrees, subjectively, people value economically productive work as a mode of life. For those who enjoy a privileged position by virtue of wealth or education, which is usually in turn dependent on wealth, there are opportunities for large income from profitable undertakings, especially when there is ambition and types of work enjoying high prestige, such as intellectual work, artistic performance and work involving high levels of technical competence. For those sharing in the fortunes of profit-making enterprises, there is the risk to the individual's own capital, as well as his own opportunity for profit, combined with the valuation of rational acquisitive activity as a "calling". On the contrary, those without substantial property run the risk of going entirely without provisions, both for themselves and for their dependants.

Vocation or "calling" was emphasised by Weber, as it could be significant as proof of the individual's own achievement. He looked upon this motivation both as a symbol and a means of autonomous control for individuals who engage in social actions like business. Alternatively, he regarded it as control over economic advantages that are culturally or materially important to many people. Now is there a difference between the market economy and capitalism?

Weber first points out that the "capitalistic" orientation of profit-making activity, meaning the orientation to capital accounting, can take a number of qualitatively different forms, such as the following:

1. Profit possibilities in trade and speculation in different currencies, in the taking over of payment functions of all sorts and in the creation of means of payment; the same with respect to the professional extension of credit, either for consumption or for profit-making purposes.
2. Opportunities for predatory profit from political organisations, or persons connected with politics, including the financing of wars or revolutions and the financing of party leaders by loans and supplies.
3. Profit opportunities in continuous business activity, which arise by virtue of domination by force or of a position of power guaranteed by the political authority: (a) colonial profits, either through the operation of plantations with compulsory deliveries or compulsory labour or through monopolistic trade; and (b) fiscal profits, through the farming of taxes and of offices, whether at home or in colonies.
4. Profit possibilities in continuous buying and selling on the market; "trade" with free exchange.
5. Profit opportunities in: (a) purely speculative transactions in standardised commodities or in the securities of enterprises; (b) the execution of the continuous financial operations of political bodies; (c) the promotional financing of new enterprises in the form of sale of securities to investors; (d) the speculative financing of capitalistic enterprises and of various other types of economic organisation with the purpose of a profitable regulation of market situations or of attaining power.

Types (4) and (5) were peculiar in the occurrence of modern or Western capitalism – this is the gist of Weber's argument. The other types have occurred all over the world for thousands of years as the possibilities of exchange and money economy (2) and money financing (types 3 and 4) presented themselves. In the Western world they have not been of such dominant importance as modes of profit-making as they were in Antiquity, except in times of war. It is only in the modern Western world that Weber finds the large-scale capitalistic type of organisation of purely voluntary labour, as the typical and dominant mode of providing for the wants of the masses of the population, with the separation of the workers from the means of production and the appropriation of the enterprises by the owners of securities. It is also only here that he finds public credit in the form of issues of government bonds, the "going public" of business enterprises, the floating of security issues and financing carried on as the specialised function of rational business enterprises, trade in commodities and securities on organised exchanges, money and capital markets, monopolistic organisations as a form of rational business organisation of the entrepreneurial production of goods and not only of the trade in them (Weber, 1991b).

It was clear to Weber from the very beginning that the politically oriented events and processes that open up the profit opportunities exploited by political capitalism are irrational from an economic point of view. It was further clear that purely speculative profit opportunities and pure consumption credit are irrational from the point of view of both satisfaction of want and the production of goods, because they are determined by the fortuitous distribution of ownership and of market advantages. Besides the rational capitalistic enterprise, Weber included the monetary system and the commercialisation of ownership shares in enterprises through various forms of securities as unique for the modern economic order. He puts up Western rationality against oriental traditionalism, and he can only find a decisive source of this separation in religion, as what separates men and women in terms of orientation in action is the degree of purposeful rationality. Weber never displayed any racist tendencies, although he wrote much about "Western", "Eastern", and "occidental and oriental" modes of action or behaviour.

If it were necessary to describe in one way or another the relation of Islam to the world, then it would be that Islam is a religion that masters the world. In short, for Weber the Asiatic religion is magically enchanted by the world, Confucianism adapts to the world, Buddhism rejects the world by flight, the Jews look upon the world with hope and the Moslem masters the world (Weber, 1978: V, §12). When comparing Islam with Judaism and primitive Christianity, Weber states that Islam adapts to the world, but in a totally different sense. At other places, we have seen that he admitted Islamic predestination, the rejection of the world by the Islamic warrior, the existence of ascetic sects and active asceticism, which all belong to Islam and monotheistic religions, including Protestantism, without, however, Islam reaching the occidental rationalisation. Yet, it must be emphasised that Weber's overall assessment of Islam was a very negative one. One reads the following section from Weber:

> A similar primary focus upon religion appeared very clearly in the case of Muhammad, whose program of social reform, which Umar carried through consistently, was oriented almost entirely to the unification of the faithful for the sake of fighting the infidels and of maintaining the largest possible number of warriors. (Weber, 1978: 444)

The religion of Mohammed, which is fundamentally political in its orientation, and his position in Medina, which was in between that of an Italian *podestà* or that of Calvin at Geneva, grew primarily out of his purely prophetic mission. A merchant, he was first a leader of a sort of pietistic bourgeois conventicles in Mecca, until he realised more and more clearly that the ideal external basis for his missionising would be provided by the organisation of the interests of the warrior clans in the acquisition of booty (Weber, 1978: 444). One should actually pose the question whether Weber really succeeded in remaining objective and neutral in his analysis of the world religions, which is a relevant question given the emphasis of Weber himself upon scientific neutrality and objectivity (Weber, 1988d; Weber, 1949).

Conclusion

When enquiring into the causes of the economic retardation of the Muslim civilisation, then, one may follow one of two possible research agendas. Either one argues that Islam as a religion hinders economic rationality, or one claims that traditional Muslim institutions slowed down economic expansion. Weber followed the first approach, linking Islam with oriental feudalism and the quest for looting among the Muslim warriors. Later research has taken the second approach, examining the rules of economic interaction in Muslim countries. The recent emergence of Islamic finance on a major scale indicates that modern capitalism can be combined with Islam. Economic expansion has taken place in several Arab countries as well as in non-Arab Muslim countries such as Malaysia. The great difficulty with modernisation in Islam lies as a matter of fact altogether elsewhere, viz. in politics, the lack of rule of law, human rights and democracy in the Moslem world.

In perhaps the most discussed social science treatise ever – *The Protestantic Ethic and the Spirit of Capitalism* (Weber, 2001, first published 1904) – Weber linked the developmental advantage of the Western world with one of its Christian sects, Puritanism. The immense attention that the short book provoked stimulated Weber to spend years substantiating his thesis, writing monographs on Judaism, Hinduism, Buddhism, Confucianism and Taoism. Weber's comparative research into the economic consequences of religious creed resulted in his sociology of religion succinctly summarised in *Economy and Society* (1978). In this chapter we have enquired into whether the retardation of the Muslim civilisation is critically due to the impact of one of the world religions, which Weber neglected, namely Islam. Our question is, however, broader: can the present turbulence in the Muslim world be seen as the inevitable outcome of the confrontation between modernity, or post-modernity, and Islam?

Today the rapid spread of so-called Islamic economics or Islamic banking raises again the question of the impact of religion upon economic life. It concerns not only the framing of commercial law and the nature and role of interest on banking loans in Muslim countries, but Islamic finance may have global consequences for the cooperation between civilisations (Nomani, 2007).

SECTION IV
Paths of Muslim Modernisation

The modernisation of society entails developing an urban and industrial or post-industrial economy based upon the existence of vibrant markets. Thus, modern capitalism is partly synonymous with modernisation, but one also needs to take other aspects of modernisation into account, such as the rule of law and the enforcement of human rights. The process of modernisation started in Western Europe with the emergence of modern capitalism. The crucial period of economic modernisation occurred at different times in various Western European countries, beginning in England in the eighteenth century. Political modernisation or the call for democracy did not surface until much later in most Western countries. Let us follow this separation between economic and political modernisation when analysing the Muslim civilisation. Economic modernisation took the form of modern capitalism, which has included the Muslim countries in a global market economy. A few Muslim countries have even become leaders in the global market economy, especially in its financial sector.

Chapter 9
The Modernisation of Arabia

Introduction

In this chapter, we will analyse how a few Arab countries have conducted successful policies of modernisation in order to promote *inter alia* the arrival of modern capitalism, or the market economy. It is to be strongly emphasised that Islam did not hinder these efforts at catching up in relation to the occidental countries. If there was a major hindrance, then it was the colonialism of the Western powers. The neo-Weberian idea that Islam adopts techniques without the technology, the science without the spirit of rationality, modernity without its culture, is seductive. However, it does not observe the many autonomous subsystems, neglects their diversified development and underestimates the logic that animates them and erases obstacles created by fundamentalist reversals. When Islam is said to be exceptionally rebellious against modernity, it transforms the religion of Islam into a daily and commonplace drama. Understanding modernity in Arabia requires an effort to analyse the roads along which the search for rationality has orientated itself, as well as how it has gone astray within Islam. Weber's study gives little information about the modernisation of Islam since 1800, as he concentrated upon the original and medieval Islam to the neglect of modern Islam.

The Arab state is typically described as authoritarian, a strong state in a weak society, following Migdal's (1988) concepts. The modernisation project initiated in Arabia in the nineteenth century was without doubt a state-led effort. However, many Arab states built sectarian, familial, tribal and suppressive monopoly states. The Arab failure to construct states that provide for all their citizens resulted in governments characterised by suspicion, intelligence services, internal conflict and total fear, where one segment devoured the share of all the others. The building of states of "winners vs losers" became a major weakness due to the lack of accountability, citizenship and democracy to protect peoples' rights and freedoms. This leads to the theory of Ayubi about the fundamental weakness of the Arab state (Ayubi, 1996).

The *rentier* state is a conception from sociological theory, dealing with the impact of fiscal institutions, and is relevant to several Muslim countries. It gives the same role to the rent from petrol as the fiscal tapping of agriculture in the Middle Ages. Then, the rent was squeezed out of peasants and serfs in the medieval agrarian economy, whereas it is now extracted from underneath the land and sold in the international market. In the former case, the rent was divided up among several stakeholders, including the nobility, the clergy and the prince. Now the state is the unique receiver of all the income. In short, the medieval governments extracted, while the petro-governments allocate, but the impact upon society is just as large in both cases.

Modernisation: The Market Economy and Democracy

Weber said that no country can resist the introduction of modern capitalism when it is ready for the battle. The Islamic world was prepared for the arrival of modern capitalism towards the middle of the nineteenth century, especially the Arab countries. At this point in time, numerous reforms were started, which removed obstacles to the introduction of large-scale modern capitalism. In the late twentieth and early twenty-first centuries, capitalist developments have been extremely strong in several Muslim countries, as their governments have proved their ability to transform the economic rent from fossil fuel extraction into large-scale capital ventures.

The most relevant question now becomes: what are the factors that hinder the Islamic countries in developing further towards post-industrial societies? More specifically, we wish to enquire into why the Islamic world does not endorse the rule of law, modern democracy and its institutions. In a post-modern perspective upon Islam, the focus is not upon the arrival of modern capitalism, but the resistance to both the rule of law and democracy – a displacement of the logic of the Weberian argument onto another topic that is truly relevant today.

One may point out that the rationalisation of the Occident has proceeded in determined spheres and in a particular direction involving a methodical conduct of life (*Lebensführung*), which incarnates the representations of life within institutions that have a certain autonomy structurally and functionally. It is this institutional incarnation in autonomous subsystems that identifies post-modernity (Habermas, 1986: 3; 1987: vol. 1, 231). In order to compare historically the process of modernisation of societies, one must examine which spheres have been rationalised, according to what internal or external factors, as well as searching for the directions the process of rationalisation did take, and its driving forces (Zubaida, 1989: 129–130). Let us first separate economic and cultural modernisation and then examine the logic of political modernisation.

Economic Modernisation

The modern capitalist enterprise could be accommodated during the emergence of modernity within Islam. Medieval Islam encouraged private appropriation (*kasb*) and the colonisation of the land, which it subsumed under "settlement of land" (*imarat al-'ardh* or *imarat al buldan*). Even usury interest rates (*riba*), which the puritan Islamic ethics forbid, were redirected without bad consequences by the wisdom of legal reason, which multiplied fictions in order to validate its use within commercial transactions. From the moment that no ethical mortgage weighed upon the capitalisation of the economy, the Arabs could enjoy the adoption of modern tools of economic management. Khayr Eddin has for a long time praised the freedom of trade, finance and industry. One single quotation may be enough:

> it is this spirit or freedom to initiate activity which has multiplied in Europe all kinds of societies – civil, commercial, financial, industrial, maritime and agricultural. It has also created admirable scientific institutions or institutions of charity as well as the most beautiful establishments of modern industry. Finally it contributed to the exploitations of mines and sandpits, canals, railroads and banks, as well as many other enterprises which would not have existed without it. (Khayr Eddin, 1987: 152)

Shidyak underlined that work constituted a vocation within Europe, which honoured the craft in itself as "there existed no other source of joy than work". A science without work is "like a tree without fruit and like a river without water" (Shidyak, 1995: 38–39). The Arabs put themselves to work, as testified by the birth of modern economic institutions in the nineteenth century.

In the early twenty-first century, Islamic finance is flourishing in financial institutions, with some $250 billion in assets – a 40-fold increase since 1982. This may appear strange, as Islam is considered incompatible with the global economic order. Why do institutions that are suspicious of interest operate within a global financial system? Modern Islamic finance emerged in the early 1970s with the oil boom. The Organisation of the Islamic Countries movement (OIC) from 1970 promoted the idea of updating traditional Islamic banking, which had preoccupied Islamic scholars, particularly in Pakistan (Mawdudi). Research institutes focusing on Islamic economics and finance began to spread throughout the Muslim world, including the inter-governmental Islamic Development Bank (IDB), and the Dubai Islamic Bank. A distinctive feature of Islamic banking is its focus on developmental and social goals. Islamic finance promises to benefit local communities and draw into the banking system people who had shunned *riba*-based finance as well as to contribute to *zakat* funds earmarked for a variety of charitable and social purposes. The first Islamic banks were partnership finance – *mudaraba* (commenda partnership) and *musharaka* (joint venture) – though most of their operations consisted of cost-plus operations. Islamic finance has thrived in the new world, with its downgrading of interest income, financial innovation and blurring of distinctions between commercial banking and other areas of finance. The downgrading of interest has allowed Islamic bankers to sidestep the controversial *riba* issue. Until the 1970s financial institutions could sell only a narrow range of financial products. With the lifting of constraints on products that could be devised to suit every need, religious or not, Islamic products could be created (Kuran, 2004).

Cultural Modernisation

Most Arab countries have adopted the primary role of science in society as well as the principle of the mastery of nature. Medieval Islam made reason holy and glorified the sciences. Universities and academies of all kinds have been developed since the nineteenth century at a steady pace. The content of education has been modernised through the introduction of the learned disciplines, especially the hard sciences, with groups of specialised scholars who are relatively autonomous in their function (Mansfield, 1992; Hourani, 2005).

The Arab-Islamic culture differs from other cultures in terms of its Islamic source, the Arabic language and the judgments of the *ulema*. Western culture draws on Greek thought, Roman law, the Latin language and the Christian heritage. The Arab-Islamic civilisation balances mind and emotion, rejecting the Mu'tazila's elevation of the mind and the *sufi* exaltation of feeling. It preserves a strong link with the Koran and the Sunna. One component of the Arab-Islamic culture is the belief and trust in the *umma*, as their *umma* is "the best of peoples, evolved for mankind". Faith in Islam preaches love or brotherhood and faith teaches equality among people. This is why education has been the basis of the Arab-Islamic culture. Another component of the Arab-Islamic culture is the Arabic language. It is primarily a language of thought and intellect. Although they preserved their national languages, the peoples and nations which embraced Islam have adopted the Arabic language as a means of cultural and intellectual advancement, and have used the Arabic alphabet to write their languages. However, education tends to be more and more secularised and dominated by the sciences as taught at Western universities.

There is one exception to the generally unfulfilled modernisation, namely the autonomy of art. Only blindness could contest the emergence within Islam of new expressive forms in theatre, the novel, paintings, museums, modern music, the press and the cinema, although what supports these activities (the markets for art, the mass media, the critical press and self-expression) tends to be restrained in Muslim countries. One can discuss the quality of work, be happy about the strength of the emancipatory movement that evolves in it, or on the contrary complain at an art that is *mort-né*, but within art the expression of value is never disassociated from its technical support, and the expression of subjective authenticity or even the production of a counter-culture is often subversive. Let us analyse a few cases of successful modernisation policies.

The Modernisation Policies

During the nineteenth century, attempts at modernisation were made in Turkey, Egypt and Tunisia. All these three countries were at that time governed by elites who had a distinct modernisation enterprise in mind concerning the necessity to reform the institutions in order to overcome the colonial ambitions of the West.

By emphasising the modernisation drive, these countries could balance Western superiority. Weber never paid attention to these reform trends with which he was a contemporary. Thus, unravelling these trends, which encompassed several spheres of life, such as the economy, culture and law, would correct Weber's analysis. In short, as a result of these modernisation policies the economy became more market oriented, society more modern, culture more secular, law more formal and authority less personal.

Turkey became the centre of the Islamic world in the sixteenth century and contained the site of the caliphate up until 1923. As the Ottoman Empire grew increasingly weak, it was looked upon as a target by the colonial powers in the West and Russia. Towards the nineteenth century, real reforms were initiated under external pressure, especially under the rule of the sultan Mahmud II (1808–1838) and his son Abdelmagid (1839–1861). Politically, these reforms were orientated towards the core of patrimonialism, namely the military order, linked with the feudalism of rents or *benefices*. Thus, the Janissaries were abolished by a proclamation on the 17 June 1826, parallel with the establishment of a new army, according to a modern format. A code of regulation adopted a European style of clothing for the army in 1828, which was extended to civilians a year later. A census as the basis for military conscription was created on the French model of St Cyr.

The next reform concerned the feudal system of rents. The rule of the nobility in the valleys and the provinces, based upon feudalism, was abolished in 1831, including the *timar*, or the granting of land to the *spahi* or the tax collectors. At the same time, the *waqf*, controlled by the Ulema, was first rationalised under a new directorate in the form of a ministry and later on formally abolished. In 1858, a code governing rights over land was elaborated that contained more than merely a collection of Hanefit rules. This well-known code required, among other things, the identification of private property, which removed land from the arbitrary decisions of the sultan, who often made land change hands by moving it from one *spahi* to another. Thus, the rights of use, possession and ownership of land were identified and became guaranteed. The abolition of the prebendal economic system went hand in hand with the arrival of modern capitalism. Thus, a series of committees for agriculture, trade, industry and public works were established in 1838. The economic infrastructure was modernised with the introduction of a postal system in 1834, a maritime company in 1844, the telegraph in 1855, the railways in 1866, as well as an Ottoman Bank in 1863.

From a legal point of view the most important impact was the reduction of the arbitrary patrimonialism of the sultan. The reform of the state changed its theocratic nature, as religious men who promoted Islam lost their position. Thus, the sultan in 1826 dissolved the dervishes, that is, brotherhoods that were either merchants or fatalistic men, often looked upon as a cause of the decline that had beset the Ottoman Empire. Also the position of the *ulemas* as the major official voice of Islam was changed step by step. They lost their control over education and the judicial process stopped being administered by the religious jurisconsultants (*mufti*). Furthermore, newspapers began to appear, including the first issue of the *Official Gazette*. Modern schools were founded from 1832 onwards, including a medical school (1827), the Imperial Ottoman Lycée (1868), a school of finance (1878), a school of law (1878) and schools of commerce (1882) and civil engineering (1884).

The legal institution of the *mufti* was bureaucratised through the creation of an office and a department of the Chief Mufti, making him a government official, in 1826. The rendering of *fatwas* was handed over to a committee of legal specialists in this office. This reform is similar to other reforms of the state, introducing a Western or formal style of administration. In 1835, the agents of the state were classified into three categories: civilians, militaries and legal/religious men. Other aspects of modern government appeared as well, such as the Ministry of Foreign Affairs (1935) and the High Council for Judicial Ordinances (1838). Last but not least, a Premier replaced the Grand Vizier, the provincial administration was given a new form as the *pashas* and the tax collectors were abolished (1840 and 1864).

In addition, there was the reform called the *Tanzimat*, or Reorganisation, based upon two edicts, one in 1839 and another in 1856. These two proclaimed modern civil and political rights, such as the security of life, honour and property, the rationalisation of taxation and the equality of all persons under the law. The special tax paid by non-Muslims was abolished (1855). Thus, social relations were not closed off from the exterior and the communities co-existed with a society based upon the formal equality of all individuals. One must especially underline the vast reforms of the legal system. Here, civil and criminal courts including the Courts of Appeals that were independent of the religious authority replaced the dual jurisdiction. At the same time, the theocratic law – Sharia – was reformed through the codification of secular law, as with the promulgation of a new penal law in 1840, a commercial code in 1841, a maritime code in 1863, a civil code (*Mejelle*) in 1870 and a municipal code in 1877. The *Mejelle* became the civil law all over the Ottoman Empire until it was replaced by separate civil codes in Lebanon (1932), in Syria (1949) and in Iraq (1953). In Turkey, the *Mejelle* was replaced by the Swiss civil code in 1926.

Moreover, constitutional developments resulting in a new constitution from 1876 were added to these modernisation efforts. A Council of State came into operation in 1867 and a new Parliament was elected in 1877. The first constitution was actually suspended as early as 1878, but a new one was introduced in 1908. The climax of reform came when the Republic of Turkey was proclaimed in 1923, including the abolition of the caliphate. The religious courts were abolished in 1924 and the institution of polygamy in 1925. The Constitution of 1924 was revised in 1928, when Turkey was declared a secular state. Chiefly four men carried out the modernisation of Turkey: Mustapha Rashid Pasha (1800–1858), Ali Pasha (1815–1871) and Fuad Pasha (1815–1869), before Mustafa Kemal (1881–1938) finalised it as President of the Turkish Republic (Lewis, 1968; Mardin, 1962; Ahmad, 1993). Thus, one may conclude that many of the structural hindrances to the emergence of modern capitalism had been removed, or at least made considerably weaker.

The new institutions did not always resist attempts at conservative restoration, but the modernisation effort did attack the roots of the hindrances to development, namely the feudalism of rents, mercenaries in the army, Islamic law, patrimonial domination and the arbitrary sultanismus. The same thing can be said about Iranian reformism, with the *ulema* movement protesting against colonial hegemony and refusing the introduction of tobacco. At the same time a Constitution was promulgated in 1905, an Assembly in 1906 (Keddie, 1981, 1995) and in Islamic India, with its huge Muslim minority, legislative councils were established (Malik, 1963; Qureshi, 1962; Ahmed, 1964).

The same modernisation drive, although less spectacular and of more of an economic character, was conducted in Egypt by Muhammed Ali (1769–1849), who governed the country from 1805 to his death. The modernisation accomplishments included the creation of a modern army on the European model, with a naval force, military schools, war material factories and the industrialisation of the economy. Egypt relied in particular upon cotton, the production of which increased rapidly. The modernising Ali Pasha also made use of the Nil in order to increase fertile land, including the project of the Suez Canal (1858–1869), with Frenchman Lesseps. The textile industry was diversified so that it also covered the production of linen and silk. Textiles became major export items besides sugar, indigo, glass and paper. Modernising Egypt also entailed the creation of a central bank in 1856, along with other administrative functions controlling economic life. In addition, the printing industry made inroads in Egypt, with the first newspaper appearing in 1829. Modern ministries were put in place in 1837, but the legal reforms were initiated somewhat later. The education system was reformed in 1875, resulting in several new specialised schools.

In 1883 a number of codes were introduced following the pattern of French law covering penal, civil, commercial and maritime matters to be applied by special tribunals outside of the religious courts. Moreover, a law on property was introduced in 1891 and a law modifying the *waqf* in 1893, although the private *waqfs* were left outside this modernisation effort until 1952. Thus, law was secularised more and more; for instance, family law was reformed in 1929, in accordance with Turkish law. Although the civil code from 1949 accepted a reference to Sharia law when there was a lacuna in the code, it was decided in 1955 to do away with this duality. An assembly of non-elected delegates was introduced in 1866, but the new constitution was suspended in 1878 (Fahmy, 1954).

In Tunisia, the modernising efforts were driven by Ahmed Bey (1837–1855) and Mohammed Saduq Bey (1859–1882) along similar lines as in Egypt, with an emphasis upon legal and administrative matters. Thus, the army was modernised as well as the economy. A military academy was founded in 1840 and the manufacture of textiles was promoted through the introduction of steam power in 1844. Similarly a central bank was introduced in 1847. The modernisation effort in Tunisia included a new system of taxation with the imposition of direct income tax and the removal of other taxes that hindered exports and production as well as certain taxes collected by the regions (governors, sheiks). The *waqfs* were centralised in 1874, but it was not until Tunisia became independent in 1956 that these were abolished. A land law was promulgated along lines similar to the Turkish land law of 1858, although it was done in 1885 during the French protectorate that wanted to stabilise land ownership. In addition there was a reform of the educational system, as religious education at the University of Zeytouna was reformed and a modern school at the Lycée Sadiki was created in 1875, which played a major role in educating the future modernising leaders of the country. The *ulemas* became functionaries. In 1860, the printing press started to operate with the first newspaper, *al raid-al-tunsi*. The legal reforms implied the secularisation of the courts, including the creation of a labour tribunal in 1877. A constitution from 1861, but suspended in 1864, restricted the powers of the monarch, preceded by the fundamental pact of 1857, inspired by the Turkish reorganisation in 1839, and the law introducing communes in 1858. Two key persons behind Tunisian modernisation were Khayr Eddin (1822–1889) and Ahmed ibn Dhiaf (1802–1874) (Brown, 1974; Van Krieken, 1976; Green, 1978).

Islamic Renaissance

These modernisation efforts indicate that the Muslims were preoccupied with the question of the advancedness of the Occident, asking themselves what caused their retardation and looking into their culture and history. The problem was posed in a succinct manner by emir Shakib Arslan (1870–1946), who in 1930 asked: "Why are the Muslims regressing whereas the others are advancing?" The word *nahdha*, meaning renaissance, is the key concept in the nineteenth century, representing a broad movement covering the arts, history and culture. First, there were the Christians in Lebanon and Syria who took up the modernisation of the Arab language, poetry and prose. Moreover, the movement developed into politics as various groups started to demand the emancipation of the Arab world from the Ottoman Empire. It may be pointed out that this cultural movement of Syrian and Lebanese Christians also contained a revision of their Christian roots, launching new forms of scepticism, agnosticism or even atheism. However, at the same time as these modernisation efforts took place, there appeared a religious reformism called *Islah*, which aimed at a renaissance of Islam by means of making a "subtle correspondence between the given scriptures and present reality" (Merad, 1987: 31). One calls this movement salafism meaning going back to the ancients, or *islah* meaning fundamentalism. The basic model was elaborated by the reading of the Koran by M. Abduh (1949–1905). In his commentary *Tafsir al-Manar* upon the Koran, the holy book is no longer a book of miracles, but a spiritual book with a relevant moral message today (Jomier, 1954). Abduh argued that the Muslims should engage in intellectual and social reforms to become better Muslims, and that they could respond to the challenges of modern society by turning to the Koran by means of a scientific interpretation. Muslims in Asia, such as Sayyid Ahmed Khan (1817–1898) (Rahbar, 1956), Abu l-Kalam Azad (1875–1938)

(Kamali, 1959: 5–18), Muhamad Iqbal (1876–1939) (Iqbal, 1968, 1980), or in Egypt, such as Tantawi Jawhari (1862–1940), endorsed this model of rejuvenation of Islam. It was even suggested that the Koran comprises all that the sciences have discovered and will discover. In any case, the religious ethos was directed towards the daily world, which one should reform (Rahman, 1982: 43–82; Esposito, 1987: 30–57; Ahmed, 1967).

In its entirety, the *Nahdha* was more than a period (Antonius, 1939). Consisting of two currents, it involved a complete resurrection of the entire Islamic space (Merad, 1987). The impact of the Enlightenment and the French Revolution was obvious. The attempts to rejuvenate religious images in order to have an impact upon the real world were also very important (Lewis, 1968; Hourani, 1983; Redissi 1991, 1992, 1994; Grunebaum, 1962). The major concern for the modernisation movement was the decline of the Muslim societies. Abderhmam Kawakibi (1845–1902) was the first author to elaborate a systematic taxonomy of the causes of the decline. Originating in the city of Alep in Syria and fleeing the Ottoman rule, he found a place of rest in Cairo where he published two books, one on the decline of Islam and another on despotism. In the first book – *The Mother of Cities* – he imagined a symposium in Mecca, consisting of 23 people representing Islam, in which 86 causes of the decline of Islam were suggested, classified in three sections: religion, morals and politics. Although we cannot go into this detailed list, we wish to underline that the modernising efforts in the nineteenth and twentieth centuries were far-reaching (Turner, 1974: 144), attacking several of these causes of backwardness. Among the religious conditions for decline mentioned here, one finds the fatalistic spirit inherent in predetermination, the popular nature of Sufism, the spread of magic, as well as the pietism and the conservatism of the *ulemas*. The moral conditions related mainly to Arab laziness and a lack of motivation for education, both stemming in part from the difference between life on earth and the promise of eternal life after death in paradise. Finally, there were the political conditions, relating to the strong position of despotism in Arab society. This is actually the same theme as his second book, *Characters of Despotism*, in which he rejects despotism as immoral, tyrannical and wasteful. Kawakbi ends his *The Mother of Cities* with a call for a foundation devoted to the education of Muslims (Haïm, 1962: 3–72).

The modernisation literature in Arab countries resulted in a clear message, namely that Islam as a civilisation had enormous problems with modernity. One finds it in the work of all the influential authors: Khayr Eddin, Qacem Amin (1863–1908), J. Eddin Afghani (1838–1897) (Keddie, 1972; Kedourie, 1997), M. Abduh and Shakib Arslan. Thus, Qacem Amin attributed Islamic lethargy to its negative posture towards women, whereas for Khayr Eddin it was a matter of the conservatism of the *ulemas* and the ignorance of the population at large. Afghani attributed the decadence to the deviation from the caliphate in the form of the arbitrary sultanate and the divisions of the community along religious schisms. Arslan on the other hand insisted upon the ethnic and political causes, such as the degradation of customs, the ignorance of the clergy and the political despotism.

They all argued in favour of reform, but they differed as to whether reform would come through a return to a purified form of Islam or whether the road ahead was to make Islamic countries more similar to occidental ones. We may here quote from the analysis of A. Laroui, saying that: "the Arabs were in search for a something during the last century: themselves, their past, a universal *raison d'être*, or just an adequate way of expressing themselves" (Laroui, 1977: 4). One may conclude that the modernisation drive did not entirely succeed. Why?

Modernisation from Above

First it may be pointed out that modernisation in the Arab world was implanted from above, as it was initiated by a dictatorial state in an authoritarian manner. Here we may refer to the model of Barrington Moore, stating that there existed three roads to modernity, namely *laissez-faire* capitalism, state capitalism and the communist road. Let us quote:

> the earliest one combined capitalism and parliamentary democracy after a series of revolutions: the Puritan revolution, the French Revolution and the American Civil War … The second path was also a capitalist one, but in the absence of a strong revolutionary surge, it passed through reactionary political forms to culminate in fascism. The third route is of course the communist one. (Moore, 1966: 413)

The modernisation movement in Islam belongs to the second type, as state bureaucracy, allied with the aristocracy and reacting to the extreme weakness of the domestic bourgeoisie, wanted to industrialise the country from above and without revolution. However, in a few countries in the Muslim world there were elements of the first type. According to one scholar, the Middle East is different from Western European modernisation. As with China and Russia, the Ottoman Empire was basically agrarian, and the impulse towards modernisation was rather weak, but no peasant revolution took place, as, in the course of the twentieth century, army juntas rose to power and established military regimes. Only in two of these societies, Lebanon and Turkey, did parliament democracy take root (Gerber, 1987: 7).

The lack of a revolutionary movement of peasants was due to the land system in the Middle East, which was essentially a very dispersed one. However, it should be pointed out that the peasants were never treated in such a brutal manner as to provoke a revolutionary spirit. Thus, the military putsch replaced social revolution. The Turkish developments towards semi-democracy are to be understood against the background of a bureaucratic bourgeoisie that emerged during the nineteenth century. In Lebanon, the abolition of the feudal system in 1861 led to the transformation of the social stratum linked with the large estates into a commercial and urban class favourable towards democracy. Modernising governments engaged in extensive reforms in several Muslim countries. Yet, colonialism from the West restricted what could be accomplished.

Colonialism left its strong marks upon the Islamic world in the nineteenth and twentieth centuries, where the Muslim countries may be compared with Japan, which managed to keep colonisation out. The modernising reforms targeted the increasing colonial pressures. Thus, it is not an accident that they all started with the modernisation of the army. However, these reforms were also recommended by the colonial powers, mainly Britain and France (Lewis, 1968: 116). Often the intention of the colonial powers was ambivalent, as they initiated reforms but abandoned them when they were on the way to being implemented, like for instance, the removal of Khedive Ismail in Egypt in 1879, one year after he had established a modern constitution.

Modernisation and Colonisation

The occidental powers were able to put pressure upon the Ottoman emperors by means of financial measures resulting from the extensive borrowing of the sultans from the West. From the eighteenth century up until the middle of the twentieth century, the Ottoman Empire exhausted itself in wars against Russia, Great Britain and France. The final outcome was the loss of all occidental and oriental territories, first at the Berlin Congress in 1878 and later in the peace Treaty of Sèvres in 1920.

Thus, Great Britain and France took over Moslem territories, directly or indirectly, with the sole exception of Turkey: Algeria in 1830, Tunisia in 1881, Egypt in 1882, Morocco in 1906, Libya in 1912, Lebanon and Syria as well as Iraq and Palestine in 1920. The monarchies in the Gulf were not yet in their present form – Saudi Arabia, Bahrain, Kuwait, Oman, Qatar and the United Arab Emirates, which is also true of Syria, Lebanon, Iraq and Jordan. All these countries were governed by various arrangements involving Great Britain or France (Hourani, 1991: IV and V).

The modernisation efforts, initiated in the Arab world, before and after the First World War, changed the basic antipathy towards modernity and capitalism in Islam. The reforms made in the state and in the legal system opened up the possibility of rapid industrialisation along Western lines, especially in Turkey, Tunisia and Egypt. The Middle East accepted to a large extent modern capitalism as an economic system. From a post-modern perspective, the key question then changes, namely, why is capitalism in modern Islamic society not combined with a democratic political culture? In other words, why is authoritarianism so strong in the Arab world today? This question about the lack of democracy and rule of law in Islamic societies is more relevant for understanding today's realities than the late arrival of modern capitalism.

Yet, it was not until the middle of the twentieth century that modernisation took its normal course without interference from colonial powers. The major developments occurred from the inter-war years up until the 1970s, from international interests to national ones, from agriculture to industry and finance, from private sector to public sector issues (Issawi, 1966: 505–516). These trends reflect major processes of change in decolonisation, industrialisation and the coming of nationalism and socialism, the rudiments of which may actually be documented even for the period between 1800 and 1914 (Owen, 1981), including the increase in population, investments in capital and the emergence of urban groups, including both the proletariat and the bourgeoisie. In addition, there was strong emphasis upon political consciousness in order to resist external attempts at hegemony (Owen, 1981: 290).

Modernisation and Democracy

The relationship between modernisation and democratisation has been much researched. Although both democratisation and modernisation constitute complex processes, one may enquire into how they condition each other from a dynamic point of view. In order to answer this question in relation to the Muslim countries, we will draw upon the basic ideas in the literature, analysing regime changes in the last 20 years. Modernisation allows a traditional society to transform itself to a modern society, based upon progress, performance and the differentiation of spheres of life. The passage to modernity and the transition to democracy obey the same logic, involving favourable and unfavourable conditions, a succession of phases as well as a number of objectives (Touraine, 1992: 375–431). Whereas the democratisation of a country focuses upon government and the state, the modernisation process is far more encompassing as it involves *inter alia* industrialisation, urbanisation and educational advances, besides reforms increasing political participation. This process, including its many different forms, can play itself out in various contexts. However, modernisation has a tendency to result in a pressure for democratisation, as shown in Europe, Latin America and Asia (Lipset, 1959). Democratisation assures the passage from an authoritarian regime, whatever its nature may be – one-party regime, military dictatorship, dynastic oligarchy or a charismatic dictator – to a regime based upon three principles: citizenship, the personal classical liberties of the person and political participation (O'Donnel and Schmitter, 1993: 7–8; Huntington, 1991; Ingelhart, 1997; Weiner and Huntington, 1987).

As soon as a strong connection between modernisation and democratisation is established, the question may be posed: what conditions hinder the passage from modernisation to democracy? One finds in the literature on regime transition two answers, one dealing with certain democratic preconditions and the other dealing with interaction. Let us relate the Arab countries to these two theories. The argument about preconditions points to the importance of affluence driven by a middle class and a pluralistic society, as well as to a political culture which is tolerant. It also includes the importance of a spirit of compromise, shared by the political elite. The interactionist argument emphasises only this latter condition. We would be inclined to say that the Arab countries are not at odds with these preconditions. The level of development is sufficiently high that one may steer between an alarming pessimism on one hand and a naive optimism on the other hand. Yet why then is the modernisation of the Arab world not followed by its corollary, the democratisation of traditional or authoritarian power structures?

The argument underlining the economic structure as a condition for democratisation may single out either the GDP or the level of industrialisation as being critical. Industrialisation and GDP growth tend to go together, but in the Arab countries the level of industrialisation is not high despite an average growth in the GDP of about 1–3 per cent in the 1990s. The Arab countries have different economies and one may identify four types: (1) the petrol economy; (2) the mixed petrol economy; (3) the diversified economy; and (4) the agricultural economy. Thus, we have the following classification: (1) petrol economies – the six monarchies in the Gulf and Libya; (2) mixed petrol economies – Algeria, Iraq and Iran; (3) diversified economies – Egypt, Tunisia, Morocco, Jordan, Syria and Turkey; (4) and agricultural economies – Sudan, Yemen, Mauritania (Economic Trends in the MENA Area, 1998).

If one looks at all the Islamic countries – 57 in all – then the distance between the weakest economies – Pakistan, the Comoros, Yemen, Bangladesh, Sudan, Mauritania, Djibouti and Afghanistan – and the most affluent ones – Bahrain, the UAE, Qatar and Kuwait – is enormous (Human Development Report, 1996). This fact implies a challenge to the economic theory of democracy, as the rich Arab countries have not entered the typical path of development towards democracy (Przeworski and Limongi, 1997: 155–183; Salamé, 1991). Why is this so? One theory that has been much discussed concerns the exceptional nature of the Gulf States.

The *Rentier* State

The first element in the concept of the *rentier* state is that state revenues originate abroad and drive the GDP. The second element is that the *rentier* government can deny their citizens political rights, such as participation in the decision-making concerning the affairs of government, because there is no taxation . Thus, taxation and participation are closely connected in the model of the *rentier* state. Indeed, the enormous state revenues from abroad legitimate a non-democratic system of government. The second element in this theory may actually receive support from the evolution of Western institutions, where the rights of Parliament were connected with their assent to taxes and charges. This connection is sometimes expressed as being "no participation without production or as no representation without taxation", and it is often accepted in Arab literature (Khuldun Naqib, Yussef Saigh, M. Ghanem, Al-Rimihi in Ibrahim Saad-Eddin, 1987: 361–390). Yet one could counter this by saying that the petrol in the first place belongs to the state and that the citizens are the principals of the state, which would make them stakeholders in the oil resources. In any case, the *rentier* state hinders the growth of a broad middle class that would be active in industrial production and transform the gains from economic activity into private holdings of capital.

Mahdawy (1970: 428–467) made the first study on the *rentier* state. The petrol state is much stronger than its society. Being independent of social forces and sometimes also tribal ones, the petrol state imposes a guardianship in the form of authoritarianism, as well as a kind of consumerism, which is fuelled by both ostentation and imitation. In this kind of society, the work ethic is hurt, because the relationship between work effort and gratification is no longer transparent or obvious. The petrol state is at the same time a welfare state, a social state, an employer and a distributor. And the key question becomes whether the state spends the rent prudently or whether it squanders it. The structure of the society in a petrol state is neither a pyramid with a minority of rich families, a middle class and a majority of poor, nor a diamond with a broad middle class. On the contrary, it has an abnormal structure in the form of an inverse pyramid with a large idle class of rich people at the top and with a smaller lower class underneath it, consisting of groups that have been left behind, such as Bedouins, agricultural populations and foreigners. One of the most conspicuous institutions in this class structure is sponsorship or *kafala*, which involves foreigners being allowed to engage in economic activities only if natives sponsor them. This system has resulted in social tensions as foreigners experience segregation, lacking citizenship rights. One may argue that such a society, dominated by a petrol state, cannot embark upon a road toward democratisation, as the nature of the state must first and foremost be changed, becoming dependent upon the internal creation of affluence in society.

The petrol state may not last forever. If the rent is reduced for one reason or another, or if the population increases, then the functional argument no longer holds as the petrol state will not be able to handle the social conflicts generated by modernisation. The political logic will make itself obvious, meaning that the regime is forced to reform the economy and give up its power to new elites. This logic was played out when the Pahlavi regime in Iran was brought down through a conservative revolution from underneath. It has been suggested that the religious state that replaced the Shah regime continue its *rentier* feature. The Islamic Republic could remain for quite some time as another kind of *rentier* state with the *ulemas* handing out alms on a large scale in return for moral conformity (Skocpol, 1982: 280).

However, the same logic spelled out above applies to the religious regime. When the rent is reduced, then the economy will be transformed into a modernised domestic one where the state must be based upon internal production. This is what has happened in Algeria, where lower oil revenues forced the praetorian state to start a democratisation process, although it has failed as the country has fallen into a kind of civil war or anarchy with dismal consequences for the population. Although authoritarianism has re-emerged in Algeria (Entelis, 1994: 219–251; Entelis and Naylor, 1992: 1–30), the future depends upon reforms such as privatisations, deregulation and foreign investment (Herb, 1999). Even Libya, where there is a kind of personalised state based upon an anti-state tradition, seems to follow this same logic (Altunsik, 1996: 49–63). Yet a lack of flexibility within these regimes can always be compensated for, if the state is a military-authoritarian one, as it used to be in Iraq.

It must be emphasised that the states with a diversified economy should have the best chance of becoming democratic, because they create to a large extent their affluence by means of productive activities in the domestic economy. The concept of a *rentier* state is so broadly defined that it covers almost all the Arab countries, with the exception of Tunisia, Morocco and Egypt. Thus, even countries that are classified as having diversified economies in the international statistics, are described indirectly as *rentier* states without petrol or as "quasi-*rentier*" states. The reason is either that they receive massive help from remittances from abroad or they employ many immigrants as foreign labour (Entelis, 1997: 127–140; 141–176).

The main difference between the pure petrol states and the quasi-petrol states is that the state does not capture all the revenues, as is the case in the petrol states. However, this hardly helps us understand why the quasi-petrol states also do not embark on the road to democracy. Luciano maintains that the rent has a decisive influence and Waterbury speaks of selected affinities between these two regimes and how they utilise resources (Luciano, 1990a; Owen and Waterbury, in Salamé 1992: 199–232, 155–276). Yet, although it is hardly conceivable that countries having a low GDP per capita of around 500 US dollars, could have a pluralistic political life, one could still argue that some Muslims cannot wait until affluence arrives in order to demand human rights, including liberty.

Civil Society in Muslim Countries

The classes behind democracy are the middle classes and the working classes – this is an undeniable fact about the process of democratisation in Western Europe. However, in Islam the individual is linked with the community of the faithful – the *umma*, which is a supra-national non-ethical bond derived not from custom but from religion. This bond is stronger than the allegiances between classes following economic cleavages within a society. Here we have a key difference between the occidental societies and the Muslim ones in the structure of social groups. The former are structured on the basis of material or rational interests, based upon rational or secular agreements between independent persons, which has been conducive to the emergence of a broad middle class and a large working class, and the flourishing of civil society. Yet, it should be pointed out that Islam as a religion has broken down much of the tribal nature of Arabic society, claiming that religion trumps ethnicity. Of course, however, Islam has only been partially successful in reducing the relevance of ethnic ties, such as family, clan and tribe.

We earlier examined the role of the bourgeoisie in the Muslim societies from a historical perspective. We now must examine the present position of the middle classes and the working classes. The recent interest in the civil society in Muslim countries is stimulated by the theory of democracy, singling out civil society as a key factor enhancing the prospects of democratisation (Bill, 1996). The key prediction is that civil society will need to be strengthened in order for social groups to be able to embark upon the road toward democracy. Yet how to promote a vibrant civil society when the individuals carry traditional (ethnic) or religious (sects) allegiances (ascriptive), instead of expressing their individual personal interests (achievement)? It should be pointed out that the weight of primary cleavages – ethnic and confessional – is quite substantial in most of the countries. For instance, tribalism creates conflict in Sudan between the *khatmiya* and the *mahdiya*, as well as in Yemen between the *hashed* and the *baqil*. Syria, Iraq and Lebanon have a mosaic of confessional differences. Ethnicity surfaces in Morocco and in Algeria with the Berber population (Balta, 1991).

The ethnic background in the Middle East involving *ethnies*, tribes and nations is to a large extent a heritage from the medieval period. The changing strengths of different ethnic groups have had strong repercussions for the state, as the Ghaznavids replaced the Buyids, the Seljuks in turn replaced the Ghaznavids, the Mongols flooded from the East and the dynasties in the Maghreb succeeded each other to the extent that one may speak of the nomadic exceptionalism (Crone, 1993: 372). The continued relevance of ethnicity in modern times is a striking feature of the Middle East. It is true that these ethnic cleavages were to a considerable extent transformed into national consciousness in Turkey. Yet, national identity remains fragile in the Muslim world, as it is challenged by tribal allegiances as well as by ethnic and religious cleavages (Bocco and Velud, 1995: 10–12; Yeor, 2002). This limits the contribution of civil society to democracy. When civil society theory is applied to the Muslim world, then the question is whether the Muslim society can emancipate itself from ethnic and religious restrictions in the future (Norton, 1994–1995; Schwedler, 1995; Sajoo, 2002; and, concerning Indonesian civil society, Hefner, 2002). In some Muslim countries there is a civil society distinct from the state and organised in the form of associations. Although these associations are not strictly speaking autonomous, they do exist. Even in the authoritarian Arab regimes, it is inconceivable that there would not be professional associations for doctors, engineers, women or charitable organisations that operate according to their own logic. Let us quote from a recent study on the civil society in the Middle East:

> In a region where freedom is circumscribed and hollow, where governments are endemically suspicious of independent forms of association, civil society cannot be described as robust. This does not mean that civil society is absent. Associational life is richer in the Middle East than is commonly assumed although there are significant variations among states, as well as among classes. (Norton, in Schwedler, 1995: viii)

From the moment that one speaks of civil society in the civic sense, then one refers to associations of free citizens who have the constitutional right to organise themselves in an autonomous manner, finding their own goals and practices with the right to participate in political life or in public affairs. Civil society articulates itself around the public sphere, which is to be found between the family and the constitution, where the debate is orientated by the free employment of reason concerning moral issues among independent persons. However, civil society in the Middle East remains disorganised and often controlled from above. The political regime matters, as this kind of civil society is almost invisible in the Gulf states, is weak and controlled in countries such as Iraq under Saddam Hussein, Syria and Tunisia, but active in Morocco, Jordan and Kuwait, yet undermined by Islamic fundamentalists in Egypt, or by tribalism in Sudan and Yemen (Norton, 1994–1995; Schwedler, 1995). Citizens who wish to defend their rights in Arab societies have to approach the authorities and ask them to intervene, instead of themselves associating to get things done, which hinders the development of these societies.

Summing up, one may say that there are two theses about the civil society in Arab countries, one cultural and the other structuralist. The cultural thesis is defended by classical orientalism, as with Bernard Lewis denying that Islam has any experience with a civil society. He states:

> in most Middle Eastern and other non-Western societies this intermediate level did not exist; its emergence was characteristically, and for while an exclusively Western phenomenon. (Lewis, 1964: 48)

Thirty years after this statement was made, Lewis repeated the same idea (Lewis, 1997a: 118). He is right only in relation to historical Islam, in which there is little room for civil society. However, this cannot be taken for an essentialist thesis about the nature of all Islamic societies. The structural thesis on the contrary searches for the obstacles to hinder the full-scale development of a civil society in the Arab world, arguing that the foundations exist in modern times. The key question then becomes identifying why the existing civil society cannot emancipate itself from the religious grip of ascriptive allegiances in Islam.

Conclusion

The religions, which Weber bypassed in his search for the sources of rationality in human conduct – Hinduism and Catholicism – today live in coexistence with democracy. Why not also Islam? Such coexistence is only possible if there is a civic culture that promotes the respect for ideas, tolerance, flexibility and pragmatism. Thus, Islam must be made to accept the equal rights of women and non-Muslims. Here, we face the crux of the matter: is Islam fundamentally anti-democratic? We would argue that in some visions Islam might incorporate the theory and the procedures of the democratic regime. Such a vision must develop a conception of Islam that accepts liberal procedures and does not only rely upon the idea of a Muslim community. The tension between procedures and community would be typical of an Islamic democracy, but the tension is not fatal.

Is it possible to democratise a country without a pluralistic culture? The political culture may be studied as a code carrying meanings such as the belief systems of citizens, expressive symbols and values that define the situation where political action occurs. A society with a political culture that underlines the values of obedience and authority, hierarchy as well as community of some kind (tribe, *ethnie*, religion), is less likely to democratise than a society that cultivates the opposite values of individualism and equality between individuals and the vibrant operations of free associations. Can Islam accommodate these values which reinforce civil society?

Several factors have to co-exist in order to have a climate conducive to system transition, creating a complicated process where the outcome is uncertain. It has been argued over and over again that there is one factor that is unique and determinant, which hinders the diffusion of democratic norms, namely Islam. It is, like the Asiatic religions (Buddhism/Confucianism, Shintoism), inherently negative towards the liberal notions of the Occident, which would explain to a large extent the failure of the many waves of democratisation in the Islamic world since 1800 (Huntington, 1991, 1997). Again, we wish to state our reservation in relation to the cultural theory. It is true that the long experience of a Muslim culture puts a country into a special position, but one cannot interpret this historical legacy as an essential truth about Islam. If one transforms this experience from a certain historical legacy into an essential argument about the incompatibility of Islam with democracy, then one is simply reiterating the Weber thesis for politics. One cannot conclude that Islam is a fundamental hindrance to democracy merely from the absence of democracy in Arab countries.

The medieval extraction of rent hindered economic development, it is true, but the modern extraction of rent in the form of gigantic oil revenues blocks the road to democracy. In the Ottoman period, the subjects were pressured by many charges, but now they are being almost infantilised by the petrol rent. The subjects in the Ottoman Empire lived under the so-called *millet* system, millet being a confession, whereas the subjects in the Gulf monarchies live under a system of classes related to nation and non-nation. The sultans ruled praetorian regimes without much concern for the economy. The modern rulers in the petrol state operate according to a different logic according to which the stability of the regime is inversely dependent upon the opportunities for political participation. When it comes to the relation between rent and work ethic, then the impact is the same. Just as the extraction of rent was hostile to a work ethic in the views of Smith and Marx, so the petrol rent does not enhance a strong work morale (Beblawi, 1990: 86). Whereas the Europeans transformed environment, economy and politics into a miracle (Jones, 1981: 90–96, 232–237; Beachler et al., 1988: 6–19, 20–38, 39–65), the Arabs on the contrary turned the petrol dollars, a gift from heaven, into a mixed blessing.

Chapter 10
Separation Between State and Religion?

Introduction

The separation between religion and politics may be made in two ways, speaking in terms of principles. On the one hand, there is the conception of the lay sector in society, guaranteed by the legal separation between Church and state, as well as by the neutrality of the state and the principle of religious freedom. On the other hand, there is the sociological separation between religion and politics in the form of growing secularisation, meaning the withdrawal of daily life and thinking from religious domination. Yet, whether this separation takes the French form of a clear identification of the lay sector, or the English form of a secularisation trend, it is confronted by three major difficulties in the Muslim society, which we will analyse below.

First, we will discuss three major difficulties of such a separation within the Arab countries as they have been put forward in several comments. Second, we will see how contemporary Islam has adopted a position towards the separation between secular and non-secular, which is in fact neither religious nor lay. Finally, we will argue not only that this ambivalent position is not without its flaws, but also that a separation is possible.

A Triple Impossibility

The first impossibility refers to one essential thing about Islam, namely that Islam does not recognise the formal separation between Church and government that is typical of Christianity. More precisely expressed, religious and political authority is traditionally mixed in one person, the caliph. Yet, Islam does not endorse a theocracy, like for instance in Judaism, as such a regime was defined by the Jewish historian Flavius Josephus in the text *Contra Apionem* (II, 16, 21–22): "where the priests have a rigorous surveillance over the Law, as they are the judges and they themselves punish the culprits" (quoted from presentation in Locke, 1992). The difference is to be found in the fact that the leader of the Muslims is not a priest but a lay person, a kind of *primes inter pares*, who respects the religious restrictions and governs his subjects who are equals in terms of religion. This is what is to be understood by a well-known expression by the orientalist Louis Massignon: "Islam is a lay theocracy, without a Church and egalitarian" (Massignon, 1975).

A Church in the sense of a community of believers exists in all religions, but the key question is why all the major world religions did not arrive at the occidental solution with the Church as a formal organisation apart from the political organisation of society. The idea of the caliphate meaning succession, or the imamate meaning direction, was the rationalisation of power in the golden age of Islam. The main outline of this classical idea is the following. The caliph replaces, as his name indicates, the prophet. He has a double mission: one is religious, to safeguard religion, and the other is secular, to administer worldly matters. It is from this one man alone that all other kinds of authority in the state flow, including judicial power with the exception of Sharia. The caliphate and Sharia are at the same time linked and separated in an ambiguous manner. On the one hand the caliphate is considered as a contract between the sovereign and his subjects, which is regulated by Sharia, because the caliph must apply the law of Allah. The Koran implies that the caliph must be obeyed in this respect (Koran 4: 59), but on the other hand Sharia is above the caliph, who may be de-throned if he does not observe the five basic commands of all Muslims. This duality between the rulers and Sharia explains why Muslims over several centuries have, willingly or not, accepted life under various dynasties, tyrants, holy men and warlords, as long as they have enforced Sharia. The duality has been conducive to the view that Islam is essentially both religion and politics, spiritual and secular. In addition, there were more secular frameworks for the identification of State power in the form of the mirror of the prince literature of indo-Persian or hellenistic origin (*Fürstenspiegel*) on the one hand and on the other certain conceptions from Greek philosophy, that had been turned into an Islamic form (Redissi, 1998).

The second impossibility refers to a historical fact, namely that the separation between religion and state belongs to history proper. It is unique to Europe. The process of secularisation has taken two routes, schematically speaking, but with similar consequences. The first is the Protestant route and the second is the Enlightenment, which, as a radical movement, was anti-clerical and eliminated religion from social life and did away with the power of the Church. Thus, one observes two roads towards secularisation: the evolutionary model in Protestantism and the revolutionary model in the French notion of a lay society. The outcome of both these historical roads toward secularisation is the arrival of a society in which the economy is driven by modern capitalism, unfettered by religion, and the state is governed by means of rule of law. It is true that this outcome had to be imposed upon the Catholic Church through a long and painful process of wars, uproars and letters of tolerance. In comparison, the Islamic societies remained with oriental despotism, which received interpretations by Montesquieu, Hegel, Marx and Weber – see K. Wittfogel's analysis (Wittfogel, 1964; Anderson, 1974).

The third version of the impossibility theme is sociological, suggesting a bridge between theology and history. One meets it in a most succinct form in the argument that Islam exhibits caesaro-papism, which hinders its evolution towards a religion of salvation. Thus, one may say that caesaro-papism is a sociological opposite to the theocratic essence of Islam, as well as in accordance with the historical tradition of oriental despotism. Gellner distanced himself from this interpretation, but he arrived at the same conclusion in any case, namely that Islam is hostile towards secularisation (Gellner, 1983: 81; 1989: 218). Let us now examine how modern Islam has coped with this triple impossibility.

Neither Lay nor Religious

The intellectual polemics around the notion of the secular as well as identification of Islam as a state religion lend credence to the argument that Islam has become too mixed up with politics, making the religion neither completely religious nor sincerely lay. In the nineteenth century, the Islamic countries were touched by a vague constitutionalism of an occidental origin, as during the same period modern ideas entered into the universe of Islamic languages. The word "lay" was introduced from the French word *laïque*, which was taken over in its French form (*layik*), translated into an Arab word (*dini* = non-religious) or interpreted in Arabic (*ilmani* = mundane). The first academics to explicitly used these words were the two Christian Lebanese in Cairo, Shebli Shmeil (1850–1917) and Farah Anton (1874–1922) (Abdel-Malek, 1965: 128–131, 132–135), as well as the Turkish sociologist Zia Gokalp later on (Gökalp, 1959). All three argued for a clear separation between state and religion, Farah Anton even accepting the French model of the Third Republic with its law of 1905 establishing the secular nature of France and the French state.

Yet, although Turkey left its Islamic medieval past, the Arab world rejected the road towards a militant lay conception of society. The two Lebanese scholars arguing the case of modernisation were much opposed by the fundamentalists. Thus, Chebeli Chmeil was accused of atheism by the father of fundamentalism J.E. Afghani (1839–1897) and of having popularised the ideas of Darwin. Farah Anton was heavily criticised by the disciple of Afghani, Mohammed Abduh (1849–1905) in a well-known text called *The Answer to Anton*, where he argued that Islam is a civil religion, meaning that it already had a civil society and that was the only one it needed. More about the usage of the concept of the lay is to be found in Lewis (1988) with regard to Turkey and in Hourani (1983) in relation to the Arabs.

The controversy over the policies of Ataturk was born when Ali Abd al-Raziq, a legal scholar at the theological university of Al-Azhar, published his book *Islam and the Foundations of Power* in 1926 (Abd al-Raziq, 1994). It contained a message along the lines of Mohamed Abduh, whose position he radicalised. He hardly ever used the term "lay society". He said what a liberal Muslim, engaged in the interpretation of the Koran, could say at that time: there exists no political theory in Islam, because power in Islam stems from a separation between state and religion, and is thus a non-religious phenomenon (Enayet, 1982: 52–58). The prophet was not a king and did not create a state, as he had transferred a message that was purely spiritual. The caliphate must be interpreted in the same spirit, which means that the caliphate is a historical invention, responding to certain circumstances as a temporary solution to the vacancy created when the prophet died. On the other hand, it was an instrument used by the dynasties to legitimate power, which in fact rested upon violence. The conclusion of Abderrazak was that the caliphate is not a religious duty. The Muslims would thus be free to organise political life according to modern principles. This thesis provoked a general outcry. The consequences for Abderrazak were highly negative, as he had to face a disciplinary tribunal as well as appear before court. Moreover, he was expelled from the *ulemas*, the jurisconsultants and prohibited from occupying any public employment.

Abderrazak denied that the confusion between religion and politics must be a burden weighing upon the holy scripture and its interpretation. The opponents took the other view, stating that without a caliph there could be no implementation of Sharia as it had been conveyed through tradition, from Mohammed until modern times. Consequently, Islam would lose its theological identity. Islam is based upon a paradox: how can it be that a religion that so much bypasses ecclesiastical matters is so resistant to the separation between the two spheres? It is possible that Islam is so close to a lay conception that it has become a state religion or that it looks upon daily life so much through religion that it also endorses a religious state.

It must be emphasised that the polemic concerning Islam is internal to Islam itself. The very idea of Islam, as both a religion and a government, forms a line of development in Islamic thought that transcends the intellectual and ideological borders between various traditions. It can be found with authors as different as Khomeiny (Algar, 1981; Khomeiny, 1979), the spiritual guide of the Iranian revolution, and Ashmawy (1989, 1994), a liberal Egyptian lawyer. The same applies to historians like Mohamed Arkoun and Abed al-Jabri. Moreover, there is also in contemporary Islam a hostile spirit toward lay radicalism, based upon an essentialist argument, historical reasons and methodological obstacles (Hanafi et al., 1990; Arkoun and Sanson, 1989).

Yet, there is another line of argument that defends the opposite idea. It takes two forms, one internal and another external. According to the internal argument, Islam is seen basically as, if not lay, then as not determining the form of the state. This thus implies that nothing prevents acceptance of the separation between religion and politics, except religious conservatism or a wrong reading of the tradition. According to the external argument, there is nothing that prevents one from importing lay principles, except that these principles come from abroad, the acceptance of which constitutes a condition for Islamic societies to enter modernity. The two versions tend to become entangled (Filaly-Ansary, 1997, 1999; Zakariya, 1991; Ferjani, 1991; Ben Achour, 1993; Azmeh, 1992, 1996). Thus, there is an intellectual movement within contemporary Islam that is favourable towards a lay society.

As one observes, the debate on the impossibility of a lay society within Islam is internal to Islam itself, and consequently those who believe, for one reason or another, that a lay society, as it has emerged in occidental thinking, could not possibly serve as an approach in the Islamic world, are simply wrong. They add to the actual impossibility of a lay Islamic society the impossibility in normative terms, which is erroneous. In reality, neither Anton nor Abduh has prevailed, which is also true of Abd-al-Raziq as well as his critics. This polemic, which has lasted for a century, indicates how Islam did not arrive at the lifting of the theological mortgage. The solution that now predominates is a lukewarm mixture of separation and confusion, of historical religion and spheres of modernity. One meets this in both the legal–political and in the sociological domains.

It is nonsense to say that Islam cannot go through the same sequences as the Occident. It is not necessary, in order to have lay Islam, to wait until Islam has experienced a Voltaire who ridiculed religion, Protestants like Luther and Calvin who removed the magic from the world, or Jewish scholars, such as Spinoza and Moses Mendelssohn, who initiated a critical reading of the scriptures, in order to accomplish enlightenment. Such a perspective amounts to historicism and entails a teleological view, as it imposes the occidental development upon non-European societies. Islam must find its own way to an acceptance of post-modernity.

State and Religion

The conception that several Islamic governments have made of their states is communitarian. This means that the state has not been modelled in accordance with a liberal or procedural approach, where the state is a neutral power holder on the basis of universal values held in common in an abstract manner such as freedom and equality among unencumbered selves. The Islamic state should rather translate, at least to some extent, the spirit of the people, its communal beliefs and values. As the state is situated in Islamic tradition, there must be recognition of the Islamic nature of government.

Only Turkey is explicitly a lay state. The second article in the constitution reads as follows: "The Turkish Republic is a state with democratic law, lay and social orientated towards the nationalism of Ataturk". However, this lay state is protected by the armed forces of Turkey (TAF) by means of a decree, the Inner Service Act, which organises the TAF, although the TAF is to be supervised by the council of ministers, according to article 117 in the constitution. With regard to the other countries in the Middle East the situation is different. Almost all the Arab countries have constitutional documents, with the exception of Libya, where the Resolution of the General Congress of the People from 1977 replaces a constitution. The point to emphasise is that these constitutions are neither lay, according to the French model, nor neutral in the sense of allowing for universal religious freedom and thus prohibiting the government from favouring one religion ahead of another. On the contrary, all the constitutional documents from these countries acknowledge Sharia, but at the same time push, at least formally, for the acceptance of a few lay principles. We wish to underline two important points.

The first is that Islam is the religion of the state and Sharia as the Holy Law is the basic source of legislation. According to one typical formulation, the constitutions say simply that Islam is the religion of the state: Jordan 1952, article 2; Tunisia 1959, article 1; Iraq 1968, article 4; Algeria 1996, article 2; Morocco

1996, article 6; Mauritania 1991, article 5. However, Islam cannot be equated with Sharia. This position entails that the state reserves to itself the right to legislate norms, which are not in conformity with Sharia. In the same vein, a judge should keep track of what positive law says, if there is no disposition which explicitly allows or commands him or her to employ Sharia. Sometimes one finds exactly such a disposition which makes Sharia prevail, as in Saudi Arabia, where the basic law proclaims that "the Constitution is the book of Allah and the sunna of the prophet" (constitution 1992, article 7).

In the constitutions of the other countries, it is indicated in one way or another that Sharia has a special position, as an "exclusive source", a "principal source" or a "major source" in relation to State legislation: Mauritania, the preamble; Oman, the constitution of 1996, article 2; Yemen, the constitution of 1994, article 3; Bahrain, the constitution of 2002, article 2; Egypt, the constitution of 1971, article 2; United Arab Emirates, the constitution of 1971, article 7; Kuwait, the constitution of 1962, article 2; Qatar, the constitution of 2003, article 1; Syria, the constitution of 1973, article 3; Iran, the constitution of 1979, article 2. Libya on the other hand only recognises the Koran: "the Holy Koran is the law", as it does not include other parts of Sharia, such as the tradition of the prophet, his doings and sayings or consensus and reasoning by analogy.

The second point is that in Arab countries it is necessary to adhere to Islamic belief if one wishes to hold public office. This is true even when the constitution does not explicitly say so, as such a rule follows from the very nature of an Islamic state. Only two constitutions in the Middle East remain silent on the question of the characteristics of state and the head of state in relation to religion, namely Lebanon with its 1926 constitution and Djibouti with its 1992 constitution. Thus, for example, Christian Egyptians, the Copts, are often heard complaining that they are almost virtually excluded from public office in a country where they make up 10 per cent of the population. It may be pointed out, however, that the Christians in Iraq were better protected under Saddam Hussein than is presently the case, where anarchy and anomie dominate.

It must be emphasised that the trend towards withdrawing state and society from religion is strong in social interaction, despite being embryonic in the legal sphere. This trend in the Arab societies dates back to the ninth century. Today, one observes that several domains of social life are placed outside of the religious sphere. In politics, one observes several lay manifestations such as a constitution, political parties, Parliament, the tribunals and formal procedures in law and administration. The economy, more than any other sphere, is guided by a teleological rationality that is utilitarian and instrumental. Also the arts manifest secularised forms of aesthetics such as novels, movies, sculpture and painting. Society itself has invented its proper syncretism, which is a mixture of tradition and modernity that one observes everywhere in various conspicuous signs of modernity. Some specialists in Islam state that radical Islam in paradoxical manner confirms the ongoing secularisation of Islam. Here one may wish to call upon the relevant distinction between institutions and cultural secularisation. It calls attention to the fact that the Arab societies are today anchored in secular lifestyles at the same time as the separation between state and religion remains a *sacrilegium* or at least a taboo.

In Tunisia, for instance, Islam is the official religion, but Sharia is not a fundamental principle of law. The family code in Tunisia from 1956 is entirely secularised, as polygamy is prohibited and qualifies as a crime. Marriage is based upon mutual consent between man and woman, and divorce is legally recognised as valid upon a request by one of the two parties, or on the basis of mutual understanding. Only heritage is influenced by Sharia. Distancing himself from the sharp separation between any lay and religious spheres, one Tunisian sociologist wrote: "the political religion and the religious politics present themselves as pluralism, constituting multiple layers of interaction and complex strategies" (Kerrou, 1998: 100).

Coexistence Between Religion and Politics

Generally speaking, the state exchanges the obedience of their subjects for its allegiance towards Islam. It increases its power by multiplying the signs of its loyalty towards Islam. This is the tradition in Islamic societies and it enters into the very heart of its history. What needs to be discussed is whether this exchange is a zero-sum game: gift contra gift? It is always possible to negotiate coexistence between religion and politics. In the case of the Muslim countries it may be argued that the state has been too much involved in handling religious matters, which has resulted in a solution where there is confusion between what is political and what is religious. The outcome is that the state can provide neither religious obedience, nor individual freedom. The putting in place of the sacred that lacks a religious core is revealed as a form of deception. In sum, the state is criticised for doing too much or not enough. Alternatively, perhaps the state pretends merely to protect religion, because it is in any case far beyond what it can take on. In any case, there is no substantial unity between religion and the state, and the state is as far from securing a lay society, as it has to respect the Holy Law. Thus, we may say in other words that the project of a "lay Islam" according to which "Islam rules theocratically, but the lay governments rule democratically" (Sanson, 1983) is a failure.

This Islamic state, in all its ambiguity, tends definitively to be a weak state, meaning a state that cannot penetrate into society, transform it and direct it by its policies. It becomes a predator state that is forced to restrain itself, accepting the primarily religious society despite all its authoritarianism. The outcome is a weak, but authoritarian, government (Migdal, 1988). When the government in the Islamic state gives itself the task of modernising society, then it is supposed to break up tradition with the help of new elites, to improve the quality of life and enhance the equality between man and woman, through the implementation of public policies. In these conditions, the two bases of legitimacy – the accomplishment of modernisation and the acceptance of religion – come into conflict, as they exemplify two different rationalities, one utilitarian and one affective. The complicated and difficult task becomes a source of deep frustration when the state does not succeed in modernising society and at the same does not act in conformity with the historical religion of the people.

A state may proclaim that its religion is Islam and its legislation follows Sharia, but it is not enough that the head of state is a Muslim, because Sharia requires other essential conditions, such as that he be just and knowledgeable in religious matters. However, it is not difficult to find evidence that people who have little knowledge of religion govern the Islamic countries. At the same time a number of Islamic countries that pretend to adhere to Sharia do not apply it in all its manifestations in life. Thus, most of these countries accept interest rates and the consumption of alcohol, while the punishment for theft is prison and not the amputation of the arm. Moreover, disloyalty in marriage – the *zina* – is punished by prison and not stoning (of women), and non-Muslims no longer pay the poll as they used to do in the classical age, at the same time as slavery is forbidden, even in the most conservative Islamic countries.

Thus, the idea of Islam as the religion of the state is in reality both an impossible programme to implement and a practice that is impossible to avoid. The secular challenge remains, but the state does not want to accept the neutrality of politics towards religion. If it proclaims itself lay, then the consequences will be that the government will not control the mosques any longer, the ritual will no longer be administered by a religious bureaucracy, and religious matters will become private ones. The fear of governments is that nature will not leave this space empty, as other groups will invade this area and attempt to make both power and society Islamic. Here we face a true vicious circle, confronted by a logic of fear, where each protagonist is driven by suspicion in relation to another. Only if one moves beyond the repressive interaction, where one or the other employs organised violence in order to handle this conflict, can one conceive of a liberal interpretation of Islam, which is currently being debated (Choudhury, 1997b; Gresh and Ramadan, 2002; Kurzman, 2002; Laroui, 1997b; Shadid, 2002, Charfi, 1999; Talbi and Jarczyk, 2002).

With the exception of the ritual and the things that are prohibited, including the untouchable metaphysical rules, Islam does not determine the nature of social relations. A tolerant and progressive spirit, it has often been said, drives Islam in one version. We are here confronted by a comprehensive vision of a liberal Islam that is different from both the fundamentalist view and the secular perspective. Yet the question arises of who decides between different interpretations: the intellectuals, in an open debate, or the institutions. It is a third solution that has been the prevailing one, viz. the Islamic state monopolises the power to interpret Islam in an authoritarian and arbitrary manner, rejecting all other opinions as heresy and thus illegal. An alternative mechanism has been suggested recently by Mohammed Charfi, former minister of education in Tunisia (1889–1995), consisting of creating beside the three powers (legislative, executive, judicial) a fourth power in the form of a religious authority that would be depoliticised, but run in accordance with democratic principles. Such a solution would avoid the politicisation of religion by either the Islamic fundamentalists or those in power (Charfi, 1999: 192–202).

Yet the search for an honourable separation is confronted by the difficult problem of accommodating a communitarian Islam. Involved here is again a vicious circle as the separation within a communitarian approach becomes impossible and at the same time risky. Another alternative remains open, namely to accomplish a higher degree of neutrality of the state institutions while leaving Islam as it is, a community of faithful, practising religion in traditional forms (*umma*). The attempts to reconcile Islam with the preconditions of a modern state have thus far only resulted in comprehensive interpretations of Islam mixing religious, moral and philosophical ideas. Each of the participants in this debate looks for a general solution based upon metaphysical premises. However, the only practical solution possible is to be found in an institutional approach, where one should focus upon the rules governing the state.

There are similarities in the present debate in Western Europe concerning the rights of increasing Muslim communities in relation to the secular state, although this kind of debate is easier to conduct when the Muslims do not constitute a majority of religious believers, as in the Arab countries. Multi-culturalism in Western Europe includes a strong component of Muslim communities. They demand the *politics of mutual respect*, which goes beyond the mere neutrality of the state. For instance, the issue over the veil in French schools is an indicator or omen of future conflicts between state and religion in Europe.

Conclusion

One cannot illuminate Islam if one does not liberate oneself from one's own preoccupations. This emancipation does not have to come in the form of a development of Islam along the road that Protestantism has travelled towards secularisation. In relation to the basic values of Islam, one may target the rejection of violence, fanaticism and the use of religion for political objectives. The putting in place of neutral institutions and formal democratic procedures, which arbitrate between rival political pretensions, could back this pact about religion and politics in Islamic societies. It is up to the key actors to show prudence, firmness and openness when supporting this pact, which is by its very nature unstable and ambiguous.

What is needed is a broad negotiation that results in a pact between the contending parties. It will have to pin down the values of the community and the neutrality of the state. The ideal should be that one could arrive at a substantial agreement concerning Islamic values but leave government open to democratic elections, as has occurred at times in Pakistan and Bangladesh, although failing to attain political stability. There is a link between the separation of religion and politics on the one hand and the acceptance of democracy on the other hand, although the terms of debate are not the same. To say that Islam in itself is secularised does not resolve the problem of the lack of democracy in Muslim societies. The institutional approach to the problem of separating religion and politics underlines the democratic regime and does not aim at a metaphysical solution. It opens up the possibility that one may be either an ardent Muslim or adhere to post-modernity in a Muslim society. Yet, Islamic fundamentalism is a very real threat to the modernisation of Muslim societies. The next chapter examines its sources of strength (Roy, 2007, 2008; Kepel, 2008).

Chapter 11

Towards a New Fundamentalism

Introduction

Islamic fundamentalism has become so relevant today that we must enquire into its sources. When did this form of religious fundamentalism emerge? And why has it proven so lethal? It may be interesting to point out that Weber, when speaking about Islam, never used the term "fundamentalism" as we now know it today. He argued that Islamic sects, including the Karijites or Shiites and the Mahdism sects, made a strong linkage between dogma and politics. He also stated that Islam is marked by mundane concerns from its beginnings, that is, as a religion of warriors who sublime *jihad* less to conquer the world than to get economic advantages from people (*looting*) forced to accept Islamic power. Contemporaneous fundamentalism makes a new link, but for other purposes, between sectarianism and combat, or practical ethics and violence. We distinguish below between various stages of fundamentalism and three rationalities, looking into how to connect them.

Four Types of *Jihad* and Three Kinds of Fundamentalism

There have been several waves of fundamentalism in Islam, which may be related to what Rapaport has described in his history of terrorism (Rapaport, 2001: 419–424). For Rapaport, the first wave of terrorism belongs to French and Russian history in the nineteenth century; the second begins with national self-determination movements (1920–1960), whereas international terrorism (1970–9/11) describes the third wave, which uses hijacking and religious ingredients. However, this history is "external" to Islam and is far from describing it in Islamic words. In fact, the nature of Osama Bin Laden's challenge – al-Qaeda – is different (Dunn, 1998: 23–28; Wiktorowics and Kaltner, 2003: 76–92).

In contemporary Islam fundamentalism has changed its face several times, so one cannot speak about one definition. Four stages can be separated. In the first stage, fundamentalism was not radical and did not use *jihad*. In the second, we had nationalist *jihad*, but without fundamentalism. In the third, fundamentalism linked radical Islam to *jihad*, but still limited the objectives to national territory and for domestic targets, seizing power by revolution for instance, or killing despots. In the fourth, fundamentalism separated *jihad* from its national background and transformed it into a global movement, recruiting militants anywhere for international terrorist acts, disseminating threats to the whole world (Khosrokavar, 1995).

The first period in the nineteenth century saw an intellectual fundamentalism, looking for an Islamic adaptation to the modern world through religious reform, or *Nadha*, meaning awakening, rebirth or renaissance of its background. The fundamentalists faced at the same time colonial hegemony and official Islam, which was scriptural, quietist, conservative and authoritarian. For *Nadha* the question was why Islam was in decline while other civilisations were in progress. The remedy was to go back to the origins of Islam, but purged from traditionalistic interpretations, Sufism, popular ritualism or *kismet*. The enemy was traditionalism but, paradoxically, it promoted a return to the fundamental Islam of the beginnings. The adherents of this ethos were quasi-clerical or intellectual scribes, reformists such as the Indo-Pakistanis Shah Wali Allah, Sir Ahmed Khan, Jamel-edine al-Afghani, Muhammed Iqbal, the Egyptian Muhammed Abduh, the Tunisian Prime Minister Khayr Eddin and the three Turkish Ministries Mustapha Rashîd Pasha, Ali Pasha and Fouad Pasha. They attempted to cooperate with Western civilisations and to adapt their developmental model to the requirements of modernisation. Their method was not revolution or *jihad*, but rationalism, which was not considered, in all cases, to be in contradiction with the spirit of the Koran. They were deeply convinced of the superiority of the West, calling upon the Muslim civilisation to catch up.

The Muslim world could not avoid colonialism for structural and cultural reasons. The second stage began then as a fight against the invaders, *inter alia* the French and English in Muslim countries from Asia to the Maghreb. This was a new beginning for classic *jihad*, or the Holy War, not against the Occident as a whole, but against colonial oppression. This is what Pipes called the "autonomism" of Islam. In contrast to India, which accepted colonialism and then subsequently fought against it, Islamic autonomism first of all pushed Muslims to fight in the name of legalism. They could not imagine themselves living in "the house of the war" (*dar harb*) and under another rule than Sharia. However, Pipes adds that Islam is not anti-modern, but being Muslim means greater difficulty in coming to terms with Western civilisations. Islam is not by nature anti-progressive, but being Muslim entails greater difficulty accepting the philosophy of technology that might lead to colonialism or imperialism. Islam is not xenophobic or irrational, but autonomism and legalism complicate the task of Muslims trying to cope with the West (Pipes, 1983, 190–193).

A deep ambivalence went along with Arab nationalism: it was secular but called for a great *jihad*. Here we have *jihad* as a path, not for profit, but for national dignity. It was also Holy War, but without fundamentalism, because the nationalist leaders in all Islamic countries were well educated, modernists, westernised and secular. Typical representatives include Bourguiba and Nasser. This period is named *thawra* (revolution). The question was: why have Arabs been colonised? The response was "because of our own colonisability, because of the betrayal of traditionalist leadership". How to get independence except by revolution, fighting against colonialism? Thus, the independence war was a secular one, but its background also had Islamic roots. Even though the nationalists were modernists, it was easy for the nationalists to focus on communitarian membership, as well as to recall *jihad*.

The third stage is better known by what all commentators have named "radical Islam". At this stage, Arabic states were independent and the task was post-national modernisation. The kind of leadership running modernisation was made up of urban and educated elites or countrymen, conservatives or modernists, servicemen (military) or civilians, nationalists or proto-nationalists in occidental countries. In various Islamic countries solutions were different. In all cases, radical Islam was a response, but an inadequate one, to the post-colonial nation-state, which turned out to be a weak state, neither secular nor Islamic, which failed to modernise and democratise itself. A great effort was devoted to explaining its religious roots, its causes and its claims. The plethora of literature about radical Islam can be located in the "postulate of failure": failure of modernisation, secular legitimisation, liberalisation and democratisation. Islamic violence was explained as a natural reaction to structural and symbolic violence, terror from society against terror of the state. Sequential phases, psychological frustrations and socio-historical factors explained the emerging violence (Hafez, 2003).

This period has been named *sahwa Islamiyya*, or Islamic awakening. The question is why Islam is losing its faith and legacy in its own territory, and the answer is *taghut*, a Koranic word for tyrannical government. Islamising society again endorses *jihad,* which is an Islamic duty, but in a generous mood, as it is not included in the pillars of Islam or the personal five duties. To clarify the subject, in classical Islam there are two kinds of duties – personal ones, incumbent on every individual Muslim (the five pillars), and collective ones recommending collective obligations, such as the search for science, encouraging everything that is good and *jihad*. Personal duties (*fardh'ayn*) are imperatives as conditions of being Muslim, while collective duties (*fardh kifâya*) are facultative and may be discharged by volunteers and professionals. Thus, nobody is personally asked to fight, if others fight for collective purposes. However, when enemies attack Muslim lands, *jihad* can become a personal duty. Yet radical Islam enlarges personal duties and transforms collective *jihad* into a precondition of being a true Muslim (Jansen, 1986; Brière and Carré, 1983).

Typical representatives of radical fundamentalism are young people educated in technical skills, living in cities and suburbs, but deeply rooted in religious beliefs that Sharia on one hand and technology on the other are the solutions to Islamic disease. People such as as Mawdudi in Pakistan, Al-Banna and Sayyid Qutb in Egypt, Ali Belhadj in Algeria and Sheikh Fadhlallah in South Lebanon belong to this kind of leadership (Carré, 1984; Haddad, 1983; Leveau, 1993; Leverrier, 1993). A great effort was devoted to explaining that radical Islam is not, in its own fashion, against modernity and modernisation, democracy and democratisation. Some of them are radical extremists, others only fundamentalists, dealing with modernity on Islamic grounds (Dekmejian, 1985; Hunter, 1988; Sivan, 1985; Tibi, 1998; Kepel, 1986) as well as with post-modernity (Ahmed, 1992). As proposed by Lerner, since "Mecca or mechanisation" has failed, the new dilemma is another one: modernisation of Islam or modernising Islam? Some have tried not to exaggerate the threat, as radical Islam in Sunnite countries did not succeed in taking power, stating simply that we are entering a "post-Islamist" period (Roy, 1994; Kepel, 2000). Even *jihad* has been considered as being over, but this is not the case. We are, after 9/11, in the fourth and ultimate stage, as Islamic fundamentalism becomes an international connection, with a deep hostility to the West and its allies.

While the first fundamentalism was an intellectual movement and the second a populist party, the third was a network. *Jihad* as a way to achieve independence or to obtain power has been disconnected from its targets. The New Fundamentalism closes a cycle, passing from classic *jihad*, shared by conservative governments and popular feeling, and from modern terrorist actions against a Pharaonic tyrant, to becoming terrorism against Westerners. At this moment, violence is disconnected from the struggle over national territories, as it has no definitive political programme, no social project, no logical aims, no specific claims, no territorial limits, only a blurred enemy. We are confronted with a network, acting in a total anomie, only oriented by an imaginary *umma* without any borders.

Al-Qaeda

The new terrorist network saturates Islam in establishing the "big vehicle" between the warmongering of the radicals and the conservation of Islam, from which the intellectuals of the nineteenth century emerged, thus closing the circle. The first adjunct of Bin Laden, the "brain" of al-Qaeda, is Dr Aymen al-Zawahiri, one of the leaders of the Egyptian *jihad* and involved in the assassination of Sadat in 1981. His second adjunct, Suleiman Abu al-Ghaïth, is an official renegade of Islam and had been a functionary of the state of Kuwait, an imam of a mosque financed by the state. Speaking on behalf of Bin Laden and al-Qaeda, Suleiman Abu al-Ghaïth, in a talk transmitted by Arab TV al-Jazira, said on 13 October 2001 that "*Jihad* had become a personal duty" (*fardh'ayn*).

In maintaining excellent relations with Pakistani and Saudi officials, the new fundamentalism, contrary to the radical Islam of the past, is not breaking up with society and has no obsessive fear of the secret services. It is not living from the poor princes' generosity, as did the first fundamentalists, nor from the militant collection of a poor radicalism, but from a *rentier* economy, generally deviating funds allocated through the monarchies of the Gulf to charitable organisations. The new fundamentalist has also learnt to manipulate the most wicked techniques of the international financial system, how to yield profit from capital, how to store interest (illicit in principle, but approved by the good cause) and how to avoid controls (Galloux, 1997; Gold, 2003). Bin Laden, welding parts of the system together, acts as the link between several Islams: bourgeois Islam, official Islam, diplomatic Islam, the Islam of intelligence and radical Islam. Son of an extremely wealthy family of merchants, brother-in-law of Bin Tenfus, one of the biggest

Saudi bankers, and linked to Prince Turki al-Fayçal, head of the Saudi intelligence services – fired only a few days before 9/11 due to his suspect relationship to Bin Laden – he fell under the influence of the *jihad* group and decided to create al-Qaeda in 1987, whilst fighting against the Soviets in Afghanistan with the active approval of the Americans. Thus, he brings to the Islamic network the honourability of ascendancy, diplomatic coverage, the experience of war and the secrets of information, as well as the financial prudence that was missing in early radicalism (Bergen, 2002; Blanc, 2001; Bodansky, 2001; Corbin, 2002; Robinson, 2002).

Al-Qaeda is different from the Islamic version of the damned of the earth (F. Fanon), a gang of *mustazifin*, the deprived waiting for glory, even if social *träger* is not homogeneous and often disconnected from social roots. Recruited on a worldwide scale, the terrorists of the 9/11 age are of different nationalities (although mainly Saudi Arabians) and social provenances. They are anonymous in a crowd, live with an intense inner rage, discreetly go to mosques and Islamic centres, and sometimes lead a dissolute life outside, going as far as drinking alcohol. They are the new *parias*, stateless persons dethroned from their nationality (Bin Laden and al-Ghaïth), clandestine militants just arrived from the Middle East, finding the European refuges a place to be on standby. Whilst fundamentalism of the first kind was grateful towards the Occident, the second tended to be sectarian and the third was ungrateful. From now on, however, a binary split separates the *mujahidin* core living outside of a humanity without borders from the rest of the world, including the modern house of *reconciliation* (*dar solh*) where the Islamists, chased from their countries, find a peaceful refuge to freely express their beliefs. They abandon their show of the beard and of the *jellaba* and exchange their PhDs against useful studies (aviation, biotechnique) of which they only retain the basics, because they are in such a hurry to join paradise. Why learn from birth to death like the ethical Islamic adherent who thinks he is eternal? Contrary to the famous personalities of initial fundamentalism and mediated radicals, they can hardly be found. They travel, if necessary with falsified documents, get training somewhere and finally depart for the war territories – and Islam is at war in many places.

The fundamentalism of the third type, intellectually poor, derives its resources from radical Islam. Compared with the exegesis books of the nineteenth century, *The Principles of Exegis* of Sir Ahmed Khan, the *Reconstruction of Religious Thought* of Muhamed Iqbal, *Tafsir al-Manar* of Muhamed Abduh, including also *Fi Zilâl al-Quran* (in the shadow of the Koran) by the radical Sayyid Qutb (Lee, 1997), the *fatwa* of Bin Laden, in 1998, would have been ridiculous if it had not been followed up by application. The key question now for the fundamentalists is who to kill? The answer is, it seems, first of all, Westerners. Bin Laden has given through his *fatwa* "Declaration of the World Islamic Front for *Jihad* against the Jews and the Crusaders", on 23 February 1998 a "license to kill". His *fatwa* holds that "to kill Americans and their allies, both civil and military, is an individual duty of every Muslim who is so able in any country where it is possible, until the Aqsa Mosque (in Jerusalem) and the Haram Mosque (in Mecca) are freed from their grip and their armies depart from all lands of Islam". The core of this new fundamentalism is a linkage between *jihad* as personal duty of the second period on the one hand, and the sacrilisation of Islamic land of this last stage, on the other hand. We have already explained the difference between private and collective *jihad*.

Let us explain what we mean by sacrilisation of Islamic land. As Durkheim said, sacralisation has two characteristics: it consists of taking out things, sites and persons from the world to consider them as prohibited to touch, either absolutely or in certain circumstances. Here there is an association, contamination and transformation from the profane to the sacred and vice-versa. Bin Laden refers to the sacred territories, but extends the conception of contamination to all Islamic territories, Iraq, Egypt, Sudan and Palestine.

In classical Islam things were different. From the sacred point of view, the House of Islam is divided into three parts: sacred lands (Mecca and Medina), part of Hijaz and profane land. On Saudi Arabian territory, notably only Mecca and the part of Hijaz where Medina is located are considered sacred (*haram*). Mecca as the "mother of cities" (the Koran 6: 92) is sacred since Abraham, the father of believers (the Koran 14: 35–40) had his locus or house (*beit*, Béthel; Genesis 12: 8) there. It is a sanctuary or temple into which every one may enter in security (the Koran 3: 96–97), where the Kaaba and Haram mosques are located. Mohammed added Medina to the sacred lands, which were profane when called *Yathreb*, saying that Abraham has sacred Mecca and me Medina in an inner circle of 10–12 miles, according to some sources. Hijaz, a territory that stretches from Mecca to Tabuk, including Medina, Khaybar and Najran, is only sacred to some extent. It was the second Caliph Omar (634–644) who, in the year 641 (20 years after Exil-Hijra of Muhammed to Medina), removed Jews from Khaybar and Christians from Najran to fulfil an injunction of the Prophet, as reported by his wife Aisha, not to allow two religions in Arabia. Jews were resettled in Syria, and Christians in Iraq, Islamic lands but non-sacred. The people of the Book can enter or stay for three days in Hijaz, but not settle as permanent residents. The third part is not sacred at all. It contains all other conquered lands that Arabs call *sawad* (black) because of the fertility of their soil. Among these territories, surely Iran and Iraq, and naturally all other Islamic lands are included. That is why some scholars have said that *jihad* is a holy war, but terrorism is an unholy war (Esposito, 2002; Lewis, 2003b).

Sacred territory (Mecca, Medina and partially Hijaz) is identified by five privileges: first, nobody enters except in a sacred status, that is, as a pilgrim or by pious purpose, except people bringing food, water and such like; second, fighting with the inhabitants should be avoided as far as possible; third, hunting is prohibited except for the killing of dangerous animals; four, cutting down natural trees is prohibited and human culture is not allowed without authorisation; five, non-Muslims or the unfaithful cannot enter or settle, and neither can they be buried. It is an offence to profane sacred territories. Sacralisation presupposes that there will be sanctions against any act of profanation, but non-Muslim persons must only be expelled or suffer discretionary punishment (*ta'azir*) as classical Islam is explicit that it is not allowed to punish an intruder by death (Al-Mawerdi, 1982: 356). That is why Bin Laden, connecting medieval Islam with modern politics, in *a mood doom and gloom*, as Sivan said (Sivan, 1985: 1–15), could not accept American soldiers in Saudi Arabia fighting against Saddam Hussein. However, in a radical interpretation, he enlarges the *intra muros* sacred lands to all Islamic territories, and enlarges the *extra muros* house of war to the rest of the world.

Now, fundamentalism adds the metaphorical return to the origins of Islam terrorism as the linkage between religious faith and *jihad*, even though one can claim that Islam is not fundamentalism and *jihad* is not terrorism. Fundamentalist thinking with the intellectuals of the first period, interpreting Islam in a new anti-traditionalistic mood, was able to deal with modern rationality, looking finally for a "rebirth" of Islam. A nationalist of the second period can be a radical Islamist, anti-imperialist, anti-American, anti-Israeli or aware of pan-Arabic solidarity, like Nasser or Saddam Hussein. A fundamentalist could even be non-violent, attempting only to Islamise people by propaganda like the international movement of *Tabligh* (predication or proselytism), because the Koran had said to Mohammed that his ethical mission was to inform or to exhort people and not to dominate them. It is also true that Saudi Arabia, in order to avoid and the political consequences of radicalism, had founded its foreign politics upon financing Islamic proselytism by a global network around the world, giving money to Islamic movements, both charitable and civil institutions, constructing mosques, as well as developing the "cultural duties of the Sharia". The Americans were immunised from political tactics, as the terrorists would not attack America because of the harsh consequences of such acts, but they could not expect that Islamists, pursued by authoritarian regimes, expelled from their national countries and some of them deprived of their own nationality, would find a refuge in the West for such a strategy.

These Islamists tried on one occasion to destabilise their own regimes without any real success. This was the case of Sayyid Qutb, responsible for terrorist acts in Egypt and assassinated by Nasser. Now, they discharge their violence against their host countries, mentors of these regimes. The Saudis wrongly thought that Islamic violence was a card in their hands against foreign countries, immunising them as a religious sanctuary and excluding terror from their own territory, a sacred land that could not be transformed into a profane land or contaminated by Bin Laden's action, killing American military and innocents in Saudi Arabia. Finally, new Islamism is less interested in looking for domestic power than disseminating Islam through the whole world either by *tabligh* mission or through a global Holy War, without any borders.

Conclusion

In fact, we do not yet have a label for this period of Islamic global terrorism. Perhaps it is an aterritorial terror, *irhab 'alami* (global terrorism) vs the planetary village (Gabriel, 2002; Scruton, 2002; Feldmann, 2003). However, it is a real one, not a metaphorical *jihad* considered only as a resistance against McWorld as Benjamin Barber considered it. Bruno Etienne said terrorists represent actually a "thanotocracy" (government of death), but can we say that when we face people looking for murder and not for government? Gilles Kepel and Olivier Roy declare that radical Islamism is over. The first speaks about "neo-fundamentalism" in a global world, very different from "national Islamism"; the second speaks about a new "salafism–jihadism" meaning salafism as Saudi traditional fundamentalism mixed with *jihad.* Fukuyama finds a new occasion to recall his message in *The End of History* (1992), except that Islam "resists modernity" and that it is the only cultural system that produces people like Bin Laden. He has responded to Huntington (1997), rejecting his theory of a clash between civilisations, saying that Islamic and Asian exceptionalism is "an illusion". Edward Said (2003) reiterated that there are many Islams.

In any case, what is happening is a defeat for those shortsighted politicians who thought that Islamic violence could be politically correct or only oriented to domestic targets in Islamic countries. Yet it is also a defeat for those Islamic social science scholars who have spent a major part of their energy on explaining that radical Islam is modern and democratic or that Islamism has failed to obtain power. Nowadays, the media and journalists criticise them for their blindness. Martin Kramer, one of Daniel Pipes's fellows, has opened a debate over this issue. Kramer is the editor of *The Middle East Quarterly* and former director of The *Moshe Dayan Center for Middle Eastern and African Studies*. Kramer considers that Middle Eastern studies have become too pro-Arab and too dovish, idealising Islam and fundamentalism, even though they are, in fact, anti-modern, anti-semitic and anti-Western. Esposito represents this tendency to idealise Islamism, insisting on the fact that Islamic threat is a myth "just as there is a Western threat or a Judeo-Christian threat" (Esposito, 1992: 168–215). After 9/11, the paradigms of American Middle Eastern scholars "have been swept away by events" (Kramer, 2001: 2). He resumes the "conspiracy theory", developed by Pipes in an article before 9/11 (1992) and later slightly modified in its formulation in *Hidden Hands* (1996), according to which hidden forces undermine the Arab Nation. Conspiracy theories are grounded on five broad assumptions: "conspiracies drive history; power is the end; benefit indicates control; nothing is accidental or foolish; appearances deceive" (Pipes, 1992, 1996: 251–262). Now, Kramer exaggerates Edward Said's impact, but the question, as Gausse said, remains "who lost Middle Eastern Studies?" (Gausse, 2002: 164–168). However, Muslims cannot avoid their responsibilities. Fouad Ajami has said:

> Bin Laden and Zawahiri and Abu Geith and Atta did not descend from the sky: They are the angry sons of a failed Arab generation. They are direct heirs of two generations of Arabs that have seen all the high dreams of Asr al Nahda (the era of enlightenment) and secular nationalism issue in sterility, dictatorship and misery. The secular fathers begot this strange bread of holy warriors. (*The Wall Street Journal*, 16 October 2001)

The emergence of Muslim terrorism at the end of the twentieth century has placed first and foremost Muslim civilisation under the formidable threat of retardation in relation to other civilisations. Thus, it promotes a vicious circle where backwardness supports fundamentalism that in turn results in retardation. Despite the outcome of the 9/11 attack, one can claim that this last type of Islamic fundamentalism is mainly a threat against the evolution of the Muslim civilisation itself. It makes democracy much less likely in Muslim countries, reinforcing authoritarianism in order to control Islamic fundamentalism. It also pushes Muslim minority communities around the world into tension with other civilisations, reinforcing Muslim isolation, even though major groups do not support Muslim terrorism, as it goes against the efforts of many Muslim countries to find a *modus vivendi* with other civilisations.

Islamic terrorism could be a temporary phenomenon reinforcing the search for moderation and balance in the long run. However, it could also turn into a lasting phenomenon turning Muslim civilisation away from the politics of moderation and the rationality of post-modernism. This question depends upon the Western response to Islamic terrorism and the outcome of the Iraq invasion.

SECTION V
The Problems of Muslim Civilisation Modernisation

The basic argument in this book has been that Muslim civilisation needs to find a peaceful and stable solution to its understanding and endorsement of political modernity, that is, human rights, the rule of law and democracy. While Max Weber focused upon Islam and economic modernisation in the form of modern capitalism and the market economy, we emphasise the impact of Islam upon the state and political modernisation. We argue that political modernisation is much more difficult to achieve in Muslim countries than economic modernisation. Let us pin down where the main problems of post-modernity in Muslim civilisation lie.

Chapter 12
Islam and Democracy

Introduction

The acceptance of democratic rules and values in Latin America, South East Asia and the former USSR and Eastern Europe has been so quick that one no longer speaks of the transition to democracy but instead of democratic consolidation (O'Donnel, 1996; Özbudun, 1996). In contrast to this, the transition to democracy in the Muslim world and the Arab countries is like a blind alley in a region that is unprepared (Cantori and Bianchi, 1991), where the prospects for democratic transition appear very meagre with a few exceptions (Huntington, 1984; Diamond et al., 1990). Except for a small number of countries (Korany, 1994), the situation in the Arab world has been described as an immobile transition (Lopez, 1992), democracy in eclipse (Salamé, 1992) or scattered development (Leca et al., 2001). One may ask if there are any Arab countries that can claim that they have taken definitive and certain steps towards the rule of law and human rights.

It should be pointed out that all is not gloomy, as a few Muslim countries practice democracy, such as Mali, Senegal and Malaysia. One could perhaps claim that India, with its huge Muslim minority, shows that democracy may work within a partly Muslim setting. Yet, democracy is almost non-existent in the Arab world and is fragile in Muslim Africa and Asia. Democracy is not impossible in a Koranique country, as the recent events in Pakistan and Bangladesh show, but when finally democracy arrives in a Moslem country, then it tends to be an unstable regime. In this chapter we will analyse the conditions necessary for stable democracy in the Muslim world.

Why Authoritarianism in Arab Countries?

Looking at the 22 Arab League countries today, one may in effect establish that eight monarchies are governed by families of a tribal origin whose origins go back to the eighteenth century at least if known sources are consulted. This applies to the family of al-Khalifa in Bahrein (1783), the Al-Sabah in Kuwait (1754), the *al-thani* in Qatar (1878), the six Emirates (from 1790 to 1892), the Alids in Morocco (1666–1674) and the Al-Busaid family in Oman (1755). Two traditional regimes came later: the Al-Saoud in Saudi Arabia (1932) and the Hashemites in Jordan (1946). With the exception of Jordan and Morocco, these royal dynasties are super rich and govern sparsely populated countries.

The tribal roots of these traditional regimes are often related to each other. Thus, the three dynasties in Saudi Arabia, Bahrein and Kuwait come from the tribe Anza, and the Qatar dynasty comes from the tribe Banu Tamim that dates back to pre-Islamic times. Certain dynasties, like that in Jordan and that in Morocco claim descendency from the Prophet, as they originate with the tribe of Banu Hashem, which was a branch of the Mohammed family, or with the family of Ali. In these countries the key posts are reserved for members of the ruling family or tribe with the exception of Jordan and Morocco, which are constitutional monarchies where civil society participates in government, although under the tutelage of the monarch (Naqueeb, 1990).

The Arab republics are poor and overpopulated, keeping only a facade of republicanism. They tend towards authoritarianism to varying degrees. Some are openly authoritarian whereas others uphold a facade of multi-partism, like Egypt since 1971. A few have improvised a political pluralism that fails to flourish, as with Lebanon and its confessional democracy, or as with the restrained competition in Yemen and Mauritania. In the case of quasi-democracies, the electoral rhetoric fulfils three functions: first it legitimates the governing elites who base themselves on traditional allegiance – *bay'a*; second, a limited participation occurs which resembles in a strange manner the classical consultation in Islam – *shura*; finally, there is the ideological function that masks the solitary exercise of power. Arab nationalism has been employed by the *Baath* parties to install praetorian regimes in Syria and Iraq. Typical of Arab nationalism is its strong authoritarian bent – the *Baath* party in both Syria and Iraq has not hesitated to conduct massacres against opponents. Despite the (short-lived) Arab federation between Egypt and Syria, Arab nationalism has not emerged as a uniting secular ideology, the *Baath* seeming thus to strive for a unity that appears rather as a modern myth (Sivan, 1995). On the contrary, Syria and Iraq have been enemies and the *Baath* ideology has recently orientated itself towards incorporating the Koranique dimension (Hinnebusch, 2001).

In the Middle East there is hardly a modern state in the sense of a nation-state that acts in accordance with a legal order – the *Rechtsstaat*. Instead one finds proto-states, for instance when anarchy ends in the collapse of the state, such as in Somalia, Sudan and Algeria (Zartman, 1995). Alternatively one finds nominal states, which hardly merit the designation state except as a courtesy when they are governed tribally under a state flag. Finally, there are the praetorian states where the military rules to the benefit of a nomenclature that may be tribal, ethnic or familial (Bull, 1977; Tibi, 1998).

Several factors have been identified in the literature as being conducive to authoritarianism. On the one hand the multiplication of divisions necessitates a centralisation of power without sharing among groups, resulting in the domination of one sector over the others: the military over the civilian society, the urban over the rural, one tribe over another, and so on. On the other hand, if the culture is homogeneous, then it counteracts pluralism. When there is much heterogeneity, then it cannot be translated into a body of rights. The Arab states are not only often described as authoritarian, but in addition the governing elites are sometimes described as irregular ones who "criminalise" or privatise politics.

Habermas divides the countries of the Third World into two worlds: on the one hand there are weak states that are governed by mafia forces, often threatened by fundamentalism, and on the other hand there are strong or authoritarian states, among which he counts the Gulf states (Habermas, 1996). None of these two types belong to the first world, where states handle their national interests in accordance with normative criteria about universal cosmopolitan citizenship. According to Robert Jackson, the quasi-states demand from the international community that it fulfils towards them all the relevant duties, including respect for sovereignty and financial assistance. Yet these quasi-states hardly honour within their borders and in relation to their population international standards concerning legal matters or moral and humanitarian requirements (Jackson, 1990: 13–31, 109–163).

A similar diagnostic may be made in relation to Muslim countries that are not Arab: Turkey is under the surveillance of the army, being lay but only semi-democratic; Iran admits a kind of democratic competition between the religious groups as long as there is Shia control; in Pakistan, Bangladesh and Indonesia, periods of democracy alternate with periods of military dictatorship, whereas Malaysia adheres to a kind of semi-democracy (Bumiputras or non-Bumiputras). Whether a Muslim country is a monarchy or a republic, it still only achieves a sort of quasi-democracy. Take the examples of Morocco and Tunisia. Despite much pressure, neither of these countries has achieved stable and consolidated democratic procedures. In Morocco the royal family does not allow a constitutional monarchy to develop, whereas in Tunisia presidential prerogatives cannot be curtailed in accordance with constitutionalism. Developments in Turkey and Senegal are more promising, but one cannot yet speak of the consolidation of a democratic regime. The hope of democracy is present in Bangladesh, Malaysia and Indonesia, but hope and reality are different things in the Muslim world of regime instability.

Developments in poor and Muslim-dominated Mali appear promising though. After a long period of one-party rule, a 1991 coup led to the writing of a new constitution and the establishment of Mali as a democratic, multi-party state. Mali is the seventh largest country in Africa, bordering Algeria on the north, Niger on the east, Burkina Faso and the Côte d'Ivoire on the south, Guinea on the south-west, and Senegal and Mauritania on the west. The country's economic structure is focussed upon agriculture and fishing. Some of Mali's natural resources include gold, uranium and salt. Mali is considered to be one of the poorest nations in the world. Present-day Mali was once part of three West African empires that controlled trans-Saharan trade: the Ghana Empire, the Mali Empire and the Songhai Empire. In the late 1800s, Mali fell under French control, but gained independence in 1959 with Senegal, as the Mali Federation. A year later, the Mali Federation became the independent nation of Mali.

None of the experiments with democracy in the Muslim world has resulted in a stable and uninterrupted regime adhering to the values of democracy. To put the case bluntly, there is a lingering doubt as to the possibility of combining democratic procedures with the traditions of Islam, such as Sharia, with its discrimination against women and the separate treatment of religious minorities. Yet Islam and the traditions of Islam are not the same things, meaning that one must ask whether there is a fundamental opposition between democracy and the Koran.

The exceptionalism of the Arab countries is based upon the contradiction between political modernisation as democracy and the religious traditions of Islam, which emerges in different ways. First, the theocratic and fatalistic orientations of Islam are at odds with a democracy as a culture of mutual understanding of differences on the one hand and as offering institutions for power alternation and bargaining on the other. Second, despite all divergences between religious groups and sects within Islam, there is no established doctrine of tolerance similar to the occidental spirit of tolerance. Third, the tribal nature of the Arab societies works systematically against the emergence of a broad-based middle class deriving its sources of strength from civil society. Finally, the Arab economy with its basis directly or indirectly in the oil industry controlled by the state and its generation of a rent hinders the cultivation of a vibrant and autonomous civil society. The question for the future is whether these circumstances – historical legacy and the economic orientation towards the petrol-rent – exclude the emergence of democracy in Arab countries. One way to elucidate this question is to look at how Islam has reacted to democracy in the past. There have been at least two such interactions in the past.

Islam and Ancient Democracy

It is not known whether the Arabs translated Aristotle's *Politics*, which suggests a more favourable evaluation of democracy than that offered by Plato, who linked this regime with anarchy, resulting in tyranny sooner or later. Although Aristotle favoured *monarchia mixta*, which combined monarchy, aristocracy and democracy, democracy was identified as a political system that had been tried several times. Yet, one finds few traces of democratic thinking with the major Arab philosophers interpreting Plato and Aristotle. With the philosophers Farabi (872–950), Avempace (died 1138) and Averroes (1126–1198), the meaning of democracy is particular. The Arab words used to convey this special sense include *al jamaîya, al juma'iya* and *al jima'iya*. These Arab words mean literally "the city of the masses, the luxurious city and the fertilising city". One finds all theses interpretations in the history of Arab thought where Arab philosophers relate to Plato and Aristotle (Rosenthal, 1956, 1958; Dieterici, 1900; Badawi, 1972: vol. 2; Walzer 1985; Najjar 1980).

One can only speculate about why these major Arab philosophers did not employ the Arab words for some form of community, such as: *shaab* (people), *umma* (nation) and *al-jamaa* (community). Perhaps they wished to maintain the secular essence of democracy, while reserving the Arab words for political communities with a religious orientation? Or they simply stayed close to the Greek reality as they portrayed it: the luxurious city. Thus, the Arab philosophers looked upon Athens as the city of splendour, whose government was, despite its freedom and popular participation, prone to decay and tyrannical rule. Democracy according to the Athenian model was thus rejected by the Arab philosophers as a bad city, opulent but not quite serious. Avempace defines democracy as the government of the masses, whose intelligence is still the prisoner of the senses. The city of the masses is merely a conglomerate, whereas the opposite implies the road of the imam-philosopher (Avempace, 1994; Dunlop 1945). To Farabi, democracy belongs to the ignorant city, which is one of four forms of mistaken human co-existence: the ignorant city (*jahiliyyah*), the immoral city (*fasiqa*), the versatile city (*baddala*) and the lost city (*dhalla*). All of these bad cities had one thing in common, namely that their populations lacked the insights of the philosopher-king. In a democracy liberty is pushed to its limits. Averroes speaks about the community where everyone is free of all constraints (Rosenthal, 1956: 207). It is debatable which rulers Averroes intended to attack by using the image of four cities (Rosenthal, 1956). Suffice it here to mention that he was disappointed with the evolution of politics within Islam: "most existing states are democracies today", that is, popular cities that change into tyrannies (Rosenthal, 1956: 235, 214).

Islamic Constitutionalism: Consultation

The great Islamic philosophers adhering to the Plato position rejected ancient democracy according to the city-state model. However, the universal acceptance of human rights in the twentieth century puts Islam in the position that it must re-evaluate its stand on the rule of law and democracy. The argument of the great philosophers seems to be of little relevance in this process of rethinking democracy in Arab countries. Instead one may ask whether there are parts of Islam that may be employed to build democracy. It should be pointed out that there are in Islam certain mechanisms that are conducive to a spirit of adaptation and accommodation, in contrast to the image of Islam according to the fundamentalist interpretation. Here we wish to underline the following:

1. The separation between the unchangeable rituals – *'ibadat* – and the changing social relation – *muamalat*, which depends upon interpretation from time to time – *ijtihad*.
2. The orientation of Islam towards a civil religion for a community of believers that leaves the more detailed question of the political regime open, to be resolved through consultation – *shura*.

Underlining these two features, democracy in Arab countries could take the form of a "*shuracracy*", which would be a most relevant alternative to Islam as a theocracy. The Koran mentions consultation in two connections. First, it points to the community of believers within a verse entitled "Consultation" as the group of people who deliberate on their common concerns (Koran 42: 38). Second, the Koran makes consultation a duty as a consequence of the following event: the prophet had consulted his followers about a problem of warfare, and he ended up having a different opinion. As the events proved him wrong and his followers right, he drew the conclusion that one must always consult the community of followers (Koran 3: 159). In the two cases where consultation is referred to, it is up to the *imam* to decide on the usefulness of the advice rendered.

It is among scholars debating Islam in the nineteenth and twentieth century that one finds the consultation idea emphasised. Thus, Tahtawi (1801–1873) refers in his book *The Gold of Paris* (1834) to consultation as *shoura* and Parliament as the council of consultation – *diwan al-shura*. Khayr Eddin defines democracy as the regime that trusts the people with deciding matters, corresponding to the doctrine of consultation in Islam. Others develop these notions in terms of constitutionalist Islam in the twentieth century. According to constitutional Islam, one may develop the concept of consultation in various directions involving elections and consultative bodies. We refer to one of the chapters in *The Caliphat* by Rashid Ridha (1865–1935), which has the title "the people who discuss the present situation" (Ridha, 1988: 65–76; Kedourie, 1963: 208–248). The most spectacular example of Islamic constitutionalism is the book by the Egyptian Mahmoud Aqqad, *Democracy in Islam* (1952).

The moderate Islamic adherents often refer proudly to the agreement between *shura* and democracy. Yet, it should be pointed out that the positive evaluation of *shura* is a recent phenomenon (Esposito and Piscatori, 1991: 427–440; Kramer, 1993: 1–8). The classical books on public law in Islam recommend only that the caliph should be elected by the procedure of consultation, but it is not a procedure that may invalidate a candidate. They recommend equally consultation in relation to the command of troops when it is a matter of warfare, such as the location of the troops and the direction of the attack. The Islamic moderates actually changed consultation by first increasing its content and secondly transforming *shura* into an imperative duty. The basis for the new interpretation was a kind of speech-act, stating that the Koran contains the working mechanism of voting ("Consult them in affairs"; Koran 3: 159). Thus, the effort to find the missing link between Islam and modern democracy is focused upon the possibility of finding a link between the concept of consultation – *shura* – and the key institutions of modern democracy – the vote and the participation of the people in relation to the religious elite including the caliph – "the people who bind and unbind". With regard to the people, then, it is a matter of the *umma*, or the religious nation, which is in the ultimate possession of the divine speech. When asked why the Arab countries have failed so miserably in implementing this scheme of *shura*, the adherents of this doctrine answer that the historical legacy of patrimonial rule in Arab countries is the main cause of this divergence between theory and practice.

Against this modern and second effort to combine Islam and democracy, one may underline that it leaves certain questions unanswered, such as the lay nature of democracy. How can Islam be reconciled as a fervent religion with a truly lay conception of society, involving full religious tolerance? Could one really vote on matters relating to Sharia law? Here one finds an interesting idea in the conception of a theodemocracy by the Pakistani scholar Abou Ala-al-Mawdudi, invented in the 1930s. According to theodemocracy sovereignty (*siyada*) and the law (*Sharia*) are of divine source, whereas power (*sulta*) belongs to the people who exercise it in a non-sacred manner through the use of consensus (Esposito and Piscatori, 1991: 436; Kramer, 1993: 6). The notion of a theodemocracy is to be found in the present Iranian constitution: God is equally sovereign as the people, represented by an elected assembly that is controlled by the religious leaders. Such a regime is, however, not in agreement with Western democracy, as the legitimacy of the mullahs is not derived from the people but from their insights into the Koran (Dunn, 1992). The Iranian ideologue Ali Shariati has made several attempts to establish the position that what he calls the people – *al-nas* – is the true receiver of the Holy Message. He uses the image of Cain and Abel in a way similar to Frechman Dumesil, stating that the official forces of Cain – political, economic and religious power – are opposed by the trinity of Abel in the form of Allah, the Koran and the people (Shariati, 1979, 1982). The same solution is basically to be found in Bani Sadr (1989), declaring that the sovereignty belongs with the people, who have however received the *imam* as a gift from God.

Yet, the Islamic fundamentalists fail to see the link between democracy and *shura*, as to them Islam and modern democracy constitute a contradiction. To radical Islamism Western democracy is an impiety or apostasy, as with the Sunnites Sayyid Qutb and Ali Belhaj, the Shiites Khomeiny and spiritual leader of Hezbollah Sheikh Fadhlallah (Fadhlallah, 1986: 170–178). Following the electoral success of the FIS in Algeria, Sheikh Abdelkadar Moghni declared in a triumphant speech that "the Algerian people had given the victory to Islam and the defeat to democracy, which is nothing but an apostasy" (Dunn, 1992: 16). In the view of some of the regimes in Arab countries, democracy is an occidental phenomenon which when exported elsewhere amounts to a cultural invasion. For instance, King Fahd declared in 1992 that "the democratic system that prevails in the world is not suitable for us". To former Syrian leader Hafedh al-Assad, occidental democracy was corrupt and individualist (Heydeman, 1991: 27). One may thus summarise the relations between democracy and Islam in modern times as either *consultation*, *theodemocracy* or *impious democracy*. We have earlier established that ancient Islam took a negative view of ancient democracy, reiterating Plato's position that Athenian democracy was the rule of the mob.

What we must now discuss is whether modern Islam can find a *modus vivendi* with modern democracy. Is this combination possible in Arab societies today? Or perhaps the distance between medieval Islam and ancient democracy resurfaces in an equally large distance between modern democracy and modern Islam? One finds in the literature adherents of all possible positions concerning Islam and democracy. There is the argument by Kedourie, which entails the basic incompatibility thesis. To him medieval Islam is a version of oriental despotism and modern Islam expresses a form of enlightened despotism (Kedourie, 1994:

83–105). Although some facts give support to this argument, one must distinguish between circumstances and principles. Liberals in Islam would counter-argue that historical circumstances do not constitute the fatality that Kedourie speaks of (Binder, 1988), as it is possible to find both a strong modernisation current in the Arab countries and traces of rationalist philosophy in Arab culture.

We conclude by noting that several Western scholars have recently argued that the opposition between Islam and democracy is not a fatal one. Thus, it is argued that when Islam is said to *imply* or logically entail authoritarianism, it is interpreted in an absurd manner, if not with prejudice (Binder, 1988; Esposito and Piscatori, 1991; Esposito, 1992; Salamé, 1992; Esposito and Voll, 1996; Abootalebi, 2000). Even Huntington admits that he accepts the compatibility between Islam and democracy, although he says that he cannot find many existing examples (Huntington, 1991). Also Fukuyama admits that Islam is compatible with the principle of universal equality (Fukuyama, 1992). Similarly, Lewis keeps repeating that it is wrong to attribute the democratic failure in Arab societies to the theological politics of Islam, although he also points out that in Muslim societies the mechanisms of self-rule, such as for example communes or parliaments, have not had a strong standing historically (Lewis, 1997b). What is at stake here is how conclusions are to be drawn about historical circumstances, especially in relation to exegetic statements about the essence of Islam or the Koran. It remains an undeniable fact that democracy occurs in several Moslem countries, although nowhere has this regime been consolidated so far.

Conclusion

We wish to state a reservation in relation to this optimistic argument, claiming that none of the great world religions are at odds with democracy. It is the circumstances that decide. We believe that democracy and Islam presents a problem of compatibility. However, this incompatibility is not impossible to handle, but it requires changes on the part of Muslim believers. It is not modern capitalism or the market economy that is favoured by Protestantism and counteracted by the other world religions, as Weber would have it. It is the compatibility between democracy and religion that is today the crucial question. Here Islam is not in a favourable position, especially if Islamic fundamentalism prevails. Yet Islam is rich in variations, the Muslim civilisation comprising also liberal interpretations that go together with modern democracy.

The solution to the problem of accommodating Islam to modernity is not so much to be found in the resistance of Islam to the market economy, which is what Weber emphasised. The problem lies elsewhere, namely in the opposition between a fundamentalist interpretation of Islam and the universal recognition of human rights. Thus, Islam must be interpreted in such a way that it accepts basic principles within universal liberalism. We believe that such an interpretation is not only possible but also that there are Arab scholars who attempted to combine faith and reason a long time ago, starting with the great philosophers of medieval Islam. Thus, rationalism and Islam are not irreconcilable and people who adhere to the message of the Koran can at the same time fully accept the requirements of universal human rights as defined by the United Nations, for example. We predict that Arab societies will in this century accept a trade-off between Islam and democracy just as they accepted the market economy in the late nineteenth and early twentieth centuries. Our message is basically an optimistic one despite the events of 9/11 (New York), 3/11 (Madrid), 7/7 (London) and 11/26 (Mumbai), since we are convinced that Islamic fundamentalism cannot possibly be the core interpretation of the message of the Koran.

Chapter 13

Islam and Politics: Where the Principal Difficulty of Post-modernity Lies

Introduction

The political aspects of modernisation and a post-modern society encounter two main difficulties in the Muslim world. First, there is the lingering relevance of traditional authority, which Weber pointed out and which still stands strong a hundred years on. Second, there is the charismatic model of politics inherent in the Koran, which is completely at odds with secularisation and modernisation. The rise of Islamic fundamentalism in accordance with the teachings of Sayyid Mawdudi (1903–1979) and Sayyid Qutb (1906–1966) has only reinforced this charismatic model of politics in Islam as involving a complete rejection of the legal–rational authority typical of the modern state and bureaucracy.

The traditional and charismatic model of politics within Muslim civilisation constitutes major hindrances for the modernisation of these countries. Only a different interpretation of Islam and the Koran can open them up for modernity or post-modernity. What must occur is that a rational interpretation of the Koran needs to become accepted once more, as it was in the Medieval period, and traditional authority must lose its legitimacy. The aim in this chapter is to discuss the major hindrances towards political modernisation in Muslim societies. The difficulty of modernity in Islam can be located either at the bottom of society in the conception of the *umma* or at the top of society in the institution of the caliph (imam). Thus, the traditional conception of *umma* entails a threat to political tolerance, whereas the caliphate – or imamate – heritage implies a fundamental bias in favour of hierarchy.

The Caliph as the Classical Model of Politics

The prophet Mohammed is given such a dominant role in Islam that the "successor problem" presents itself with a vengeance. Immediately the prophet died, the question of who to obey or follow took on an immense proportion. As already emphasised, Mohammed was both an ethical and exemplary prophet. He was both a religious and worldly leader, and he was the commander-in-chief of the troops of the new Arab nation. How could such a father be replaced by anyone in particular or by an elected leader?

The solution to the successor problem in Islam was the institution of the caliph, who is both a spiritual and a worldly leader. The caliphate became almost immediately hereditary, meaning that it took on the features of patrimonialism. In fact, the caliphate was not a successful institution, as it quickly turned into a vehicle for feuds between families, clans and dynasties. It was surrounded by court intrigues and was at times replaced by the rule of eunuchs and military slaves. Although the Ottomans kept the caliphate as a empty institution, they ruled in their capacity as sultans, whose power was again both secular and sacred. Whether in its Arab version or in its Ottoman variant, the caliphate actually failed completely to generate a set of institutions that would provide limited government and a predictable state.

The caliph institutions underline the unity of command in a Muslim society. There is one commander of the army, one leader of government and one sheik responsible for religious matters. These roles all converge onto one person. Whether the caliphate is hereditary or elective, it expresses the omnipotence of oriental despotism. There was bound to be fierce struggle about who became the caliph, and when these struggles could not be ended, several caliphates emerged. When the title of the caliph was supplemented by other titles such as the Sultan, the Khan, Emir, Pasha, then the same focus fell upon one person and many roles emerged. The same negative dynamic applies to Shiism and its hierarchical focus on the *imam* or the spiritual leader.

Politics *von oben* has always characterised the Muslim countries. Hierarchical domination is not conducive to rule of law and representative institutions. Even when secularisation reached the Muslim civilisation, the tendency towards top-heavy politics continued to focus upon charismatic leaders such as Nasser, Sadat, Khadaffi, Bourgiba, Rahman and Mahatir. There is one leader or there is anarchy – the heritage of the caliphate and the imamate.

The caliphate institution pulls Islam towards authoritarianism through its concentration upon one man. A few major movements or traditions in Islam emerged – the Sunni, Shia and the Kharitjs – which all in turn display different versions. However, the hierarchical tendency is strong in all, especially the Sunni and Shia. It is no coincidence that the present King of Morocco calls himself "Commandeur des croyants", claiming a direct blood relation to the Prophet. Thus, Mohammed is the eighteenth king in the Alawite dynasty, which has reigned in Morocco since 1666. He also carries, according to the Moroccan constitution, the title of *Amir al-Mu'minin.* With the Shiites and their idea of the *imam* or the *Mahdi* the hierarchical bias of Islam is merely brought to its extreme.

The *Umma* as the Model of the Community

Von unten things also look dismal for the values of post-modernity, namely toleration, heterogeneity and multi-culturalism. It is often maintained that Islam does not recognise this tolerance of heterogeneity, or that it refuses to recognise it.

The community or society in Islam is conceived as a coherent body characterised by religious compactness – the *umma*. However unrealistic this conception may seem, and the although Muslim civilisation is in all its countries divided against a background of ethnic and religious divisions, it remains true that the conception of the *umma* may be developed into a religious society where Islam rules everything.

The *Umma* argument is often stated in the form of a comparison with Christianity, where one finds the separation between the temporal kingdom and the Eternal Kingdom already in the New Testament, to be elaborated by Saint Paul and receive its classical expression in Augustine's philosophy in *The City of God*. However, the Christian distinction between the two swords, *imperium* and *sacerdotium*, is not the same as a recognition of tolerance. It took Christianity several hundred years and much conflict to arrive at a doctrine of non-state intervention in religious affairs. The process of secularisation was not initiated within Christianity but against the Church. One may thus ask whether the Muslim civilisation could generate from within a similar process of secularisation as the Christian civilisation achieved, despite the opposition from religious groups. We believe not. The Muslim civilisation with its concept of *umma* and sacred law (or *umma* shaped by a sacred law) does not permit the same secular evolution as Western Europe experienced with the Renaissance and the Enlightenment.

However, it must be emphasised that the *umma* concept does not rule out democracy within the Muslim civilisation, because despite this *umma* concept, the Muslim civilisation has always displayed much heterogeneity and many divisions. Is the *umma* either Sunni or Shiite, or both? What is lacking in Muslim civilisation is not heterogeneity or conflict of views but the institutionalised mechanisms for arriving at peaceful results, however temporary they may be. Thus, the caliphate or imamate and its hierarchical tendency are more negative for political modernisation than the *umma*. If the *umma* is (correctly) reconceptualised as diversity, then the road to democracy is opened.

An acceptance of secularisation is to be found only among the Alawis in Turkey. The makeup of Turkey includes numerous minorities besides Christians. The assertion that Turkey is 90 per cent Muslim overlooks the fact that this population includes groups that see themselves as minorities – Alawi Kurds, Turkish Alawis and Sunni Kurds as well as Arabs. The Alawi Muslim minority is estimated at roughly 12 million people. Alawis allege discrimination concerning the teaching of Islam, complaining of a Sunni Muslim bias in religious affairs, which opinion classifies the Alawis as a cultural, rather than a religious, group. Alawis are followers of a belief system comprising both Shia and Sunni Islam as well as the traditions of other religions found in Anatolia as well. Alawi rituals include men and women worshipping together through oratory, poetry and dance.

The Alawites in Syria, along with the Druzes and the Ismailis (a Muslim sect in Syria), are remnants of a wave of Shiism that swept over the region a thousand years ago. An "Alawite" is a "follower of Ali", the martyred son-in-law of Mohammed, venerated by millions of Shiites in Iran and elsewhere in the Moslem civilisation. The Alawites' resemblance to the Shiites constitutes one of their heresies in the eyes of Syria's majority Sunni Arabs; perhaps more serious is the Alawite doctrine's affinity with Phoenician paganism and also with Christianity. The Alawites celebrate Christian festivals, including Christmas, Easter and Palm Sunday, and their religious ceremonies make use of bread and wine. In reality, heterogeneity is a typical feature of many Muslim societies. Table 13.1 exemplifies this fact by looking at the map of minorities in the Middle East.

Table 13.1 Middle East: Pattern of Minorities in Arab Countries

Country	Religious Adherence
Bahrain	70% Shia, 30% Sunni
Iraq	60% Shia, 32% Sunni, 3% Christian
Jordan	92% Sunni, 6% Christian
Kuwait	45% Sunni, 40% Shia
Lebanon	70% various Moslem, 30% Christian
Oman	75% Ibadhi Moslem
Qatar	Sunni
Saudi Arabia	Wahabbi Sunni
Syria	74% Sunni, 16% other Moslem, 10% Christian
United Arab Emirates	80% Sunni, 16% Shia
Yemen	Shaf'i Sunni, Zaydi Shia
Palestinian Territory	Gaza Strip: 98.7% Sunni
	West Bank: 75% Sunni, 17% Jewish, 8% Christian

The Arab world is not a monolithic one, as it displays both religious and ethnic diversity. It has often been stated that unity is not the distinguishing feature of Arab politics, as disunity is all the time displayed in the Arab League, for instance. Arab complexity derives not only from different strategic calculations in power politics among Arab leaders, exemplified time and again in the course of events during the twentieth century, but also from the multi-cultural nature of the Arab society In the Middle-East religious heterogeneity characterises not only the Arab societies but also the non-Arab countries (Table 13.2).

Table 13.2 Middle East: Pattern of Minorities in Non-Arab Countries

Country	Religious adherence
Afghanistan	84% Sunni, 15% Shia
Iran	89% Shia, 10% Sunni, Zoroastrian and Christian
Israel	80% Jewish, 14% Sunni, 2% Christian
Turkey	99.8% Sunni including 15–20% Alawis

The Moslem population in the Middle East is made up of two large groupings, Sunni and Shia, but there are several kinds of Shia, as Islam displays many divisions and sects. The Sunni Muslims constitute the largest group in Islam, making up 90 per cent of the religion's adherents. This brand of Islam has dominated almost continuously since 661, when the Shiites departed from the main fold. Sunni Islam claims to be the strict continuation of Islam as it was defined through the revelations given to Mohammed as well as through his behaviour. In the Middle East and North Africa Sunni Muslims dominate, as in the populations and rulers of Iraq, Kuwait, Saudi Arabia, all the Persian Gulf States such as Qatar, Bahrain and the Emirates as well as Egypt, Libya, Tunisia and Algeria. The majority population of Syria is Sunni, but the ruling power belongs to the Alawite minority. In Morocco the population is Sunni but the rulers claim descendency from Ali. In Jordan and Palestine the majority and the rulers are Sunni.

The Shiite Muslims represent the largest non-Sunni branch of Islam, as the Shiites in their various forms represent some 10–15 per cent of Muslims. The term *Shii* refers to the partisans of the fourth caliph, Ali, who was Mohammed's son-in-law through his daughter Fatima and the last caliph to be elected, as well as the last to be drawn from the original nucleus of converts from the Mecca–Medina period. The Shiites are significant minorities in Lebanon, Syria, Saudi Arabia, Yemen, Bahrain, the Gulf States, Pakistan and India. They make up the overwhelming majority (88 per cent) in Iran where Shiite Islam has been the state religion since the sixteenth century. The Shiites make up the population and the rulers of Iran as well as the poorer minority populations in the Persian Gulf states. They constitute a majority in today's Iraq, living mostly in southern Iraq (Basra area) and they are the largest religious community in Lebanon (including the Hesbollah)

The Alawites (in Arabic: *'alawî*) constitute an Islamic sect, stemming from the eleventh Shia Imam, Hasan al Askari (died 873), and his pupil Ibn Nusayr (died 868). They live mainly in Syria, mainly in the mountains near the city of Latakia, but many also live in the cities of Hama and Homs, and in recent decades there has been a migration to Damascus. Their exact number is not known, but is estimated to be between 1.5 and 1.8 million, most living from agriculture. The Alawites are central in the leadership of Syria, as its president, Bashar al-Assad, is an Alawite as was his father, Hafez al-Assad. The Alawites remain the ruling class in Syria. Besides the Alawites there are the Druze or Druse (in Arabic: *durzî*), which is a religion comprising about 350,000–900,000 adherents. They live mainly in Lebanon, but are also to be found in Syria, Jordan and Israel, often in mountainous regions. There are also important Druze communities abroad, living in Europe and the United States. While the Druze are not regarded as Muslims by other Muslims, they do regard themselves as Muslims. Their origin is from a group of Shiites, the so-called Ismailis, that is, the followers of Ali who accepted only seven *imams* (the seventh being Ismail in the seventh century; the sixth accepted by all Shiites was Ja'far al-Sadiq, who died in 765), but they have diverged much and they believe in esoteric truth beyond canonical islam. The Druzes call themselves *muwahhidun*, 'monotheists'. In Turkey there is a special form of Alawi religion, which has a strong secular drive and is practised outside the mosque. It is strong in areas where the population used to be Christian.

The Nizāriyya are the largest branch (90 per cent) of the Ismaili. They are the only Shia group to have their absolute temporal leader in the rank of the imamate, which is currently invested in Aga Khan IV. Their present living *imam* is Mawlānā Shah Karim Al-Husayni who is the 49th *imam*. The Ismailis and Twelvers both accept the same initial *imams* from the descendants of Mohammed through his daughter Fatima Zahra and therefore share much of their early history. However, a dispute arose on the succession of the sixth *imam*, Ja'far al-Sadiq. The Ismailis are those who accepted Ja'far's eldest son Ismail as the next *imam*, whereas the Twelvers accepted a younger son, Musa al-Kazim. Today, Ismailis are concentrated in Pakistan and other parts of South Asia. The Nizari Ismailis, however, are also concentrated in Central Asia, Russia, China, New Zealand, Papua New Guinea, Australia, North America (including Canada), the UK, and in Africa as well.

The Kurds are the largest ethnic group in the world (roughly 25 million) without a homeland. "Kurdistan" is an immense territory covering southeastern Turkey, northeastern Syria, northern Iraq, western Iran, as well as parts of Azerbaijan and Armenia. The clear majority of Kurds are Sunni Muslims, but a small group of less than 100,000 living in Iraq (small communities scattered in Turkey, Iran and Syria too) are *Yazidis*, the so called "devil worshippers". The Kurds predominantly live in rural districts.

The Christians in the Middle East are made up of several minorities. Thus, we have a large Coptic Christian (Orthodox and Catholic; 10 million) population in Egypt, a large Maronite Catholic population in Lebanon and elsewhere in the Arab world, Melchites or Greeks (Orthodox and Catholic) in Lebanon, Syria, Egypt, Jordan and Palestine, Chaldean Christians (Catholic) in Iraq, Syria, Egypt and Lebanon, Syriac Christians (Orthodox and Catholic) in Syria, Egypt, Lebanon and Iraq and small Arab Anglican and Protestant groups. Armenian Christians are found in Turkey, Syria, Lebanon, Iraq and Egypt and Latin communities (Roman Catholics) in Syria, Lebanon and Palestine. The above Christian communities are also to be found in Israel. Finally, there are the Zoroastrians in Iran, a tiny minority that practises the ancient religion of Persia. Most Zoroastrians live outside of the Muslim world.

Given such a complicated background of majorities and minorities in the Muslim countries in the Middle East, it is perhaps not astonishing that conflict is so omnipresent. However, where there is no religious fragmentation or homogeneity in a Muslim country, there is still a hierarchical structure of politics. See the examples of religious homogeneity in northern Africa in Table 13.3.

Table 13.3 Northern Africa: Religious Homogeneity

Country	Religious adherence
Algeria	99% Sunni
Egypt	84% mostly Sunni, 16% Coptic Christians
Lybia	97% Sunni
Morocco	98.7% mostly Sunni
Tunisia	98% mostly Sunni

Thus, whether a Muslim country is homogeneous or heterogeneous, it is still typically governed without the rule of law or democratic politics. At most, one may hope for the rule by law. In homogeneous Muslim societies there may emerge, with dire consequences, a basic rift between the secular state and the army and the religious community, as for instance in Algeria.

It should be pointed out that the *umma* might adhere to one religion but the rulers to another. Surprising consequences arise in Arab politics when this happens, as in Syria in particular, where the governing group is Alawite. The population of Syria in 2003 was about 17.1 million with 90.3 per cent Arabs and 74 per cent Sunni Muslims. The Alawites, that is, the religious group that broke away from Shiite Islam in the ninth century, numbered about 1.7 million, about 13 per cent. The powerful president Hafez Assad is a member of this sect and the Alawites govern Syria, to their own advantage it is often claimed. In Morocco, King Mohammed VI states that he is the latest in a long line of Fatimid Alawites who claim direct descent from the prophet through his daughter Fatima. The prestige that a claim of descent from Mohammed lends may perhaps help explain why this group of Fatimid Alawites has survived. There is though an anti-monarchist Islamic opposition in Morocco and the Independence party advocates curtailing the absolute power of the King; however the disinterest of the Berbers in political Islam seems to have prevented wholesale polarisation as in neighbouring Algeria.

Whether the *umma* is fragmented into different religious groups or homogeneous, there is still no political modernisation. Whether the *umma* coexists with other religious minorities or is monolithic, there are few signs of the rule of law and democratic contest. The problem with political modernisation lies elsewhere, not at the bottom of the political system but at the top. Many countries in the world today are multi-cultural, and so are Moslem societies. A truthful recognition of the heterogenous nature of the *umma* would pave the way for an endorsement of the value of pluralism in the Muslim civilisation.

The Succession Problem

Politics in Islam is extremely focused upon leadership. It is as if there can only be one leader of the country. What Muslim countries lack is a set of institutions to disperse political power onto several groups and stabilise peaceful succession from one leader to another. The struggle for power tends to be a game of everything or nothing – this is the caliphate or imamate heritage. When a charismatic leader dies or leaves power, then the succession problem arises: who will come after the leader? There is no guarantee whatsoever that the successor of a charismatic person will have the necessary qualifications and thus institutional mechanisms emerge. However, in the Muslim civilisation this has never occurred.

Leaders in several Muslim countries tend to exercise total power, or power with few real constraints. Islamic fundamentalism merely reinforces the hierarchical nature of Islamic politics, as anything but a grip on the state is unacceptable to the Islamic fundamentalists. It is the control of the repressive power of the state that counts in Islamic politics. Controlling the state is a *sine qua non* as otherwise other groups will destroy the power holders. The missing link to democracy and the rule of law is political tolerance and safeguards for the losers in this zero-sum game.

Semi-religious or residual tolerance exists to a certain extent in Islam, but political tolerance was never known in the period when the caliphate operated in a real sense, and it never existed when the caliphate was abandoned, although not formally, and replaced by the sultanate. Thus, after the Mongol destruction of the caliphate in Baghdad in 1258, there came for instance the Mamluk sultanate in Egypt from 1250 to 1517. A mamluk was a slave soldier who converted to Islam and served the Muslim caliphs and the Ayyubid sultans during the Middle Ages. Over time, they became a powerful military caste, often defeating the Crusaders. On more than one occasion, they seized power for themselves. Ottoman rulers used primarily the title of Sultan and the title of Caliph only sporadically, but Mehmed II used it to justify the conquest of Islamic countries. Later on, Ottoman rulers, beginning with Selim I, began to claim the authority of a "Caliph". Thus, the Ottoman rulers employed "Caliph" merely symbolically on certain occasions, but this practice was strengthened when the Ottomans defeated the Mamluk sultanate in 1517 and took over much Arab land.

When Islam was introduced into non-Arab countries, it retained this fundamental lack of political tolerance towards competitors. Either a leader controlled political power or he would be eliminated, just as there could only be one caliph and imam, or successor of the prophet. It is the fundamental lack of political tolerance within the political elite of opposing contendings that marks the politics of most Muslim societies.

Political Tolerance and Multi-culturalism: Bumiputras and the *Millet* System

It is often stated that Islam is not tolerant towards other religions. Thus, for instance, when a person marries a Muslim, then the following rules apply: a man can marry a non-Muslim woman from the "people of the Book", but a Muslim woman cannot marry a non-Muslim except if he converts to Islam. Neither permitted to leave Islam for another religion (apostasy), nor to actively proselytise for other religions among Muslims. No fewer than 11 Arab states outlaw proselytism by non-Islamic faiths, and at least nine Arab countries outlaw apostasy. Many Muslim countries, such as Saudi Arabia, tend to proscribe the construction of churches on their territory. Christian worship is prohibited to foreigners stationed in these countries. In the majority of Muslim countries, the entry or residence of Christian priests is almost impossible, because any proselytism is prohibited under penalty of immediate expulsion. In Europe, however, Muslim proselytism is accepted as a human right and partly financed through the construction of mosques by the authorities. Yet Islam can cope with social heterogeneity. Take the present Malaysian society with the Bumiputras and non-Bumiputras or the historical *millet* system in the Ottoman Empire.

In present Malaysia different communities live together in a flourishing society. Here the division that is present in everyone's mind is that between those coming from the native soil – Bumiputras – and those originating from outside, the non-Bumiputras. In general, the Bumiputras include the Muslims and the Christian Malaysians, whereas the Chinese and Indian populations make up the non-Bumiputras. Although tensions exist between these two groups and communal violence has occurred, Malaysia has managed to develop strongly economically. Thus the *umma* may accept other people. Malaysia is considered to be a semi-democracy as political elections do take place but they are mastered by the single governing coalition, including the representatives of the three major groups: the Malayians, the Chinese and the Indians. Under Mahatir's rule there was a strong concentration of power in one person – the caliphate principle. However, Malaysia is a more open society that the Arab ones. Indonesia is also multi-cultural and multi-religious. One can here add the five Indonesian constitutional principles named Pancasila (*panca*: five, *sila*: principles): monotheism, humanism, national unity, democracy and justice.

The Ottoman Empire was truly multi-ethnic and multi-religious in its social composition. For much of its 600-year existence it managed to rule effectively over a large set of diverse peoples. Institutionally speaking, these minorities were regulated by government in terms of the *millet* system, but the truth of the matter is that these flexible rules allowed for self-regulating and autonomous communities. At the height of its power (the sixteenth and seventeenth centuries), the Ottomans ruled over three continents, controlling much of southeastern Europe, the Middle East and North Africa. It encompassed the Strait of Gibraltar (and in 1553 the Atlantic coast of Morocco beyond Gibraltar) in the west and covered the Caspian

Sea and Persian Gulf in the east, stretching from the edge of Austria, Hungary and parts of Ukraine in the north to Sudan, Eritrea, Somalia and Yemen in the south. The empire included 29 provinces, in addition to the tributary principalities of Moldavia, Transylvania, Wallachia and Serbia. In addition, it temporarily gained authority over distant overseas lands through declarations of allegiance to the Ottoman Sultan and Caliph, such as the declaration by the Sultan of Aceh in 1565; or through the temporary acquisitions of islands in the Atlantic Ocean, such as Lanzarote (1585), Madeira (1617), Vestmannaeyjar (1627) and Lundy (1655). How could the rulers in Instabul govern all the *ethnies* and sects living in this central part of Eastern Euroe, the Middle East and North Africa?

The Ottomans' success in achieving long periods of peaceful coexistence was due not only to the resort to naked power but also depended on the employment of a pragmatic style of governing, There was broad autonomy granted to the various ethnic and religious groups – the *millets*. Thus, the Ottoman government intervened in the internal affairs of its minority communities to a very limited degree. The vast majority of Ottoman subjects were actually shielded from contact with the state by their own community leadership. Popular grievances were first and foremost directed at the community leaders, while the state was called upon to mediate internal disputes (http://www.osmanischesreich.com/Geschichte/Artikel/Religiose_Koexistenz/religiose_koexistenz.html).

Broad communal autonomy allowed these groups to live according to their own customs and preserve their own languages and cultures. The minorities enjoyed not only wide religious and cultural freedom but also considerable administrative, fiscal and legal autonomy. The word "*millet*" meant both a religion and a religious community. Later it also came to denote nation and nationality. The Ottoman *millet* system had its origins in earlier Middle East countries, both Muslim (Umayyad, Abbasid) and non-Muslim (Persian, Byzantine). The Ottomans allowed each group to conduct its internal affairs, although the Ottomans attempted the centralisation of government as far as security and taxation were concerned. The Ottomans respected the internal affairs of the minority communities and they supported the community's leadership. The *millets* were even permitted to collect their own taxes.

Ottoman patriotism comprised their empire as essentially Muslim, but the two elements of pluralism and equality before the law were grafted onto it. The purpose of Ottomanism was to blur the traditional perception of Ottoman society as divided between a ruling people, Muslims, and non-Muslim subject peoples. A new term, *milel-i erba'a*, was coined by the Ottomans, namely "the four communities", denoting the officially recognised four religious communities that constituted the Ottoman polity: Muslims, the Greek Orthodox, Armenians and Jews. Thus, the Ottoman Empire was a plural society in which the minorities' special status was officially recognised. The minority communities maintained their houses of worship, often with the help of tax-exempt religious endowments. They also operated their own educational institutions. The curriculum and language instruction in these schools were determined by the community. Each community could also set up its own welfare institutions, which depended on its own financial resources. Although state taxes were collectively assessed by the local Ottoman authorities to the local community as a whole, based on the number and wealth of its members, the real collection of taxes was done by community-appointed tax collectors. The amount of taxes was generally set through negotiations between the community leadership and the local authorities. The community could appeal to the state courts or the central authorities. Each *millet* possessed an amount of judicial autonomy, operating courts in order to adjudicate among its own members on a wide range of family and civil matters, such as marriage, divorce, inheritance and financial transactions (Ursinus, 1989).

It may be pointed out that there were rather open boundaries between the different communities, as there were quarters where the population was mixed. In addition, public spaces existed where the entire population mixed freely, such as the *bazaar* where shop owners, bankers, entrepreneurs, craftsmen and shoppers from the *ethnies* and sects came together to engage in business. Yet the Muslims and the other minorities typically lived in their own urban as well as rural areas, congregating around their houses of worship and community institutions. Considerable mobility from one quarter to another as a result of population trends emerged. Thus, it must be pointed out that the different groups lived largely segregated, although within every community there were important segments that interacted with other groups. Christians and Jews often did services for the powerful and wealthy, including the sultan's palace, as physicians, bankers, merchants and craftsmen. Education in their own schools allowed each group to preserve its own language, customs and culture, and to observe its festivals and holy days. As the *ethnies* and sects harboured sentiments of rivalry, distrust, prejudice and even hostility towards the other groups, communal tensions sometimes led to open conflict and violence.

Contacts between segments of each community with other groups led to considerable acculturation and borrowing, which affected language and every other aspect of culture and daily life. Intercommunity relations gave rise to multi-lingualism, especially among the minorities' professional and commercial classes, which contributed to cultural synthesis. Yet Christians and Jews paid higher taxes than their Muslim neighbours and they were barred from most government positions, as well as suffering from a variety of legal and social disabilities. They were able to compensate for these restrictions by their professional skills and their strong sense of community identity.

The economic decline of the Ottoman Empire, the growing corruption and disintegration of its state apparatus, the breakdown of public order, and the worsening relations between ethnic and religious groups prepared the ground for ethnic mobilisation and strong nationalist movements in the Balkans in the nineteenth century. The early signs of this new threat induced the Ottoman government to attempt sweeping reforms to modernise the administration, the economy, the military, education and public health, trying to persuade the minorities not to attempt to form small national successor states. Despite the Ottoman attempts to reshape and redefine the very nature of the Ottoman polity and to modernise the Ottoman state, improve the quality of life and establish greater equality among its various ethnic groups, separatist nationalisms gained strength throughout the nineteenth and early twentieth centuries, leading to wars and huge territorial losses for the Sublime Porte, until the First World War brought down the empire (Quataert, 2005).

Political Power in Islamic Fundamentalism: Arab Traditionalism and Political Power

Islamic fundamentalism rejects both Western modernity and Arab patrimonialism. However, support for Arab patrimonialism does not imply any form of endorsement of democratisation. The kingdoms of Arabia operate according to the same logic as the caliphate and imamate, that is, they are extremely hierarchical political systems where the stakes are high, meaning that there is a tendency for the winners to take all and the losers to get nothing.

One may speculate about the sources of Arab traditionalism in politics. No doubt oriental societies are in general less prone to endorse political change than Western societies. Yet, the strength of the position of kings and emirs is astonishing, as they tend to monopolise opportunities for their families. Perhaps part of the explanation of the strength of Arab traditionalism is that it is in perfect agreement with the caliphate heritage. The king or the emir is not only the guarantor of the political stability of the country, but also the guard of the religious integrity of Islam.

When Arab political traditionalism is rejected, an alternative model of government has been sought not in democratic politics but in authoritarian socialism. In Egypt, Libya, Iraq and Syria we may find the same caliphate heritage, although the outer formula is now either Arab socialism or charismatic politics. The caliphate heritage weighs heavily upon politics in the Muslim civilisation. It explains better than the *umma* why the institutional setup of the modern state – rule of law and democracy – has not been introduced or consolidated in most Muslim countries. The struggle for political power tends all the time towards an all-out game where the stakes only comprise two alternatives, total win or complete loss.

The caliphate is the union of all kinds of power into one person: religious, administrative and military. It is the simplest solution to the successor problem that the prophet left behind at his death. It does not matter whether one stays with the Sunni tradition or goes outside of it to the various sects following the tradition of Ali. The Shiites and the Alawites display the same focus on the leader with total power, called the *imam* or *Mahdi*. Only the Alawis in Turkey accept the demands of modernity, although it is true that an election mechanism was conceived with the Kharijites. However, the Kharijites may have endorsed democracy but they have never accepted political tolerance. Kharijite theology is a form of radical extremism, preaching observance of the teachings of the Koran in defiance of corrupt caliphs and princes. Under the Umayyad caliphate they preached the equality of Moslems and proclaimed that the leader of the Muslim community could be any good Muslim, even a slave, provided he had the support of the *umma*, in opposition to the aristocracy of the *Quraysh*. They also spread their views by violent conflict, which they considered to be righteous and the sixth pillar of Islam. Anyone who commits a grave sin is no longer a Muslim and is subject to excommunication, warfare and death unless the person repents. Having a strong emphasis on the need to depose unjust rulers and believing that the current leaders of the Muslim community were guilty of grave sins, they withdrew themselves from the rest of the Muslim community, banding together against their enemies.

The concepts of rule of law and democracy have been imported into Muslim civilisation through contact with Western powers, which came in the negative form of colonialism. There are rudiments of these concepts within Muslim thought and in the Ottoman Empire with its system of *millet*. However, their full-scale development is hindered today mainly by the emergence of Islamic fundamentalism, which has a conception of political power that is totalitarian in nature. It is not a coincidence that Muslim fundamentalism received a major push ahead from the elimination of the caliphate by Ataturk in 1923. The reaction to the loss of this special Muslim institution, though merely of symbolic relevance for centuries, came in the form of the creation of the Muslim Brotherhood in Cairo in 1928, which has developed into one of the chief vehicles of Islamic fundamentalism. Can fundamentalism be contained in Muslim countries? If not, then there can be no hope for political modernisation.

Conclusion: Accepting and Endorsing Diversity

Politics in Muslim countries tends has particular characteristics. It lacks many of the features of a modern polity, for example, the constitutional state, legal–rational authority and human rights. Few countries where Islam is the major religion score high on democracy. Some Muslim countries are semi-democracies or are in a process of transition to democracy, but most have more or less authoritarian regimes, traditional or modern. This creates an enormous pressure on the politics of these countries as well as upon the globalisation process.

Islam and political modernisation has become an acute problem with the American invasion of Iraq. Can a democracy be put in place in a core Arab country in the same way that Germany and Japan were democratised after the Second World War? Or will the situation in Iraq deteriorate towards civil war when the Americans withdraw? If Islamic fundamentalism gains support, then the internal politics of Muslim countries will be turbulent, to say the least. However, there is nothing in Islam according to the Koran that negates political modernisation. This is our essential point.

The main framework for analysing the social consequences of religion remains that of Weber. However, his framework cannot be applied to understand this major question of Islam and political modernisation, as it only explains economic modernisation. Bendix writes in *Max Weber: An Intellectual Portrait* (1977):

> In Asia, no Messianic prophecy appeared that could have given plan and meaning to the everyday life of educated and uneducated alike. It was this Messianic prophecy in the countries of the Near East – as distinguished from the exemplary prophecy of the Asiatic mainland – that prevented the countries of the Occident from following the paths of development marked out by China and India. Weber's study *Ancient Judaism* was, therefore, the cornerstone of his attempt to explain the distinguishing characteristics of Western civilization. (Bendix, 1977: 199)

Against the interpretation of Bendix linking Western civilisation with the birth of a Messianic religion, it should be pointed out that Islam is as Messianic as Judaism but it is Islamic fundamentalism that poses a true challenge to political modernisation in Moslem countries today. Islam has the same features of rational prophecy and rejection of magic that Weber emphasised in Judaism and Christianity. Yet Muslim countries have hardly been receptive to the basic ideal of Western civilisation, namely the constitutional state as well as democracy. One must thus ask in relation to Bendix's interpretation whether monotheism, eschatology and prophetism are sufficient conditions for the emergence of Western modernity.

In any case, the democratic potential in the Moslem countries is squeezed by the two opposite forces of Muslim traditionalism on the one hand and salafism or religious fundamentalism on the other. Whether the outcome of the collision between these two major Moslem forces is neo-patrimonialism, neo-sultanism, Arab socialism, authoritarian republicanism, military government, Shiite theocracy or simply charismatic domination, constitutional democracy and the rule of law with free and fair elections resulting in representative institutions is not likely. Democratic improbability does not depend upon Islam in itself, as who can say what is the correct reading of the Koran? It all depends upon interpretation and a liberal approach is as possible as a fundamentalist one. To demonstrate how small the space is for democracy in Moslem societies, we will now turn to one part of the Arab world that has been somewhat neglected by the social sciences – Maghreb, although these northern African countries are very important both economically and geopolitically.

SECTION VI
State and Religion in the Maghreb

What obstacles prevent non-Western countries from adopting modern values? Why is it that, despite genuine efforts to modernise their societies, these countries have not been able to achieve higher levels of social welfare? Why do these countries flout human rights and seem to be so reluctant to espouse democracy? Finally, how could they become democratic? Beyond local specificities, these questions seem to be common to almost all non-Western countries. In the social sciences, the "democratic consolidation" paradigm (O'Donnel, 1996) focuses on elements that would enable democratic rules and procedures to prevail. According to this paradigm, countries in Latin America, Asia, Eastern Europe and parts of Africa that are said to have achieved a democratic transition should only be considered as "semi-democratic" as they still include authoritarian tenets like strong executives, limited participation and illiberal laws (Diamond et al., 1990). On the African continent, some countries – like Nigeria and South Africa – can be considered to belong to the democratic consolidation paradigm, while others are still staggering under authoritarian rule, irregular regimes and electoral shifts. Against this background, the democratic prospects of the North African (Maghreb) countries seem to be very meagre. These countries belong both to the African and the Middle East third-world spheres which, apart from a few sub-Saharan exceptions, represent the strongest resistance to democracy, with Arab countries taking the lead (Cantori, 1991; Breynen et al., 1995; Ehteshemay, 1999).

Chapter 14
Religion and Human Rights: Constants and Constraints

Introduction

The focus in this chapter will be on the structural and cultural variables touching on religion, democratisation and human rights. Apart from some common features, each of these countries represents a different case. Thus, Algeria stands for a *rentier* state in armed hands, Libya is an irrational state under international pressure, Morocco has a neo-patrimonial monarchy negotiating its own historical domination, Mauritania stands for liberalisation in an ethno-tribal fragmentation and Tunisia represents liberalisation in a corporate state.

A Genuine Theoretical Distinction

Let us start from the distinction between values and processes. Thus, while religion, modernity, democracy and human rights represent values, religious transformation, modernisation, democratisation and liberalisation are considered as processes. If we focus on religion, we can see that, as a value, religion is a system of beliefs (*credenda*), cults (*cultus*) and ethics (*moralia*) (Locke, 1992: 151) It is also a "système solidaire de croyances et de pratiques relatives à des choses sacrées, c'est à dire séparées, interdites, croyances et pratiques qui unissent en une même communauté morale appelée Église, tous qui y adhérent" (Durkheim, 1994: 65).[1] Weber, in his *The Economic Ethic of World Religions* (1913), argues that a culture (*Kultur*) is equivalent to religion, which is taken here to include all aspects of life, anxiety of death, economic ethics and social support groups (*Träger*) (Weber, 1996b: 331–378). From a dynamic perspective, however, religion begs the following question: does it further democratisation or does it rather represent an obstacle to it?

The same applies to human rights. Since the coming into force of the Universal Declaration of Human Rights (adopted in 1948) and subsequent international treaties, human rights have become an independent set of norms by means of which

1 A solidary system of beliefs and practices relative to sacred – i.e. separated, forbidden – things, beliefs and practices, which unite into the same moral community called a Church all those who adhere to them.

states are judged.[2] Respect for human rights has become a prerequisite, which does not take the development level into account. Hence, no state is allowed to deny them in the name of alternative norms such as welfare, security, social goods or political stability. According to John Rawls, basic liberties such as liberties of conscience, expression, religion and movement, the rights to access to offices and self-esteem have two characteristics: (1) they cannot be abandoned in the name of utilitarian ends or any ideal vision of the world; and (2) they have a lexical priority over social justice such as reducing inequalities (Rawls, 1971: §8). Accepting this kind of liberal doctrine entails priority of international consent about civil and political rights, such as the CCPR, over economic and social treaties.

How to conciliate between human rights as values and a transitional theory to attain democracy? The doctrinal/normative approach and the dynamic/empirical approach are not mutually exclusive. Nowadays, both local and international networks play a key role in the human rights socialisation processes by generating human rights norms, implementing them and finally pressurising political attitudes towards compliance and legitimacy (Keck and Sikkink, 1998). In this respect, a five-stage transitional model has been created by social scientists. It unfolds as follows: (a) repression of opponents and activists; (b) denial or refusal of human rights as a criterion for international qualification; (c) tactical concessions; (d) human rights as a prescriptive status invoked by actors; and (e) rule-consistent behaviour conforming to international standards. This model, however, has been criticised as linear. It is indeed almost impossible to identify pertinent cases to illustrate such an on-going strategy (Risse et al., 1999). Rather, political attitudes toward human rights are believed to consist of a swing between actions and reactions, between repression and concessions, between the denial of human values and their institutionalisation.

Islam does not represent in itself an obstacle to the transformation of values into processes, but the connection between independent variables (normative values, social processes) must in each case be empirically questioned within a network of causalities and meanings.

Democratisation, Modernisation and Modernity

The literature on modernisation focusing on the transitional status can help us to understand what the obstacles are to the modernisation of North African countries and what the areas may be where social and historical transformations are needed. Democratisation refers to the processes "whereby the rules and procedures of citizenship are either applied to political institutions previously governed by other principles (e.g. coercive control, social tradition, expert judgment, or administrative

2 Among the most important treaties are the CCPR (International Covenant on Civil and Political Rights) and CESCR (International Covenant on Economic, Social and Cultural Rights), 1976, and the Convention against Torture, 1984.

practice), ... or extended to cover issues and institutions not previously subject to citizen participation (e.g. state agencies, military establishments, partisan organisations, interest associations, productive enterprises, educational institutions, etc.)" (O'Donnel and Schmitter, 1993: 8). Although no linear process guarantees the irreversibility and sureness of the processes, there are strong empirical reasons to believe that democratic transition on the one hand and modernisation and liberalisation on the other are interrelated. *Modernity* is a normative notion, even when considered as a cultural understanding of Western values. This has to do with the new era we live in, which is marked by the alternative concepts of universal reason, subjectivity and an agenda of new values. However, *modernisation* is also a complex transition process from a traditional society to a modern one, from a rural and agrarian economy to an urban and industrial or post-industrial one. Along the process, rigid and holistic social structures become flexible, and evolve into autonomous and differentiated spheres, institutions are adapted to the rapidly changing functions, and politics increases its capacity to reach new goals and respond to genuine demands for participation and rights (Apter, 1965: 67; Black, 1966: 7; Levy, 1966: 35). Liberalisation, therefore, is also an economic and political process. Economically, liberalisation implies a gradual shift from a bureaucratic and state-controlled economy to one based on the law of the market. Politically, it is "a process of making effective certain rights that protect both individuals and social groups from arbitrary or illegal acts committed by the state or third parties" (O'Donnel and Schmitter, 1993: 7). American Middle Eastern studies minimise the normative meaning of modernity or substitute it with modernisation as a transition process from a "traditional" to a "modern" society. In this framework, the content of modernity is turned into a simple cultural value, among other independent variables that can help modernisation take place. Westernisation is interpreted as a movement describing the Middle East in the nineteenth century supplanted by the theory of modernisation in post-colonial societies (Lerner, 1958: 45), for Arabs who want to be modern without being French, American or English (Halpern, 1963: 33–36). Some studies indifferently assimilate modernity with Westernisation and modernisation (Lewis, 1997b: 114–130) or enclose it between quotation marks. The theory of modernisation poses the same questions as the normative theory of modernity: is the history of Europe unique or does it repeat itself in non-European countries? (Przeworski and Limongi, 1996: 155).

If one argues that modernisation is conducive to democratisation, then are there pertinent criteria and preconditions to identify a gradual successful transition, capture this uncertainty, and limit its indeterminacy? When and how should a country – which starts a transitional process of modernisation, and liberalises its economics and politics – still be considered behind a democratic transition, in so far as the process does not alter the structure of authoritarian rule?

Structural and Cultural Prerequisites

It is assumed here that there are structural and cultural factors, which can help or hamper the democratic process. Structural factors consist of economics, social stratification and political interaction. Cultural factors are those related to political culture as a set of "empirical beliefs, expression of symbols, and values which defines the situation in which political action takes place" (Verba, 1965: 513). Religion stands out as a pertinent cultural factor. The opposition between cultural interpretation (Ross, 1997: 42–80) and structural configuration (Katznelson, 1997: 81–112) is well known in comparative politics. Nevertheless, these two kinds of explanation may be used individually or simultaneously. However, whether one favours the structural explanation or the cultural interpretation, democratic prospects are generally dependent upon both structural and cultural preconditions. Thus, scholars argue that the emergence of democracy in a society is helped by a number of factors: "higher level of economic well-being; the absence of extreme inequalities in wealth and income, greater social pluralism, including particularly a strong and autonomous bourgeoisie; a more market-oriented economy; greater influence vis-à-vis the society of existing democratic states; and a culture that is less monolithic and more tolerant of diversity and compromise" (Huntington, 1984: 214). For the Middle Eastern area, the cultural approach (Hudson, 1995) and the political economy explanation (Anderson, 1995) compete with each other.

Each of these two positions is backed by strong arguments. It is for this reason that the attempt is made here to make use of both of them in order to be able to understand the genuine relation between religion, democratisation and human rights in Maghreb. What is at stake is: do Islam and Sharia represent obstacles to a democratic transition respectful of social pluralism and international human rights standards? Two positions emerge here. The first one considers that Islam (as a religion, a culture and a history) stubbornly opposes democracy. Islam here is viewed as a theocracy, characterised by confusion between religion and politics. It is thought to be fatalistic, communitarian and authoritarian. So long as democracy is conceived as secular and based on individualism and pluralism, its association with Islam sounds like an oxymoron or a *contradictio in adjectum*, due to what Binder calls "the cluster of absences" (lack of associations, of a middle class, of revolution, of civil rights) (Binder, 1988: 226).

The second view considers that religion is neither democratic nor undemocratic, and that all religions are "multi-vocal", pluralistic in rituals and meanings (Stepen, 2000). According to the Weberian theory, only Protestantism transformed its religious ethos into a secular one and helped modern capitalism to give birth to its own economic ethos. Other cultures failed to achieve this. Hence, Confucianism is the *literatis*' tradition, the monks of Buddhism reject the world, the *gurus* of Hinduism contemplate it, Judaism is a religion of "pariah", Islam enjoys the world and Catholicism encourages passive ritualisation of salvation (Weber, 1985: 1968). Now, this theory is hardly relevant to new world developments, as Asian cosmogonic religions have developed a new modern capitalism, which in some cases has proved superior to that of Protestant countries. Catholicism in Latin America together with Eastern orthodoxy have contributed to the democratisation of their societies. However, in the case of Arab-Islamic countries, only a few deserve to be described as "semi-democratic" (e.g. Turkey, Mali, Bangladesh and Indonesia), and none can claim to be taking further steps toward democractic consolidation.

Logic of the Maghreb Situation

Independences in the 1960s gave priority to modernisation in Maghreb, but it was modernisation from above. There are three paths leading to a modern society, namely the capitalist–democratic route, the reactionary capitalist route and the communist route. The "revolution from above" flourished mainly in Germany and Japan. When state bureaucracy and its aristocratic ally are weak, it is the peasant revolution that takes its place, and the "third route is of course a communist one" (Moore, 1966: 413).

In the case of North African countries, the bourgeoisie did not exist or was very weak (no democracy without bourgeoisie, says Moore, quoting Marx). It is for this reason that the bureaucratic states managed a revolution from above in the 1960s, with civil and urban petit bourgeoisie in Tunisia, traditional scriptural elites in Morocco and Libya, ethnic traditionalism in Mauritania and revolutionary armed peasants in Algeria, each of them combining modernity and tradition in a specific manner. All tried to control the economy, integrate corporate bodies into society and monopolise religious faith. However, in the 1970s, their legitimacy was so weak that they were obliged to liberalise the economy and to grant some political rights. Unfortunately, this was not to be a specific route with respect to the following scenario: modernisation from above, followed by liberalisation from below, followed by a democracy. It is still liberalisation from above, without democratisation. Thus, religion has come back forcefully with Islamist movements as a *revolutionary path from below*, beginning with the Islamisation of society, moving from political compromise to popular upsurge. To deal with this dilemma (secularisation vs Islamisation), North African governments hesitate between *recognition*, *repression* and *cooption* of radical Islam. They are dealing with Islamists in a pragmatic way, including some of them and excluding others, to maximise their assets and reduce their loss.

Modernity as Contamination

To a certain extent, the Maghreb (etymologically *the West*) with its five states – Algeria, Morocco, Tunisia, Mauritania and Libya – represents a somewhat isolated area of the Arab World. Because of its geographical remoteness, it has been excluded from major events that have shaped the Mashriq (East). Nevertheless, the Maghreb represents a significant component of the Arab world with almost 60 million people, according to the 1990 estimates, constituting 30 per cent of the Arab population. Tunisia is the smallest of the five countries with an area of 164,150 km^2 and a population of 9 million people. Algeria has a huge area of 2,381,741 km^2 and a population of 34 million. For the other countries, the figures are: Morocco, 458,730 km^2 and a population of 34 million; Libya 1,759,540 km^2, and a population of 6 million; and Mauritania, 1,025,520 km^2 with 3 million. The main resources of Tunisia are agriculture and tourism. For Morocco it is phosphate, for Mauritania iron and fisheries, and for Libya and Algeria oil and gas.

The North African region Berber witnessed many invasions before it was integrated into the Islamic world and culture shortly after the death of the prophet Mohamed (632 AD). Its religious character is predominantly Sunni (orthodox and traditional) Islam, characterised by a strict abidance by prophetic tradition as a puritan, anti-dogmatic and anti-intellectual Islam. However, the Maghreb is also part of Africa and the Mediterranean area. This latter dimension has lately acquired more importance and is due to grow even further. The five countries constituting this area are very dependent on trade with Europe (about 70 per cent of trade exchanges). In the nineteenth century, all were colonised by France, except for Libya, which became an Italian colony.

The relation of Maghreb to modernity was contaminated by colonialism. The Maghreb discovered modernity as a colonial enterprise that brings domination together with new ideas, values and ways of life, or what Taylor (1995), speaking about the West, calls "the kernel truths", i.e. Western reference to the world, the Other, time and good. Colonialism not only represented a territorial appetite, a colonial domination over the earth, which, in the Maghreb, was a heavy "fardeau de l'homme blanc" and elsewhere a light "white man's burden". It was above all a "colonisation of the world of life", what Germans call "Lebenswelt", i.e. "a product of traditions where he (someone) finds himself, communal groups to which he belongs and the processes of socialisation in which he grows up" (Habermas, 1986: 147–148). As a result, the concepts of modernity and the West were historically affected, distorted and disturbed by colonialism. Even though modernity is not identical with the West, Arabs have experienced them as the two sides of the same coin, right from the nineteenth century (Lewis, 1984).

The Maghreb countries became independent in the 1950s and 1960s: Libya in 1953, Morocco and Tunisia in 1956, Mauritania in 1961 and Algeria in 1963. The first years of independence were a period of modernisation from above, or mobilisation. All observers noted the average increases of economic growth and political capacities of these countries, which moved from utter poverty to a better situation thanks to industrial projects, urbanisation, and the achievement of social goals, political mobilisation and bureaucratisation. The Maghreb countries took different modernisation paths: a peasant-led path based on revolutionary legitimacy in Algeria, a liberal tendency articulated by aristocratic and religious legitimacy in Morocco and Libya, a swing between liberal and socialist orientations in Mauritania and a path based on the exceptional charisma of Bourguiba in Tunisia (Amin, 1970b).

The Failure of Legitimacy

In *Arab Politics: The Search for Legitimacy*, Hudson (1977), identifies a crisis in Arab politics, which he considers as its "unstable" and "volatile" quest for legitimacy. Going beyond the classical views of legitimacy as a docility, which turns power (*Macht*) into an accepted domination (*Herreschaft*) (Weber), or "a diffuse support in favour of both the authorities and the regime" (Easton, 1965: 278), Hudson puts the emphasis on three specific prerequisites for Arab modern politics: the ability of a regime to exert authority, the ability to express a collective identity, i.e. a sense of corporate selfhood, and the ability to respond to aspirations of equality (Hudson, 1977: 4). Twenty-five years later, this crisis persists in a pervasive manner that has eroded the ability of the regimes to exert authority and has weakened their capacity to maintain identification with a political community. Worst of all, these regimes are far from meeting the public demand for political accountability to those who are governed, for civil and political participation, and for the respect of human rights. Although using different methods, these countries were forced, a few years ago, to liberalise their politics (privatisation and, to some extent, the recognition of civil rights). Now, they all face the same pressure: democratisation, not as a "natural" correlate of a modernisation process, but rather as a by-product meant to handle the erosion and the collapse of their legitimacy (Entelis, 1998). Can the Maghreb democratise? Or can authoritarian rulers reinvent extraordinary resources in order to stay in power and prevent political disasters similar to those in Algeria?

The initial legitimacy of socialist, anti-imperialist and populist Algeria has given in to social protests and Islamic activism. Tunisia has always done well in economics, but by narrowing the public sphere in an "irrational authoritarian manner" political participation does not take place along with social modernisation. Morocco is trying to strike a balance between economic reforms and a viable political life, and has to a certain extent succeeded in doing so. Mauritania, a poor agrarian country, cannot do better on the economic plane than in the political arena, and Libya, because of hydrocarbon revenues and eccentric handling-power style, is missing out on being rich as well as liberal. However hard they express their commitment to republican socialism (in the case of Algeria and Tunisia in the 1960s), to Arab nationalism (Libya), to liberal traditionalism (Morocco) and to ethnic particularism (Mauritania), legitimation failure is a result typical of North African political structures and cultures: a failure of a speedy, constant and strong modernisation; modernisation from above, followed by a liberalisation in response to social pressures and economic shortages, and not representing the outcome of a normative conviction; liberalisation without democratisation; a rejection of core components of liberal democracy; limited liberalisation without free, transparent and honest elections; an inveiglement of a minimal civil society insufficient to frighten governments; repression of Islamic revivalism or its "political patronage" by official parties and by authorities; inclusion and/or exclusion of political opposition. In all cases, modernisation never goes with democratisation, welfare is considered prior to democracy, security or stability is deemed more important than pluralism (the latter being usually identified with discord), liberalisation is either limited to economics or, when it goes further to grant some guarantees to individuals or public rights to non-trading organisations, remains an immature process controlled by "liberalised authoritarianism".

Why have North African regimes lost or weakened their bargaining power, their flexibility and their capacity to control their societies? How does the situation vary from one case to another? Beyond common features, each North African state comes with its own specificities. Economically, Algeria and Libya are *rentier* states, Tunisia and Morocco have diversified economics and Mauritania is a poor agrarian country. Politically, Morocco is a traditional constitutional monarchy, while the four others have chosen a republican regime. Culturally, Morocco has a religious pluralistic political culture, and Mauritania an ethnical one, while Tunisia and Algeria have a monolithic authoritarian culture. However, all of them have combined modernity with tradition and face an Islamist upsurge, which they can neither eradicate nor fully recognise.

Algeria: *Rentier* State in Armed Hands

Algeria is a *rentier* state, i.e. a state is in which most revenues originate from a natural resource. A *rentier* state is said to be an "*allocative state*" as opposed to a "*productive state*" in which prosperity comes primarily from the taxation of a domestic economy, which is grounded on the creation of wealth and the labour of citizens. With the "*allocative state*" the golden cycle (work, domestic production and taxation) is reversed: it is the state revenues that determine the GDP (Luciano, 1990b: 70; 1994; Beblawi, 1990: 86). According to the IMF, the hydrocarbon sector in Algeria still accounts for 95 per cent of export revenues, 60 per cent of state revenues and 30 per cent of GDP. The social and political consequences are that, as taxation is connected with representation (no representation without taxation) and democracy is linked to the bourgeoisie (no bourgeoisie, no democracy), the *rentier* state, freed from social pressures coming from below, is stronger than its society. A *rentier* economy breaks the inner relation between work and gratification, allowing the state to deny political rights and to hinder the growth of the bourgeoisie and the middle class. This state subsidises the economy and allocates revenues to patrons, clients and relatives. This is the case of traditional Gulf states were "all is in the family: absolutism, revolution and democracy" (Herb, 1999). Since its independence in 1962, Algeria has been a *rentier* state in armed hands, a military power in a technocratic rule (Entelis, 1982; 1992: 1–30; 1994: 219–215). "In most countries the state has its army, but in Algeria the army has its state" (Mortimer, 1993: 37).

However, a *rentier* state is not fatal, nor is military rule an irreversible situation. When oil revenues drop, a *rentier* state may collapse, and when social revolt, riots and manifestations occur on a large scale, military rule is obliged to reform or resign. In Algeria, oil revenues fell from $40 per barrel in 1979 to $10 per barrel in 1986, which obliged the praetorian state to agree to political pluralism. However, it was too late to avoid a civil war (Entelis, 1994: 226–230; Entelis and Naylor, 1992: 1–30). The dilemma of any *rentier* state is that it has to negotiate its authority and reform its economics, or else vanish.

Under the leadership of Haouri Boumediene (1965–1978) and Chadli Benjedid (1978–1991), the country focused on heavy industries, "industrialising industries" and collectivist agriculture, but industrialisation failed and agriculture was neglected. The resulting situation was summed up by an observer in the following terms: "Algeria had long been plagued by serious problems of overpopulation, inadequate housing, over urbanisation, unreliable food production and supplies, a decrepit transportation system, chronic water shortages, overcrowded schools, poor-quality medical facilities and health services, an uncontrollable birth rate with one of the world's youngest populations, and consistently high rates of unemployment and underemployment" (Entelis, 1992: 15–16). In fact, as long as the price of oil remained high, the Algerian state could maintain an apparent prosperous welfare state in "exchange for political docility of a society that was cared for from the cradle to the grave" (Layachi, 2000: 20). In 1986, oil revenues slumped, and in October 1988, thousands of young people took to the streets, demonstrating to reject the political system. The apparent strength of the state was deceptive. Social turmoil stimulated a new trend of policy in political life and economic management. A year later, in 1989, a relative liberal constitution replaced the authoritarian *Charte* (1976). About 50 parties were recognised, and freedoms of speech and of the press were to be granted. Despite the fact that Algeria was a *rentier* state, some observers expected an ongoing democratisation process, which would have encouraged a transition from an allocative economy to a productive one. Unfortunately, Algeria had waited too long before it initiated the reforms, and its chances of success within such a short period of time were reduced to nil. When the reform of the social system became the only alternative left, it was carried out in chaotic circumstances. Municipal elections were held in 1990 and were dominated by the Islamic Salvation Front (FIS), which further consolidated its stand in the legislative elections of 1991. Consequently, army "hard-liners" organised a coup in January 1992 and deposed Chadli Benjedid. The state of emergency was declared in February, the FIS was banned in March and its leaders were arrested and imprisoned, and many of them were interned in concentration camps in the Sahara desert. This was the start of a civil war in which 150,000 people were killed and 10,000 were reported missing.

With a persisting economic crisis, Algeria was obliged to sign a stand-by agreement with the IMF according to which the state committed itself to privatising its economy, mainly its state-owned enterprises (SOEs). The legal framework for privatisation was established with the Complementary Finance Law (articles 24/25, May 1994), enabling private individuals to acquire up to 49 per cent of the capital of a firm, and transferring the management of SOEs into the hands of private entities. However, despite the scarcity of available official data, it can be safely claimed that little has been done. Today, the overall results of the privatisation efforts remain insignificant. This failure is accounted for by a number of structural obstacles, and by the presence of a residual, but powerful, pseudo-charismatic, nationalist and bureaucratic leadership, which has taken control of the post-independence "triangle of army–state–FLN" (National Liberation Front). This collectivist and revolutionary legitimacy, in fact, conceals intense struggles and constant conflicts between armed clans, corrupt elites and political patrons, all trying to capture and control SOEs, the public sector, oil and gas revenues, just to satisfy private ends and clientelistic advantages. This irregular elite understandably stands against any change that would touch upon economic management, the redistribution of wealth, resources and structures of power, thus making any coherent reform strategy impossible (Werenfels, 2002: 2–3). Consequently, privatisation was attempted in a difficult context characterised by a disorganisation of the state and a dramatic upsurge of violence that followed the interruption of the legislative elections of December 1991, including the nullification of the results of the first round of the elections won by Islamists. These developments show the extent to which political crisis and economic crisis are interrelated. In this context, the weakness of the private sector and its inability to meet social demands led to the emergence of a parallel informal economy, under the close control of members of the Islamic network (Martinez, 2000). In the words of Dilman, "a *rentier* state pursuing dirigist policies prevented a productive private sector from emerging by monopolising resources and by failing to stem a drain of resources to a clientalistic private sector operating on the fringes of the formal economy" (Dillman, 1998: 4). This situation is bound to undermine the reforms: "the real problem was the lack of effective institutions and the rule-of-law within the Algerian state, both in political and economic spheres and the fact that violence itself was in part an outcome of the politiced structure of the economy" (Joffé, 1988: 48).

Human Rights: Between Repression and Compliance with the Norms

Rejecting the model proposed by Risse et al. (1999), Schwarz argues that the Algerian model swings between repression and compliance with the norms (Schwarz, 2002), to which one can add that the model is also characterised by a hiatus between norm prescription and practical behaviour. After the political and economic opening of 1989, and with the cancellation of the second round of the January 1992 elections, Algeria entered a phase which Amnesty International called "10 years of Grave Rights Abuses",[3] and the French organisation Reporters sans Frontières qualified as a "Livre noir de l'Algérie".[4] It became obvious that liberalisation was a survival tactic used by an ageing authoritarian military clan to secure and maintain its power. President Ben Jedid was dismissed and an HCS

3 A.I.: Algeria, 10 Years of State Emergency, 10 years of Grave Rights Abuses, AI MDE 28/003, 2002.

4 Reporters sans Frontières (1995): Le Livre Noir de l'Algérie. Paris: La découverte.

(Haut Conseil de Sécurité) was created on 14 January in which figured five of the most prominent army generals.[5] Then, the HCE (Haut Conseil d'Etat) was created, headed by Mohamed Boudhiaf, a charismatic FLN leader, who returned from his exile in Morocco. After he was assassinated in June 1992, the HCE appointed General Ali Kafi, and then Liamine Zeroual in December 1993, who was subsequently confirmed as an "elected" President in December 1995. To deal with a deteriorating situation, a decree issued in October 1992 created special courts, which constituted a breach of constitutional provisions. Along the same line, the state created and armed militia groups in order to curb terrorist attacks. In short, the regime lost its state character: the monopoly of violence.

It is worth noting that repression and liberal measures went together, hand in hand. Just when the country was grappling with a civil war in which nobody could tell whether the killers were Islàmists, civil militiamen or soldiers, a referendum on a new constitution was held in November 1996, followed by legislative elections in June 1997, regional elections in October 1997, the founding of a new second chamber in December 1997 and finally, a presidential election in April 1999. In these elections, Abdelaziz Bouteflika, another army-backed charismatic leader, was appointed in supposedly free elections. His opponents withdrew from the campaign, criticising it. Another referendum was held on September 1999 to ratify the Loi de la Concorde Civile (Law of Civil Harmony), which amnestied some armed groups and excluded from the death penalty those who agreed to give up their arms. This law was subject to criticism from the Commission of Co-ordination for Truth and Justice. which was acting on behalf of the families of the victims of terrorism (Bouandel, 2002: 32).

In this context, civil society became as weak as the state. Although two independent human rights NGOs, namely the Ligue Algérienne de la Défense des Droits de l'homme (LADDH, created in 1989) and the Ligue Algérienne des Droits de l'homme (LADH created in 1997) filed many complaints about cases of torture and missing persons, the civil society was in a dilemma. In spite of the fact that it represented a gigantic authoritarian rule, it supported the military rule in order to put an end to the development of Islamic groups. Lawyers, journalists, intellectuals, women's organisations, the Rassemblement pour la Culture et la Démocratie (RCD), the communist party (Ettahadi) and the trade union organisation, Union Générale des Travailleurs Algériens, were all fighting for democratic rule, but they were all also just as afraid of terrorism. The society was weak, but the army was also weak as it could neither put an end to the civil war nor meet the popular demands for social goods.

5 These were: Khaled Nezzar, Abelamalek Ghenazia, Mohamed Lamari, Mohamed Mediane and Mohamed Belkheir.

Towards a Limited Inclusion of Moderate Islamism

Since 1992, Algeria has claimed to work for the eradication of terrorism, but could there be a third path between eradicators and terrorists (Redissi, 1998: 125–142)? In the meantime, the military rule has made two concessions: the "Harmony" project in 1999, which failed as it could not stand the rate of massacres and attacks (between 200 and 300 people were killed per month) that hampered political life even during the presidency of Bouteflika (Zoubir, 2000), and the second project – which has had a relatively better outcome – aimed at the integration of moderate Islamists. These are organised into two movements, Hamas led by Sheikh Mahfoudh Nahnah and Nahdha, led by Abdallah Jaballah. As Islamists, they share the Egyptian Muslim Brotherhood ideology. They call for an application of the Sharia and are hostile to secular parties such as the RCD (Rasemblement pour la Culture et la Démocratie) and the FFS (Front des Forces Socialistes). Ennahdha was present in the St Egidio pact (Rome, 1995), a meeting of the Algerian opposition, which adopted a "Platform for a political and Peaceful Solution to the Algerian Crisis". Like the FIS, Ennahdha endorses but also criticises democracy and pluralism (Willis, 1998: 57). However, unlike the FIS, it accepts dialogue with the government and rejects violence. Defeated by the FIS in the 1990–1991 elections, Ennahdha did not take part in the subsequent bloody spiral of terror and eradication. Nahnah participated in the presidential elections of 1996, and both Hamas and the Nahdha took part in the legislative elections of 1997, and obtained some seats in parliament.[6] However, Algeria is still under pressure: it is expected that the crisis will linger on as long as armed resistance persists, political prisoners are not released, and electoral legitimacy is not accepted. Anyway, the example of the relative inclusion of moderate Islamists could eventually be followed by that of radical Islam, if the latter enhances its capacity to rationalise an absolutist religious agenda.

Libya: Irrational *Rentier* State under International Pressures

When the officers in Libya seized power in 1969, they put an end to the Sanusi dynasty (1951–1969).[7] The country was very poor and 94 per cent of the population was illiterate; infant mortality reached 40 per cent. Politically, the Libyan revolution played the card of Arab nationalism, and economically that of a socialist egalitarianism hostile to the law of the market. In fact, Libya is a *rentier*/distributive state. What happens when a state is freed from taxation? And how does this luxury affect the state building process, which, under different circumstances,

---

6 Ennahdha obtained 34 seats.

7 The *sanousiyah* is a mystical brotherhood founded by the Algerian Mohamed Ben Ali Sénoussi (1787–1859). It played a political role when it opposed the Italian colonisation in 1911. Its leader Idris became the king of Libya when the country gained independence.

would have been the outcome of the construction of national unity and integration, the capitalisation of the economy, class struggle and the conflicts and compromises between leaders? As was the case with Algeria, Libya became a *rentier* state just when such processes were starting to take place (Vandewalle, 1998), but this structural interpretation runs up against the example of the Gulf *rentier* states, which faced the same constraints. However, in the case of the Gulf countries, the state revenues, the independence and the family dynasty went together, whereas in Libya oil revenues were going to finance the Arab nationalist claims of Gaddafi, his anti-imperialist policy and his personal eccentricity. Here too, however, the *rentier* state cycle ends with an economic crisis. Even the Libyan state which J. Davis qualified as "anarchist" founded on an anti-state-control tradition seems to have learned the lesson (Altunsik, 1996: 49–63).

Economic Adjustments

Between 1988 and 1990, Libya took measures to liberalise its economy: trade and agriculture were liberalised, the number of public service officials was reduced, bankrupt public firms were closed down, private firms benefited from bank-financed schemes, etc. The embargo imposed on Libya by the Security Council in 1992[8] eroded the redistributive capacity of the regime: the Libyan Dinar was devaluated *de facto*, average wages stagnated and commodities became increasingly scarce. The embargo equally caused the country to collapse into an informal and parallel economy. However, as is the case with the other North African countries, this parallel economy was beneficial to the clients of the regime, particularly the 10,000 members of the "revolutionary committees" and the 40,000 soldiers of the Republican Guard (Ouanès, 1994). In order to eradicate the plague of speculation and corruption, the regime launched a populist campaign with "purification committees". The 1994 Purge Law against corruption allowed the state to confiscate "excessive private assets". Another 1996 law advocated the death penalty for foreign currency speculators.

As Libya verged on general chaos, a debate broke out between soft-liner bureaucrats advocating structural adjustments and hard-liners, who preferred to carry on with their hostility to the West and the market economy. After a long silence, Gaddafi took "the road to redemption", calling, in his September 2000 speech, for a new "era of economy, consumption, markets, and investments. This is what unites people irrespective of language, religion, and nationality" (Takeyh, 2001: 62–72). From the moment the suspended embargo could no longer work as

8 Accusing it of having perpetrated the Lockerbie attack (Scotland, 1988), the Security Council imposed a number of sanctions on Libya: an air embargo, the reduction of its foreign diplomatic personnel, the freezing of its assets, and the banning of the export of weapons and a number of oil products. In 1999, Libya handed the two attack suspects over to an international court in Holland, following which the Security Council suspended its embargo.

a justification for the economic and social crisis, the *Jamahiriya* (a republic ruled by the masses) was bound to make political adjustments. These took two equally irrational directions. The first was internal, inspired by the anti-state-control tradition of the *Jamahiriya*. The second was a spectacular reversal of Libyan foreign policy, which was henceforth directed towards Africa.

Political Adjustments

On the political plane, Gaddafi decided in January 2000 to adopt the communal councils and the "popular committees" (*shaabiyat*) instead of the *Jamahirya* (masses state) system proclaimed in March 1977. In March 2000, he reduced the government to its simplest form (Ministry of the Interior, Foreign Affairs, Finance, Information and African Affairs). In order to understand this development, we have to keep in mind that the Libyan system is based on "direct democracy": the grass-root congresses known as the *Congresses of the People*, the *People's Committees* and the *Professional Unions* elect representatives who gather into a *People's General Congress*. This latter elects the General Secretariat, which acts as the Council of Ministers, consisting of a Secretary-General (Prime Minister) and several secretaries (Ministers). In 1979, Gaddafi created the "revolutionary committees", which were going to control the basic congresses, track opposition members, eliminate Islamist contestants and spread fear. Between 1995 and 1998, these committees dealt ruthlessly with Islamists. It was only after the end of the embargo that Gaddafi shifted the control of the society from the "revolutionary committees" to the popular and social commands of the town councils, and to the "popular committees". This shift was due to the implication of the "revolutionary committees" in the repression of opponents and also the fact that the committee members were recruited from among tribal clans close to power (Khaddafia, Warfallas, M'agherba). In doing so, Gaddafi modified the structure of the elites and of the social basis, since these new committees are led by the heads of the tribes.[9] Thus, as is the case in Morocco, tradition has been reinvented by reviving tribal forms of allegiance.

Refocusing the Foreign Policy

The embargo (1992–1999) made Libya turn even more towards Africa (Djaziri, 1998; Haddad, 2000). In fact, sub-Saharan Africa has always represented an interest for Libya, if only because Gaddafi thinks that Libya belongs to three concentric circles (the Arab world, the Islamic world and the African world).

9 This modification in the structural rule seems to be behind the failure of the "Gaddafi assassination attempt", which was led by Khalifa Henaish, head of the security troops, a cousin of Gaddafi from the Gaddafa tribe, who was disenchanted when a member of his tribe was cut into pieces and sent to his family because he had questioned Gaddafi's authority. *Defence & Foreign Affairs Strategic Policy*, vol. 30, no. 4/5, April/May 2002.

Nasser, his inspirer, said the same about Egypt. However, until the embargo, his hegemonic temptation was a mixture of aggressive policy and financial assistance, or "*commandos and credits*" (Bugeat and Lalande, 1996: 105). For a long time, Libya supported African subversions in Niger (1976–1982), Gambia (1981), Mali (1982) and Sudan, among others. Its military adventure in Chad, which was started in 1973, finally failed in 1987, just like its intervention in Uganda in 1979. Financially, from 1973 to 1978, Libya underwrote more than 50 per cent of the Arab assistance to Africa, in addition to the creation of 10 banks and 40 government-controlled corporations, encouraging African countries to break their ties with Israel (Otayek, 1986: 78–105). It is difficult to understand the reason why Gaddafi invested so much money and political support and for such a long time in the control of sand and rocks without locating this irrational politics within the framework of a widespread struggle for supremacy along the fringes of the Islamic world (Burr and Collins, 1999).

The politics of Libya has changed, but not its African dream. In a speech delivered on 1 September, marking the thirty-first anniversary of his revolution, Gaddafi said, "Libya is small, but great things have small beginnings" (*The Economist*, 16 September 2000). On the doctrinal plane, this change consisted of toning Arab nationalism down in favour of the Africanity of Libya. Politically, it involved moving from an aggressive diplomacy to an active one, based on dialogue, the resolution of conflicts and financial assistance.

This political shift is due to the isolation of Libya, combined with the fact that it did not get the support it expected from Arab regimes. Taking into account the failure of previous Arab union experiments (the Charter of Tripoli in 1969, which brought together Sudan, Libya and Egypt, the Union of Arab Republics in 1971, between Libya, Syria and Egypt, and the union between Tunisia and Libya in 1974), it becomes easier to understand how, disappointed, Colonel Gaddafi turned to Central Africa, with which he shares the Sahara through Chad and Niger. The African countries, on the other hand, broke the embargo by organising air flights and by concluding several cooperation agreements with Libya. This movement was crowned by the decision taken at the third OAU summit (9–10 June 1998), which invited African countries to break free from the Security Council sanctions. Following this decision, Libya abolished its ministry for the Arab Union in September 1998 and created in its stead the ministry for African Union in March 2000. It also dropped the OAU contribution arrears of certain African countries, and granted UNESCO $200 million to finance grants for African students and other projects. More significant still was the creation of the Community of the Sahelo-Saharan States (COMESSA) in 1998, financed by Libya up to 75 per cent, the incorporation of legal status of the African Union in Lome in 2000, and finally the extraordinary summit meeting in Syrte in March 2001. Libyan hegemonic ambitions, however, ran up against the reserves of Algeria, Nigeria and South Africa, all having large ambitions for Africa (Darwish, 2001: 23–25).

Certain elements cast a shadow over this reversal, however. First, there were the September 2000 riots against African nationals, which claimed the lives of a hundred Africans and led to the expulsion of thousands of others, an illustration of the gap between Gaddafi's African ambitions on the one hand, and the *rentier* and moralistic[10] Libyan mentality, largely hostile to foreigners, on the other. Also, there was the tension between Libya and Mauritania following Mauritania's establishing of diplomatic relations with Israel (28 October 1999). Lastly, there was the discrete support which Libya is still giving to the Tchadian opposition in spite of the fact that Libya accepted the decision of the International Court of Justice of the same year (1994), which allotted to Chad the Aozou strip, after a 20-year long conflict between the two countries. Thus, with regard to the unforeseeable character of Gaddafi, a new reversal of his policy is not to be excluded.

Human Rights

Although information is scarce, there have been reports on harshly repressed guerrilla attacks and ambushes against symbols of the regime (Deeb, 1999, 2000). According to Libyan legislation, however, arbitrary arrests, detention and deprivation of liberty are prohibited under the terms of article 14 of the Promotion of Freedom Act No. 20/1991. According to articles 30 and 31 of the Criminal law Procedure, no one can be arrested except by order of the competent legal authorities (article 30). Article 435 of the Penal Code forbids torture. With regard to the misuse of power against individuals, article 431 of the Penal Code stipulates that any public official who uses violence against an individual is liable to a prison sentence.[11] Despite this judicial apparatus, human rights reports insist on "extrajudicial, arbitrary or summary executions, arbitrary arrest without trial on suspicion of belonging to or supporting Islamic movements, systematic torture, kidnapping and elimination of dissidents". A "Charter of Honour" allows for the punishment of anyone who shelters or helps "criminals".[12]

Apparently, "the non existence of abject poverty, the absence of social mobility, the systematic effort to obliterate economic differences, and the nonmonlothic political system have tended to hamper the rise of a dominant militant Muslim opposition in Libya" (Deeb, 1996: 190). Nevertheless, since the mid-1980s, fragmented movements have emerged, inspired by the Egyptian model and Algerian violent upsurges. Trying to destabilise a regime weakened by the international embargo, these movements are the National Salvation Front, the Muslim Brotherhood, the Jihad, the Islamic Liberation Party, the Tabligh (the

10 The justification for the riots was that Africans were spreading diseases and taking to prostitution.

11 Third periodic report of state's parties due in 1995: Libyan Arab Jamahiriya, 15 October 1997. CCPR/C/102/Add.1 (State Party Report). Human Rights Committee. Considerations of reports submitted by state parties under article 40 of the covenant.

12 UN Human Rights Committee Report, concluding observations at its 1720th meeting, 2 November 1998.

Warning), the Takfir wa al-Hijra (Apostasy and Migration), the Libyan Islamic Group and the Islamic Martyr's Movement (Deeb, 1996; Joffé, 1988).

Yet the most important events that have shaped the country's modern history (the Libyan resistance to Italian colonialism (1911), the Sanusi monarchy established upon independence (1951), in the person of Idris, the first and the last king, and even the first period of the revolution (1969–1973)) are based on an alliance between politics and traditional Islam. The Libyan resistance and the Idris monarchy are in fact intertwined. The Idris monarch was a descendent of Sayyid Muhammad Ali al-Sanusi (1787–1859), founder of the Sufi order of Sanusi. He was an Algerian who settled in Libya when he realised that he could no longer go back home after France colonised Algeria (1830). He created the first *zawia* in 1843. His relatives, Muhamed al-Mahdi (died 1902) and Ahmed al-Sharif (died 1933) continued his apostolate, a mixture of traditional Islam (sunnit and malikite) and reliance on *ijtihad*. Idris's religious political legitimacy, however, mostly derives from the fact that al-Mahdi and al-Sharif fought against the Italian occupation. After independence, traditional Islam continued to shape Libya's political culture.

Until 1973, the claim made by Carl Brown remained true: "as a symbol of unity and identity, Islam is to North African what Arab nationalism is to the Arab East" (Brown, 1973: 32). Idris kept tribal cleavages intact. He did not modernise the country and refused to integrate the urban middle class into the country's political structure. His failure to handle and contain the tensions resulting from the discovery of hydrocarbons led to Gaddafi's coup in 1969. During the first years of the revolution, the political system remained deeply rooted in Islamic tradition. Gaddafi often consulted the clerics, who kept their traditional control over the legal, judicial and educational spheres. Arabic became the only language for official and non-official documents, and the Hijra (Exile) calendar was adopted instead of the Gregorian one. In fact, it seems that among the multiple causes undermining the union between Libya and Egypt in 1972 and 1973 was Gaddafi's attempt to declare the Sharia as the source of legislation in the new draft constitution.

However, by 1973, Gaddafi had dragged his country into his famous Third Universal Theory. Presented in his *Green Book*, a small book issued in three instalments, 1976–1978, this theory is a mixture of Arab nationalism, socialism, populism and egalitarianism, which constitute the Republic of the Masses. But Gaddafi equally pretended that his theory derived from a new interpretation of Islam, that it was rooted in Islam and that it was as universal as Islam (Anderson, 1983, Bleuchot, 1982, Deeb, 1978). The clash between the *ulemas* and Gaddafi could not be avoided, and degenerated, a few years later, into an armed conflict between Gaddafi and Islamists. The *ulemas* criticised the *Green Book*, arguing that the socialist agenda was contradictory to Islamic law, which never prohibited trade and property rights. During a debate with the *ulemas*, Gaddafi declared that he considered the Sharia as "a positive law", meaning non-sacred like Roman and French laws. He even threatened to adopt atheism if the *ulemas* rejected his *Green Book* (Djaziri, 1996; Deeb, 1996). Worse, Gaddafi eroded religious influence by expropriating religious endowments, declaring that Islam does not recognise the priestly class and rejecting prophetic Hadiths as a source of legislation. Only the Koran, he argued, could be considered as such. The situation worsened in the 1990s. An armed insurrection began in Djebel Akhdar, between 1995 and 1996. It was stifled in blood in 1999 (*The Economist*, 30 October 1999). The choice of this mountain as the location is significant as it was the stronghold of the Sanusi brotherhood opposition to the occupation forces. After the coup, the revolution chased out the Sanusis, who are still resentful. The Islamists thus represent a junction between confreric and maraboutic Islams (Martinez, 2000: 8–9).

This repression was accompanied by a policy taking over Islamic sentiments. In 1994, Gaddafi stated that the Sharia was to be implemented and extended to corporal punishment and heresy offences. At the same time, the regime encouraged the Islamisation of Africa through the *Jama'has al-dawa wal al-Islam* (Society for the call to Islam), founded in 1972 and based in the Cathedral of Tripoli. This policy was characterised by the distribution of grants to African students studying in Libyan universities, the propagation of Islam through the use of missionary caravans, and financial help for the building of mosques, hospitals and Koranic schools. This foreign policy was very much like that adopted by the Saudis, except that Libya was working on two planes: religious proselytism but also support for the laic and the Marxist-influenced subversive revolutionary regimes in Ethiopia and elsewhere.

Just like the situation in Algeria, Islamism seems to have been brought under control. However, if in both countries, a local, low-intensity conflict could be contained thanks to the revenues of hydrocarbon export, Libya lacks the military clan that represents the backbone of the state in Algeria. Gaddafi governs alone, without allies, without army and increasingly without tribes. The constants of the Libyan policy were cynically synthesised by John Davis and Lisa Anderson (Anderson, 2000, 2001). Its major trait is Guaddafi's rejection of state control. Since he came to power in 1969, "he sustained a campaign against the Libyan state, and against the systematic, scientific theories of politics that are associated with modern government" (Anderson, 2001: 515). This campaign against the state looks like a permanent revolution. This is all the more paradoxical as Gaddafi rose out of the army, an organisation renowned for order, discipline and the weight of hierarchical structure. "So Gaddafi resolved to rule without a state", conceptualising and realising "a stateless polity in a world of states" (Anderson, 2001: 515–516; 2000: 12). His eccentric character, his extravagances and his utopia are only explained by the state revenues he and those close to him are able to administer. In other *rentier* states, these revenues are shared among those who govern (the military clans in Algerian and Nigeria) or among the reigning families (Gulf states). As for Gaddafi, the leader of the revolution, he is constantly trimming the structures of the state, while holding the reigns of power alone.

The anti-state control policy deprives the Libyans of any form of allegiance except to the family and the tribe. Under these conditions, only Islamism represents an alternative to, on the one hand, the absence of the state and, on the other hand, forms of allegiance to entities smaller than the state. However, on account of the fact that only the army constitutes an organised force, one can expect an alliance between the peripheral urban classes that have represented a fertile ground for the Islamist upsurge and army officers, coming from tribes and from rural areas. Maybe "the long-term beneficiaries of Gaddafi will be the Islamists, who are the guardians of dynamic ideology and have survived the regime's repression. Post-Gaddafi Libya is likely to be a state governed by military officers who retain a close association with the orthodox Islamic establishment" (Takyeh, 2000: 164).

Morocco: Neo-patrimonial Monarchy

The Moroccan political system is based on a twofold, traditional and constitutional, centrality of the monarch. From the point of view of tradition, monarchy rests on the triple unity of God, the caliph and the *umma* (community). Two concepts are fundamental in this context: the caliphate and the Makhsen. The caliphate rests, understandably, on the califal model whereby it is traditionally considered as a natural, rational and legal necessity. The king, of prophetic descent, is "the commander of believers", who owe him allegiance (*bay'a*). The enthronement of King Hassen II on 3 March 1961, who took over from his father, Mohamed V, was the occasion to bring out once again contested Hadiths (words of the prophet), which claim that "he who dies without having proclaimed his allegiance dies like those who lived in the polytheist era", or "the sultan is the shadow of God on earth". The investiture ceremony consists of two phases: the first takes place in private at the seraglio in the presence of the members of the royal family, the regime dignitaries, the *ulemas*, the ministers, the state bodies, the armed forces and the heads of the political parties. In a second phase, the allegiance moves from the private to the public, and the ceremony from the seraglio to the mosque, where the king chairs a solemn prayer, which consecrates the allegiance of the people. The second concept is that of Makhsen, which refers to the royal home and its traditional extensions (tribes, brotherhoods, territorial authorities, families, allies), but which also comes to encompass the modern administration. The alliance between religious legitimacy and political domination makes the Makhsen the politico-administrative locus of power. This same tradition is thus articulated around a modern kind of legitimacy.

The constitutional framework granted by the Monarch is unstable (five constitutions), but it provides the country with an elected Parliament, grants basic freedoms, and allows legally recognised parties to compete for the exercise of part of the power. However, this constitution imparts the monarch with the competences and the power of the head of state of an authoritative republic by making him the pivot of all institutions. This centrality is consecrated in the famous article 19 of the constitution: "le Roi, commandeur des croyants, représentant suprême de la nation, symbole de son unité, garant de la pérennité et de la continuité de l'État, veille au respect de l'islam et de la constitution. Il est le protecteur des droits et libertés des citoyens, groupes sociaux et collectivités".[13] This centrality, which extends to the Makhsen, makes Morocco a "neo-patrimonial State", which is different from medieval authority identified by Weber. Weber defines Islamic power during the classical age as patrimonial, sultanic power, characterised by an arbitrary personal authority exerted over the subjects, "just like any object that could be possessed", based on a military order, a personalised administration and the distribution of favours (Weber, 1995: vol. 1, 308–309). Through discharge, the prince delegated the collection of resources to military and mercenary orders (Weber, 1991a: 85–92). In modern times, this power becomes neo-patrimonial, i.e. this unequal and asymmetrical relation survives in the context of post-colonial modernisation (Eisenstadt, 1973: 323–324; 1984: 48–49; Bill and Springborg, 1990: 152–176). Thus, the Makhzen integrates alternative forms of allegiance, of patronage and of distribution: from the unequal, but symbolic, exchange of Baraka (Hammoudi, 1997) up to the material donations of the concessions and the unlawful activities of those who are close to the palace.

Under these conditions, the functional tumbling down of monarchy is at once its strong point and its weakness. True, constitutionalism and political liberalisation partake in the consensual legitimacy of monarchy, but, since negotiation takes place in the palace, they run up against the very limitations of a monarchical, supra-constitutional power. Finally, the fact that the monarchy is based on a religious legitimacy heightens religious sensitivity. This calls for a greater harmony between the religious discourse and the political practice. As a result, Islam from above ran up against Islam from below, a situation where government, which is already Islamic, is required to really conform to the precepts of Islam.

A Fragile Economy

Morocco has resorted to the strategy of modernisation from the top since the Abdallah Ibrahim government (1958–1960). In the 1980s, the country was affected by a severe recession. The resulting food shortage led to rural migration, a drop in GDP, the decline of investments and a restriction in the subsidising of essential products. A series of riots and popular demonstrations broke out in 1981 under the leadership of the CDT (Confédération Démocratique des Travailleurs: Democratic Confederation of Workers) supported by left-wing parties and notably the USFP (Union Socialiste des Forces Populaire: Socialist Union of Popular Forces). The leaders of these organisations were arrested and charged. USFP decided to withdraw from parliament. It was replaced by a pro-monarchy party, the RNI. In 1983 the growth of the GDP was about −5.7 per cent, the deficit of the balance of payments about −6.3 per cent and the unemployment rate about 14.5 per cent; 26 per cent of

13 The king, commander of believers, supreme representative of the nation, symbol of its unity, guarantor of the perenniality and the continuity of the state, sees to it that Islam and the constitution are respected. He is the guard of the rights and freedoms of the citizens, social groups and communities.

the population lived below the poverty line. It is in this context that the legislative elections of 1983 were held. A "national union" made up of six parties obtained seats in Parliament and had representatives among government members, but riots continued in 1984. By 1999, the country was still affected by an economic crisis. The annual growth rate of GDP was about 1.2 per cent, agricultural production declined by 1.2 per cent, unemployment reached 15.4 per cent, and over 50 per cent of the population aged over 15 was illiterate. A program of structural adjustment imposed by the IMF and intended to rationalise the political economy was initiated between 1983 and 1993. It comprised the reduction of expenditure, the disengagement of the state, the abandoning of price subsidy, the devaluation of the currency and the encouragement of exports. Before this second scheme was completed, however, Morocco was called upon to start a third plan relative to the association agreements of a partnership between the European Union and the North African countries belonging to the South Mediterranean (Tunisia, Algeria, Morocco and Libya; the agreements were ratified in 1995 with Tunisia, in 1996 with Morocco and in 2001 with Algeria). The plan, meant to "upgrade" the economies of the three Mediterranean countries, is scheduled until 2010. It consists of adapting economic structures to international standards with a view to confronting the challenges of globalisation and the generalised liberalisation of exchanges, but it is too early to tell whether the process will succeed (Al-Aoufi, 1999: 36–52).

Limited Political Reforms

Since the 1960s, and owing to the fact that political power is in the hands of the king, Morocco has been in a "motionless transition". The Istiqlal and USFP parties, which took part in the fight for national liberation, have always had a variable representation in Parliament. Therefore, the country can claim what Ehteshami calls "relatively open or politically significant elections" (Ehteshami, 1999: 210). In the 1980s, a number of reforms constitutionalised the monarchy even further. These touch upon human rights,[14] the legitimate state[15] and social dialogue.[16] However, as every expert in political science knows, "economic crisis stimulates political exchanges and creates consequently the conditions for the acceleration of economic and democratic demands" (Moutadayne, 2001: 70). These reforms thus came as an answer to the persistent economic crisis and the pressures of opposition parties for the reform of the political system. They took place through the October 1991 memoranda of the Istiqlal and the USFP parties and the May 1992

14 Creation of the Consultative Council for Human Rights (decree 1-90-12 of 20 April 1990) and of the Ministry in Charge of Human Rights in 1993.

15 Creation of administrative courts (decree 1-91-225 of 10 December 1993 promulgating law 41-90) and of the Constitutional Council (decree 25 February 1994 promulgating law 29-93).

16 Creation of the Council for Social Dialogue (announced on 24 November 1994).

memorandum of the democratic block called Koutla.[17] These memoranda asked for a revision of the constitution to reinforce the Prime Minister's prerogatives and Parliament's competencies. The king accepted the reform of the constitution, submitted to popular vote in 1992, although Kotla decided to withdraw from a process that did not take its demands into account. Because of constant pressure from the opposition, another revision followed in 1996, again, without touching on the supremacy of the king. Finally, the legislative elections of 1997 allowed the left-wing opposition to share power with the other represented parties. This political opening was crowned by the nomination of the head of the USFP left-wing party, Abderrahman Youssefi, who came from the "contreculture" (Entelis, 1996), as a Prime Minister on 4 February 1998, following the victory of the left in the legislative elections of December 1997. Yet this opening is only relative, if only because the king is still the one who appoints key ministers (the Interior, Foreign Affairs, Justice and *Habous* properties or *waqf*).

Selective Inclusion of Fragmented Islamism

The panorama of Moroccan Islamism is complex, because of the fragmentation of movements that are constantly changing their names. There are at least three types of Islam: the official Islam of the *ulemas*, the Sufi Islam of the brotherhoods and militant Islam (Dialmy, 2000). The first Islamist movement used as a breeding ground for militant Islamism was the Achabiba Al-islamiya (Islamic youth), created by Abdelkarim Moti, which appeared in November 1972. First marginalised after having been implicated in the murder of a leader of the USFP in 1975, the movement was finally prohibited and broke into many competing factions. Since 1983, a group intent on breaking with the Achabiba al-islamiya, led by Abdallah Benkirane, has come onto the scene. These Islamists first renamed themselves all Al-jamaa' al-islamiya (Islamic group), then Al-islah wa al-tajdid (Reform and Renewal) in February 1992, before they organised into a party Hizb al-tajdid al-watani (National Renewal Party) in May 1992. In the meantime, they accepted the legitimacy of the king, renouncing the use of violence. Some of them even participated in the constitutional referenda held in 1992 and 1996, supporting the king against official parties. The government tried to include moderate Islamism into the official political arena. The solution adopted was to insert Al-Islah wa al-tajdid, led by Benkirane, into the MPDC (Mouvement Populaire Démocratique Constitutionnel) led by Al-Khatib, a former leader of the struggle for independence, a former minister and president of the Chambe des Députes, who created his party in 1967 and won three seats in the 1977 legislative elections, before he decided to leave political life. His comeback into politics was characterised by the co-opting of Islamists, but the Islamists' credo was "affiliation without dissolution"

17 This coalition is made up of the following parties: the Istiqlal Party, the USFP, the Organisation for Democratic and Popular Action (OADP), the Progress and Socialism Party (PPS) and the National Union of Popular Forces (UNFP).

into the MPDC, or "coalition and not integration" (Willis, 1998: 48). They took part in the communal elections of June 1997 as independent candidates and in the legislative elections of November 1997, in which they obtained nine seats. In the legislative elections of 2002, moderate Islamists obtained about 30 seats, while Al-Islah wa al-ihsen (Justice and charity), led by the charismatic Sheikh Yassine, was still banned. Sheikh Yassine, with a Sufi origin, had a spectacular entry into politics in 1974 when he published his famous open letter to the king, "l'islam ou le déluge" (Islam or the flood), asking the king to apply Islamic law. He was confined to a mental hospital until 1979. When he came out of hospital, he created a first association then a second, i.e. Al-Islah wa al-ihsen, in 1987. He belongs to the radical Islamic tendency preached by the Egyptian Islamist Sayyid Qutb (1906–1965). He considers that the Muslim society is pagan and calls for *jihad* against non-Muslims and a potent tyrant (*taghut*).

If constitutional legitimacy implies liberalisation, then religious legitimacy supposes the exclusion of Islamism, since the king himself proclaims his religious fundamentalist origins. However, with the presence of several tendencies and associations resulting from the breaking up of Islamist movements, the monarchy opted for a selective strategy to include some and exclude others. The integration of Islamists can succeed only as long as it remains an ongoing process of "conditional integration" in which every partner makes an effort to reach a mutual consensus over the rules of the game. In brief, between inclusion and exclusion, allegiance and revolt, there is a fragile balance between the traditional Makhsen and the neo-traditional Islamist movements.

Mauritania: Ethno-tribal Fragmentation

Mauritania became independent in a difficult regional context. Its first president, Mokhtar Ould Daddah (1960–1978), was obliged to battle for recognition, as Arab countries were largely supporting Morocco's claims over Mauritania's territory. In addition, he had to compete with Morocco over the former Spanish colony of Western Sahara. During the 1970s, Mauritania was accepted as a sovereign state by both Africans and Arabs. The construction of the state started along the modernisation model. The only trouble was that modernisation might not mean very much for a poor, semi-arid country, with few natural resources, except fisheries and some iron ore reserves.

Ould Daddah decided to develop his economy from above in an authoritarian manner. As he was the one who negotiated independence, he created his *Parti du Peuple Mauritanien* (PPM) in 1961, and made it a complex federation which absorbed all pre-independence political clans. In the economy, he introduced a national currency in 1973–1974 after he withdrew from the French-led Communauté Financière Africaine (CFA) and expropriated the Societé Anonyme des Mines de Fer de Mauritanie (MIFERMA). However, Ould Daddah's misfortune came from the outside. When in 1975–1976 he reached an agreement with Morocco over the partition of Western Sahara, he could not imagine that the Saharan natives would resist and organise into an opposition led by the Polisario. Yet if Morocco was strong enough to stop Polisario incursions supported by Algeria, Mauritania was a weak state that could not resist attacks with an economy resting on the sole revenue of iron ore mines. In 1977, Ould Daddah was deposed by a military coup, imprisoned and finally exiled. His party was abolished to make room for a Comité Militaire de Redressement National (CMRN), itself replaced, in 1979, by the Comité Militaire de Salut National, which governed the country until the April 1992 elections. Three military leaders followed one another at the head of the country: Colonel Mustapha Ould Mohamed Sale (1977–1979), Mohamed Khouna Ould Heydallah (1979–1984) and Colonel Ma'awiya Ould Sid'Ahmed Taya (1984–2005). The analysis below will read this history as a series of social conflicts in the context of economic shortages.

Ethno-tribal Identity

The social structure of Mauritania is less homogenous than that of Libya, Tunisia (with 99 per cent Arabs) or Algeria (with an Imazigh minority). It is as fragmented as that of Morocco, while both are less so than sub-Saharan African social structures. The provisions of the Mauritanian constitution (articles 1 and 6) recognise ethnic pluralism and forbid any racial or ethnic propaganda. In front of international organisations, the Mauritanian state proudly highlights its social pluralism, its tolerance, the abolition of slavery and its respect of the law. Thus, three associations promoting African dialects (Pular, Sninké and Wolof) were recognised,[18] and the UN Committee on the Elimination of Racial Discrimination noted huge progress towards the eradication of slavery and discrimination in Mauritania.[19]

Mauritania's ethno-tribal identity is made up of a number of dichotomies: Arabs vs Africans, whites vs blacks, Arabs vs native Berbers, and, among Arabs themselves, Arab-whites vs Arab-blacks. At the top of the hierarchy, we find the Arab white tribes of Maqil called Banu Hassan. These are Arabic-speaking warriors who arrived in the thirteenth century and ruled the country until the French colonisation in the 1890s. At the bottom end, we find the minority of non-Arab black African groups such as the Fulanis, the Bamabaras and the Wolofs, who speak their own dialects. They are situated almost outside the Arab-Berber social group. Between these two extremes, and immediately after Banu Hassen in the social hierarchy, come the clerics. They result from interbreeding between Arabs and Berbers and get their social rank from their function as *marabouts* (Zawiya). They form a caste of clerics teaching traditional Islam. Next come the Znagas, a

18 Cinquièmes rapports périodiques des Etats parties devant être présentés en 1998: Mauritania, 26 October 1998 CERD/C/330/Add.1 (State Party Report).

19 Conclusions du Comité pour l'élimination de la discrimination raciale: Mauritania, 12 April 2001. CERD/C/304/Add.82 (Concluding Observations/Comments).

group of defeated Berbers who had to pay a tribute called *horna* to Banu Hassen's hegemonic warriors up until the twentieth century. Among speakers of Arabic we find whites called Bidan and black moors called Haratin who used to be slaves (Gerteiny, 1967, 46–56, 88–101).

The first president of the country, Ould Daddah, was not an Arab, but an Arab-Berber member of an important *marabout*, the Zawiya of Boutilimit (at the southeast of Nouakchott), which is also a tribe (Ould Berri). His successors, Colonel Mustapha Ould Mohamed Saled (1977–1979), Mohamed Khouna Ould Heydallah (1979–1984) and Colonel Ma'awiya Ould Sid'Ahmed Taya (1984–2005) have reinforced the power of the Banu Hassen warrior tribe against the *marabouts*, the Haratin former slaves and black Africans. Although independent Mauritania condemns slavery, white Arabs continue to exert their hegemony. Mohamed Khouna Ould Heydallah was deposed on 12 December 1984, not for his partiality, but upon suspicion of closeness to the Polisario. However, the main trait of political life remains the tensions between Arab-whites and their black counterparts. The Haratin themselves are threatened by ethnic dislocation, notably by the Forces de Liberation Africaine de Mauritanie (FLAM), close to Senegal, which represents non-Arab Blacks in Mauritania. FLAM was accused of fomenting a coup against Taya in December 1987, and was harshly repressed according to international human rights reports. Ould Taya had also to face an upsurge of Arab nationalism, notably among the Mauritanian section of the Baath Socialist Party, which emerged during the 1991 Gulf Crisis. These constraints may represent some of the forces pushing Ould Taya to recognise Israel in 1999.

Limited Liberalisation

Squeezed between Arab nationalism and Black secessionism, Ould Taya chose to abandon military rule. In April 1991, he announced a new trend of reforms. Thus, without prior debate, a new constitution was approved by voters in 1991. Freedom of speech and association were restored. Presidential elections were held 1992 in which Ould Tay obtained 63 per cent of the votes, while his three challengers shared the remaining 37 per cent. These results show how tribal divisions continue to shape and undermine political life. Thus, the principal challenger Ahmed Ould Daddah, leader of the Union des Forces Démocratiques (UFD) (33 per cent of the votes), is the brother of former President Mokhtar Ould Daddah, while Mustapha Ould Mohamed Salek (3 per cent of the votes) is a former CMRN chairman. The legislative elections of a bicameral Parliament (lower house and upper house or Senate) were held between March and April 1992, with a large victory to the presidential Parti Republican Démocratique et Social (PRDS). This party won almost 280 districts in the Municipal elections of 1994, while 34 went to the opposition. Frustrated by these results, the opposition declared that the presidential and legislative elections were fraudulently conducted. Six years later, the outcome of the presidential elections, boycotted by Ahmed Ould Daddah, was an inevitable success for Ould Taya and his party. Thus, economic liberalisation began with a new civilian government conducted by technocrats, but Mauritania still suffers from a shortage of business tools, funding and basic infrastructure. Politically, human rights are not really respected, and the opposition, like the UFD, the Union pour le Progrès et la Démocratie (UPD) and the baathist party Parti d'Avant-garde Nationale (PAGN), is still persecuted. In September 1994, 60 members of the Umma Islamist party were jailed.

Although Mauritania has shifted from a military rule to a civilian government, and has made some steps towards political and economic liberalisation, the country remains "deeply traditional, geographically dispersed, ethnically divided", and the regime remains corrupt and grounded on tribal and family loyalties, "manipulated for the benefit of the presidential office" (Pazzanita, 1999: 53–56). In 2005 and 2008 there again occurred military coups in the Islamic Republic of Mauritania.

Tunisia: Economic Liberalisation in Authoritarian Regime

Independence under the leadership of Bourguiba, in 1956, endowed Tunisia with a particular profile, which, in some respect, is still valid. The neo-destour (1932) (new constitutional party), the political vehicle by means of which independence had been achieved, was to become a single state-party in 1964, subordinating social institutions like trade unions, employers and agricultural organisations, and prohibiting other parties. At the same time, the national construction process, under the lead of a single bureaucratic party, was undertaken by Ahmed Ben Salah (1963–1969), who adopted a socialist approach characterised by land expropriation and capitalisation of the economy. The country was close to bankruptcy when Bourguiba dismissed Ben Salah and appointed Hédi Nouira in his stead, the former director of the Central Bank. As a prime minister, Nouira (1971–1980) initiated a liberalisation process in the 1970s, which however remained confined to the economic field. Thus, opposition parties were still forbidden, freedom of expression non-existent, trade unions repressed and the leftist opposition harassed. When Hedi Nouira fell sick, Mohamed M'zalli took over (1980–1986). He managed to liberalise political life by allowing a relative freedom of expression, negotiating with the UGTT (Trade Union Organisation), tolerating an Islamist movement (Islamic Tendency Movement) and recognising a liberal opposition made up of elements who had left the ruling party and organised into the MSD (Social Democratic Movement). Unfortunately, M'zali failed in the economic sector. Riots over the increase in the price of food broke out in 1984 and degenerated into social protests a year later. The country witnessed its second structural crisis. A new prime minister (Rachid Sfar) was appointed before Zine al-Abidine Ben Ali deposed Bourguiba in a constitutional coup, in November 1987. In 1986, a stand-by agreement was ratified with the IMF ($125 millions). This agreement purported to restructure the economy, reform a plethoric public sector, stabilise the balance of payments, reduce the budget deficit and encourage domestic and international investments. Since then, Tunisia has been doing well in its economy, especially compared with other North African countries (Dillman, 1998; Layachi, 2000).

Authoritarian Continuity

The structural adjustment program intended to liberalise prices and trade, reform the tax system, and boost the private sector, managed to stabilise the economy, diversify exports and generate strong growth. By the 1990s, inflation had been brought down to 4 per cent, and the budget deficit to 2 per cent, while GDP growth reached an annual rate of 5 per cent in an increasingly diversified economy, based on agriculture (14 per cent), manufacturing (20 per cent), services (37 per cent) and hydrocarbons (6 per cent). In 1995, the Tunisian government signed a partnership agreement with the European Union to create a free and integrated trade zone over a period of 12 years starting from 1998. According to this agreement, the Tunisian government was due to dismantle trade restrictions, in exchange for European financial support and funds to help upgrade the national economy and make it meet European standards. Tunisia has thus reduced its public sector, privatised public enterprises, encouraged private investments and upgraded a selected list of competitive private enterprises, despite a slow-moving bank sector.

This economic success, however, is paradoxically undermined by an authoritarian political rule. From independence (1956) up until Ben Ali seized power (1987), Tunisia was governed by a complex president/party rule. Ben Ali managed to depose Bourguiba on the basis of disability, thus applying the Tunisian Constitution, which specifies that the prime minister be automatically declared president in the event of the illness, death or disability of the president. President Ben Ali promised political reforms of pluralism, freedom of the press and the rule of law. The president indeed started to take some public measures to restore the rule of law. Hence, the Security of State Court was abolished (1987), police custody reduced (1987), a law regulating political parties was passed (1988), articles in the constitution limited eligibility for presidential elections to two consecutive times (1988), two new parties were recognised, the UDU (Union Démocratique Unioniste) and the RSP (Rassemblement Progressiste Socialiste) (1988), amnesty declared (1988), and, last but not least, a national pact binding political parties and civil society was signed (1989).

For some time, observers thought that Tunisia was making a transition from an authoritarian rule to a democratic system. They were all proved wrong. Ben Ali chose to govern with the ruling party, renamed the RCD (Rassemblement Constitutionnel Démocratique), in an extraordinary congress, held in 1988. Legislative elections demonstrated that nothing had really changed, as the RCD obtained 80 per cent of the votes and the totality of the seats in the National Assembly (141). The officially illegal, but tolerated, Islamic movement (the Mouvement de la Tendance Islamique becoming Annahdha) had 14 per cent of the votes and the liberal MDS party (Mouvement des Démocrates Sociaux), led by Ahmed Mistiri, former minister of the interior, had only 3 per cent of the votes. In order to remedy the hegemony of the single ruling party, which was subject to domestic and international criticism, the legal opposition was allowed to enter parliament for the first time, albeit in an insidious and even bizarre manner. Out of a total of 163 seats, 144 went to the RCD due to the system of election-on-a-majority-basis, while 19 seats were, by virtue of the law, reserved for the opposition and allotted proportionally to the number of votes at the national level. This proportion increased to about 20 in the legislative elections of 1999.

Despite cosmetic measures, "the ostensibly pluralising reforms put in place by Ben Ali actually appear to be making the ruling party's exercise of power more authoritarian" (Angrist, 1999: 91). In the meantime, two major events occurred. The first was the eradication of the Islamist movement. All of its militants were imprisoned, jailed, tortured and exiled. The second was a new constitutional reform (2002), reinforcing Ben Ali's grip on power by allowing him to stand indefinitely as a candidate in presidential elections (articles 39 and 40).

Bourguiba tried to proclaim a secularist regime in which Islam was by-passed, marginalised or taken over by the state in so far as the constitution stipulates that Islam is the religion of the state (article 1). For instance, Bourguiba outraged public opinion by encouraging people to stop fasting for the month of Ramadan, basing his argument on a historical precedent whereby fasting was interrupted during the Holy War. Economic development, Bourguiba argued, was the new form of *jihad*. He went as far as drinking a glass of water in a TV transmission during the fasting time. This triggered a conservative reaction, then an Islamist upsurge in the 1970s. Bourguiba's handling of this group swung between toleration (1970–1978 and 1980–1986) and repression (1979–1980 and 1986–1987). As for Ben Ali, he moved from toleration to eradication. Initially, he tried to contain them (1987–1991). For instance, he tolerated their activities, and allowed them to publish a weekly newspaper (*Al-Fajr*), but after the April 1989 legislative elections, he became afraid of their hypothetical electoral success in the following elections. Islamists, on the other hand, opted for confrontation, thinking they could overthrow the president with a popular revolt. During the second stage, eradication became a national policy (1991–2002).

Tunisian politics comes down to a good economic performance in iron hands. A stable regime, an almost *de facto* single party for more than 40 years, a cohesive homogenous and technocratic elite, facing a docile and weak opposition. Yet why has Tunisian politics remained unchanged for such a long period?

From Charismatic Leadership to a Corporate State

Bourguiba had a long reign from 1956 until he was deposed in November 1987 by the present president Ben Ali. This period was marked by a charismatic, personal and capricious leadership. Political crises were handled in a personal and authoritarian fashion. When rivalries arose within the state, between him and ministerial colleagues, he forced them to resign, or imprisoned them, after which he called them back, rewarded them for their silence and gave them new portfolios. However, when conflicts opposed the state to the society, harsh and violent solutions were the rule. In Tunisia, the state is stronger than the society. Tunisia, like Morocco, has always had the basic structures of a united state; this is not the case for the other North African countries.

What characterises Tunisian authoritarianism most is neo-corporatism. The term stands for an interest-representation system within which the state creates, recognises and allots the monopoly of socio-professional representation to a limited and hierarchically organised number of constitutive bodies. In return, these bodies act as a support for the state that dominates them (Chalmers, 1991: 59–81). The features of this neo-corporatism are the following: the first is the confusion, or the lack of a clear distinction between the structures of the party and those of the state; the second is the link between the electoral populism and the organisation of the electoral consultation; the third is the state–party–president control over the historical block of national organisations that have been in power for 40 years: the workers (UGTT), the industrialists and tradesmen (UTICA), the farmers (UNA), women (UNFT) and the youth (UTOJ). This thesis has again been brought up by Emma C. Murphy. Nevertheless, she is mistaken when she addresses the role of the army in Ben Ali's corporatism, which she calls a "government of soldiers and technocrats" (Murphy, 1999). The recent thesis of Stephen King, according to which the party, using the state as its vehicle, has merged into the urban middle class since the structural adjustment of 1986, is equally wrong (King, 1998: 59–86). The middle class in Tunisia remains weak. It is a *rentier* middle class that has been created by the state. Its structure is based on the family unit, and its standard enterprise is the small or medium-sized company. It is organised around the fragile UTICA (*L'union tunisienne de l'Industrie, du Commerce et de l'Artisat*), and its major fear is tax control (Bellin, 1991: 45–65). The Tunisian neo-corporatism is equally characterised by a selective and discriminatory pluralism. It is selective in the sense that the government chooses its opponents. The parties that were recognised before Ben Ali came to power were the Communist Party (1981), the MDS (*Mouvement des Démocrates Sociaux*) and the PUP (*Parti de l'Unité Populaire*). In 1988, the UDU (*Union Démocratique Unioniste*), the RSP (*Rassemblement Socialiste Progressiste*) and the PSL (*Parti Social Libéral*) were equally recognised. To this list was added the Democratic Forum in 2002. However, the rule which prevails in neo-corporatism for the granting of the management monopoly equally applies for the functioning of the parties. This means that, in case of internal conflicts, the government intervenes in favour of or against the secessionists. On the other hand, other movements like left-wing extremist parties and Islamists are outlawed.

Finally, corporatism is a movement that brings society under state control. This inevitably creates pockets of resistance from the bottom, which, in turn, causes a counter-mobilisation from the top. Economically, authoritative modernisation by means of bureaucratic capitalisation (1964–1969), made way, since the Nouira government (1971–1980), for the logic of the market (Camau, 1984: 8–38), but this was only a redeployment strategy of what Weber calls the "politically directed" economy. The situation is such that it could be argued that only the association agreement between Tunisia and the European Union (1995) could bring it to an end. The bringing of civil society under state control was consecrated by the promulgation of the 1959 law on associations, which is still effective in spite of the 1988 reorganisation schemes. Nonetheless, the civil society stood out in the 1970s against the three intervention attempts of the army in political life (1978, 1980 and 1984; Zghal, 1991: 208). State control over the feminine question was achieved by means of a state feminism that boasts the emancipation of women from the yoke of tradition thanks to the Code du Statut Personnel (1956). This, however, did not prevent women from objecting to it (Chekir, 2000).

The state control over religion hits at the basis of traditional Islam (the selling off of *waqfs*, the dissolution of *charaïc* courts and the weakening of popular Islam). It integrates the cultural socialisation institutions within the state machinery (the *mufti* of the Republic, the University of Zeitouna, the management of mosques and religious schools (Nouira, 2001). It creates new institutions, such as the Republic's Higher Islamic Council in April 1987 and the ministry for Religious Affairs in 1992 (Kerrou, 1998: 81–102; Fregosi, 1997: 103–123). This "caesaro-papism" has equally created a double radical resistance: an Islamist inflation against the attaturkist laicism of part of the democratic left (Al-Ahnaf, 1989).

The political exclusion of Islamism in Tunisian can be explained by the economic success of liberalisation, while its inclusion in other North African countries is due to difficulties in managing social constraints. One could say that "when the economic crisis is managed with relative success, political inclusion tends to be minimal, and when the crisis and the reforms worsen social and economic conditions, relative political inclusion become necessary" (Layachi, 2000: 15). Thus, the case of Tunisia totally validates the law-like generalisation according to which, when the economy is well managed, the state maintains its authoritarian politics. One must therefore wait for a profound crisis to see some changes in Tunisian politics.

Conclusion

Religion by itself is neither a favourable factor nor an obstacle to democratisation. It all depends on the existence of a genuine relationship between structural and cultural factors. Fundamentalism and radical Islam are recent phenomena from which North Africa was spared for some time. One has to take into account that the liberal, secular and democratic middle classes strongly believe that radical Islam is a threat and an anti-democratic alternative to the quasi-secular, albeit authoritarian, states. If they were to choose, some of them would prefer a pervasive secularity and a private security to religious political programs and collective anarchy. However, the linkage between normative behaviour and the interactive political game must lead protagonists, in a pedagogical manner, to a realistic deal between "hard liners" and "soft liners". That would result in a sort of limited and explicit "partial-inclusion pact" that would involve moderate Islamic trends upon the condition that they accept a modest and secondary role. Could the different protagonists, governments and parties, accept such a deal? (Zartman, 1992: 190; Sivan, 1997: 112). Mauritania and Morocco, following the lead of other countries (Egypt, Jordan, Yemen, Turkey), are moving in that direction. Algeria still has to struggle with political instability, stemming from the enormous confrontation between the Islamic movement FIS and the military that won independence from France – see Chapter 15.

How to choose between integration into the Arab world, into Africa or into Europe? While the Mashriq (Orient) seems to be self sufficient, the Maghreb is harassed by the search for unity with the Mashriq or Africa. The cases of Libya and Mauritania are more than noteworthy. Even the articles of the convention of the "Arab Maghreb Union" (UMA, 1989) make room for the membership of other Arab and African countries, but the future may be different. In fact, the European Union is now proposing to the 12 southern Mediterranean countries a new deal in the creation of a "free trade zone". Tunisia, Morocco and Algeria have already ratified the convention, unlimited in time, which stipulates in section B that, in return for assistance to reform their economies, the partners have to respect human rights and to encourage democracy as an integral part of the agreements. Could North Africa at the beginning of the twenty-first century escape from its "Eastern " destiny, or will it "chew over" its incapacity to stand for itself (*bei sich*): the Maghreb, sunset (*Abendland*) of the East and daybreak (*Morgenland*) of the West. The Maghreb is a distinctive part of the Arab world that perfectly mirrors the political dilemma of the Moslem civilisation today: on the one hand are the various forces of authoritarianism – traditional monarchy, military intervention and *coups*, unrestrained presidentialism and charismatic leadership. On the other there is the growing strength of salafism with its call for the Islamisation of society and government. Not even the most modernist country in the Arab world, Tunisia, having abolished polygamy and *qadi*-justice, has found a middle way between these two paths.

Chapter 15
Islamic Politics and the Military: Algeria 1962–2008

Riadh Sidaoui

Introduction

Algeria, with its population of some 35 million people, is a global player on the energy markets for oil and gas. The political development of the country after independence illustrates how religion may collide with a major secular force in many Muslim countries, namely the military. When such a collision occurs, then the prospects for democracy are slim indeed. The Islamic movement in Algeria before the confrontations with the army began in the 1970s and was mainly reform-oriented (Al-Ahnaf et al., 1991). The "Association of Reform Ulemas" worked for decolonisation, the Arab language and Islam. The *ulemas* had been supporting the FLN (National Liberation Front) in its struggle against France and the French community in Algeria, but at Independence Day in 1962 they were not willing to endorse Ben Bella's victorious formula: "Islamic Socialism". The association "Al Quiyam" proclaimed that nationalism should be combined with an Islamic society, built upon Sharia Law. Thus, the Algerian problem – *ulemas* contra military strongmen – emerged early and became quite conspicuous when army leader Boumedienne removed Ben Bella in a coup, promising to introduce a socialist economy in Algeria. The concern among older *ulemas* was private property, and the landowners started to support religious causes, attempting to halt the "agrarian revolution".

However, one cannot speak of radical or fundamentalist Islamic movements before the 1980s. Only in 1981 did the first violent action, orchestrated by radical Islam, take place in Algeria. This first attempt by an armed Islamic group, having armed itself in 10 regions of the country, was crushed in 1987 by the state and its leader put to death. Already in 1988 the attempt was materialising with the creation of the powerful Islamic Salvation Front in Algeria.

The background of the new organisation of radical Islamists was the attempt of the Algerian president to introduce democracy. President Benjedid made a number of reforms aiming at the separation of the state and the military. A democratic constitution was created in 1989, introducing multi-partism. The Islamists tried to form a broad-based Islamic party, but differences among the key personnel resulted in the formation of a smaller group, the FIS. Numerous groups of Islamists were forthcoming at the same time as a referendum legitimized the role of law constitution, but the FIS regarded itself as the leading "front" for completing the national revolution by introducing an Islamic state. The FIS immediately embarked upon electoral success, as it won almost half the commons and three-quarters of the villages in the municipal elections of 1990. The following year the FIS was strong enough to challenge the government by occupying key areas of Alger. The military intervened, suppressing the rebellion, but it was decided to hold general elections in 1992, despite the arrest of several FIS leaders.

Confronted by the electoral victories of FIS in the first round of the 1999 elections, the army staged a coup d'état, removing president Benjedid and cancelling the second round of elections. Thus, the confrontation between the Islamists and the military effectively killed of democracy in Algeria, setting the stage for a civil war that cost some 200,000 people their lives. The struggle between religious groups and one secular force, the army, is not unique to Algeria, but can be found in several Arab or Muslim countries. Which states were involved?

The FIS

From the outset the FIS included Islamists who had early engaged in armed struggle against the state, but the FIS also included mass support. One can distinguish between different layers of support.

Social Composition

The elite of the FIS is to a large extent composed of professionals: engineers, doctors, medical staff, etc. The dominance of scientifically trained people appears in the success of the FIS in the elections to the scientific councils in Algeria. The recruitment of large numbers of university-trained people into the FIS follows the general model in the Muslim world of Ph.D. + beard = young dynamic skilled people (Etienne, 1987). In Algeria, the FIS recruited its elite more from students in the non-theological faculties than those in religious schools. This was no doubt facilitated by the rapid expansion of higher education after Independence.

In Algeria, the new emerging elites, trained in various disciplines to help build the future of the country, found themselves blocked by the military. It kept its firm hand on power and state long after the FLN (National Liberation Movement) had achieved independence. The first generation of military was confronted by a second, well-trained generation, who looked for their share of state advantages. Frustrated by the army's grip on politics, they searched for a different approach, Islamic politics.

The middle classes in Algeria were caught in this confrontation between the army and the FIS. They divided their support between the protagonists according to the economic interests at stake. Thus, the small shopkeepers and peasants supported the FIS, whereas the upper bourgeoisie went for the army. Moreover, the bureaucracy had to take the side of the army, as any form of protest would result in the loss of their secure jobs. The adherence of the small businessmen to the FIS reflects the symbiosis between the state and the large enterprises in the Algerian economy, dominated by the energy sector.

Finally, there was the support among social groups with low income for the message of the FIS. There is a relationship between the voting support for the FIS and the level of unemployment, at least at the district level. Despite having an energy-based economy, Algeria suffers from very high rates of unemployment, in the 40 per cent range in several areas of the country. As often happens, the benefits of a petrol economy are not distributed to the lower income groups, which explains the link between unemployment and support for the FIS (Fontaine, 1992). Yet the support for FIS was in no way restricted to the groups left behind, as the FIS could draw upon votes from all kinds of social groups. Radical Islamic groups were actually on the move politically in several Muslim countries, following the defeats of the Arab world in the Israeli wars and the taking of power of the Shias in Iran. How does the ideology of the FIS compare with the currents of Islamic fundamentalism in other Muslim countries? Let us discuss how the FIS relates to the doctrines of the so-called radicals – the salafists – and the moderates – the *Djazaristes*.

Political Programme

Ali Belhadj is the key representative of the salafists. They refer to the medieval Ibn Taimiya and the contemporary Sayyid Qutb, whom Nasser imprisoned and executed, both looking into the past for a model of the future. They reject Western concepts of development as conducive to ignorance or deviation from the correct path of pristine Islam of the four Rightly Guided Caliphs. To get on the right classical track, the political leaders who are not obeying Sharia and are collaborating with the West may be removed through *jihad*, i.e. holy war. The fundamentalists aim at an Islamic state, although participation in democratic elections may be a means to that goal.

The modernists believe in the adaptation of Islam to Algerian realities, as they reject the import of radical Islam from for instance Egypt, Saudi Arabia or Iran. The Djazaristes connect to the struggle for Algerian independence, staying away from a universal concept of the *umma*. They search for an interpretation of the Koran that allows for modernisation on the basis of Algerian nationalism. The modernists strongly favoured participation in the democratic elections in 1991–1992, despite the arrest of leaders Abbassi Madani and Ali Benhadj. After the military coup, many modernists were arrested, although some managed to flee abroad to Europe, the United States and Canada, given the fact that they often had good professional training.

Lack of Charismatic Leadership

The FIS has had three major leaders: the moderate Abassi Madani, the fundamentalist Ali Benhadj and the modernist Abdelkader Hachani. Some look upon Madani as a charismatic leader, but this is debatable. His background was actually the FLN, to which he belonged from its creation in 1954. Although he had to stay in prison during the liberation war period (1959–1962), his support for political Islam did not go down well with either Ben Bella or Boumedienne. His organisation, the "Society of Values", was short-lived, as created in 1963 it was dissolved in 1970. In the 1980s, Madani activated himself within the FIS, again having to spend time in prison. When the FIS was at its peak of influence in 1991–1992, Madani's leadership was contested by the radical wing of the FIS, the Armed Islamic Groups (GIA). Today he cannot be considered the leader of FIS, which has dispersed into moderate and radical factions. The GIA does not accept his authority, for instance.

The second personality in the FIS hierarchy is the fundamentalist Ali Benhadj – called "The Number Two". Born in Tunis in 1956 and originating in southern Algeria, his education is basically religious. Being a professor in Arabian, he has studied theology with Sheikh Arbaoui, and he is well versed in Muslim law, both Sharia and comparative jurisprudence. As he was close to the Algerian Islamic Movement (MIA) of Mustapha Bouyali, he was imprisoned from 1983 to 1987. Together with others, he created actually the FIS and entered its governing board in the 1980s. On 25 June 1991, he called the Algerians to arms, which led again to a prison term.

Benhadj is in possession of a certain charismatic talent, his discourse being more poetic than rational. He has a capacity to mobilise the masses, being trained as an agitator in preaching in the mosques, like Al Sunna de Bab-el-Ouad and Ben Badis de Kouba. Benhadj is hardly an organisational man, as his message is simply salafism, i.e. mobilisation according to *jihad* and no *bidaa*, i.e. renovation.

The third person with power in the FIS was Abdelkader Hachani, who favoured Islamic modernisation and was prepared for compromise. He originated in Constantine and trained with the national petrol company of Algeria (Sonatrach). His father was active in the revolutionary organisation from which FLN emerged. Adhering to Djazara, Hachani was very active in promoting the participation of FIS in the national elections in 1991. He had to serve a long prison sentence during the 1990s, which left him in relation to the FIS more fundamentalist as a reaction to the repression of the state. In 1999, Hachani was assassinated by an Islamist from the GIA, which implied that one personality interested in conciliation with the strongman, president Bouteflika, was gone.

In fact, the FIS cannot deliver a charismatic leader, reflecting to some extent the difficulty of this Islamic movement in searching deep into the social roots of this country. In this regard, the FIS deviates from organisations in Muslim countries, where charismatic leaders have been forthcoming. In Algeria, there is a tradition against strongmen, buttressed by one the one hand the legacy of clan power typical of Arab society, and on the other the more recent experience of a modern revolutionary and egalitarian movement, the FLN. In this respect, there is a parallel between the FIS and the FLN, despite the first being religious and the second secular in orientation.

Early Success of the FIS

It is undeniable that the FIS scored massive support temporarily in the municipal and legislative elections of 1990 and 1991. One may also interpret the long civil war from 1992 to 2001 as indirect support for the FIS, because the army could not eradicate the Islamists despite the possession of massive resources of retaliation. How to account for the popular support for the Islamists?

In the 1990 municipal elections, the FIS took 850 of the 1500 communes in the country with a total majority of 59 per cent of the vote. The FLN only received 28 per cent of the votes, while at the same time 35 per cent boycotted the elections. This surprisingly large vote in favour of the FIS indicates that the regime faced a legitimation crisis, where a general call for change favoured the Islamists. Table 15.1 shows the election results.

Table 15.1 Algerian Municipal Elections in 1990

Party	Votes	Percentage
FIS	4331472	54.25
FLN	2245798	28.13
FFS	–	–
Independent	931278	11.66
RCD	166104	2.08
Others	310136	3.88

Note: FIS = Islamic Salvation Front; FLN = National Liberation Front; FFS = Socialist Forces Front; RCD = Rally for Culture and Democracy.

It is hardly surprising that the process of holding national elections in 1991 became tumultuous. The government decided to change the number of seats in Parliament, from 295 to 542, which it was hoped would favour the FLN. The FIS responded with a general strike, to which President Chadli reacted by declaring martial law and moving the elections ahead in time. The FIS declared *jihad* against the army, which led to the arrest of Madani and Benhadj, accused of conspiracy against the state. The national elections were finally held on 26 December 1991, with a surprising result in the first round of elections (Algeria used the French method of two rounds of elections). Table 15.2 shows the results.

Table 15.2 The 1991 National Elections

Party	Votes	Percentage
FIS	3260222	47.27
FLN	1612947	23.38
FFS	510661	7.4
Independent	309264	4.43
RCD	200264	2.9
Others	1004358	14.56
Hamas	386697	5.35
Small Parties	635761	9.21

Note: FIS = Islamic Salvation Front; FLN = National Liberation Front; FFS = Socialist Forces Front; RCD = Rally for Culture and Democracy.

One can interpret the outcomes in two ways. Either one interprets the victory of FIS as a defeat for democracy. Or one sees it as a confirmation of the wish of the population for more popular control over the distribution of the huge rent from the energy sector.

Table 15.3 The 1995 Presidential Elections

Eligible: 15261731		Percentage
Voters	11500209	75.4
Eliminated votes	347722	2.28
Zéroual	6834822	61.29
Nahnah	2907356	26.06
Sadi	996835	8.94
Boukrouh	413032	3.7

In the elections after the elections after the elimination of the second round in 1991, the support for the FLN increased. Thus, Table 15.3 shows the presidential elections in 1995. The victory of President Zéroual may be seen as a quest for stability among the Algerian people, favouring the role of the army over the attempt to establish an Islamic state. The decline in the proportion of abstentions may also be seen as a preference for law and order over the anarchy that could result from the dismantling of the FLN hegemony.

One observes in Table 15.3 the strong support for Mahfoud Nahnah, who received 26.6 per cent as the leader of the moderate Islamic movement, Hamas. In reality, Hamas captured a large portion of the support for the FIS in 1991, increasing from 386,697 votes to 2,900,000 votes in 1995. Thus, the Islamic support was in no way dead with the dissolution of the FIS by the military. This was confirmed in the legislative elections on 5 June 1997 – see Table 15.4.

Table 15.4 The Legislative Elections 1997

Parties	Seats
RND	156
Hamas	69
FLN	62
Nahda	34
FFS	20
RCD	19
Travailleurs	4
Independents	11

Note: RND = National Rally for Democracy; NAHDA = Islamic Renaissance Movement; FFS = Socialist Forces Front; RCD = Rally for Culture and Democracy.

The results indicate a profound reorientation of Algerian politics. The new party, RND – "Rassemblement National Démocratique" – scored a huge victory with President Zéroual, at the same time as the two Islamic parties, Hamas and Nahda, managed to score a strong presence in Parliament with 103 seats. The FLN changed its leadership in order to come out as supporting the regime. Thus, a coalition government was formed, comprising RND, Hamas and FLN. However, the FIS did not endorse these developments. Its voice abroad, *La Cause*, rejected these elections as illegitimate. Thus several articles in *La Cause* denounced these elections as masquerades in order to hide the real dictatorship of the military. Yet, it is clear that the elimination of the FIS had not wiped out the religious vote in Algeria. The moderate Islamic movements continued to be active openly, whereas the FIS had to go underground.

Tactics of FIS

The astonishing political mobilisation of the FIS reflects two circumstances: first FIS pursued a special tactic of political mobilisation; second, the FIS employed a discourse that fascinated the younger Algerian masses.

The FIS engaged in mass political mobilisation through several means. Fuller (1997) lists these tools of political mobilisation as education, economic support, targeting of municipal voting groups, the spreading of a clear and simple message and the build-up of a vast network of sympathisers, some of whom came from the FLN itself (Fuller, 1997: 73).

The tradition of Islamic teaching emerged in Algeria with the Association of the *Ulemas* in the 1930s. The domination of Arab-Islamic groups within the FLN led to an emphasis upon the Arabisation of culture and the integration of religion into all forms of education. It was in the 1980s that several Islamic networks appeared at the university faculties. Thus, public prayers were held on the university campuses, in gymnastics halls as well as in theatres. However, the appearance of Islamic movements in public places divided the opinion of the regime, as some like president Bendjedid endorsed it whereas others saw the politicization of the faculties as a threat to the state. Although it is true that the rise of Islamic groups in Algerian universities reduced the attraction of the left, it also started the new phenomenon of Islamic mobilisation besides the official avenues, like the Association of *Ulemas*. The young Islamists bypassed the traditional religious structure, having the courage to render their own interpretation of the Koran. Thus, they challenged the status of other authorities, including their parents, the regime and the sheiks, only relying upon a "revolutionary" approach to Islam and the Koran.

Several scholars and commentators have underlined the role of foreign financing of the FIS, but also other religious groups. The strong flow of money from Saudi Arabia began in 1980 in order to counteract the Iranian Revolution and limit its consequences, rejecting its claim to be the major paradigm for Islamic renewal.

The exact information about Saudi financial support to Islamists in Algeria is perhaps only known by the regimes' secret police. One is well aware, though, of the fact that Saudi money has been distributed broadly – confirmed by their daily paper in London: *Al Hayat*. It is also noteworthy that the Saudis started to favour moderate Islamic movements like Hamas ahead of the FIS, when the FIS came out in support of Iraq and Saddam Hussein in the first Gulf War. Yet the FIS could also draw upon local financing. Carlier (1992) argues that a considerable portion of the population participates in this, including newly rich people, workers, merchants and small entrepreneurs. This local pattern of financial support reflects the broad implantation of the FIS among various social strata.

The Algerian regime clamped down upon the financial support for FIS. Thus, the government contacted both Saudi Arabia and the United Arab Emirates, reminding them of the dangers for all Arab countries of Islamic fundamentalism. Locally, the Algerian authorities used the state power to grant licences for business as an effective tool of curbing local financial support for the FIS. Thus, they required that shopkeepers and independent entrepreneurs showed evidence of no link with the FIS.

The FIS never had its own television channel or a radio station. Not even a press outlet was in their possession, but the agitation and propaganda touched all of society. The principal mechanism of communication was access to the mosques.

By and by the government and its Ministry of Religious Affairs lost control over many religious establishments, especially when the rent from the energy sector was not distributed widely or in an egalitarian manner. FIS employed the strategy of always being present on the street, mobilising its militants every Friday for prayer, thus dominating the public space and the mosque.

In *Les Frères et la mosquée* (1990) Ahmed Rouadjia analysed how the FIS during the 1980s managed to mobilise a large number of firm adherents, acting from the mosques. It is estimated that the number of militants grew from 2000 at the ear of independence to around 11,000. Despite the law from 1971 that allowed the state to control the activities in the mosques, the Islamists occupied these places, using them for politicisation and mobilisation. First, the FIS constructed its own mosques, often financed by external charity. Second, the FIS made good use of the weakness of the state at the end of the 1980s, when the government hesitated to enforce the law giving it control of the mosques, their construction and activities. As the government-controlled media proved ineffective in relation to the strategy of the FIS of targeting the local street level, the regime changed its strategy, trying to isolate the activists from the mosques and appointing state-sanctioned imams, all helping in a continuous political surveillance of the local situation.

A key element in the strategy of FIS is the employment of networks in order to penetrate society. The Algerian researcher Aïssa Khelladi has presented a highly original idea about what united the militants of FIS. His argument is that the social link that unites the Muslim brothers is not to be found in tribalism but is based upon the locality. The members of the FIS tended to meet each other regularly in the mosques, which became the start of local interaction, as friends and sometimes resulting in marriages. Often these marriages were never rescinded by the state, as they remained only religious ones (Khelladi, 1995). Somewhat astonishingly, the Islamists decided during the victorious period of 1990 to legalise many of these marriages, which worked against them when the government later decided to clamp down upon the FIS in 1992. Actually, access to the information about the networks among the Muslim brothers (and sisters) helped greatly in the efforts of the secret police to arrest some 30,000 militants. Of course, this led the members of the FIS to change strategy when forming their networks (Khelladi, 1995).

The discourse of the FIS merits an analysis. It is based upon transmitting a very particular image of the Algerian regime. Let us pin down some of the key points in the propaganda of the FIS.

Spokesman Madani monopolises Islam in his discourse, repeating that "the people is us and we are the people, because it only recognises itself within Islam" (Al-Ahnaf et al., 1991: 341). Thus, the basic message is that only the FIS can be considered the legitimate representative of the Algerian people. At first this message went down well, as the FIS mobilised more and more support. Typical of the street-level tactics of the FIS is to put blame on people who refuse to follow the ideal of an Islamic state, being "the only road to salvation for all the levels of the Algerian people" (Al-Ahnaf et al., 1991: 32).

The propulsion of the FIS was very explicit, as it tried to put itself in the shoes of the FLN, the Algerian liberation movement that had become more and more ossified with the years. An expert states:

> By adopting the unifying language of the liberation movement, the FIS attempted to impose a hegemonic discourse, cancelling out the ossified message of the FLN and the regime, and bypassing the multitude of new parties that emerged around 1990. (Al-Ahnaf et al., 1991: 32)

Can one then say that FIS had a complete and well-defined program? In fact, Madani had a simplistic diagnosis of the crisis of the Algerian society as well as a superficial set of remedies. The basic idea is that, contrary to Western ideologies, radical Islam perfectly unites religion, conscience and science (Madani, 1989: 26). The official programme of the FIS – 38 pages long – does not analyse political questions at any length. Instead, it focuses upon economic and social matters. The political message targets the position of the military, calling for the elimination of despotism through the application of Islamic Shura. Yet Madani underlines the importance of the respecting the electoral law in order to have free and fair elections. Moreover, the discourse of FIS is characterised by the Manichean opposites: good–bad, positive–negative, etc., almost as if FIS had adopted the political theory of Carl Schmitt: friend–enemy. The FIS looks upon politics as the mobilisation of compact groups in terms of a perspective of display of force (Mos'ad, 1994: 156). One may say that FIS was confronted with a hiatus between its simple religious ideals and a complex socio-economic reality. Its response was to engage in forceful mobilisation on the one hand and to stress on the other hand the respect for rule of law and the rights of all to political opposition. Let us exemplify the contradictions in the propaganda of the FIS.

In relation to democracy, the FIS like other salafists look upon this political regime as a tool for conquering power, only to abandon it immediately afterwards, because democracy does not flow from the divine law (Sharia). For Benhadj, for instance, the value of democracy is purely instrumental, i.e. it is good as long as it promotes the end of an Islamic state. He is quoted as saying in 1989 (23 February) that:

> multipartism is unacceptable because it is the result of an occidental vision … There is no real democracy, as the sole source of power is Allah and the Koran, not the people. If the electorate votes against the law of God, then that is nothing else but blasphemy. If this happens, one must kill the false believers. (Lacoste, 1995: 10)

For the so-called Jazaristes, this same democracy constitutes a noble end and a real objective when it truly expresses the wishes of the people.

The Algerian researcher Lahouari Addi does not believe that there was a strong democratic hand in the FIS. He looked upon the double language of FIS as reflecting the deep contradiction that the Islamic movement had to experience as its support started to increase dramatically:

> on the one hand, democracy with FIS was an expression of the masses having a say in the political process of Algerian, but on the other hand, FIS did not have the ideological means to make this aspiration concrete. (Addi, 1992: 68)

This type of discourse, sometimes rational, sometimes tactical, is criticised by the authors of the book Algeria according to its Islamists (Al-Ahnaf et al., 1991), who interpret the propaganda of FIS as purely a matter of tactics. Their argument is simply that, when the FIS arrives in power one day, it will turn around and abolish democracy. They state:

> on the basis of the written propaganda of the FIS, it is permissible to suppose the legalism of this movement is mostly a temporary phenomenon. (Al Ahnaf et al., 1991: 85)

Thus, if the first stage of democratic power ascension would work, then in the second stage there would be the strong diffusion of a discourse embracing all society, tempered only by the Islamic version of weak representation, the shura (Al-Ahnaf et al., 1991: 85). One could perhaps argue that the ambiguity of the FIS towards democracy reflected splits within this broad based popular movement. Yet it is more correct to interpret it as a tactically motivated double language.

One important aspect of the discourse of the Islamic movements, like for instance the FIS, consists of the mobilisation of the masses against the Occident, or Western countries. The defeat of the Arabs in the Six-Day-War contributed strongly to nourishing this discourse. The sense of overwhelming force on the part of Western powers and Israel was made ever more credible by the 1973 war and the war in Lebanon. The first Gulf War split the Arabs as how to react to Western interference (Madani, 1989: 20).

The Algerian regime, condemned to counteract the FIS on all sides, found itself caught in a dilemma vis-à-vis the occidental image of the FIS. On the one hand, the diabolisation of the Occident was actually a key feature of the propaganda of the FLN. One may recall that Algeria during the 1960s and 1970s presented itself as the anti-imperialist bastion, at least in official discourse. The Algerian regime supported socialist liberation movements around the world, and invited many times the leaders of Third World countries to visit the country, as a token of its ambition to assemble a united front against the Occident.

One may find reminiscences of the strong anti-imperialist position with the FLN also with the present government. It does not hesitate to launch support campaigns against Western neo-colonialism, although this message has become more and more toned down. In the 1990s, for instance, this message was thrown at the international organisations and NGOs when they pressed the regime to conduct enquiries into the massacres and atrocities that were typical of the Algerian civil war. Thus, one could claim that the FIS took over a propaganda theme already well elaborated by the FLN.

However, this message is not easy to manipulate, as contradictions may arise. The FIS on the other hand often searched for support from the international community, such as Amnesty International, as the state repression rolled slowly but mercilessly over its members. Similarly, the present coalition government between FLN and Hamas often appeals to the West in order to obtain support when terrorist groups strike.

One may reflect somewhat more upon the strategy of the FIS of inviting foreign support, despite its anti-occidental message. Let us mention Mostafa Hamza, writing in *La Cause*:

> The assassinations seem to replace the arrests. This is the conclusion of the most recent reports from Amnesty International … Amnesty notes the grave fact that the number of executions by the security forces extrajuridically has increased. (Hamza, 1995)

La Cause looked for the support of leading occidental intellectuals, such as Pierre Guillard, publishing his article "FIS, a democratic party" (Guillard, 1993). An article by Pierre Rossi, who was the general secretary of the European Association of Human Rights, was also published, stating a similar message (Rossi, 1995: 1 September).

The French intellectual François Burgat presented himself as the defender of the "just" cause of FIS in his article, published in *La Cause*. Burgat was interviewed in *La Cause*, providing him an opportunity to attack the FLN and express his sympathy with the FIS (*La Cause*, 30 September 1994). One may, however, turn the tables and ask why the Algerian regime had to employ such fierce repression in order to eliminate the FIS.

It is well known that the Algerian state is in the possession of a very solid police apparatus as well as considerable secret police with a good reputation (Lacoste, 1995: 7). To understand why the crack-down upon FIS became so bloody and difficult for the regime, one can point to both subjective and objective factors. First, among the subjective factors there were:

1. A culture of resistance and fighting with the Algerians since the liberation war against the French had fostered heroism and martyrism. The FIS could draw to some extent upon the same culture as that of the FLN.
2. The direct impact of the emergence of global Islamic fighters – *mujahedeens*, coming out of the Iranian revolution and the Afghan war against the Soviet Union.

In addition, one may point to objective factors, which somehow are linked to the above-mentioned subjective ones. Thus we have:

3. The territory of Algeria is no doubt very large. The north of the country is characterised by mountains and forests, which make this part suitable for guerrilla operations. Just remember that France during its Algerian war put some 500,000 men into action but failed to defeat the FLN guerrilla, far inferior in numbers and equipment In the south of the country there is vast desert, where the villages are also difficult to survey in detail.
4. The Algerian army, just like the French one, was not trained or equipped for guerrilla-type warfare. It took considerable time for it to adapt and develop a strategy toward the FIS, which went underground.

Repression of the FIS

According to C. Tilly, there exist several types of state repression. The government may directly target the leaders of the revolutionary movement. Or it may indirectly try to weaken it, for instance by spreading disorder in the organisation or preventing it from using its resources (Markov, 1986). One may say that the Algerian regime and its military embarked upon all three strategies.

The arrival of President Zéroual at the summit of the Algerian state marked two important changes. First and foremost, he was instrumental in consolidating the state, its institutional framework as well as the adaptation of the army to the civil war with the FIS. In reality, the army was not prepared for the guerrilla warfare that ensued after the annulations of the second and decisive round of elections. Second, the FIS started facing mounting difficulties in keeping its organisation with the many networks intact, politically and militarily. Together these two changes transformed the situation, weakening the possibility of an Islamic revolution recurring in Algeria. From 1995 and onwards the new strategy of the military bore its fruits, although the human cost turn out to be ghastly.

The Algerian army proved more and more effective in counteracting the Islamic movements, launching vast cleansing operations and destroying the bases of the FIS. The army includes some 180,000 men and constitutes an effective combat force, because it can quickly call up reserves prolong the term of military service. In addition, the state is in possession of a 60,000 man-strong special force, recruited from the police and the army (Boularès, 1995: 192). During the years 1992–1995 the army operated in a traditional manner, with tanks and heavy equipment, as it was trained by the Soviet advisers. This may have worked when it came to dissuading Morocco in the border tensions between the two countries, but it was ineffective against armed Islamists using urban guerrilla tactics. Thus, the army suffered losses in relation to the mobile and lightly equipped Islamic *mujahidins* (De Salies, 1997).

From 1995, the army could employ two complementary operations. The first was the traditional heavy clamp down with heavy equipment. The second was the subtle employment of sudden and secret small-sized operations, all the time harassing the Islamic groups in a variety of ways. This combination proved too strong for the FIS, and it collapsed at grassroots level.

The number of men in the local guards was increased from 15,000 in 1995 to 100,000 in 1997. These local guards could prevent the Islamists from regrouping due to their detailed local knowledge. The guards were trained by the army and were highly instrumental in cutting the links between FIS and the local population.

In addition to the new local guards, there was a new second type of threat, the groups for self-defence. In 1997, it was decided that the regional prefect could create such groups with the permission of the security forces and after demand from the local population. These self-defence forces grew rapidly in numbers, reaching about 100,000 men in 1997 (De Salies, 1997). They were coordinated through an agency in the Ministry of the Interior.

This massive build-up of armed forces besides the regular army did not go unnoticed. Thus, the democratic opposition accused the regime of a "privatisation of the civil war", claiming that they were very active in the tragic mass slaughter of innocent people that became typical of the Algerian civil war. In essence, these guards and self-defence groups made it even more urgent to demand rule of law in Algeria, as some of these forces could operate any opposition group and even seize ordinary people's property.

After 1995, the losses for the Armed Islamic Groups (GIA) started mounting. The hard-liners were mostly killed whereas the others accepted the offer of "*rahma*" or clemency, introduced in 1995. Today, the Islamists live under difficult conditions, as they cannot mobilise support any longer.

It must be emphasised that the methods of repression employed by the regime met with protests from the international organisations working for the respect of human rights. The association Reporters sans Frontières published the book *Le livre noir de l'Algérie* in 1995, and later in 1996. The Committee of the Militants for Human Dignity and Human Rights published *Le livre blanc sur la repression en Algérie (1991–1995)*. Both these books condemned the repression, presenting information about the numbers killed, tortured and harassed.

Besides the violent repression against the rank and file of the FIS, the regime attempted to split the fundamentalist movement into two factions, the GIA and the AIS (Armée Islamique de Salut). Actually, this effort met with success, as the AIS under the command of Madani Mazreg, operating in the western and eastern parts of Algeria, declared a unilateral peace with the army on 1 October 1997. He was given grace by president Bouteflika on 10 January 2000, which took place at the same time as the AIS was dissolved.

It may be pointed out that the FIS groups who lived abroad also experienced this major split. Thus, Rabah Kebir, operating in Germany, was favourable to the peace whereas United States-based Anwar Haddam rejected it. In Algeria, it seems that the adherents of FIS began to align behind the Nahnah. There were also some permanent people in the FIS who rallied behind the regime, such as Ahmed Marrani, Ben Azzouz Zebda, Saïd Guechi, Elhachemi Sahnouni and Béchir Feqih. The Algerian regime managed to integrate FIS leaders into the state approaches, like ministries or the Council of the Nation, resulting in a severe loss in the leadership capacity of the FIS. Given the total state occupation of the political space in Algeria and the severe repression, it is hardly surprising that the defections from the FIS became numerous. Yet, the regime did not eliminate entirely the armed Islamists. Even today there is a constant threat of violent actions in Algeria.

Explaining the Failure of Political Islam

How, then, to explain the failure of the FIS to take control over the state approaches? One may point to the reliance on both internal and external factors.

First, among the internal factors one must mention the strengthening of the position of the Algerian regime, especially with the election of President Zéroual. To the strategy of his government of on the one hand favouring the Islamic moderates and on the other hand eliminating the Islamic fundamentalists, the FIS had no reply. French historian Yves Lacoste has underlined how complex the links, positive or negative, are between the Algerian state and the Islamic networks (Lacoste, 1995).

Faced with this double tactics from the Algerian regime and the military, the FIS published a letter in *La Cause*:

> Brothers, men of Islam in Algeria, we live in a period of estrangement from the reality of the Message. This led us to examine our errors like those of others, and work for reconciliation as much as possible, by adopting the principles of coalition, patience and magnanimous gesture, tolerating opinions that we may find surprising. It could be the case that a counter-opinion to ours is founded upon a validity that we have missed. Allah has declared: You have only been given a little bit of knowledge. (*La Cause*, 1994: vol. 1, no. 6, 30 September)

As a matter of fact, the support of the government for Hamas meant that the rug was pulled from under the feet of the FIS. Thus, the leader of FIS, Mahfoud Nahnah, came in as number 2 in the presidential elections of 1995 with a strong 25 per cent of the votes. Hamas then entered the government with seven ministers. The same strategy included a third Islamic movement, the Nahda, and its president, Abdallah Jaballah, although with less enthusiasm from the government. As a consequence, the FIS was cut off from its popular support in its earlier vast network.

Among the domestic conditions that reduced the capacity of FIS to take action for its ideal of an Islamic state one must mention the repression with various types of armed forces, including some 200,000 in local militias besides the regular army.

One may also wish to point out that the Algerian military did not hesitate to support the regime against the Islamists. The homogeneous support of the army for the regime reflects its FLN legacy. Algeria belongs to these countries where the military is widely considered as providing the cement of the state, which is not uncommon in the Arab world.

It is impossible to analyse the confrontation in Algeria between the state and the Muslim Brotherhood without taking into account the economic rent from the energy sector. The enormous resources derived from the selling of oil and gas on the world market helped the regime when setting up its guards and strengthening the military. This rent stabilised the regime, financing the conflict with Islamists and enhancing the homogeneity in the ruling elite, anxious to protect its vested interests.

The Algerian economy is extremely dependent upon the energy revenues. It is also volatile due to constant inflation pressures. It seems that the economy started to do better in the second half of the 1990s with the rate of economic growth improving while the rate of inflation decreased. The external balance of the country began to show considerable surpluses, with the Bank of Algeria announcing consequently large dollar asset holdings. Let us quote an expert from the IMF:

> President Zéroual had every reason to keep a straight political course during those years, refusing all compromises. The economic upturn contributed to the isolation of the Islamic movement from the rest of society. (Ellyas, 1997)

In reality, the Algerian economy was reinvigorated not only because of a higher petrol price. The economy was being better managed with less corruption and red tape in the state bureaucracy and a reduction of the accumulated state debt.

One may mention that the revenues from oil and gas climbed to some $10 billion between January and June 2000, which amounted to double that in 1999. The energy company, Sonatrac, could deliver substantial resources to the state coffers. Some 90 per cent of Algerian oil is for export, and although the country is especially rich in gas, its petrol exports amounted to more than 1.5 million barrels/day in 2000. When in 2006 and 2007 the oil price skyrocketed, the Algerian regime found itself in an extremely fortunate position. The minister for Energy and Mining, Chakib Khelil, declared to the AFP in 2006:

> The total value of oil exports from 2000 to 2006 reached the level of 204 billion dollars, where 45 billion dollars were the revenues for the first ten months of 2006. The export of oil has increased from 124 million tons (TEP) in 2000 to 145 million tons (TEP) in 2005, constituting a 17 per cent increase. (AFP, 19 November 2006)

One may conclude that Algeria benefited exceptionally not only from the global energy shortages but also from increasing efficiency in its state-controlled energy-producing sector. This could not be without political implications.

Among the external conditions that were disfavourable for the FIS one must count the growing international hostility towards salafism, or Islamic fundamentalism. This holds not only for the occidental powers, but also for most of the Arab states.

France supported the Algerian regime when it collided with the Islamic fundamentalists, although hardly taking a coherent stand during the early stages of the conflict. It was only when the socialist government was replaced by the Balladur government with Charles Pasqua as the head of the Ministry of Interior that France began to back the Algerian regime strongly. The position of the new president, Chirac, was no less favourable to the Algerian government (Provost, 1996). For France, the Algerian crisis had to be placed into the international fight against terrorism and the Islamic networks, which explains the high general support of some 4 billion francs to Algeria during 1996–1998 (Provost, 1996). France restricted visas to Algerians, helped the country to produce or provide essential goods, and restricted comments upon the Algerian situation (Provost, 1996).

The French assistance met with a fierce reaction on the part of GIA, and counter-operations against French people in Algeria were initiated in 1993, involving killings, the taking of hostages and the destruction of property. There were armed attacks also on French territory, but the most spectacular event was the execution of seven nuns in 1996 in the Algerian region of Médéa and the assassination of the bishop of Oran on 1 August the same year. The FIS used its press to wage war against France:

> The Algerian people is at war! For the second time since 1 November 1954 it is in arms against the oppression. It has taken up arms in order to complete its independence which France has tried to suppress to the very last hour. (Moufdi Belgacem in *La Cause*, vol. 1, no. 2, 4 November 1994)

Mostafa Hamza published an article "What does France want?" in *La Cause*. He asked whether the support for the government meant that France sought to maintain its presence, its language domination and its economic interests. Or perhaps France dreamed about cutting up Algeria into parts, as it had in 1930. He claimed emphatically:

> The army and repressive forces have received not only support but also advanced materials from France in order to fight the Islamists. (Hamza, *La Cause*, vol. 1, no. 9, 18 November 1994)

One finds several articles in *La Cause* with similar accusations against France. There is an exception, however, namely Abdelhamid Ibrahimi, earlier prime minister under the president Bendjedid. Although he was not a militant for the FIS, he argued that "the best help France could provide Algeria would be to leave its democracy develop its free course so that the Algerian people could elect the leader the people had confidence in". Moreover, he stated:

> the economic help that France speaks about is not for Algeria but to help Algerians buy French products. As a matter of fact, France has created a network of contacts in both the Algerian state and the army based upon corruption and illegal operations. (*La Cause*, vol. 1, no. 5, 16 September 1994)

The United States took a negative stance against the FIS. In May 1994, President Clinton declared that the enemies were extremisms and oppression and not Islam, but in 1995, Washington and Paris had come to the same position concerning Algeria, both countries supporting the so-called Saint-Egidio Platform, like Germany (St John, 1996). Step by step, the United States improved its relations with the Algerian government. The same attitude was found with the UK and German governments, who opted for a policy of restraining the possibility of the Algerian Islamists operating from their territories. The EU decided at the end of 1994 to increase the economic assistance to Algeria to the sum of 5.5 billion Ecus for five years, to be compared with the 7.5 billion promised for Eastern Europe (St John, 1996).

As a result, the relationships between the FIS and the Western powers deteriorated. The Islamists, including the moderates, orchestrated on their side a media campaign against the Occident. Mohamed Iqbal, for instance, accused several countries in *La Cause* of opposing change in Algeria, even democratic change (*La Cause*, vol. 2, no. 20, 9 June 1995).

> On our side, we believe that the Occident should balance its arrogance and act prudently so that this conflict does not result in a clash between civilisations.

Moreover, *La Cause* rejected all forms of external assistance to the generals in Alger: "As we have many times declared in our columns, the help in various forms from some European countries to the repression in Algeria becomes more and more concrete" (*La Cause*, vol. 3, no. 24, 4 August 1995).

The terrorist attacks on 11 September 2001 led to a complete break between the Islamists in the Arab world and the Occident, especially the United States. The intelligence services in the Western countries turned to the Algerian state in order to receive information about presumed terrorists, and the Algerian government declared that it was prepared to enter an American-led coalition against terrorism (*Le Matin*, 20 September 2001). In fact, the Algerian regime benefited from 11 September by becoming an acceptable partner to Western governments. Thus, the UK government sent its undersecretary for foreign affairs to Alger: "The main aim of this visit was to lay the foundations for the construction of an international solidarity after the attacks" (*Le Matin*, 25 September 2001). Undersecretary Bradshaw declared in Alger: "We are from now on in the same boat". Nicolas Sarkozy, at that time mayor for the RPR regretted during his visit to Alger: "that Algeria finds itself alone in the fight against this scourge acting in a very important strategic zone" (*Le Matin*, 30 September 2001). He went so far as to say that: "France and the other European countries have acted so as to overshadow the danger from these networks" (*Le Matin*, 30 September 2001). President Bush signed a decision to freeze the property of terrorists, among whom he counted the GIA and the GSPC in Algeria. The result of the cooperation of the intelligence agencies in the West and the Algerian government was that the leaders of FIS outside of Algeria were under surveillance with the risk of arrest. As a global police campaign was launched against the extreme Islamists, Alger became a vital source of information for all countries in this campaign. One may say that the events of 11 September led to the final victory of the regime over the FIS everywhere.

The majority of the Arab states took a position in favour of the Algerian regime. Tunisia and Egypt were the most ardent supporters in the region, on the belief that a victory for the Algerian regime would significantly reduce the Islamic threat that had existed for a long time in their own countries. Libya and Morocco were the exceptions, as Libya had supported the FIS up until the end of October 1995 while Morocco behaved inimically towards the Algerian regime from the start of its confrontation with the FIS. Colonel Gaddafi manifested the sympathy of Libya for the FIS early in the 1990s, especially for its two main leaders: Abassi Madani and Ali Benhadj. These two were invited to Tripoli and prayed behind Gaddafi, which was much exploited by the Libyan television for its own propaganda purposes. As Algeria accused Libya of housing Algerian Islamists, training them and sending them back over the border, the tension between these two countries increased step by step. However, the 15 October 1995 marked a fundamental change on the side of official Libya. The GICL – Fighting Islamic Group in Libya – claimed responsibility for bloody attacks in Benghazi, Libya's second largest city, some months before. Gaddafi started a new policy of prevention after this, and collaborated closely with the Algerian intelligence agents in order to eliminate the Islamists in Libya (*Ouazani*, 23 June 1998).

The animosity of Morocco towards Algeria started with the so-called War of the Dunes in 1963. The support of Algeria for Polisario, demanding the independence of Moroccan Sahara, could only increase the hostility between the two countries. Morocco began to use the FIS as a way to get revenge, although its support stayed a secret affair. The ex-minister for defence, Khaled Nezzar, published an article in the newspaper *El Watan* with the title "The game of the king", where he accused Hassan II of Morocco of delivering logistical support to the GIA (Nezzar, 2 February 1998). Yet, with exception of Morocco, the Algerian regime received backing from all Arab countries. It was Tunisia and Egypt that provided the most assistance when it came to security.

The Algerian islamists, conscious of the massive support officially from the West and the Arab regimes in favour of the Algerian government, could do nothing other than try to strengthen their domestic propaganda in order to mobilise the "Muslim youth in Algeria" in the civil war. Thus, *La Cause* published an "open letter to the young Muslims in Algeria", stating:

> It is certainly true that you are not confronted with a local or regional confrontation, but you are more party to a total war declared by numerous local

> and international actors who would like to see the defeat of the Muslims in their search for self-determination. These groups all have an interest in such a defeat, without any major sacrifice on their part, taking place in a war of brother against brother, attracting the youth by an intelligent war of words that will ultimately result in the employment of arms. (*La Cause*, vol. 1, no. 6, 30 September1994)

Conclusion

The support of most Arab regimes for the Algerian government could be explained with reference to their self-interests. A victory for the Muslim Brotherhood in Algeria would have political consequences for all Arab states. Thus, they were eager to recognise the positive impact of the Algerian military upon the entire region. Tunisia was the first country to express comfort from the success of the Algerian clamp down. Morocco was more ambivalent, but in this country hostile to Algeria there was also relief on the part of the authorities.

Actually, the lessons from the Algerian confrontations between state and religion, secularisation and salafism, were quickly drawn in Morocco. Thus, on the one hand, the Moroccan regime, moderately modernising the country albeit underlining the king as "commandeur des croyants", seems to have decided to clamp down upon the Islamists, if they pose a serious threat. On the other hand, the Islamists in Morocco learned from Algeria that an open confrontation with the Moroccan regime could be a most costly and unsuccessful path. The Moroccan Islamists underlined instead "Islamisation from beneath", putting the emphasis upon charity and the promotion of solidarity, bypassing a direct confrontation with the king. In Egypt as well, the Muslim Brotherhood as well as other Islamic groups backed down from an explicit political strategy of creating an Islamic state, favouring "Islamisation from beneath".

Perhaps, one may venture to say that all radical Islamic groups in the world were affected by the Algerian civil war and its dismal outcome for the hopes of an Islamic state. On the domestic front, the Islamists in several Arab countries toned down their radicalism. Some of them even pledged international support of the NGOs by adhering to Amnesty or Reporters sans Frontières, the Socialist International or the European left. For the internal development in Arab countries the outcome of the confrontation between the Algerian military and the FIS played a more important role than global Islam and Al Qaida.

Epilogue

The Muslim societies confront today the challenges of a post-modern society. The crucial question is whether these countries can combine their religion with the two key sets of institutions of post-modernity: the market economy and the rule of law or human rights. We suggest a cautiously optimistic answer, but such a developmental path is only one of several future scenarios. Islamic fundamentalism pushes these countries in another direction. The Muslim civilisation has shown that it can accommodate the postmodern society in countries like Tunisia, Morocco Mali, Senegal, Bangladesh, Malaysia and India with its giant Muslim minority. However, post-modernity is hardly accepted in several other Muslim countries where the threat of Islamisation is all the time present. Several future roads of development are possible in the future for different Muslim countries. The key challenge comes from politics and not economics, as Weber believed.

Chapter 16
Islam – *A Religion of Warriors?*

Introduction

The Moslems, making up a population of more than 1 billion globally, face unprecedented challenges to their civilisation, as the politics of several Muslim countries experience, to a greater or lesser degree, either internal or external turmoil, if not violence or war. Political conflicts derive their strength either from *fitna*, meaning internal divisions among Moslems, or from external sources, such as foreign intervention like in Iraq and Afghanistan.

External Intervention

The second Iraq war was conducted with rapidity in the spring of 2003 by the American army supported by the UK but also backed by Spain. It was in many ways different from the first Iraq war or the Gulf war. We cannot go into a detailed analysis of the legitimacy of the second Iraq war, which presents serious questions from the perspective of Public International Law. Here we shall deal only with the consequences for the Muslim civilisation in general and for the Arab civilisation in particular.

Two extreme interpretations of the invasion of Iraq or the liberation from Saddam Hussein come to mind. On the one hand one may argue that the second Iraq war is basically a rerun of the Western conquest and domination of Arabia in step with the demise of the Ottoman Empire or an enlargement of the American involvement in the Persian Gulf, replacing the British after the Second World War. This is the neo-colonialism interpretation. What speaks against it is the official motivation for the entire project *Iraqi Freedom*, which is to remove an authoritarian regime and make it possible for a large Arab country to embark upon economic and political modernisation. However, motivation is one thing but outcomes constitute something else. One intention may very well have been to remove a brutal dictatorship, but it remains an open question whether the Americans will succeed in introducing democracy in Iraq, or a stable government at all in this society, fragmented as it is along both ethnic and religious fault lines. In addition, the costs to the Iraqi people have become so huge that even the benefits from the introduction of human rights could not outweigh them.

On the other hand, the second Iraq war may not merely be the completion of the first Iraq war, when for some reason or other Saddam Hussein was not removed – a mistake supposedly corrected in 2003. The intention may be for the Muslim world to embark upon a path towards modernisation and democracy, the liberation of Iraq being the first country in a long-term evolution bringing the countries with Islam into agreement with post-modernity. Successful regime change in Iraq would entail that the impossible has become feasible, namely that democracy and human rights can operate in a Muslim country. If Iraq becomes democratic, then why should other countries such as Tunisia, Egypt or Pakistan not follow suit? The liberation interpretation would be in agreement with American history in the twentieth century, doing for Iraq something similar to what was handed down to the Germans and the Japanese after the Second World War.

Is either of these two extreme interpretations true? Or is the reality to be found somewhere in between liberation and neo-colonialism? The evaluation of the second Iraq war is a complex business, where *ex-ante* considerations mix with *ex-post* considerations. *Ex-ante*, the case for invasion appears very weak, using the norms laid down in Public International Law as the benchmark criteria. Strictly speaking, war may be resorted to only in self-defence or as part of collective defence against an attack, *de facto* or imminent. Since the United Nations did not authorise the invasion, the argument of collective defence has little validity, especially if one considers the likely French, German and Russian veto of the invasion. No link between al-Qaeda and Saddam Hussein has been proved, which would have legitimised the United States invading by itself. Thus, the argument about self-defence appears equally weak, especially when it has proved impossible to find any weapons of mass destruction after the invasion.

The argument about hidden motives, mainly oil and future petrol revenues, would support the neo-colonialism thesis, but is it really true? The monetary costs of the second Iraq war have become so burdensome for the United States that they constitute a threat to the economic stability of the country. It is better to pay for the petrol than to make war in order to steal it. It is difficult to tell what the basic motivation was, as the intentions change from one group to another as well as over time. What is crucial from the perspective of this volume – the modernisation of the Muslim civilisation – is how the American occupation of Iraq is looked upon by Arabs and other Muslims. As the resistance against the occupation authority increased and large-scale terrorism on an ever increasing scale in and around Iraq emerged, the belief that regime change in Iraq would set off a democratic snowball in the Muslim civilisation was grimly falsified. From the *ex-post* perspective, the American–British occupation of Iraq will have to be evaluated negatively: the second Iraq war has not enhanced the position of human rights and democracy in the Muslim world. It is impossible to predict the outcome of an American withdrawal from Iraq. There is no chain reaction in the Muslim world, calling for the acceptance all over the Muslim world of the political notions of post-modernity, such as rule of law and human rights. The second Iraq war in contradistinction to the first Iraq war has reinforced the hostility between the civilisations and plunged the Middle East into even worse turmoil. In general, Muslims tend to regard the United States with distrust, expressing once again occidental superiority towards the "orientals", especially in the mastery of warfare. A majority of Muslims would probably have preferred the French approach in the Security Council, that is, multi-lateralism.

At the same time, several groups in Iraq have welcomed the removal of Saddam Hussein and his oppressive regime, especially the Kurds in the North and the Shias in the South. The probability that the new government in Baghdad will succeed in introducing a stable democratic and federal polity in the country, given its strong ethnic and religious divisions, is not high. The sufferings of the Iraqi population, especially in the capital area, are enormous, with huge numbers of people having been killed or maimed. It is difficult to foresee a stable Iraq once the Americans have left, as the Kurdish question will automatically become highly politicised, given the interests of Turkey in the region, at the same time that any balance between Sunnis and Shias will be tipped in favour of the latter, given the close presence of Iran.

The Afghan war is unravelling with greater and greater intensity, as the government of Afghanistan with the help of NATO faces stiff Taliban insurgency. The Afghan war is very different from the Second Iraq War, as it is not problem from the standpoint of legitimacy or international justice. The United States can claim that the 9/11 attack on the country was related to the Taliban regime harbouring al-Qaeda within Afghanistan. Whether Bin Laden and his associates still live secluded in the area is not known, but it is not unlikely. Yet, the Afghan war like the second Iraq war has made an imprint upon Muslim affairs, increasing violence like shockwaves from its epicentre. Thus, the Afghan war destabilises first and foremost Pakistan. With growing Taliban strength, the *mujahidin* is back.

The Afghan guerrillas fighting the Russians in the twentieth century and the Americans, Europeans and Australians in the twenty-first century resemble the tribesmen who fought the British in the late nineteenth century. Crude leather sandals in traditional Afghan pattern complement their baggy trousers and over-jackets. The brown waistcoat, worn under the blue sash and musette bag, seems standard for the guerrilla forces. Small arms like the AK47 are in considerable demand, home-made adaptations of factory models often being used, such as the bolt-action rifle. The whereabouts of Afghanistan's exiled Taliban leaders are not fully known. Some have been captured and detained by US forces as enemy combatants in the "war on terror". Many of the Taliban were able to melt back into predominantly Pashtun areas of Afghanistan in the south and east. Some are working to overthrow the current government. Many others have reassembled in neighboring Pakistan, where the Taliban movement was born, and launch attacks from there. Beginning in mid-2006, the Afghan Taliban stepped up its attacks on coalition forces, with fighters adapting Iraq-like suicide and roadside bombing tactics. Uruzgan, Helmand, Kandahar and Zabol Provinces in the east and south – regions that NATO forces have been responsible for securing since 31 July 2006 – saw some of the fiercest clashes. The resurgence in fighting has sparked debate about whether it is driven by frustration with the Karzai government or Taliban intimidation. For its part, the Afghan government asserts that the spike in attacks is the result of Pakistan providing the Taliban with a safe haven across the border.

Inexperienced younger leaders have been radicalized by al-Qaeda. Yet not all former Taliban members have joined this fight. Many heeded a call by President Karzai to disarm and have assumed normal lives as members of Afghan society. Some even won seats in the September 2005 parliamentary election, including the former Taliban governor of Bamiyan province, who was in office when the Bamiyan Buddhas were destroyed.

Given the size of Afghanistan as well as the huge numbers of people in both Afghanistan (31 million) and Pakistan (170 million), the prediction about the possibility of introducing political stability and democracy in the country must be gloomy. The obvious question for NATO is how long it will stay in the country, fighting a war that has no "natural" end in sight, as the *mujahidins* will most probably never give up. In order to avoid a serious deterioration, the NATO would have to increase its presence in the country, which may not be easily accepted back home, as the struggle with the *mujahidins* drags out.

An outside call for the democratisation of the Muslim civilisation is culture-blind, as it is a task for the Moslems themselves to decide upon how they wish to be governed. Westerners may in general argue in favour of the introduction of rule of law and human rights into Muslim countries, asking in particular for the protection of religious freedom in Muslim countries with large Christian or other minorities. Yet the employment of military force of Western powers against "oriental" states or governments must always be based upon the principles of Public International Law. The call for democracy, however attractive it may be, does *not* trump the Law of Peoples or legitimise invasions of dictatorships, all other things being equal.

Is it really true as Amin Saikal states in his *Islam and the West: Conflict or Cooperation* (2003) that the American–British invasion of Iraq has led to a situation where the modernisation of the Muslim civilisation is from now on linked with its international relations, especially to the United States (Sakal, 2003: 142–143)? The invasion runs a high risk of being counterproductive, fuelling terrorism in Iraq and abroad. Sakal suggests that the Americans and the British should hand over power to some Iraqi administration, but how could it function? A more credible alternative is to call in the United Nations on a broad front, although time is running out for that. The problem is that the forces of "evil" in Iraq may have gained such momentum that a Western retreat would soon lead to a new authoritarian regime. Sakal is right in arguing that Muslim civilisation must continue its struggle to come to grips with democracy and its implications for a post-modern society.

Internal Divisions

The externally induced conflicts in the Muslim civilisation such as in Iraq and in Afghanistan are one challenge, but even more consequential is the deepening of tensions within the Muslim community between various sects, religious groupings and political organisations. *Fitna* is an Arabic word referring to schism, secession, upheaval and anarchy at once. It is often used to refer to civil war, disagreement and division within Islam. The term originally referred to the refining of metal to remove dross, but became common in apocalyptic writings, where it referred to the first Islamic civil war, in 656–661 AD, a prolonged struggle for the caliphate after the 656 assassination of the Caliph Uthman, resulting in the Sunni–Shia split. A second *fitna* is usually identified as the 683–685 AD conflict among the Umayyads for control of the caliphate, whereas the third refers to the battle among principalities (*taifas*) at the end of the Caliph of Córdoba's rule.

A few Koranic translations demonstrate some of the confusion this term has engendered:

> So fight them until there is no more disbelief (*fitnah*) and all submit to the religion of Allah alone. (8:39)

> And fight with them until there is no more persecution (*fitnah*) and religion should be only for Allah. (8:39)

"Fitnah" means test and the "test" is for the Muslims not for the disbelievers or any other non-Muslim group (http://en.wikipedia.org/wiki/Fitna_%28word%29).

The concept of the *fitna* targets a core problem in the Muslim civilisation (Kepel, 2004). As the above note on the history of the concept shows, *fitna* has always been typical of Islam. This basic heterogeneity of the Muslim civilisation is fundamentally at odds with the strong emphasis upon homogeneity among the contending Moslem groups. The Muslim civilisation is and has been ever since the first *fitna* after the death of the Prophet fragmented into religious sects, legal schools, ethnic groupings, tribal communities, competing clans and, in the twentieth century, also secular groupings like nationalist or socialist parties. However monolithic Islam may appear, forcing its impression upon all aspects of the ways of life of Moslems, the Muslim civilisation is replete with strong divisions.

First, the Muslim civilisation harbours strong tensions among the two major sects, the Sunnis and the Shias. Although the Shias only dominate numerically in Iran, they constitute strong minorities in several countries, especially when one recognises that there are several Shia communities besides Iran. Second, the Muslim civilisation is divided between modernists and fundamentalists, albeit it is impossible to count their exact numbers. The fundamentalists are organised in different groups: the Muslim Brotherhood, al-Qaeda, etc. Third, the Muslim countries face not only religious divisions but also ethnic ones. Thus, Turkey for instance has Sunnis, Alawites and the Kurds. Finally, many Muslim countries, especially the Arab ones, are tribal societies where Islam has not been able to fully replace clan linkages.

When the troubled external relations mix with the internal divisions, then Weber's characterisation of Islam as a religion of warriors retains its relevance, although it is very one-sided. To Weber, Muslim inferiority was expressed in weak economic performance and had its basic root cause in the religion of

Mohammed, which was at odds with the requirements of modern capitalism. Nothing prevents other civilisations copying Western achievements, however, and modern capitalism has conquered Muslim civilisation almost to same the extent as Buddhist civilisation. Weber's thesis is no longer relevant, as globalisation has put a single market economy in place.

Islam does not have nearly as many sects and divisions as Christianity, but there are a few major ones. The two biggest are the Sunnis and the Shiites, with the Sunnis being the largest of all and representing the vast majority of Muslims. Shiites are a minority everywhere except Iran. After them, the two most influential sects are the Sufis and the Wahhabis. The Sufis represent a long-standing mystical tradition in Islam, whereas the Wahhabis are strict traditionalists dominant on the Arabian peninsula. Unlike churches, mosques are not denominational. Despite the differences among Muslims, traditional Friday prayer services are largely similar and Muslims of any background are welcome to attend services at any mosque. Sunnis are considered the "orthodox" believers, following the most traditional beliefs and actions.

Over time, Shiism became the largest non-Sunni sect in Islam. Sufism developed the spiritual and mystical aspects of Islam in contrast to the mainstream. An early Shia sect – the Ismailis – split from the main group because of a dispute over who should be considered the next imam. Formed by Zaid, a grandson of Husain, the Zaidis believed that the true Imam must publicly assert his claim to the title and seek to overthrow the corrupt regime run by unacceptable rulers. The Fatimids are a successor movement to the Ismailis and are descendants of Fatima and Ali through the line of Ismail. In the tenth century, those descendants asserted themselves as caliphs in North Africa, and ruled Egypt from 969 to 1171. Another sect – the Nizaris – is well known around the world, but under a different name: the Assassins. Also known as Nusayris, the Alawis are a branch of Ismailism that has gone so far along its own path that many Muslims no longer even regard it as a form of Islam. The term Alawis actually just means "followers of Ali", which is used to refer to all kinds of Shia. The Druzes comprise another sect that is not widely regarded as being "truly" Muslim. This group diverged from mainstream Islam in the eleventh century when some Ismailis started to believe that God became manifest in the personality of a prophet or imam. Bahai is another movement which is descended from Islam, but which most Muslims today no longer regard as authentically Islamic.

Sufism is the mystical orientation inside Sunni Islam. A person who belongs to Sufism is called a Sufi. Nearly all Sufis are men. Sufism's aim is to gain a closer connection to God and higher knowledge by communal ceremonies, where trance is widely used. Today there are fewer Sufis; some estimates run at less than 5 million in the whole Muslim world. Sufism's strongest footholds are now in Egypt and Sudan. Sufism got its content and its rituals from inside Islam, but it also picked up elements from older religious practices. Sufism developed gradually in the first centuries of Islam, but there is little proof of real Sufism before 800 CE (about 200 H). Sufism has been a practice mainly among ordinary peoples, and often performed without much consent from the religious elite. The core of Sufism is to leave the ordinary life, in order to close down the distance to God. By reducing the distance between man and God, man also gets closer to truth and knowledge. Few Sufis will claim that they can reach all they way to God, but knowledge and insight increase the closer one manages to get. Techniques vary, but they have three things in common: rhythm, repetition and endurance. The actual technique can be utterance of words or phrases, singing and dancing. There is little to find in the Koran to sustain the tradition of Sufism, and therefore Sufism have normally had major problems being accepted by the religious as well as the learned elite. Sufism has faced problems surviving during the modernisation processes that have taken place in most of the Muslim world.

Muhammad ibn Abd al-Wahhab could be considered the first modern Islamic fundamentalist. He made the central point of his reform movement the idea that absolutely every idea added to Islam after the third century of the Muslim era was false and should be eliminated. Wahhabism is an ultra-conservative, puritanical Muslim movement adhering to the Hanbalite law, although it regards itself as *ghair muquallidin*, non-adherent to parties, but defending truth. It arose in Najd in the Arabian peninsula during the eighteenth century. Its founder, Muhammad ibn Abd al-Wahhab (1703–1787) found a champion in the tribal leader Muhammad ibn Saud of the Dariya region, and from then on the Saudis became the main supporters of the movement. They believe that the Muslims have abandoned their faith in God (*tawhid*) and have distorted Islam through innovations (*bida*) which run counter to pure Islam. The Wahhabis accept only the Koran and the authentic Sunna, and all Muslims who do not accept their creed are regarded as heretics, especially the Shia, who are considered as archenemies of Islam. During the nineteenth century, the Wahhabis in alliance with the Saud family began to expand territorially. Within the new kingdom of Saudi Arabia, the Wahhabis became dominant in conservative control, introducing *mutawwi'un*, "enforcers of obedience", a kind of private religious police, monitoring not only public but also private conformity to Islam.

Islam and Politics: Three Problems

Can democracy and human rights be introduced from *OBEN* in an Arab country or a Muslim society? The failure of creating democracy from *UNTEN* in Muslim societies does not increase the probability that democracy from above or from the outside will be more successful. Beside the Islamic fundamentalists, there are other groups that are hesitant about external intervention into Arab affairs or a Muslim community. It is not only a matter of nationalism, as with the Baath Party, but also simply pride. The Islamic fundamentalists have managed to stage a slow but increasing movement of protest and resistance against American involvement in Iraq. This has turned into anarchy with breakdown of law and order, from which a new dictatorship will follow in due course. It is difficult to see any tenable American strategy against such a development towards unending violence and political turmoil. The opportunity, on the other hand, is clearly there for a Muslim country and an Arab society to show that democracy is a promising set of institutions for handling communal conflicts. One can turn the tables and claim that only democracy can secure religious peace and ethnic stability in Iraq. If democracy works in Iraq, then it may be imported into more Muslim countries.

The Muslim civilisation is going through a period of turbulence both inside its countries and in its external relations with countries from other civilisations. Often there is bloodshed, as the occurrence of political violence takes ever more innocent victims. In our view, this tremor reflects three basic problems within the Muslim civilisation, which relate to the consequences for state and society of its religion, Islam. These three problems have always characterised politics in Muslim countries, but the emergence of Islamic terrorism on a global scale has made them more acute and difficult to resolve. They are:

1. The nature of political leadership: religious, secular or both – the caliphate problem. Many Muslim countries had reached an acceptance of the principle of a secular state, although recognising Islam as the religion of the country. However, Islamic fundamentalism does not accept the secular state calling for the radical Islamisation of government or even the recreation of the caliphate in some form or another.
2. The nature of the religious community: homogenous or heterogeneous – the *umma* problem. The Muslim civilisation has always been split into different communities, be they sects, schools or brotherhoods. Besides all the various kinds of Alawites – followers of Ali – there is Wahhabism, Sufism and the various schools of *figh* or jurisprudence. However, Islamic fundamentalism rejects the implication of tolerance and advocates the employment of *jihad* to arrive at a religiously compact community.
3. The nature of the religious elite – the *ulema* and the *mufti*. In several Muslim countries, the religious elite plays a major political role, negating the principle of state neutrality in relation to religious matters. Only in Iran can the *ulema* be said to be the rulers, but the influence of the *ulema* and the *mufti* is so considerable even in countries with secular states that they can block any advances in secularisation. At the same time, the religious elite may easily be used by government for its own purposes, as the *ulema* and the *mufti* are not independent of the state. The sheiks directing the Friday gatherings in the mosques are public employees.

How the Muslim countries resolve these three problems will be decisive for their internal stability as well as for their external relations to their neighbours. There will be a variety of solutions to these three problems depending upon country legacies and external influence. The amount of secularisation arrived at as well as the amount of heterogeneity accepted will not be the same in the Mahgreb, the Middle East, South Asia or Far East Asia, as country-specific factors as well as different colonial legacies play a role in how these problems are handled. Yet, there is nothing in the basics of Islam, the Koran, that negates the possibility of a secular government and a tolerant community. The Ottoman Empire arrived at one such trade-off between politics and religion as well as endorsing heterogeneity among its *millets*. Compared with the Gulf states, Malaysia today displays a promising trade-off allowing for secular government and considerable tolerance among communities. The outcomes for the new Iraq are impossible to predict, but political stability will only come about if the principles of a secular federal state and tolerance among the communities are accepted. However, there is the ever present threat of Islamic fundamentalism – a phenomenon of the twentieth century.

Colonialism and its Legacy

It is astonishing that Weber did not mention the strong colonial grip of the Western powers upon Muslim countries at the time he was enquiring into the consequences of religion, especially that of Europe upon the Arab world. Colonialism as the driving force of Islamic fundamentalism is an argument that one often finds with Arab scholars. It is developed to its maximum with François Burgat (2003, 2008). He lists the number of years of foreign domination as: Algeria, 1930–1962; UAE, 1892/1916–1971; Egypt, 1882–1936; Iraq, 1920–1932; Jordan, 1922–1946; Kuwait, 1899–1961; Lebanon, 1920–1946; Libya, 1912–1951; Morocco, 1911–1956; Mauritania, 1907–1960; Sudan, 1898–1956; Syria, 1920–1946; Tunisia, 1881–1956; and Yemen, 1839–1937. One could also count the years of foreign domination of major non-Arab Muslim countries including India–Pakistan–Bangladesh, Malaysia and Indonesia. However, this argument puts too much emphasis upon the historical legacy. To understand the frustration of Muslim civilisation with the world today and the forces of globalisation, one needs to explain why Muslim civilisation is performing worse than the other major civilisations, on an economic as well as on a political level. We suggest that traditionalism in the Muslim civilisation is a stronger factor than colonialism, especially today when colonialism is a thing of the past.

The problem of the political modernisation of Muslim civilisation is, however, much more difficult to resolve than the withdrawal of the foreign troops from Iraq. The first step is to put in place and enforce daily the rule of law. The second step, which will take much longer, is to achieve a multi-party system where political competition is fully endorsed. It would be a major advance if several Muslim countries could take the first step in the coming decade, viz. the introduction of rule of law. This would entail Muslim countries coming to grips with the difficulty of reconciling religion with the doctrine of human rights. It is, we argue, not impossible.

The major question is now whether all the civilisations of the world will endorse the core of political post-modernity, that is, human rights and the rule of law. If the thesis of this book is true, namely that the retardation of the Muslim civilisation is more due to traditionalism than to Islam in itself, then the liberation argument could work. Yet, the combination of outside intervention and inside dissent propels a radical interpretation of Islam, reinforcing fundamentalism. The emergence of radical Islam, or Islamic fundamentalism, amounts to a most spectacular story, with enormous implications for both domestic and international relations in the many Moslem countries (Roy, 2007; Kepel, 2000, 2004).

Fundamentalism: *Fitna* and *Jihad*

The solution to the problem of accommodating Islam to modernity is not so much found in the resistance of Islam to the market economy which Weber emphasised. The problem lies elsewhere, namely in the opposition between a fundamentalist interpretation of Islam with the salafists and the universal recognition of human rights. Thus, Islam must be interpreted in such a way that it accepts the basic principles of mankind. We believe that such an interpretation is not only possible, but also that there are Arab scholars who attempted this a long time ago, starting with the great philosophers of medieval Islam. Thus, rationalism and Islam are not irreconcilable and people who adhere to the message of the Koran can at the same time fully accept the requirements of rule of law and universal human rights. We predict that Arab societies will in this century accept a trade-off between Islam and democracy just as they accepted the market economy in the late nineteenth and early twentieth centuries. Our message is basically an optimistic one despite the events of 9/11, since we are convinced that Islamic fundamentalism is not the core message of the Koran. To understand the emergence of Islamic fundamentalism and its new doctrine about *jihad* we will look at a few of the key personalities behind the movement: Mawdudi, Qutb and Faraj.

Throughout the history of Muslim civilization, charismatic leaders have arisen attempting to renew the fervour and identity of Muslims, purify the faith from accretions and corrupt religious practices, and reinstate the pristine Islam of the Prophet Mohammed's day. Leaders of revivals tended to appear either as renewers of the faith promised at the start of each century (*mujaddids*), or as the deliverer sent by God in the end of times to establish the final kingdom of justice and peace (*mahdi*). In modern times, a new wave of revival was initiated by the Muslim Brotherhood in Egypt, the main grassroots movement that emerged in response to the modern crisis in the Arab world. When Egypt faced the challenges of decolonialism, modernisation and a massive population explosion, the Muslim Brotherhood began calling for a return to the original fundamentals of Islam. Suppressed by Nasser in the mid-1950s, underlining socialism and nationalism rather than Islam as Egypt's main identity marker, the Muslim Brotherhood re-emerged during the Sadat era (1970–1981). Radical Islamic societies (*jama'at*) emerged out of the Muslim Brotherhood, drawing on the thought of its main ideologue, Sayyid Qutb, who endorsed a violent takeover of power. Qutb's reinterpretation of several key Islamic concepts inspired some to split off from the Brotherhood and use his writings to legitimise violence against the regime. He argued that the existing society and government were not Muslim but rather dominated by "pagan ignorance" (*jahiliyyah*). The duty of righteous Muslims was to bring about God's sovereignty (*hakimmiyya*) over society, denounce the unbelief (*takfir*) of the current national leaders, and carry out a holy struggle (*jihad*) against them.

Al-Banna, Hasan (1906–1949) founded the Muslim Brotherhood in Egypt in 1928. Under his leadership it soon became the best organised and largest political group in Egypt with branches in other Muslim countries. Al-Banna was a pragmatic and charismatic leader, as well as an exceptional public speaker and skilful organiser. Hasan al-Banna received an elementary religious education as well as state primary school. He was associated for a while with the Hasafiya Sufi order, and in 1923 started studying at a teacher's training college in Cairo, from which he graduated in 1927. He was then appointed as an Arabic language teacher at a primary school. Al-Banna was disturbed by the rapid Westernisation and secularisation of Egyptian society and preached a return to the sources of Islam and a rejection of foreign currents. He founded the Muslim Brotherhood in order to purify Islam and combat foreign domination. He sought to re-Islamise the masses as a step towards the establishment of a comprehensive Muslim order in an Islamic state. With the growth of the Brotherhood, Al-Banna became involved in national politics. In 1936 he sent a letter to King Farouk, the prime minister, and other Arab leaders, encouraging them to promote an Islamic order. Al-Banna was assassinated in 1949 by the government after the military arm of the Brotherhood was implicated in some political assassinations against the colonial administration.

A number of factors led to the proliferation of radical groups since the 1970s in Egypt and across the Muslim world. Islamic fundamentalism was a response to the impact of modernity, Western encroachment, misrule by the national elite, and massive economic and social dislocations. The result was a crisis of identity and a search for authenticity. The oil boom enhanced the power of Saudi Arabia and channelled much financial aid to militant groups, encouraging their growth. The 1973 war against Israel and the accompanying oil embargo against the West as well as the 1979 Iranian revolution further fuelled radical zeal. President Anwar Sadat encouraged the development of Islamicist societies (*jama'at Islamiyya*) as a counterweight to the Nasserist dominated professorial associations and student unions. These societies extended their influence through a network of educational and social services at a time when government services had collapsed in the face of economic crisis and rapid increases in the number of students and the overall population. The Islamic societies, offering identity and community as well as social welfare, became a recruiting field for the revolutionary radicals. During the 1970s there was a dramatic rise in the number of independent private (*ahli*) mosques, not controlled by the government, that provided a safe meeting point for militants and recruits.

All religions attempt to maintain their areas of domination, as they attempt to guard their own borders to other religions. Thus, they fear proselytism or mission or conversion campaigns by other religions, the occurrence of apostasy among their own adherents as well as the emergence of schisms or dogmatic splits within their own ranks. All the world religions have reacted with violence against these three threats. Perhaps the posture of Islam is the least open or tolerant in these matters. In the Muslim civilisation marriage, for instance, entails that a women adhering to another religion than Islam converts to the same religion as her husband. It is not difficult to find within the Koran very strong admonitions against proselytism, apostasy and schisms. The emergence of global Islamic terrorism may have a disastrous impact not only upon the countries targeted but also upon the Muslin countries themselves. As we have seen, Weber put the concept of *jihad* at the centre of Islam in his short historical analysis of the fate of this religion with the Prophet and after him. Several Muslim scholars would deny the correctness of Weber's theory of Islam as a religion of warriors, pointing to the fundamental fact that Islam has five fundamental duties, which do not include *jihad* (Otto, 1996). All the world religions have been conducive to the occurrence of large scale violence and political conflict. And all of them have developed forms of fundamentalism that are violent in the twentieth century (Juergensmeyer, 2001).

Two things should be underlined when speaking about the concept of *jihad* in the Muslim civilisation: first, *Jihad* as a core element in Islam is a concept that was launched in the twentieth century; second, *Jihad* within Islamic fundamentalism presents two different aspects: (i) violence against foreign intrusion in the Muslim civilisation; and (ii) violence towards internal sources of secularisation within the Muslim societies. Mawdudi, Abul 'Ala' (1903–1979), was the greatest architect of the contemporary Islamic revival, considered by many to be the most outstanding Islamic thinker and writer of our time. Mawdudi was influenced by Hasan al-Banna and the Egyptian Muslim Brotherhood. He founded the *Jama'at-i-Islami* movement in 1941 in the Indian sub-continent, an extremely well-organised association committed to the establishment of an Islamic world order that has played an important role in the politics of Pakistan, India, Bangladesh and other South-East Asian countries.

Fundamentalism in India: The *Deobandi* School

For Mawdudi the *Jama'at* was an elite vanguard of the Islamic revival and revolution, working for a gradual appropriation of power in the state. Mawdudi wrote many books, including a six-volume *Tafhimul Qur'an* (*Understanding the Quran*), published in 1972, which impacted Muslims all over the world, as well as *Towards Understanding Islam*, *Let Us be Muslims*, *Way to the Qur'an* and *The Islamic Movement*. Mawdudi was born in Aurangabad in south India and grew up in a traditionally religious family. He studied traditional Islam as a young man, then acquired a Western modern education on his own. He was involved in the *Khilafat* movement between 1921–1924, hoping to preserve the Ottoman Caliphate. Later he tried to revive Islam as the sole answer to the Muslim communal problem in India. Mawdudi began his public career as a journalist, a career he was involved in for many years. He left journalism in 1927 for literary and historical pursuits. In 1933 he assumed editorship of *Tarjuman al-Quran*, which became a vehicle for the propagation of his thought. In the early 1920s he studied with Abdusallam Niyazi in Delhi and later with the *Deobandi ulema* at Fatihpuri mosque's seminary, also in Delhi. He moved to Hyderabad, the last remaining Muslim enclave in India, in 1928 to lead the Muslim community there. Mawdudi was opposed to the secularist nationalist Muslim League led by Jinnah, but on the formation of independent Pakistan he emigrated there, hoping to influence a change from being merely a state for Muslims to an Islamic state. His political involvement and criticism of government policies, as well as his anti-*Ahmadiya* agitation, led to his imprisonment in 1953, but the death sentence passed was never carried out. Mawdudi saw Islam as threatened by a wave of Westernisation. He criticised the West and the Westernised Muslim elites as degenerate, and he called for a renewal and purification of Islam. He conceived of true Islam as a total comprehensive system and ideology, incorporating society, politics and the state. Mawdudi differentiated sharply between *jahiliyyah,* which included most contemporary Mulsim societies, and true Islam. His goal was an ideological Islamic state based on God's sovereignty (*hakimiyya*) and on Sharia. As an explanation for the decline of Muslim power, Mawdudi concluded that diversity was the culprit: the centuries old practice of interfaith mixing had weakened and watered down Muslim thought and practice in that region of India. The solution was to purge Islam of all alien elements and social and political ties with Hindus must be severed. Non-Muslims, for Mawdudi, were *ipso facto* a threat to Muslims and to Islam and must be contained by restricting their rights. Mawdudi and others founded the *Jama'at al-Islami* Party in Lahore, Pakistan in 1941. Mawdudi based his call to arms against those who reject Islam on Sura 2: 190–193 from the Koran and on the Hadith, "I have been ordered to fight people (*al-nas*) until they say 'There is no God but God'. If they say it, they have protected their blood, their wealth from me. Their recompense is with God".

Mawdudi envisioned a particular set of institutions for his ideal Islamic state. An Islamic state will have a President, an elected *shura* council (consisting only of Muslims who have been elected solely by Muslim suffrage), an independent judiciary and a cabinet formed by a Prime Minister. *Dhimmis* (non-Muslims living under Muslim protection) have the right to vote in lower-level (i.e. municipal) elections. They have the right to serve on municipal councils and in other local organisations, but not to serve in the larger, overarching administrative units that deal with what he calls the "system of life" (*nizam al-haya*). Mawdudi's goal was to wage *jihad* until the whole natural universe has been brought under the rule of Islam, as quoted here from *Jihad in Classical and Modern Islam* (1996):

> Islam wants the whole earth and does not content itself with only a part thereof. It wants and requires the entire inhabited world. It does not want this in order that one nation dominates the earth and monopolizes its sources of wealth, after having taken them away from one or more other nations. Islam requires the earth in order that the human race altogether can enjoy the concept and practical program of human happiness, by means of which God has honoured Islam and put it above the other religions and laws. In order to realize this lofty desire, Islam employs all forces and means that can be employed for bringing about a universal all embracing revolution sparing no efforts for the achievement of his supreme objective. This far-reaching struggle that continuously exhausts all forces and this employment of all possible means are called *Jihad*. (Peters, 1996: 128)

Modern Fundamentalism in Egypt

"Holy terror" is a term for "holy assassination" in the Middle East, applicable to the assassinations of Sadat and Rabin. The assassins of Sadat were guided by Muhammad Abd al Salam Faraj (1954–1982) and his booklet, *The Neglected Duty*, to violent behaviour. Faraj arrived at this *jihad* (holy war) duty by considering and rejecting non-violent options: participation in benevolent societies; obedience to God, education, abundance of acts of devotion, and occupation with the quest of knowledge; exerting oneself in order to obtain an important position; and democratic options such as engaging in civil liberties such as freedom of speech, the founding of a political party to compete freely with other parties in elections, and the creation of a broad base of support resulting in majority rule. Faraj believed that none of these would lead to the messianic goal of establishing of an Islamic state and ultimately reintroducing the caliphate.

The two Egyptian radical groups, the Society of Muslims (*Takfir wal-Hijra*) and the Society of Struggle (*Jama'at al-Jihad*) espoused drastically different ideologies and strategies for gaining power. The Society of Muslims (*takfir*) had a passive separatist and messianic ideology, delaying active confrontation with the state to an indefinite point in the future when it could reach a certain degree of strength. In comparison, the Society of Struggle (*al-Jihad*) followed an activist, militant ideology that committed it to immediate and violent action against the regime.

The Saudi Arabian city of Medina is known in the Muslim world as *Dar al-hijra*, the first place of refuge. In Islamic teachings, Medina is traditionally where the persecuted of Islam withdraw to begin again and return in triumph to the unbelieving lands through *jihad*. The Muslim calendar begins with the *hijra*, Mohammed's flight from Mecca to Medina in 622 AD to avoid death at the hands of "infidels" who denounced his teachings. The word *hijra* literally represents the emigration of a Muslim from hostile surroundings to a supportive population from which a *mujhidin* will then plan and regroup to launch *jihad*. It is Mohammed's *hijra* to Medina that is considered the pivotal and most sacred event in Islamic history. The spiritual manifesto of al-Qaeda, *The Neglected Duty*, by Faraj, placed enormous emphasis on the importance of the *hijra* component to a *jihad*. Al-Qaeda transplanting itself from the "hostile" lands of its origin to the supportive confines of Taliban Afghanistan was clearly a form of *hijra*. Allowing al-Qaeda terrorists to return to Medina, Mohammed's chosen place of refuge, provides a close parallel between their lives and that of Mohammed. Such a vital symbolic connection may enable a new generation of terrorist lieutenants to validate their claim to leadership by emulating the early trials and tribulations of Mohammed.

Sayyid Qutb (1906–1966) was an Egyptian and as a member of the Muslim Brotherhood, a prominent Islamist figure whose career spanned the middle decades of the century. His thought, deeply influenced by Mawdudi's revolutionary radicalism, falls into two distinct periods: that which occurred before President Nasser detained him in a concentration camp for political enemies (he was eventually executed in 1966), and that which emerged during the period of his internment. The first excerpt comes from an early work, *Social Justice in Islam*, which he wrote in 1949, translated by John B. Hardie (New York: Octagon Books, 1970: 19, 49, 66). Qutb builds on the Islamic idea of *tawhid* (the singularity of God and, therefore, of the universe):

> So all creation issuing as it does from one absolute, universal, and active Will, forms an all-embracing unity in which each individual part is in harmonious order with the remainder … Thus, then, all creation is a unity comprising different parts; it has a common origin, a common providence and purpose, because it was produced by a single, absolute, and comprehensive Will … So the universe cannot be hostile to life, or to man; nor can "Nature" in our modern phrase be held to be antagonistic to man, opposed to him, or striving against him. Rather she is a friend whose purposes are one with those of life and of mankind. And the task of living beings is not to contend with Nature, for they have grown up in her bosom, and she and they together form a part of the single universe which proceeds from the single will.

In 1964, Qutb, having suffered torture as well as 10 years of incarceration in Nasser's concentration camps, published perhaps his best known work, *Milestones* (*Ma'alim fi'l Tariq*), a work that has inspired some of the more extreme expressions of Islamic revivalism, such as *Islamic Jihad* and *Takfir wa-l Hijra*. Qutb's concept of *jahiliyyah* ("pagan ignorance") was deeply influenced by his unpleasant experience living in the United States from 1948 until 1951. He had been sent to the United States to study American educational institutions. Qutb was deeply offended by the racism he observed (and experienced first-hand) and was scandalised by the openness between the sexes in American society. In *Milestones* he wrote (Beirut: The Holy Koran Publishing House, 1980: 7–15, 286):

> If we look at the sources and foundations of modern ways of living, it becomes clear that the whole world is steeped in *Jahiliyyah* (pagan ignorance of divine guidance), and all the marvellous material comforts and high-level inventions do not diminish this Ignorance. This Jahiliyyah is based on rebellion against God's sovereignty on earth: It transfers to man one of the greatest attributes of God, namely sovereignty, and makes some men lords over others. It is now not in that simple and primitive form of the ancient Jahiliyyah, but takes the form of claiming that the right to create values, to legislate rules of collective behavior, and to choose any way of life rests with men, without regard to what God has prescribed. The result of this rebellion against the authority of God is the oppression of His creatures.

The Islamic civilisation can take various forms in its material and organisational structure, but the principles and values on which it is based are eternal and unchangeable. These are: the worship of God alone, the foundation of human relationships on the belief in the Unity of God, the supremacy of the humanity of man over material things, the development of human values and the control of animalistic desires, respect for the family, the assumption of the vice regency of God on earth according to His guidance and instruction, and in all affairs of this vice-regency, the rule of God's law (Sharia) and the way of life prescribed by Him.

Qutb could be considered the main ideologue of the Muslim Brotherhood in Egypt, one of the most widely read Islamic writers whose works have been translated from Arabic into many other languages. Qutb was born in the village of Musha near Asyut in Upper Egypt, into a family of rural nobles. His father was a delegate of Mustafa Kamil's National Party. Qutb went to the state school in the village and had memorised the Koran on his own by the time he was 10 years old. In 1921 Qutb moved to Cairo. In 1933 he graduated from Dar al-Ulum teacher training college with a B.A. in Arts Education. Qutb was then employed as a teacher by the Ministry of Public Instruction, starting his career in the provinces, and was later transferred to Helwan, a suburb of Cairo. From 1940 to 1948 he served as an inspector for the Ministry.

During that time Qutb had a liberal worldview influenced by Abbas Mahmud al-Aqqad and Taha Hussein, and wrote literary criticism as well as poetry, short stories and articles for newspapers and journals. Following a visit to the United States from 1948 to 1951 he turned to fundamentalist Islam, joined the Muslim Brotherhood, was soon elected to their leadership council and became their chief spokesman in the 1950s and 1960s. During the short honeymoon between the Free Officers and the Muslim Brotherhood, Qutb served for a short time as the only civilian on the Revolutionary Council. With the crackdown on the Muslim Brotherhood following the 1954 assassination attempt on Nasser, Qutb was arrested and spent 10 years in prison. He was freed in 1964, but re-arrested in 1965, tortured and executed in 1966. While in prison he wrote his greatest work, an eight-volume *tafsir* of the Koran, *Fi Zilal al-Quran*. Towards the end of his imprisonment he wrote *Milestones* (*Ma'alim fil-Tariq*) – the key manifesto of radical Islamic groups, providing Islamic fundamentalism with an intellectual base. His most important contributions were his reinterpretation of traditional concepts such as *hakimiyya, jahiliyyah* and *takfir*, turning them into contemporary revolutionary concepts in his Islamic ideological system.

One of the new radical Islamic groups was generally called Takfir wa-Hijra (hereafter, Takfir) by the media and by government security agencies. *Takfir* is the legal ascription of unbelief while *hijra* signifies Mohammed's original flight or migration from Mecca to Medina, serving as a model for contemporary disentanglement from the corrupt society and regime in Egypt. Takfir was led by Shukri Mustafa, a member of the Muslim Brotherhood in Asyut who was imprisoned in 1965 and joined the radical disciples of Qutb while in prison. On his release in 1971 he started building up Takfir. Following the kidnapping and murder of an ex-government minister in 1978, Mustafa was arrested and executed by the authorities. Mustafa was an autocratic leader who expected total obedience from his followers. His control was strengthened by the belief that he was the predicted saviour (*mahdi*). Given this prestige, he was able to run Takfir as a highly disciplined organisation, divided into action cells, recruiting groups, and logistic units. Faraj was the main ideologue of the radical Egyptian Tanzim al-Jihad movement, which assassinated President Sadat in 1981.

Faraj, an electrical engineer who worked at Cairo University, was born into a devout Muslim family, his father a member of the Muslim Brotherhood. Faraj, however, became disillusioned by the passivity and gradualism of the Muslem Brotherhood, and he joined activist radical groups, finally founding al-Jihad in 1979 with a complex organisational structure and a coherent ideology. Faraj recruited for his organisation mainly in *ahli* (independent) mosques in the poor quarters of Cairo, where he delivered Friday sermons. He succeeded in recruiting members of the presidential guard, military intelligence and civil bureaucracy, as well as university students. Faraj's book *Al-Farida al-Gha'iba* (*The Neglected Duty*) had an immense impact on all radical Islamic movements. Following Sadat's assassination, Faraj was executed in 1982.

Thus, the main ideologue was Muhammad Abd al-Salam Faraj, a former Muslim Brotherhood member who was disillusioned by its passivity. But al-Jihad did not restrict itself to theory alone. It quickly became involved in sectarian conflicts and disturbances in Upper Egypt and Cairo. After the assassination of Sadat at a military parade, al-Jihad supporters fought a three-day revolt in Asyut, seeking to spark a revolution, before being defeated. In contrast to Takfir, al-Jihad was not led by one charismatic leader but by a collective leadership. It built up a sophisticated organisation run by a leadership apparatus in charge of overall strategy, as well as a 10-member consultation committee headed by Sheikh Umar'Abd al-Rahman. Everyday operations were run by a three-department supervisory apparatus. Members were organised in small semi-autonomous groups and cells. There were two distinct branches, one in Cairo and the other in Upper Egypt. In recruiting, both Takfir and al-Jihad relied heavily on kinship and friendship ties, recruiting predominantly students from rural areas and from lower-middleclass backgrounds who had recently migrated to the big cities and were alienated and disoriented in their new environment. Most members were well educated, particularly in technology and the sciences. Takfir recruited mainly in Upper Egypt and was the only society to actively recruit women. Faraj recruited for al-Jihad in private mosques in poor neighbourhoods where he delivered Friday sermons.

Both groups agreed that authentic Islam had existed only in the "golden age" of the Prophet's original state in Medina and under the "rightly guided" first four Caliphs (622–661). Muslims must rediscover its principles, free them from innovations and actively implement them in the present society. This was in line with revivalist (*salafi*) views, and contradicted the traditionalist view of Islam as the total of the sacred source texts of Koran and the Prophet's example and traditions (Sunna), plus all scholarly interpretation and consensus over the ages. The ultimate goal for both groups was the establishment of a renewed universal Islamic nation (*umma*) under a true caliph, fully implementing Islamic sacred law (Sharia) as God's ideal form of Islamic government. Until the establishment of this caliphate (*khilafa*), the Islamic societies would form the embryo and vanguard of the true Islamic nation in its struggle against internal and external enemies. The takeover of power in individual Muslim states would be a necessary first step toward the ultimate goal.

The views of al-Jihad were roughly parallel: true Muslims must wage war against the infidel rulers of all states, including Muslim states. In contrast to the traditional religious scholars, who proclaimed the necessity of submission to any ruler claiming to be a Muslim, they insisted that acceptance of a government was only possible when the Islamic legal system is fully implemented. Implementation of Sharia becomes the criterion of the legitimacy of regimes. Traditional scholars viewed the concept of the "age of ignorance" or paganism (*jahiliyyah*) as an historic condition in pre-Islamic Arabia. However, "ignorance" (*jahiliyyah*) is a present condition of a society which is not properly Islamic because it does not implement the full Sharia and hence is rebelling against God's sovereignty. All the regimes currently in power in Muslim countries are thus not acceptably Islamic and it is both right and necessary to rebel against them. Takfir and al-Jihad differed in a way that made it clear why al-Jihad was the more successful organisation. Takfir claimed that both the regime and all of society were pagan and true Muslims must separate from them. Takfir included in this condemnation all four traditional schools of Islam (*madhabs*) and all traditional commentators. It labelled these schools puppets of rulers who used them to monopolise Koranic interpretation to their own advantage. They had closed the door of creative interpretation (*ijtihad*) and set themselves up as idols (*tawaghit*), serving as mediators between God and believers.

Al-Jihad, in contrast, selected certain commentators it favoured, including the famous Hanbali medieval scholar, Ibn Taymiya. His writings were interpreted as showing that societies were partly Muslim even when the rulers are pagans who legislate according to their own whims. Al-Jihad accepted the four traditional schools of Islam (*madhabs*), much of scholarly consensus and some later commentators. Consequently, it would be much easier for a Muslim to join al-Jihad or find some truth in its teachings. While traditional scholars and the Muslim Brotherhood would not denounce a Muslim as an infidel – accepting his claim to be Muslim at face value and leaving the judgement of his intention to God – both groups denounced Muslims as infidels, which could imply a willingness to attack or kill them. Since Egypt's failure to implement Sharia made it an infidel pagan state placed under excommunication (Takfir), all true Muslims were duty-bound to wage holy struggle (*jihad*) against the regime, an idea alien to traditional Islam.

Takfir and al-Jihad agreed on the emphasis on a national revolution first: only when the infidel regimes of Muslim countries were overthrown and replaced by true Islamic states could the caliphate be restored, occupied Muslim territories liberated and Shria rule established throughout the world. However, in determining the targets and enemies of its revolution, Takfir declared that not only the regime but the society itself was infidel and under excommunication. This entailed two strategic decisions that ensured that Takfir would remain more of a cult than a revolutionary organisation. First, it entailed a personal withdrawal from society, which required a choice that few people would make and a burden beyond what its infrastructure could sustain. Second, it meant a delay in action, which indefinitely postponed active militancy. Islamic doctrine was always critical of the killing of fellow Muslims and viewed a government professing Islam as an acceptable ruler. Al-Jihad argued that killing Muslims and overthrowing a Muslim-led government was the correct interpretation of Islam. While al-Jihad enthusiastically endorsed this position, its leaders knew that theirs was a distinctly minority view. Faraj criticised other groups – most importantly, the Muslim Brotherhood – for their gradualist strategy and involvement in the political system. Such behaviour, he insisted, only strengthened the regime. He also rejected widely accepted arguments that *jihad* should be postponed (as Takfir claimed) or that this concept required only defensive or non-violent struggle (a widely held Muslim position). In response, Faraj insisted that active, immediate *jihad* would be the only strategy for achieving an Islamic state. Instead of seeing Jews and Christians as protected communities (*dhimmis*) and "People of the Book", the two groups viewed them as infidels both because they had deliberately rejected the truth and because of their connections to colonialism and Zionism. They were accused of serving as a "fifth column" for external enemies; Takfir stressed an international Jewish conspiracy and the need to fight it, whilst al-Jihad viewed Christians as the first enemy to confront and was heavily involved in anti-Coptic activities. Sheikh Abd al-Rahman issued a religious legal edict (*fatwa*) legitimising the killing and robbing of Christians who were said to be anti-Muslim. Both groups saw the Christian West, Jewish Zionism and atheist communism as planning to corrupt, divide and destroy Islam, the rulers in Muslim states being puppets of these forces, leading their countries into dependence and secularisation.

Both groups saw themselves as messianic. Takfir believed that the world was nearing its end and Mustafa, Takfir's leader, was looked upon as the *Mahdi*.

Mustafa would be the caliph who would found a new Muslim community. The West was in decline, and would soon be replaced by true Islam. Leadership should be given to the best Muslim in the community, presumably al-Jihad's leadership. After its suppression by the government and the execution of Mustafa, the members of Takfir joined other underground groups such as al-Jihad. In contrast, al-Jihad survived repression. Despite the imprisonment and execution of al-Jihad's leaders following Sadat's assassination, offshoots managed to regroup, declaring *jihad* against Mubarak's regime. Al-Jihad has continued to be linked to terrorist incidents and outbreaks of communal violence ever since. One wing seems to be loyal to Abbud al-Zammur, one of the original founders, now imprisoned in Egypt. Another wing is called Vanguards of the Conquest or The New Jihad Group led by the well-known Afghan war veteran, Dr Ayman al-Zawahiri.

Abd al-Rahman, 'Umar (1938–) is a blind Egyptian religious scholar and fundamentalist leader, a graduate of al-Azhar. He was taught as a mosque preacher in a poor rural area but returned to studies in al-Azhar, obtaining a Master's degree in 1967 and a faculty appointment in 1968. He was connected to the Muslim Brotherhood in the 1960s. He completed a doctorate in 1972 and lectured at al-Azhar and later at the Azhari Institute in Asyut where he was sympathetic to the Muslim Brotherhood student organisation, the Jama'a al-Islamiyya. He left Egypt in 1977 for four years in Saudi Arabia as Professor of Koranic Studies at Saud University. After his return he was arrested for his leadership role in the Jihad Organisation involved in the assassination of President Sadat. However, he was acquitted by the court and released in 1984. Abd al-Rahman emerged in the 1980s as a leading figure in the Islamist movement in Egypt. His book *Mithaq ql-'amil al-Islami* (*Charter of Islamic Action*) expressed his affiliation with the radical groups aiming at the overthrow of the secular state. He also became linked to the Jama'at al-Islamiyya as their chief *mufti* and spiritual guide. In 1990 he emigrated to the United States and was arrested there in 1993 as being linked to the bombing of the World Trade Center in New York. He was put on trial and sentenced to imprisonment. He had kept his influence in al-Jihad as well as in the other radical movement, al-Jama'at al-Islamiyya, operating both in Egypt and abroad. In the 1980s members of these societies, like other radical groups in the Arab world, fought alongside the *mujahidin* in Afghanistan against the Soviets, gaining valuable experience in warfare and often specialist training from US agents. After the Soviet withdrawal from Afghanistan, many returned to their home countries, reinvigorating the violent struggle against the regimes in power.

Ayman al-Zawahiri joined the Muslim Brotherhood at age 15, was caught in the Nasser dragnet after the 1965 assassination attempt on the Egyptian leader and was thrown into jail. An April 1968 an amnesty freed most of the Brotherhood, and Ayman, in that regard following in his father's footsteps, went on to Cairo University to become a physician. He obtained his degree in 1974 and practised medicine for several years. By the late 1970s, he was back fulltime in the Islamist revolution business, agitating against the Egypt–Israel peace treaty (concluded in 1979). In 1980, on the introduction by military intelligence officer Abbud al-Zumar, he became a leading member of the Jama'at al-Jihad of Muhammad Abd-al-Salam Faraj. Faraj, like al-Zawahiri, argued along the familiar lines that acceptance of a government was only possible and legitimate when that government fully implemented Sharia, or Islamic law. Contemporary Egypt had not done so, and was thus suffering from *jahiliyyah. Jihad* to rectify this, was not only the "neglected obligation" of Muslims, but in fact their most important duty. Following the Sadat assassination, al-Zawahiri was arrested on a minor weapons possession charge and spent three years in jail. In 1985 he left Egypt for Saudi Arabia and later Peshawar, Pakistan, where he was joined by Muhammad al-Islambuli, the brother of one of Sadat's five assassins, 24-year-old artillery lieutenant Khalid Ahmed Shawki al-Islambuli. There, connections were made with the groups of Palestinian Islamist Abdullah Azzam and the latter's one-time student Osama Bin Laden, by then fully engaged (with well-known CIA support) in assisting the *mujahidin* struggle against Soviet occupation of Afghanistan.

Al-Zawahiri's al-Jihad was in many respects better organised and better trained than other groups in the Afghanistan theatre. Prior to the murder of Sadat, it had succeeded in recruiting members of the presidential guard, military intelligence and civil bureaucracy. Most importantly, it was in possession of a cogent and comprehensive ideology pointing beyond the Afghan struggle against the Soviet occupiers. "Afghanistan should be a platform for the liberation of the entire Muslim world" was the distinguishing creed of al-Jihad. Al-Zawahiri wrote several books on Islamic movements, the best known of which is *The Bitter Harvest* (1991/1992), a critical assessment of the failings of the Muslim Brotherhood. In it, he draws not only on the writings of Sayyid Qutb to justify murder and terrorism, but prominently references Pakistani Jamaat-i-Islami founder and ideologue Mawdudi on the global mission of Islamic *jihad.* Global *jihad* as Mawdudi had prescribed became al-Zawahiri's obsession.

After several years in Afghanistan and Pakistan, constructing there the platform from which to launch broader pursuits, Zawahiri travelled extensively on Swiss, French and Dutch passports in Western Europe and even the United States on fund-raising, recruiting and reconnaissance missions. He had close connections to Sheikh Omar Abdel Rahman. In 1995, he was behind the truck bomb attack on the Egyptian embassy in Pakistan; in November 1997, he led the Vanguards of Conquest group responsible for the Luxor (Egypt) massacre in which 60 foreign tourists were systematically murdered and mutilated; in August 1998, he organised the bombings of the US embassies in Kenya and Tanzania; and probably, in 2000, the speed-boat bomb attack on the *USS Cole* in Aden. Israeli intelligence considers him the "operational brains" behind 11 September; the fact, in any case, is that the Egyptian Mohamed Atta, principal of the Hamburg, Germany, al-Qaeda cell that was instrumental to the World Trade Center destruction, was a member of Zawahiri's al-Jihad. Osama Bin Laden had the money, some of the connections and perhaps the charisma to function as the leader of the al-Qaeda global *jihad.* It was when Zawahiri's al-Jihad in February 1998 formally joined forces with Bin Laden that the present global Islamist terrorist threat emerged. With his experience in the Muslim Brotherhood, his assessment of its failures, his drawing on Islamic religious elements, and his organisational and operational skills, al-Zawahiri is the key personality of global *jihad.* Zawahiri's Islamism seized the ideological initiative in the Muslim world against which traditional Islam has so far proved an impotent, indeed often unwilling, opponent. Young Muslims are captivated by Zawahiri Islamism, to which they attribute selfless idealism and in which they admire the ruthless determination.

Khalid Sheikh Mohammed was linked with Zawahiri, as he is known to have been a member of the al-Qaeda Council. He was born in 1964 or 1965, in the Baluchistan region of Pakistan, but he grew up in Kuwait. He studied in the United States, briefly at Chowan College in North Carolina before graduating in 1986 from the North Carolina Agricultural and Technical State University with a degree in engineering. Within a few short years he was in Pakistan and part of the Afghan mujahideen. By the late 1990s he was the al-Qaeda media director under Zawahiri. The US offered a reward of up to $25 million for his capture. In March of 2003 he was captured in Pakistan. In March of 2007 the US released a transcript from a military tribunal in which Mohammed, while denying that he ever said he was al-Qaeda's military commander, takes credit for planning the 9/11 attacks.

Al-Zawahiri has come forward with a book that has been smuggled from an Afghan cave to the border city of Peshawar and then to London. The book is divided into three sections and has the title *Knights Under the Prophet's Banner* and the subtitle *Meditations on the Jihadist Movement*. The knights to whom he alludes are the leaders and members of the fundamentalist movements. The title is a response to a name widely used in the Middle Ages to describe "the Knights of the Holy Tomb", during the Crusades in the Middle East. His main ideas include (Mansfield 2006):

> *The universality of the battle*
>
> The western forces that are hostile to Islam have clearly identified their enemy. They refer to it as Islamic fundamentalism. They are joined in this by their old enemy, Russia. They have adopted a number of tools to fight Islam, including the United Nations, the friendly rulers of the Muslim peoples, the multi-national corporations, the international communications and data exchange systems, the international news agencies and satellite media channels and the international relief agencies, which are being used as a cover for espionage, proselytising, coup planning and the transfer of weapons. A fundamentalist coalition is taking shape made up of the *jihad* movements in the various lands of Islam as well as the two countries that have been liberated in the name of *jihad* for the sake of God (Afghanistan and Chechnya). A growing power is rallying under the banner of *jihad* for the sake of God and operating outside the scope of the new world order, free of the servitude for the dominating occidental empire. It promises destruction and ruin for the new Crusades against the lands of Islam. Ready for revenge against the heads of the world's gathering of infields, the United States,

Russia and Israel, it seeks retribution for the blood of the martyrs, the grief of the mothers, the deprivation of the orphans, the suffering of the detainees and the sores of the tortured people throughout the land of Islam, from Eastern Turkestan to Andalusia (Islamic state in Spain). Thus, our age is witnessing a new phenomenon that continues to gain ground. It is the phenomenon of the *mujahid* youths who have abandoned their families, country, wealth, studies, and jobs in search of *jihad* arenas for the sake of God.

No solution without jihad

A new awareness is increasingly developing among the sons of Islam, who are eager to uphold it: There is no solution without *jihad*. The spread of this awareness has been augmented by the failure of all other methods that tried to evade assuming the burdens of *jihad*. The Algerian experience proved to Muslims that the west is not only an infidel but also a hypocrite and a liar. The principles that it propagates are exclusive to, and the personal property of, its people alone. They are not to be shared by the peoples of Islam, at least nothing more that what a master leaves his slave in terms of food crumbs. The Islamic movement in general, and the *jihad* movements in particular, must train themselves and their members on perseverance, patience and steadfastness. The leadership must set an example for the members to follow. This is the key to victory. "O ye who believe. Endure, outdo all others in endurance, be ready, and observe your duty to Allah, in order that ye may succeed" (Koranic verse).

Loyalty to the leadership

The acknowledgement of its precedence and merit represent a duty that must be emphasized and a value that must be consolidated. But if loyalty to the leadership reaches the point of declaring it holy and if the acknowledgement of its precedence and merit leads to infallibility, the movement will suffer from methodological blindness. Hence comes the importance of the issue of leadership in Islamic action in general, and *jihad* action in particular and the nation's need for a scientific, struggling, and rational leadership that could guide the nation, amidst the mighty storms and hurricanes, toward its goal with awareness and prudence, without losing sight of its path, stumbling aimlessly, or reversing its course.

Mobilization (tajyyish) of the nation: Its participation in the struggle, and caution against the struggle of the elite with the authority

The *jihad* movement must come closer to the masses, defend their honour, fend off injustice, and lead them to the path of guidance and victory. It must step forward in the arena of sacrifice and excel to get its message across in a way that makes the right accessible to all seekers and that makes access to the origin

> and facts of religion simple and free of the complexities of terminology and the intricacies of composition. The *jihad* movement must dedicate one of its wings to work with the masses, preach, provide services for the Muslim people, and share their concerns through all available avenues for charity and educational work.

The rhetoric of Al-Zawahiri is comprehensive *jihad*, which if carried through would turn Muslim countries into battlegrounds like in Palestine, Pakistan, Afghanistan and Iraq.

> *Changing the method of strikes*
>
> The mujahid Islamic movement must escalate its methods of strikes and tools of resisting the enemies to keep up with the tremendous increase in the number of its enemies, the quality of their weapons, their destructive powers, their disregard for all taboos, and disrespect for the customs of wars and conflicts. In this regard, we concentrate on the following: (a) The need to inflict the maximum casualties against the opponent, for this is the language understood by the west, no matter how much time and effort such operations take. (b) The need to concentrate on the method of martyrdom operations as the most successful way of inflicting damage against the opponent and the least costly to the mujahidin in terms of casualties. (c) The targets as well as the type and method of weapons used must be chosen to have an impact on the structure of the enemy and deter it enough to stop its brutality, arrogance, and disregard for all taboos and customs. It must restore the struggle to its real size. (d) To reemphasize what we have already explained, we reiterate that focusing on the domestic enemy alone will not be feasible at this stage. (e) The battle is for every Muslim. In order for the masses to move, they need leadership that they could trust, follow, and understand, and a clear enemy to strike at as well as that the shackles of fear and the impediments of weakness in the souls must be broken.

Osama Bin Laden (1957–) is a Saudi multi-millionaire dissident and anti-American activist born in Medina, Saudi Arabia. He studied management and economics in King Abdul Aziz University, Jedda, and joined Islamic groups in 1973. He joined the Afghan *mujahidin* in their fight against the Soviets in 1979 and played a significant role in financing, recruiting, transporting and training Arab volunteers to fight in Afghanistan. During the war he founded al-Qaeda – the Base – to serve as an operational hub for like-minded radicals. In the beginning of the 1980s he also fought against leftists in Yemen. With Abdullah Azzam he established the office for Mujahidin Services in Peshawar, Pakistan, to help the Afghan *mujahidin*. He established *mujahidin* bases in Afghanistan, and participated in battles against the Soviets there.

The Saudi government withdrew his citizenship in 1994 and froze his assets; his own family disowned him. He had moved to Sudan in 1991 but international pressure forced him to move back to Afghanistan. His organisation sent trainers to Afghanistan, Tajikistan, Bosnia, Chechnya, Somalia, Sudan and Yemen and has trained fighters from many other countries as well. He maintains close ties with leaders of other Islamist terrorist groups, providing them with training, safe havens and financial support. Bin Laden is a principal source of funding and direction for al-Qaeda, a multi-national *jihad* movement whose leaders are also senior leaders in other extremist organisations such as the Egyptian al-Jama'at al-Islamiyya and al-Jihad. Al-Qaeda seeks a global radicalisation of existing Islamic groups and the creation of radical Islamic groups where none exist. It recruits, supports and trains fighters in Afghanistan, Bosnia, Chechnya, Tajikistan, Somalia, Yemen, Kosovo and other lands. It has been implicated in terrorist activities such as the bombing of US Embassies in Nairobi and Dar-as-Salam.

In 1996 Bin Laden issued a public statement which he termed "A Declaration of War" outlining his organisation's goals to drive the US forces from the Arabian Peninsula, overthrow the government of Saudi Arabia, liberate Muslim Holy Sites in Palestine, and support Islamic revolutionary forces around the world. The declaration was a call to Muslims worldwide to declare *jihad* against the Judaeo-Christian Alliance occupying the "holy land of the two holy places", Saudi Arabia and Palestine. According to Bin Laden, *da'wa* and armed struggle are the way to repel the greater *kufr* and unite the Muslim world. In 1998 he organised the creation of a new alliance of radical movements, the "International Islamic Front for Jihad against Jews and Crusaders", which included the Egyptian al-Jama'at al-Islamiyya and Islamic Jihad, the Harakat al-Ansar, and others. The Front declared its intention to attack Americans and their allies (including civilians) anywhere in the world.

The war on Islamic terrorism has not been without some major successes. Thus, senior Bin Laden lieutenant Muhammad Atef was killed in Afghanistan in 2001 and a CIA predator drone brought a fiery end to al-Qaeda's top man in Yemen, Qaed Salim Sinan al-Harethi, on 3 November 2002. More importantly, some of al-Qaeda's most influential commanders have been captured. Al-Qaeda operations chief Abu Zubaydah, Omar al-Farouq (a senior aide to Khalid Sheikh Mohammed), Ramzi Binalshibh, Omar al-Farouq (Bin Laden's operations chief for Southeast Asia), and most recently Abd al-Rahim al-Nashiri in Yemen, are all in US custody. The suspected mastermind of the 11 September terror attacks, Khalid Sheikh Mohammed, was arrested in one of the biggest catches yet in the war on terrorism in March 2004 in Rawalpindi, near the Pakistan capital of Islamabad. Mohammed was perhaps the most senior al-Qaeda operative after Osama Bin Laden and Egyptian Ayman al-Zawahiri. The leader of Al-Qaeda in Iraq, Al-Zarqawi was killed by US air strikes in 2006.

Conclusion

As fundamentalism with this new doctrine of Islamic terrorism becomes more widespread within the Muslim civilisation in the early twenty-first century (Roy, 2004; Kepel, 2005), Weber's perspective – Islam as a religion of warriors – is more relevant than it was hundred years ago. It could be more vindicated by the new salafists than he ever imagined himself. His concept of Islam as a religion of warriors would be verified with a terrible vengeance by the combination of salafism and *jihad*. According to Mawdudi the new theory of *jihad* entails:

> Islam is a revolutionary doctrine and system that overturns governments. It seeks to overturn the whole universal social order ... and establish its structure a new ... Islam seeks the world. It is not satisfied by a piece of land but demands the whole universe ... Islamic Jihad is at the same time offensive and defensive ... The Islamic party does not hesitate to utilize the means of war to implement its goal.

Yet, the truth is that the religious community of Muslims (*umma*) has always been heterogenous and the fusion of secular and religious power is not viable in Muslim countries (caliphate, immmate). A Muslim state can only be stable and prosperous if these two facts are acknowledged by the key religious groups, the *ulema* or *muftis*, who must accept the secular nature of a modern state in the Muslim civilisation.

Modern Islamic fundamentalism was to a significant extent conceived in the Indian *Deobandi* movement, from which comes Mawdudi, the Pakistani who inspired the Egyptians: Qutb and Faraj and the now second in command for Al Qauda Al-Zawahiri. The Muslim community in India responded to the British destruction of the Mogul Empire with a seminary in Deoband in 1866 by former students of the Delhi *madressa*, destroyed after the "Revolt of 1857".

The new seminary in Deoband aimed at (1) indoctrinating Muslim youth with Islamic values, and (2) cultivating intense hatred towards the British and all foreign (i.e. non-Islamic) influences. The seminary exposed their students only to the spiritual and philosophical traditions of Islam with the goal of islamisation of state and society in view.

However, this is not feasible in a globalised Muslim country, as Egyptian writer Naguib Mahfouz testified in his many Nobel prize winning books. In 1994 Islamic extremists almost succeeded in assassinating him. He survived until 2006, permanently affected by damage to nerves in his right hand. Mahfouz could no longer write for more than a few minutes a day, delivering fewer and fewer works.

The *Aligarh* movement would serve Moslems better than the *Deobandi* School. Aligarh became famous as a centre for various movements that shaped India with the start of the Mohammedan Anglo Oriental College by Sir Syed Ahmed Khan in

1875. This College has become Aligarh Muslim University – a hub for bridging the gulf between Islamic and Western cultures.

The life of Mohamed Atta presents an ideal-type image of a modern Egyptian fundamentalist and terrorist – "Ph.D. and beard". Born in a town on the Nile Delta in 1968, Atta moved with his family to Cairo at the age of 10. Atta studied architecture at Cairo University, and went to Hamburg, Germany in 1992 to continue his studies at the Technical University of Hamburg. Atta disappeared from Germany for periods of time, spending some time in Afghanistan, when he met Osama bin Laden and other al-Qaeda leaders. Atta and the other Hamburg Cell members were recruited by Bin Laden and Khalid Sheikh Mohammed for the "planes operation" in the United States.

In 1985, Atta entered Cairo University, where he studied engineering. As one of the highest-scoring students, Atta was admitted into architecture. In 1990, he graduated with a degree in architecture. He then worked at the Urban Development Center in Cairo with architectural, planning and building design. After coming to Hamburg, Atta became more religious. His friends in Germany described him as an intelligent man with religious beliefs who grew angry over the Western policy toward the Middle East, including the Oslo Accords and the Gulf War. After spending the summer of 1995 in Egypt, he joined the Hajj in Mecca that autumn. Before going to Egypt, he grew a beard, which is a sign of being a devout Muslim but was also seen as a political gesture.

In Hamburg, Atta visited the Al-Quds Mosque, preaching a "harsh, uncompromisingly fundamentalist, and resoundingly militant" version of Sunni Islam. He even began teaching classes at Al-Quds, as well as at a Turkish mosque near Harburg. Atta also formed a prayer group, which Ahmed Maklat and Mounir El Motassadeq joined. Ramzi Binalshibh was there teaching occasional classes, and became a good friend of Atta's. Mohammed Haydar Zammar, a German terrorist of Syrian origin, says that he met Atta at this time, bringing him into al-Qaeda.

In 2000, Atta received a five-year US B-1/B-2 (tourist/business) visa from the US embassy in Berlin. Atta arrived in June at the Newark International Airport. Days later, al-Shehhi and Atta ended up in south Florida. Atta and al-Shehhi established accounts at SunTrust Bank and received wire transfers from Ali Abdul Aziz Ali, Khalid Sheikh Mohammed's nephew in the United Arab Emirates. Atta and al-Shehhi enrolled at Huffman Aviation in Venice, Florida, where they entered the Accelerated Pilot Program, while Ziad Jarrah took flight training from a different school, also based out of Venice. Atta earned his private pilot certificate in September. In November 2000, Atta earned his instrument rating, and then a commercial pilot's licence in December from the Federal Aviation Administration. Atta and Marwan went to the Opa-locka Airport to practice on a Boeing 727 simulator, and they obtained Boeing 767 simulator training from Pan Am International. After planning the 11 September attacks travelling back and forth between Europe and the United States, Atta crashed the Boeing 767 into the North Tower of the World Trade Center.

Chapter 17
Fundamentalism and the State: Need for Mutual Explanation

Introduction: Towards a New Agenda?

The agenda set up after 11 September focused on two connected issues: the war on terrorism and the democratisation of the Arab world. The idea was that the authoritarian and stable *status quo* provides fertile ground for terrorism. The former objective is half success, while the latter is a failure. The Middle East reacted positively to the first task and participated actively in deterring terrorist sanctuaries, but it exhibited mistrust in US politics and criticised the idea of the "Broader Middle East", arguing that democracy cannot come from outside and by constraint, by rapid and brutal reforms that put the regime's foundations at risk. Therefore, the challenge is the following: gradual change or absence of change. However, nobody has a clear opinion on how to initiate and implement reform, whether through gradual reforms initiated by the existing regimes, or by radical remedies, including war. Gradualists think that democracy and political freedom are a by-product, an output of a modernising process that makes genuine progress in economic, cultural and social fields such as education, urbanisation and secularisation. Radicals think that reforms are so urgent that the Middle East has to be put in a sort of a Cornelian choice: reform or transplant a new liberal leadership. Gradualists are pessimistic, while radicals are optimistic. The Iraqi civil war is giving right to gradualists. Nevertheless, one should not be so pessimistic: the need for change is effective and appeals for human rights, voice and accountability as well as demands for democratic reforms are coming from many constituencies – liberals, secularists, women and even moderate Islamists – once again a key variable to understanding the future of Islam. Who are they? How to deal with them? Should we integrate them or ban and exclude them from any kind of political participation and on what basis? These are the main issues of the current debate.

The Inevitable Islamic Variable

Since the 1980s, a great deal has been written on the distinctions to be made between various kind of fundamentalism, Islamism and radical Islam. Islamism is a large spectrum, a network of various groups, splitting off from one another. Some are only ideologically radicals, others not only radicals but also terrorists, while a current mainstream trend is actually politically pragmatic, moderate and peaceful. Once again, a recent study tried to distinguish between religious and political activism and differentiate within the Islamic religious movements between violent and non-violent tendencies. There are three main distinctive types, each with its own world vision, modus operandi and characteristic actors (International Crisis Group, 2005).

The first is Islamic political movements (*al-harakât al-islamiyya al-siyassiyya*) that accept the nation-state, operate within its constitutional framework, refuse violence, articulate a reformist agenda and refer to universal democratic norms, although they continue to ask for the application of Islamic law. The ideal type of actor is the party political militant. Second are the Islamic missionary movements of conversion (*al-da'wa*), which are indifferent to political power and focus on Muslim identity, faith and cults. Third there is a constellation of Islamic armed groups, themselves divided into three main variants: those committed to internal struggle, i.e. combating the "near enemy", nominally Muslim regimes considered impious; those who are involved in a nationalist combat, fighting against foreign occupation; and finally, those who are attracted by global *jihad*, combating the "further" enemy, the West. The al-Qaeda network is a synthesis of worldwide *jihad* or what we have considered in this book the "third type of fundamentalism". Islamism encompasses different trends. However, there is a "family resemblance" between all variety of fundamentalisms, including Christian and Jewish fundamentalisms. A comparative study has charted the list of common denominators: anti-secularism, sacred scripture and revealed law requirements, inclusion of state and religion, recourse to the past golden age and eschatological separatism (Zeiden, 2003).

For their part, Islamic states have reacted to political Islam with various policies, balancing between two major orientation trends: exclusion and inclusion. Which of these main religious outlooks and state policies will prevail in the medium and longer term is of great importance to the future of Islam. That is why diplomats and scholarly researchers strongly appeal to a mutual understanding between regimes and Islamists in order to include at least moderate Islam in public life. This realistic trend is looking forward to "engaging Islamists and promoting democracy" (Yacoubian, 2007).

Nevertheless, criticism remains strong against Islamism, accused of being insincere, dishonest, hypocritical, two-faced and opportunistic, actually seeking to establish an authoritarian regime in an Islamic dress. Authoritarian regimes also manoeuvre by using at their convenience various policies, from rejecting Islamism on traditional Islamic principles to accusing them of being illiberal and anti-modern. Some have banned and repressed them on these bases, whereas others fully recognise them or just suspiciously tolerate them.

Instead of arbitrating between two extreme positions, there are actually issues of concern, twilight zones, indistinct and uncertain frontiers in a sense that neither Islamists nor Islamic governments have clarified. This uncertainty opens a door and even an avenue both to Islamists and for regimes to manoeuvre and operate.

Inspired by a genuine expertise (Hamzawy et al., 2006, 2007), we selected five twilight zones, at the crossroads between Islamic ideology, state policies and Islamic tradition. These "grey zones" enable Islamists to plot and states to trick: Sharia law (I), democracy (II), women (III), minorities (IV) and violence (V).

Thick and Thin Sharia

The main issue under debate is the application of the Sharia, a common denominator of all Islamists movements, whether they are radicals or moderates prompt to criticise positive law. They appeal to apply in one way or another Sharia and its legal dispositions, and it is a source of inspiration as well. Extreme versions of the Sharia may be "the Islamists' other weapon" used in the battle of the war of ideas (Marshall, 2005), while a moderate version may be compatible with modernity and democracy (Hamzawy, 2005). For their part, states also compete in this issue and are not far from respecting Sharia, either by applying legal religious statements or by making positive law compatible with the principles of Sharia. Therefore, the core issue of debate concerns the plasticity of the Sharia and the recourse to Sharia either by Islamic modern legal systems or by Islamists.

What does thick Sharia law mean? Sharia designates broadly the path of God, the lawgiver, and encompasses rules of guidance, including the sources or foundations of law in Islam (1), schools of law (2) and the rules of the Sharia (3). As far as rules of law are concerned, thick Sharia includes the five acts of worship or personal duties that make up Islamic faith: (a) the recital of the creed (*shahada*); "There is no God but Allah and Mohammed is the Apostle of God"; (b) the performance of prayer (*salat*) at the five canonical times; (c) the payment of the legal alms (*zakat*); (d) the 30 days of fasting during the month of *Ramadan*; and (e) the pilgrimage (*hajj*) to Mecca. Also, there are the collective duties that have to be implemented by the Muslim community as a whole, beyond the duties of every Muslim (the five pillars), such as *jihad* and seeking knowledge. In addition, we have interpersonal acts (*muamalat*), including family law (marriage, divorce, inheritance, slavery, etc.) and economic law (contracts, debt, hire, loan, gifts, etc.), not to mention other controversial ethical principles and political doctrine (the caliphate).

Apart from civil religious duties and civil regulations, Sharia includes definitely six cases of corporal punishments to be observed by individuals. The first is unlawful intercourse (*zina*). As a counterpart of legal polygamy, Islam prohibited intercourse between a man and a woman neither legally married nor being in a state of legal relation between an owner and his female slave. While the punishment required 100 lashes, for the man as well as the woman (XIV: 2), the jurisprudence maintained the penalty for the virgin, but for married partners it enforced the penalty of stoning to death. The legal argument refers to a prophetic sentence where Mohammed decided to stone a couple of Jews guilty of unlawful intercourse and who asked him to judge the case (V: 46).

The second case is false accusation of fornication (*kadhf*), as a logical counterpart of the severity of punishment of unlawful intercourse. The penalty laid down by the Koran is 80 lashes (XIV: 4).

Third is drinking wine (*kham*). The Koran moved smoothly from considering it God's grace to mankind (II: 219), to dissuading performing prayer in drunkenness (IV: 43), to asking Muslims to "avoid" it as an "abomination of the work of Satan", as well as gambling and divining arrows (V: 93–94), without fixing any particular punishment. It was Mohammed and his first successor, Abu Bakr (632–634), who set the tradition. Mohammed imposed 40 blows by means of palm branches and the second caliphate, Umar (634–644), increased it to 80 on the basis of false accusation of adultery because whoever drinks is able to go as far as lying and falsely accusing men and women of illegal intercourse.

The fourth is theft (*sakira*), is punished by cutting of the hand (V: 41), except in particular circumstances determined by jurisprudence, such as illness, pregnancy or necessity.

Fifth is highway robbery with violence against pacific people or travellers, to be severely punished by one of four means: cutting off the right hand and left leg, death, crucifixion or exile (V: 36). In the medieval age, such a dissuasive punishment was frequently used.

Sixth is murder, already forbidden for the Jews (V: 35) and on an equal basis: "Life for life, eye for eye, nose for nose, ear for ear, and tooth for tooth" (V: 48). In case of accidental murder, compensation may be paid provided that it is accepted by the relatives of the victim. Nevertheless, killing for "a just cause" is legal (VI: 151), in case of legitimate defence or in *jihad*. The jurisprudence extends the penalty to apostasy.

Thus, we face a "thick" and a "thin" Sharia. A thick Sharia is the entire Sharia as it prevailed in the medieval age. It is actually a sacred tradition whose rules were a result of an historical process, set up either by scriptures or by clerics as "prophets of law" that exceed even the previous statements. A thin Sharia revises some of its own regulations and refers more to principles and spirit than to legal statements. Moreover, Sharia is a complex and a plastic system of law enabling any actor to manoeuvre. Islamists felt themselves free enough to question whether to apply all traditional provisions, or some of its practical obligation to the detriment of others. For instance, some would include collective duties such as *jihad* among the conditions of being a good Muslim. Others would not. We do not intend to give a broad panorama, well documented, but rather to deliver guidelines in order make a genuine classification.

Radicals are those who claim that "Islam is the solution", but whole Islam, including naturally the implementation of the Sharia as such. This is the case of the banned Moroccan Al-Islah wa al-ihsen, led by Sheikh Yassine, the Algerian FIS and the Egyptian groups Jihad and Gamaa. Moderates are those who moved from the call for the application of Sharia to a realistic and limited acceptance of positive law. They have changed their terminology and adopted a series of accommodations. They insist on Sharia as a "reference" (*marja'iyya*) within a positive system of law. They look forward its "goals" (*maqasid*), a kind of "Zweckrationalität" or goal attainment, encompassing the intention of the God, the circumstances of revelation and the finality of law. The Egyptian Muslim Brotherhood is the most frequently mentioned case, but one may also refer to the legal Moroccan PJD (Party of Justice and Development), the Tunisian Nahdha and the Algerian Hamas led by Sheikh Mahfoudh Nahnah (died 2003) (close to the Egyptian Brotherhood) and now by Aboudjerra Soltani, that morph into The Movement for Islamic Society and Peace and the Nahdha (subsequently *al-Islah*), led by Abdallah Jaballah. This positive and welcome change remains questionable. As far as the legal system is concerned, the issue of who enacts the law is a debatable issue. Even moderate Islamists consider that the path of God is beyond discussion or violation by parliaments so that only religious authorities have the right to interpret it. They campaign to review positive codes in order to bring them into harmony with Islamic principles and demand that religious men ought to be consulted. However, "Islamic reference" (*marja'iyya islamiyya*) is so vague that it can be a cosmetic change of phraseology, since "reference" includes the four Sharia sources of law (Koran, Sunna, consensus of legists and *ijtihad*) that have performed the legal statements under discussion. It is worth noting that all Islamists focus on civil and personal status, while they are have in trouble to proclaiming openly corporal punishment. In addition, would Islamists accept a democratic due process of law at odds with this "reference" without any protest?

States are not helping Islamists to clarify the difference between thin and thick Sharia. The modern Islamic legal system maintains the same grey areas and ambiguities. Islamic states are actually divided into four categories: declared Islamic states, declared Islam as the state religion, declared secular and without any constitutional provisions (Stahnke and Blitt, 2005). Moreover, many constitutions state that the Sharia is (1) a source of legislation, (2) a major source or (3) the principal source of legislation. Such provisions enable the courts to refer to the Sharia at least in three cases of (1) formal contradiction between a positive law and the Sharia, (2) interpretation and (3) absence of a specific law. Nevertheless, domestic legislation varies and ranges from being semi-secular in civil matters to the replacement of corporal punishment by modern penalties, except for some cases, notably Iran, Saudi Arabia and Sudan. In practice, the judges are more prudent and *mal à l'aise* to endorse Sharia law. As a result, the Islamic legal system is "a composite", neither fully traditional nor openly modern.

Moreover, the international policy of Islamic states is not in total compliance with international standards. It is worth noting that Islamic states resist bringing their domestic legal system into conformity with international law by resorting to a range of artifices, including limiting it on a religious basis. They select some rights and ignore others. They upgrade economic and social rights as well as third-generation rights, while they downgrade individual and political rights or the first generation of international rights. They sign international covenants without including them in their domestic legal system by a due process of law. They adhere to international conventions but make reservations on a religious basis so that the effective application of human rights is often conditional upon its harmony with Sharia law (Badrin, 2003; Mayer, 2005). Reservations are announced by the same general formula: either the state declares its adhesion to the international treaty, "in so far as it is not incompatible with the provision of the Islamic Sharia", or reservations are made provision-by-provision.

In order to resist international pressure, Islamic states approved a "Human Rights Declaration in Islam", usually known as the "Cairo declaration", adopted in August 1990, by the 19th Ministerial Conference of Foreign Affairs in Cairo under the auspices of the Organisation of Islamic Conference (OIC). The OIC was created in Rabat in 1972 in order to "consolidate solidarity and reinforce cooperation among its members" and comprises 57 member countries. As stated by resolution 49/19 S, issuing the declaration, the "Declaration on Human Rights in Islam" is not an international treaty or a bill of rights, but just an informal proclamation that "entails global orientations of the states" (OIC, doc. (LEG.DR.TXT)-M). The declaration was an output of a huge political and intellectual movement in the region during the 1980s. The governments were under pressure from scholars, religious figures (*ulamas*), Islamists and secular groups. Various public and private institutions have initiated the Islamic declaration of rights (Mayer, 1991; Redissi, 2007), not to mention international institutions asking Muslim countries to comply with international standards in human rights issues.

The Islamic *Weltanschauung* is clearly set up in the preamble of the Declaration and some of its provisions: for instance, Islam is a "natural religion" of human kind and the Islamic community is "the best of communities". Men, who are only servants of the Lord, are vice-regents of God; life is "a gift"; commending what is good and prohibiting what is bad is a duty. This religious pattern is not necessarily at odds with human rights standards, in so far that this monotheistic point of view is now considered as one of the historical backgrounds of secular rights, namely coming from the Christian ethos. In addition, even from a Rawlsian point of view, "an overlapping consensus" may allow religious adepts to ground basic and civic liberties in a religious belief. In fact, the heart of the matter is the compatibility of the Sharia and human rights. Instead of listing the whole provisions of the declaration, it would be useful to highlight the logic entailing the three main rights set up by the declaration.

First, some declared rights comply with minimal international standards, as international treaties and documents, regardless of their basis, set them up, even though they refer to the Sharia. They are related to primary rights such the respect for life, the right to a legal capacity, to honour, to reputation and self-esteem. Others are political rights such as political participation (article 23b), or social ones such as the right to education or to a job. Moreover, the Declaration recognises the law of people, for example the right to self-government and independence.

Second, rights absolutely at odds with international norms and modern values outnumbered the first category. The declaration endorses the death penalty in the case of murder (article 2a). It incorporates among "human rights" the corporal punishments in Islamic law "*hudud*" or penal observances (article 2b). It charges women with more duties than rights (article 6). It declares that Islam is "the natural religion of man" and prohibits apostasy (article 10). It prohibits also the taking of interest payments or "*riba*" (article 14). In theses cases, we are looking at duties more than rights and more within the Islamic tradition than in a genuine attempt to set up general rights for specific cultures.

Third are preconditioned rights that should be either accepted "according the principles of the Sharia", such as the rights of children (article 7), or should not be "at odds with the principles of the Sharia", as is the case of intellectual and artistic properties (article 16). On the other hand, there are rights that must be applied "in the framework of the Sharia", such as freedom of circulation (article 12) and freedom of speech (article 21). These are the three main categories of rights.

Moreover, Sharia law reshapes the whole Declaration: it shapes rights, conditions their application and limits their effects. It is the reference in case of conflict of interpretation (article 24). In such conditions, the Declaration should have been titled the "Sharia Declaration on Human rights"! For their part, Arab secular states were active in elaborating an Arab Charter on Human Right, free from Islamic provisions, which they enacted three years later in 1994. The Arab Charter on Human Rights is an international treaty binding the 21 Arab states of the Arab League in full respect of international standards on human rights, including prohibiting the states from limiting such rights, even though the preamble refers to the Cairo Declaration as well. The treaty, amended in 2004, entered into effect on March 2008, by the signature of eight states, including Saudi Arabia, initiator of the Cairo Declaration, willing to demonstrate its positive commitments to moving towards a new policy.

In fact, the ambiguity of one group, Islamists, meets the uncertainty of the others, Islamic states. Liberal secularists are asking for the respect of basic liberties while radicals are overstressing the implementation of the Sharia. Therefore, as Weber stated it, Sharia law can neither be implemented nor dismissed. Islamic states cannot get rid of Sharia law, but are unable to respect it.

Democracy: Procedure or Values?

For years, Islamists refused democracy and were reluctant to accept political competitiveness. This was, for instance, the classical position of the Egyptian Brotherhood, from the founder Hasan al-Banna (1906–1946)'s *Autobiography* (Muzakkarat), namely through the first of the 50 proposals that planned to abolish political pluralism. In the same period, Mawdudi (1903–1979), founder of the Pakistani Jamaat-i-islami (1946) pledged rather a "Theo-democracy", a *sui-generius* invention that mismatched the sovereignty of God and the will of people. A drastic change occurred in 1970 when radical Islamists clashed with the moderates, the latter being actually the mainstream political movements in favour of accepting democratic principles. Nevertheless, it was not clear enough whether they adopted democracy as a method or as an array of values. Democracy as a procedure refers to the definition given by Schumpeter in his *Capitalism, Socialism and Democracy* (1949), according to which the democratic method is a competition between leaders for the popular vote, while democracy as a series of values encompasses the basic liberties, ranging from individual rights to political participation. Therefore, the welcome evolution remains questionable. Is it a genuine change or just a tactic to catch power?

As far as the theoretical framework is concerned, there are three Islamist approaches: democracy is an "impiety", democracy an "Islamic "consultative" principle and "theo-democracy". Radicals reject democracy as a non-Islamic system, a Western and atheist doctrine depriving God of his absolute sovereignty. This was Sayyid Qutb's position during the 1950s, followed by the Algerian Ali Belhadj, Zawahiri and Bin Laden. The Jordanian *salafi-jihadist Maqdasi,* the mentor of Zarqawi, has written a book *Democracy, A Religion! But a Fallacious One.* In contrast to this hostility, "consultative democracy" and "theo-democracy" are two similar attempts to combine Islamic tradition with Western values. The former is based on the Koran, pointing out that Muslims are a community of believers who deliberate on their matters. Once again, it was the Egyptian Brotherhoods who abandoned the initial view of their founder Hasan al-Banna and adopted this moderate position. Thus, they improved their reputation as "The Moderate Brotherhood" (Leiken and Brooke, 2007). They are followed by the Moroccan PJD, the Jordanian Islamic Action Front, the Tunisian Nahda and mainstream Islamic political groups. More representative of the spirit of Islamist movements, "theo-democracy" refers to a genuine distinction between the sacred and eternal Sharia, since it is set up by God (Theos) and the will of the people (democracy).

The move toward endorsing political pluralism is ascribed to the increasing popular support of Islamism and their spreading influence. Therefore, in order to take advantage of this audience, Islamist movements give up their grievances and adopt a realistic strategy tending to participate to political life, even though elections are considered unfair and dishonest. This is the case, for instance, for the Morocco's Party of Justice and Development (PJD), Egypt's Muslim Brotherhood and Al-Wasat Party (Center) (a split from the Brotherhood), Yemen's Islah (Reform) Party, the Jordan's Islamic Action Front, Kuwait's Islamic Constitutional Movement and Bahrain's al-Wifaq Society (Concordance). As a result, Islamists entered parliaments. In Bahrain, where the electoral assembly were restored after being suspended in 1975, Islamists won 14 out of 40 seats; in Morocco, the PJD become the third party represented in the parliament with 42 seats taken of 325; in Yemen, Islah won 46 of the 301 seats; in Kuwait, 17 of the 50 seats; in Jordan, 17 of 116; in Iraq, the list backed by Shia swept 140 of the 275 seats; in Bangladesh, 17 of the 300 seats; and in Saudi Arabia, independent Islamists got six of seven seats in a municipal election held in Riyadh.

However, if the moderate Islamist acceptance of the electoral process is no longer debatable, its commitment to basic civil liberties is still doubtful. A large zone of uncertainty is still open to discussion. The problem lies in a double doctrinal source of thought. In one hand, they declare their commitment to the rules of law, pluralism and basic liberties, including freedom of religion, since there is "no compulsion in religion" (II: 256). On other hand, they strongly reject attitudes deemed non-Islamic such as secularism, atheism, apostasy, public immorality and women's rights. Their conservatism goes as far as campaigning against "non-Islamic" ways of thinking, irreligious publications, the broadcast of liberal programs, Western music and the like. This contradictory policy is ascribed to their ideology: civic rights must be at best in conformity to Islamic "reference" or at least not at odds with "Islamic guidelines". This communitarian view of civic liberties gives precedence to duties to the prejudice of rights. It is more based on a utilitarian common good or public interest approach (*maslaha amma*) rather than on liberal and universal principles of freedom. Henceforth, moderate Islamists are democrats but "illiberal". Moreover, they are suspected of only being willing to take advantage of the electoral process in order to break it down and establish Islamic republics, once the political majority meets a strong social support. As Edward Djerejian, a veteran diplomat said when the Algerian Islamists won the elections in 1991: how do you ensure that elections do not ultimately lead to "one man, one vote, and one time". A recent International Crisis Group reported on the Islamic Brotherhood between "confrontation and integration", with a vast of area of mistrust and criticism levied against them "that their reliance on religious discourse represents a danger to national unity and alienates Christian Egyptians; that they remain committed to the creation of an Islamic state; and that, even if they came to power democratically, they would not exercise it that way" (International Crisis Group, 2008: 25). In addition, once the electoral process in Algeria was aborted, the Islamists moved toward radical and violent movements (GIA and then Salafi Group for Preacher and Combat). Conversely, the Turkish experience deserves better attention either to the hidden agenda of the Turkey's Justice and Development Party or the capacity of the Turkish army accept the rules of game. This dualistic attitude hinders the implementation of democracy on universal values.

Are Women Equal to Men?

Equality between men and women is one of the more relevant and controversial issues related to basic liberties. As for the Sharia issue, it divides Islamic societies according to new lines between liberals and conservative, since Islamic states have not made enough effort to improve women rights. As a result, Islamists have an avenue to manoeuvre and to oppose to any attempt to empower women.

As far as Islam is concerned, various regulations sharply limit women's rights. First, polygamy enables a man to marry four women provided they are treated with fairness, otherwise he is required to marry only one (IV: 3, 129). The bride has the right to a dowry (*mahr*) from the groom, but guardians or tutors on her behalf with "her agreement" conclude the contract, in the presence of two witnesses. A Moslem woman cannot marry to a non-Moslem, unless he converts, while a

Moslem man can marry a woman belonging to the possessors of the scripture (Jews and Christians). As heads of families, men are the "protectors and maintainers of women because God has given the one more than the other" (IV: 34). Marriage does not produce a community of property; thus, the man has to bear the expense of maintaining the household, otherwise his wife is in a position to ask for a divorce. A man has the right to repudiate his wife, temporarily or permanently. In case of divorce, the wife has the right to alimony and to custody but not guardianship and tutelage. In case of inheritance, the male inherits "a portion equal to that of two females" (II: 11). Women must be protected from the sexual appetites of men in the public sphere so the headscarf is considered as a religious obligation.

This traditional and unequal status is rooted in sexual and gender domination as well as in Islam and is the core of Islamist ideology. In general, Muslims declare either that Islam respects women as equal to men before God in matters of belief, or they accept woman's rights but within Islamic law and principles. They campaign so strongly that they have convinced states and secularists to accept limited rights for women and dissuade states from implementing reforms. Conversely, almost all Islamic states have tried desperately to ease the burden and to reform this traditional status. They have limited the right to abuse polygamy, established judicial divorce and enforced women rights in case of arbitrary behaviour or violence, but few have gone so far as, for instance, to abolish polygamy, establish equality in inheritance or accept that a woman has the right to transmit citizenship to her child. In such issues, religious law is ultimately the basis of legislation and jurisprudence. Among Islamic countries, Turkey remains a model and Iran a counter-model; among Arab countries, Saudi Arabia is the worst case, and Tunisia an extraordinary exception. In Morocco, when then king decided in 2003 to reform the *Mudawana* (personal status code), the PJD resisted and organised demonstrations before it accepted the law enacted by Parliament.

While the personal status is discriminatory, opening the public sphere and social activities to women is less controversial. Women are welcome in the public sphere even for Islamists, provided they are segregated, physically separated from men, dressed according Islamic rules and work in particular fields in conformity with their "nature" as mothers (medicine, nursing and education in schools for girls). Islamists in Kuwait campaigned in a 2005 parliamentary vote against the right of women to vote, not to mention being candidates (which they obtained). Nevertheless, a survey conducted among Islamist women from Hezbollah, Muslim Brotherhood, Moroccan activists and even Kuwait indicated that, while they reject "feminism", they contest inequality ascribed to social variables, and they look for a leading political role and try to balance household duties and public engagements (Abdellatif and Ottaway, 2007).

Therefore, if in the public sphere, men and women are "equal and separate", in interpersonal matters the full equality for women as private persons is accepted neither by the states nor by Islamists. As a result, two-thirds of the 65 million illiterate adult Arabs are women. In addition, the proportion of women in Arab parliaments is low. According to the UNDP report of 2003, women occupy 3.5 per cent of all seats in parliaments of Arab countries.

Three Remaining Divisions, One Citizenship

Islam pretends to unify all those embracing its faith regardless of their origins, colour and ethnic allegiances. However, Islam is actually undermined by the following three kinds of divisions or ascriptive allegiances: (1) confessional between Muslims and non-Muslims; (2) a constellation of primary divisions, whether they are ethnic (Kurds, Berbers, Pachtouns), or tribal and familial; and (3) sectarian ties within Islam opposing essentially Sunni to Shiite, not to mention the four religious Sunni legal schools. As a result, there are few homogenous Islamic countries (Tunisia, Libya, Yemen, Gaza strip; see Chapter 13). One might welcome this domestic multi-culturalism, if it was not actually destabilising the Middle East. Therefore, since political ideology and leadership are rooted in a culture that promotes hierarchy and communality, rather than individualism and civic rights, promoting a civic culture and a civil society is difficult. In addition, minorities need to be protected from tyrannical majorities.

Confessional Ties

In the medieval age, religious minorities shared one of three inequalities marking Islamic culture (between men and women, free men and slaves and Muslims and non-Muslims). Non-Muslims, at least the "people of the Book" (namely Jews, Christians and Zoroastrians) were "submitted" and "subdued": they practised their religion freely but paid a compensation or poll tax (9: 29). This *millet* system prevailed in the medieval age, namely in the Islamic and Ottoman Empires, during which religious minorities paid a special poll tax, finally abolished in the nineteenth century. Equal rights were recognised regardless of religion beliefs, including equal access to property and equal submission to taxes. Since then, for various reasons, religious minorities and particularly Jews have emigrated so that nowadays only a limited number of Christians are concerned with equality, particularly in Arab countries like Lebanon, Egypt, Iraq, Jordan and Syria. Lebanese Christians benefit from a "consociational pact" (1926 and Taïf 1992), according to which the president has to be Christian, while the president of the parliament is a Shiite and the prime minister a Sunni. Apart from this special case, the Arab state policy has a very positive attitude to this sensitive issue where Christian contribution is recognised and their presence favored by either political appointments or parliamentary quotas in parliament (Egypt, Syria, Jordan and Iraq). Unfortunately, since this representation is conceded by authoritarian regimes on an undemocratic basis, it is arguable that the status of religious minorities is a "privilege" and not a right to equal citizenship.

Islamists have more trouble with confessional ties. In theory, they are also committed to Islamic minority jurisprudence, according to which non-Muslims have the right to organise freely their own matters on issues such as worship and personal status. However, the solutions vary. In Lebanon, neither Hezbollah nor tiny Islamic Sunni groups contest the multi-confessional divisions. Similarly, they do not give up their religious propaganda and proselytise to gain more adherents. The situation is more complicated in Egypt, where Christians comprise about 10 per cent of the population (10 million). The Islamic Brotherhood demands that the head of the state must be Muslim, refuses any non-Muslim in its rank and membership and excludes any kind of "affirmative action" allowing Copts to be represented in parliament and in the executive branches. On the contrary, the tiny *Wasat* Party (Center) is more liberal, makes no difference between citizens and deliberately accepts universal principles. Otherwise, religious non-Muslim minorities are often subject to harassment, discrimination and violence, particularly in case of conflicts and political tensions, coming mainly from fanatic mobs and public opinion hostile to any religion except Islam.

Conversely, Islamists are very active and leading movements in Europe to promote "minorities jurisprudence" (*fiqh al-aqaliaat*). On the one hand, they call strongly for equality and citizenship based on universal principles. On the other, they ask positively for "collective rights". They fix legal statements, address issues and give advice for Muslims on how to practice ritual in matters of mixed marriages, food and the like. In case of conflict, they advocate respect for religion prior to obedience to citizenship. In addition, they have created private religious institutions to talk on behalf of Muslims and encourage them to defend their rights to private schooling, swimming pools, Islamic dress and mosques, as revealed in Khosrokhavar-led interviews with suspected members of al-Qaeda in French prisons to examine to what extent Islamic activism was behind their enrolment (Khosrokhavar, 2006). Therefore, a real double need for clarification is at stake: states have to recognise equal and universal rights, while Islamists must put an end to a "double standard" of a denial of minorities' rights at home and an appeal for citizenship abroad.

Primary Cleavages

The nation state is not congruent with ethnic, tribal and familial ties. Islamic states deal with them for political purposes, including legitimating their own authority. Some of them are bluntly rooted in familial and tribal ties, namely in the Gulf states. In contrast, Islamists apparently are indifferent to primary divisions, namely ethnical, tribal and familial ties that they promptly incorporate in the mainstream of Islamic magma. As a result, Islamism spreads regardless to theses divisions in so far that there is a Kurd Islamist movement, while the Taliban are rooted in Pachtun tribes. However, they are harshly hostile to any kind of separatism and refuse cultural rights to minorities, such as the Berbers in Algeria and Morocco not to mention Kashmir, where a war has been taking place since 1992 between

Hindus and Muslims. Once again, Islamism has to moderate its "unitarian" and intolerant ideology, while the nation state has to be more open to federalism and regionalism.

Sectarian Ties within Islam

Sectarianism is actually reshaping the future of Islam, even though it forms only 15 per cent of the Islamic population. In the beginning, Sunni Islamists supported the Iranian revolution, taking it for granted that a religious revolution was no more a dream or a utopia. The war between Iraq and Iran (1979), the American conquest of Iraq (2003) and Hezbollah resistance to Israel (2006) reversed the situation. Iraq, where the population is made up of 60 per cent Arab Shiites, is a good example of the dramatic consequences of any unbalanced shift between the two credos. Manipulated by Islamists, the ethnic variable opposes two main Shiite factions (the Sadr fraction and the Supreme Council for the Islamic Revolution) against a constellation of Sunni groups lead by the Muslim Brotherhood, revived under the Iraqi Islamic Party, not mentioning Kurdish subdivisions (Fuller, 2003). The situation is complicated by the interference of tribal leadership (Baram, 2005; Merr, 2006). Thus, in a series of *fatwa*, Sunni Iraqi Islamists, Wahhabi clerics and independent Islamists are more likely to condemn Shiites on a Sunni orthodox basis. The Sunni "forum of fatwa" raised on 11 April 2005 the question whether "the Shiites are impious". Two Saudi independent Islamists (Hamed al-Hamidi and Khuteir) gave their contribution, stating clearly that they are "heretical" (*rawafidh)*, impious and worse than the Jews! Al-Qaeda and foreign Arab combatants are more divided on the issue. Apparently, Bin Laden is appealing for unity against the Americans, while Zawahiri, more suspicious, would prefer to target Shiites than Americans. Moreover, the situation of the Sunni minority (9 per cent of the population) in Iran is not much better than the Shiite minority elsewhere. In Bahrain also, the Sunni Islamist movement is very hostile to the Shiites, who represent 70 per cent of the population, and is excluded from social welfare and deprived of political rights.

In this issue, the grey area is located in the tradition itself and in the way a majority is used to deal with sectarian minorities. The traditional position of the Sunni theology in medieval age was actually less or more similar: the excessive Shiite groups (*ghulat*) were excluded from the community, forcing them to balance between unsuccessful revolts and passive dissimulation of their faith. Their emergence today as a large component of Islamic faith puts Islam face to face with Islam, so that Islam vs Islam is no more a Western fantasy.

The Nearer and Further Enemy

While several religious parties are benefiting from the electoral process, other groups swing between participation in the electoral vote and violence. For example, in Pakistan, while the moderate garner not more than 5 per cent at the polls, others are attracted by what a report called the "Kalashnikov culture". Also, the Jamaat-e-Islami in Bangladesh, the Shiite Supreme Council for the Islamic Revolution and the Al-Da`wa and the Sunni Islamic Parties in Iraq, Hezbollah in Lebanon, and Hamas in Palestine balance between the poll and the sword. Data available also demonstrate clearly that some individuals of pacific movements, deceived by the moderate path, move to terrorism and leave moderate movements. This is the case for some militants of the Tunisian Nahdha or Pakistani radicals devoted to spreading Islam out of the country. Scholarly research devoted to the transnational non-violent Hizb al-Tahir (created in 1953, Jordan) evaluated the threat of a non-violent moment by explaining why Hizb al-Tahrir remains opposed to violence, while the Islamic Movement of Uzbekistan, its branch in Central Asia, embraced violence (Karagiannis and McCauley, 2006). In other words, Islamism is always ready to return to violence, or alternate between moderation and radicalism when circumstances or the balance of power change.

Is there any explanation for this conditional and inconsistent commitment to non-violent politics? Is it because Islam legitimates *jihad*? Does *jihad* involve killing the tyrants and open the door to internal and external terrorism? The issue is widely discussed and scholars and politicians do not agree on Islamists' priorities, whether they target the tyrant, are committed to national *jihad* or enlarge their combat to international arena.

Initially, radicals claim openly that Muslims have fallen again into idolatry that legitimates the murder of tyrants. Sayyid Qutb's doctrine was deemed even to have influenced the 11 September attacks (Zimmerman, 2004). He was followed by a network of extremist movements, including in the Middle East: in Pakistan Lashkar-e-Taiba (Army of the Pure), Laskar Jihad (The army of Jihad), Harakat al-Mujahideen (Movement of Combatants), Harakat ansar (Movements of Supporters) and Jaish Muhammed (the Army of Muhammad), mostly operating now in Kashmir; in Bangladesh, the Jamatul Mujahidin (Party of Holy warriors); in Algeria, the SGPC (Salafi Group for Preacher and Combat), recently reshaped as al-Qaeda of the Maghreb (Boudali, 2007); in Egypt, Jihad, al-Gamaa al-Islamiyya (The Islamic Group) and al-Takfir wal-Hijra (Unbelief and Exile); in Lebanon, Hezbollah; and in Palestine, Hamas and Jihad. A recent militant ideology atlas surveyed the mainstream trends (McCants, 2006). Once again, their ideology has been analysed (Torres et al., 2006) and refuted as "diametrically opposed to the requirements of liberal morality", regardless of its "social roots" (Meisels, 2006), their social roots examined (Abadie, 2004; Piazza, 2006; Gambetta and Hertog, 2007) along with their psychological "syndrome" (Kruglanski and Fishman, 2006). Shiite violence is singled out (Moghadem, 2007), while the comparative religious perspective stresses the monotheist destructive potentialities (Ellens, 2004). In addition, Christopher Blanchard, analyst in Middle Eastern Affairs, is periodically supervising a series of well-informed update papers on "Al-Qaeda: Statements and Evolving Ideology", published by the Congressional Research Center (USA).

A great deal has been written on "Islam and violence", but the issue is debatable how to address the question of whether violence is rooted in cultural or structural variables (Etienne, 2007). Recourse to violence has earlier been considered as a manipulation of classic and orthodox Sunni dogma, according to which obedience to the imam and praying behind him are duties whether he is pious or not. It is argued that *jihad* has at least two meanings: making an effort to fight one's defects, inclinations and the devil inside, or fighting with weapons in a holy war against infidels, but not against Muslims. The manipulation resides in the fact that radicals assume the impiety of the government and the leaders. Unfortunately, the same people who condemn this extremism are also prompt to legitimise violence against external enemies. This is the case of Hamas and Hezbollah and various Iraqi extremist movements, widely supported by Islamist movements, traditional clerics of al-Azhar and the independent religious establishment, and also Islamic public opinion. All argue that there is a difference between national resistance through *jihad* against Israel and the United States on the one hand and terrorism on the other hand. They even declare that Israel and United States are also rogue and terrorist states. Traditional clerics of al-Azhar, independent individuals and wide Islamic public opinion assume that only internal terrorism is religiously illegal. The shift comes with al-Qaeda's ideology, that moved from combating the "nearer enemy" to target the distant enemy.

West vs Islam

A recent survey by the PEW Global Attitudes Project on the "Great Divide" between Westerners and Muslims conducted in 13 countries, including the United States, in 2006, recognised that many in the West see Muslims as "fanatical, violent and as lacking tolerance", while Muslims see Westerners as "selfish, immoral and greedy – as well as violent and fanatical". Regarding Islamic violence, the survey noticed a substantial decline in the percentage of people supporting suicide bombers and having confidence in Bin Laden. Nevertheless, a majority of respondents in Indonesia, Turkey and Jordan and 56 per cent of the British Muslims do not believe that Arabs carried out the 11 September attacks. Muslims in general deplore the double standard in the Palestinian conflict and in every issue related to Islam. Islamists are thus prompt to exploit this anger and feelings of injustice and give an extraordinary amplification to the "conspiracy theory", according to which the Americans and Jews and Crusaders are plotting against Muslims in order to divide them and rob their resources.

The West has only one agenda: democratising the Middle East is the core solution to all Islamic diseases, including the war on terrorism. Nevertheless, it is doubtful that the more democratic a country becomes, the less likely it is to produce terrorism. Data available do not prove a robust correlation between democracy and absence of or decrease in terrorism. Terrorists recruit candidates for suicide in Western democratic countries, as well as in undemocratic Middle

Eastern countries. Hostility to the United States is a global and shared feeling, even among liberals and seculars who deeply disagree with US policies. Western public opinion is not doing better since Western audiences oversimplify the complexity of Islam and the Middle East.

Conclusion: Clarifying the Uncertainty

Islam, fundamentalism and Islamic states face series of dilemma. As the opposite of scholarly research that repeatedly stresses the mutual compromise between governments and moderate Islamists, it would be better to ask for a mutual clarification from states and fundamentalists as well. However, this double ambiguity is rooted in a series of causes.

First, neither the governments nor the Islamists are willing to get rid of this confusion between religion and politics. This makes it difficult for the former to accuse the latter of politicizing Islam, while each of them mismatch politics and religion. Liberals are claiming this separation but they are not strong enough and do not have enough credentials to make things move towards a modern path. Second, the genuine advantage according to which Islam is freed from an official clergy is nowadays reversed in a dramatic shortcoming. Medieval Islam shaped by a kind of Church represented by official scholars committed to jurisprudence. This was what Gellner called "Higher Islam": urban, individualistic, quietist and indulgent persons managing education, jurisprudence and ritual. In addition, "Lower Islam" is grounded on popular feelings, propelled by saints and marabous, with ecstatic and charismatic leadership. Today, the Sunni official establishment is characterised at least by three models: the Egyptian model based on "subordination and cooperation", the Saudi-Arabian model reflecting "an equal alliance" between the state and Wahhabi clergy and the Jordanian model where religious establishment is "totally subordinate to the Hashemite Throne" (Bachar et al., 2006; Redissi, 2008). Nevertheless, official Islam has actually lost its traditional antecedence so that several constituencies are in competition for the "symbolic capital" of Islam: official clerics vs freelance, political Islam vs missionaries, moderate vs radicals, scholars vs charismatic media leaders, elder generations vs newcomers, good vs bad Islamists. Each of them is issuing *fatwa* with ease, from Ben Laden to Wahhabi clergy. As Hillel Frakin put it: "The Islamist movement may mount a debate over authority as such" (Frakin et al., 2006: 2). The output is so confusing that nobody is able to differentiate between official clergy and independent and influential leaders such as Ghardawi, Umar Khaled and Safar al-Hawali. That is why the Al-Azhar religious official clergy is asking political authorities to prohibit the issuing of *fatwas* without legal credentials.

Third, the tradition of Islam is open to interpretation. In the past, *ijtihad* (individual reasoning) was surrounded by a series of conditions so that only those who were scholarly qualified were authorised to issue legal statements. However, the "gate of ijtihad" has been opened so that any actor has become able to advocate the revival of Islamic principles or to debate by quoting this or that verse of the Koran or by recalling that tradition of the Prophet. Islamists and liberals are in conflict on what Abdurrhamane Wahid, Indonesian former President and the former Head of Nadawt al-Ulama (Congress of Religious Scholars) called in 2005 the "global struggle for the soul of Islam" or the war of ideas between "right Islam versus wrong Islam" (Wahid, 2006: 5–9). In this context, while Islamists are arguing that their interpretation is the "true" Islam, liberals, secularists and modern Muslim rightly accuse them of promoting a conservative, rigid and an illiberal *ijtihad*. This current issue is of great importance for the future of Islam.

Appendix 1.1

Muslim Populations in per cent of Total Populations during the Twentieth Century

COUNTRY	2000	1995	1990	1980	1970	1900	POP 2000 (millions)
Mauritania	99.1	99.5	99	99.4	99.3	97.7	2.7
Tunisia	98.9	99.4	99	99.4	99.1	87.5	9.5
Yemen	98.9	99.8	98.9	100	99.9	98.4	18.3
Morocco	98.3	98.9	98.3	99.4	98.9	96.4	29.9
Somalia	98.3	99.7	97.7	99.8	99.7	99.9	7.3
Afghanistan	98.1	99	98	99.3	99.3	99.5	25.9
Turkey	97.2	99.2	97.2	99.2	99.1	80	66.7
Algeria	96.7	99.9	96.8	99.1	99.1	86.6	30.3
Libya	96.1	96.9	95.9	98.1	97	94.3	5.3
Pakistan	96.1	96.8	96.2	96.8	96.7	82.1	141.3
Iraq	96	96.2	95.8	95.8	95.3	89.5	22.7
Iran	95.6	99.2	95.7	97.9	98.1	98.1	70.3
Saudi Arabia	93.7	98.8	94.1	98.8	99.3	100	20.3
Jordan	93.5	92.9	94	93	93.6	94	4.9
Niger	90.7	98.5	90.4	87.9	86	45.1	10.8
Syria	89.3	89	88.8	89.6	89	83.1	16.2
Senegal	87.6	94	87.7	91	90	69.1	9.4
Oman	87.4	85.9	88.7	98.9	99.1	100	2.5
Turkmenistan	87.2	87.1	82.4				4.7
Bangladesh	85.8	86.7	85.5	85.9	82.3	65.6	137.4
Egypt	84.4	90.1	84.1	81.8	81	81.2	67.9
Azerbaijan	83.7	86.9	81.5				8
Tajikistan	83.6	85	79.8				6.1
Kuwait	83	89.9	89.6	95.1	94.6	100	1.9
Mali	81.9	90	81	80	77.7	30	11.4
Indonesia	76.5	87.2	77.2	78.9	43	44.5	212.1
Uzbekistan	76.2	88	71.5				24.9
United Arab Emirates	75.6	95.8	77.8	94.9	95.3	100	2.6
Sudan	70.3	73	69.1	73	71	62	31.1

COUNTRY	2000	1995	1990	1980	1970	1900	POP 2000 (millions)
Guinea	67.3	84.9	66.9	69	68	58	8.2
Kirghizia	60.8	69.9	53.8				4.9
Bosnia Herzegovina	60	40	45.8		33.5	34	3.8
Chad	59.1	44.1	58.5	44	42	36	7.9
Burkina Faso	48.6	30.6	48.3	43	35	10	11.5
Malaysia	47.7	52.9	47.7	49.4	49.4	48.8	22.2
Sierra Leone	45.9	60.1	45.9	39.4	38	10	4.4
Nigeria	43.9	45	43.9	45	44	25.9	113.9
Kazakhstan	42.7	47	35.4				16.2
Lebanon	42.4	66.8	42.1	37.4	35.4	20.5	3.5
Albania	38.8	65	35	20.5	27.7	68.5	3.1
Tanzania	31.8	35	31.6	32.5	31.5	7	35.1
Ethiopia	30.4	30.1	30	31.4	31	26	62.9
Ivory Coast	30.1	38.8	29.5	24	22.8	5	16
Macedonia	28.3	26	22.4		25.8	34	2
Cameroon	21.2	21.8	21.2	22	20	5	14.9
Benin	20	12	18.7	15.2	14	7.1	6.3
Ghana	19.7	30	19.4	15.7	14.2	5	19.3
Georgia	19.3	11.1	19.1				5.3
Togo	18.9	12	18.5	17	13.2	4	4.5
Singapore	18.4	15.4	18.3	17.4	18	22	4
Mauritius	16.9	16.1	16.6	16.4	16	10.8	1.2
Serbia-Montenegro	16.2	19	15.5	10.4	11	9.9	10.7
Liberia	16	13.9	16.3	21.2	19.6	1.9	3.1
Central African Republic	15.6	14.8	15.5	3.2	3	0.3	3.7
Malawi	14.8	20	14.9	16.2	16	3.1	11.3
India	12.1	10.9	11.9	11.6	11.2	13.8	12.1
Israel	12	14.3	12.3	8	8.9	83.5	6
Bulgaria	11.9	10.5	11.7	10.6	11	17.2	7.9
Mozambique	10.5	13	10.6	13	12.2	3	18.3

Source: Barrett, Encyclopaedia Britannica: Yearbook.

Appendix 1.2
Muslim Populations < 10%

COUNTRY	2000	1995	1990	1980	1970	1900	POP 2000 (millions)
Sri Lanka	9	7.6	8.9	7.2	6.9	6.9	18.9
Rwanda	7.9	1	8	8.6	8.5	0.2	7.6
Russia	7.6	2.7	7.6	11.3	11.5	11.2	145.5
Kenya	7.3	6	7.1	6	6.4	3.4	30.7
France	7.1	5.5	6.8	3	2.7	0.1	59.2
Thailand	6.8	3.9	6.7	3.9	3.9	1.5	62.8
Trinidad and Tobago	6.8	5.8	6.7	6.5	6.3	3.7	1.3
Philippines	6.2	4.3	6.1	4.3	4.3	3.4	75.7
Moldova	5.5	0	5.1				4.3
Uganda	5.2	6.6	5.5	6.6	6	2	23.3
Mongolia	4.8	6.2	4.3	1.4	1.6	1	2.5
Gabon	4.6		4.3	0.8	0.8		1.2
Germany	4.4	2.1	3.6	2.4	0.7		82
Panama	4.4		4.4	4.5	4.5	0.5	2.9
Nepal	3.9	3.8	3.8	3	2.9	1	23
Netherlands	3.8	3.2	3.6	1	0.5		15.9
Belgium	3.6		3.4	1.1	0.9		10.2
Greece	3.3	1.5	3	1.5	1.5	12.8	10.6
Armenia	2.7	2.8	4.2				3.8
Switzerland	2.7		2.3	0.3			7.2
Myanmar	2.4	3.8	2.7	3.6	3.6	3.2	47.7
South Africa	2.4	1.1	2.4	1.3	1.3	0.6	43.3
Cambodia	2.3	2.1	2.3	2.4	2.4	2.2	13.1
Croatia	2.3	1.3	2.9		0.3		4.7
Sweden	2.3		1.6	0.1			8.8
Austria	2.2		1.8		0.2		8.1
Argentina	2		1.7	0.2	0.2	0.1	37
Madagascar	2	5	2.1	1.7	1.6	0.5	16
United Kingdom	2	1.4	1.8	1.4	1.1		59.4
Ukraine	1.7		1.6				49.6
China	1.5	1.4	1.6	2.4	2.6	5.1	1.5
United States	1.5	1.9	1.4	0.8	0.4		283.2

COUNTRY	2000	1995	1990	1980	1970	1900	POP 2000 (millions)
Burundi	1.4		1.3	0.9	0.9	0.2	6.4
Congo Brazzaville	1.3	2.1	1.1	0.4	0.4		3
Denmark	1.3		1.1	0.2	0.2		5.3
Romania	1.3		1.2	1.2	1.2	0.8	22.4
Australia	1.2		1	0.2	0.2	0.3	19.1
Italy	1.2		1.1	0.1	0.1		57.5
Congo Kinshasa	1.1	1.4	1.2	1.4	1.4	0.6	50.9
Zambia	1.1		1.1	0.3	0.3		10.4
Bhutan	1		1	5	5.1	0.9	2.1
Canada	1	0.4	0.9	0.6	0.2		30.8
Luxembourg	1		1				0.4
Norway	1		0.9	0.1	0.1		4.5
Viet Nam	0.7		0.8	1	1	0.7	78.1
Zimbabwe	0.7		0.8	0.9	0.9	0.2	12.6
Hungary	0.6		0.5				10
Spain	0.5	1.1	0.4				39.9
Laos	0.4		0.4	1	1	0.2	5.3
Latvia	0.4		0.3				2.4
Taiwan	0.4		0.4	0.5	0.4	0.2	22.2
Belarus	0.3		0.2				10.2
Estonia	0.3		0.3				1.4
Mexico	0.3		0.3				98.9
Botswana	0.2		0.2				1.5
Finland	0.2		0.2		0.3		5.2
Ireland	0.2		0.2				3.8
South Korea	0.2		0.1				46.7
Lithuania	0.2		0.2				3.7
New Zealand	0.2		0.2				3.8
Portugal	0.2		0.2				10
Brazil	0.1		0.1	0.1	0.1		170.4
Colombia	0.1		0.1	0.2	0.2	0	42.1
Cuba	0.1		0.1	0		0	11.2
Honduras	0.1		0.1	0.1		0	6.4
Jamaica	0.1		0.1	0.2	0.2	0.3	2.6
Japan	0.1		0.1			0	127.1
Lesotho	0.1		0.1			0	2
Slovenia	0.1		0.1		0.5	0	2

Bibliography

Abadie, A. (2004) *Poverty, Political Freedom, and the Roots of Terrorism*. Faculty Research Working Papers Series, Harvard University, John F. Kennedy School of Government.

Abd al-Raziq, A. (1994) *L'islam et les fondements du pouvoir*. Paris: La découverte.

Abdel-Malek, A. (1965) *Anthologie de la littérature arabe contemporaine*. Vol. 2. Paris: Seuil.

Abdoh, M. (1925) *Exposé de la religion musulmane*. Paris: Geuthner.

Abootalebi, A.R. (2000) *Islam and Democracy*. New York: Garland.

Abrahamian, E. (1982) *Iran Between Two Revolutions*. Princeton, NJ: Princeton University Press.

Abramovici, P. (2002) "L'histoire secrète des négociations entre Washington et les talibans", *Le Monde Diplomatique*, 10–11 January.

Abu-Lughod, J. (1989) *Before European Hegemony: The World System A.D. 1250–1350*. New York: Oxford University Press.

Abu-Rabi', I. (1996) *Intellectual Origins of Islamic Resurgence on the Modern Arab World*. Albany, NY: State University of New York Press.

Adas, M. (ed.) (1993) *Islamic and European Expansion: The Forging of Global Order*. Philadelphia, PA: Temple University Press.

Addi, L. (1992) "Islam politique et démocratisation en Algérie", *Esprit*, August–September, 143–151.

Afkhami, M. (ed.) (1995) *Faith and Freedom: Women's Human Rights in the Muslim World*. Syracuse, NY: Syracuse University Press.

Ahmad, F. (1993) *The Making of Modern Turkey*. London: Routledge.

Ahmed, A. (1964) *Studies in Islamic Culture in the Indian Environment*. Oxford: Oxford University Press.

Ahmed A. (1967) *Modernism in India and Pakistan, 1857–1964*. Oxford: Oxford University Press.

Ahmed, A.S. (1992) *Postmodernism and Islam*. London: Routledge.

Ahmed, A.S. (1998) *Islam Today: A Short Introduction to the Muslim World*. London: I.B. Tauris.

Ahmed, L. (1993) *Woman and Gender in Islam*. New Haven, CT: Yale University Press.

Ahmed, R.S. (1991) *The Militant Prophet*. London: Riad El-Rayyes, 2 volumes.

Ajami, F. (1998) *Dream Palace of the Arabs*. New York: Pantheon Books.

Al-Ahnaf, M. (1989) "Tunisie, un débat sur les rapports État-religion", *Maghreb Machrek*, 123, October–December.

Al-Ahnaf, M., B. Botiveau and F. Fregosi (1991) *L'Algérie par ses islamistes*. Paris: Karthala.

Al-Aoufi, N. (1999) "La réforme économique: Stratégies, institutions, acteurs", *Maghreb Machrek*, April–June, 164.

Al-Azm, S.J. (1999) "Sur l'islam, la laïcité et l'Occident", *Le monde diplomatique*, September.

Algar, H. (1969) *Religion and State in Iran, 1785–1906*. Berkeley, CA: University of California Press.

Algar, H. (trans.) (1981) *Islam and Revolution: Writings and Declarations of Imam Khomeini*. Berkeley, CA: Mizan Press.

Ali, T. (2002) *The Clash of Fundamentalisms: Crusades, Jihads and Modernity*. London: Verso; In French (2002) *Le Choc des Intégrismes*. Paris: Textuel.

Al-Mawardi, Abu Al-Hasan (10th century) (1982) *Les statuts gouvernementaux*, trans. E. Fagnan. Paris: Sycomore.

Al-Mulk, N. (1960) *The Book of Government or Rules for Kings*, trans. H. Darke. London: Routledge & Kegan Paul.

Al-Najjar Fatiha Dazi-Héni, G. (2006) *Monarchies et sociétés d'Arabie: Le temps des confrontations*. Paris: Les Presses de Sciences Po.

Altunsik, M.B. (1996) "A Rentier State's Response to Oil Crisis: Economic Reform Policies in Libya", *Arab Studies Quarterly*, 18(4) Autumn, 49–63.

Al-Yassiri, A. (1985) *Religion and States in the Kingdom of Saudi Arabia*. Boulder, CO: Westview Press.

Amin, S. (1970a) *La nation arabe*. Paris: Minuit.

Amin, S. (1970b) *Le Maghreb Moderne*. Paris: Minuit.

Anderson, E.W. (2000) *The Middle East*. London: Routledge.

Anderson, L. (1983) "Qaddafi's Islam", in J.L. Esposito, *Voices of Resurgent Islam*. New York: Oxford University Press.

Anderson, L. (1995) "Democracy in the Arab World: A Critique of the Political Culture Approach", in R. Breynen, B. Korany and P. Noble (eds) *Political Liberalization and Democratization in the Arab World. Volume 1, Theoretical Perspectives*. Boulder CO: Lynne Rienner.

Anderson, L. (2000) "Entretien", *Maghreb Machrek*, October–December, 170.

Anderson, L. (2001) "Muamar al-Qaddafi: The 'king' of Libya", *Journal of International Affairs*, 54(2) Spring.

Anderson, P. (1974) *Passages from Antiquity to Feudalism*. London: New Left Books.

Angrist, M.P. (1999) "Parties, Parliament and Political Dissent in Tunisia", *The Journal of North Africa*, 4(4) Winter, 89–104.

Antonius, G. (1939) *The Arab Awakening: The Story of the Arab National Movement*. Philadelphia, PA: J.B. Lippincott; Reprinted (1945) by G.P. Putnam's Sons; Arabic trans. (1962) by N. Asad and I. Abbas. Beirut: Dar al-'ilm li al-malayin.

Apter, D. (1965) *The Politics of Modernization*. Chicago, IL: Universty of Chicago Press.

Aqqad, M. (1952) *Al-dimuqratiya fi-l islam* (*Democracy in Islam*). Cairo: Dar al-Ma'aref.

Arab Human Development Report (2002) New York: United Nations.

Arkoun, M. (1984) *Pour une critique de la raison islamique*. Paris: Maisonneuve et Larose.

Arkoun, M. and H. Sanson (1989) *Religion et laïcité. Une approche laïque de l'islam*. La Tourelle: Centre Thomas More.

Armstrong, K. (1999) *A History of God*. London: Vintage.

Armstrong, K. (2000) *The Battle for God*. London: HarperCollins.

Armstrong, K. (2001a) *Muhammad: A Biography of the Prophet*. London: Weidenfeld and Nicolson.

Armstrong, K. (2001b) *Islam: A Short History*. London: Weidenfeld and Nicolson.

Ash'ari, A. (10th century) (1980) *Maquâlât al-islâmiyyin*. Cairo: Maktabat al-nahdha al-misriyya.

Ashmawy, M.S. (1989) *L'islamisme contre l'islam*. Paris: La découverte.

Ashmawy, M.S. (1994) "Terreur et terrorisme au Moyen Orient", in R.S.A. Ashmamy and A.K. Khalil, *Contre l'islamisme*. Paris: Maisonneuve et Larose.

Avempace (Ibn Bajjah, 12th century) (1994) *Tadbîr al-Mutawahid* (*Rule of the Solitary*). Tunis: CERES.

Averroès (1996) *Discours décisif*. Paris: Flammarion.

Ayubi, N.N. (1993) *Political Islam: Religion and Politics in the Arab World*. London: Routledge.

Ayubi, N.N. (1996) *Overstating the Arab State: Politics and Society in the Middle East*. London: I.B. Tauris.

Azmeh, A. (1992) *Al-'ilmaniyya min manthur mukhtalf* (*Secularism from Different Points of View*). Beirut: CEUA.

Azmeh, A. (1996) *Islams and Modernities*. London: Verso.

Babès, L. and T. Oubrou (2002) *Loi d'Allah, loi des hommes*. Paris: Albin Michel.

Bachar, S., S. Bar, R. Machtiger and Y. Minzili (2006) *Establishment Ulama and Radicalism in Egypt, Saudi Arabia, and Jordan*. Center on Islam, Democracy and the Future of Muslim World, series no. 1, paper no. 4, Hudson Institute, December.

Badawi, A. (1968) *La transmission de la philosophie grecque au monde arabe*. Paris: Vrin.

Badawi, A. (1972) *Histoire de la philosophie en islam*, 2 volumes. Paris: Vrin.

Baderin, M.A. (2003) *International Human Rights and Islamic Law*. Oxford: Oxford University Press.

Badie, B. (1986) *Les deux Etats: pouvoir et société en Occident et en terre d'islam*. Paris: Fayard.

Balta, P. (1991) *L'islam dans le monde*. Paris: Le monde de l'édition.

Bani Sadr, A.H. (1989) *Le Coran et les droits de l'homme*. Paris: Maisonneuve et Larose.

Baram, A. (2005) *Who Are the Insurgents? Sunni Arab Rebels in Iraq*. United States Institute of Peace, Special Report 160, www.usip.org.

Barber, B.D. (1996) *Djihad versus McWorld*. Paris: Desclée de Brouwer.

Bayart, J.-F., S. Ellis and B. Hibou (eds) (1997) *La criminalisation de l'Etat en Afrique*. Brussels: Editions Complexes.

Beachler, J., J.A. Hall and M. Mann (eds) (1988) *Europe and the Rise of Capitalism*. Oxford: Basil Blackwell.

Beblawi, H. (1990) "The rentier state in the Arab world", in L. Giacomo (ed.) *The Arab State*. Berkeley, CA: University of California Press.

Becker, C.H. (1910) *Islamstudien, Vol. 1*. Leipzig: Quelle und Meyer.

Bellin, E. (1991) "Tunisian Industrialists and the State", in W. Zartman (ed.) *Tunisia. The Political Economy of Reform*. Boulder and London: Lynne Rienner.

Ben Achour, Y. (1993) *Normes, foi et loi*. Tunis: CERES.

Ben Dhiaf, A. (1963–1966) *Ithaf*, 6 volumes (Chroniques des Rois de Tunis). Tunis: MTI.

Bendix, R. (1977) *Max Weber: An Intellectual Portrait*. Berkeley, CA: University of California Press; First published 1960.

Benjamin, W. (1979) *Charles Baudelaire*. Paris: Payot.

Bergen, P. (2002) *The Holy War, Inc.: Inside the Secret World of Osama Bin Laden*. Phoenix, AZ: Mass Market.

Bergensen, A. (2007) *The Sayyid Qutb Reader*. London: Routledge.

Berman, H.J. (1983) *Law and Revolution: The Formation of Western Legal Tradition*. Cambridge, MA: Harvard University Press.

Bianchi, R. (1991) "Four Reasons for Optimism", Workshop, F.L. Cantori (ed.) "Democratization in the Middle East", in *American-Arab Affairs*, 36, Spring.

Bill, J.A. (1996) "The study of Middle East Politics: A Stocklading", *Middle East Journal*, 50(4) Autumn.

Bill, J.A. and R. Springborg (1990) *Politics in the Middle East*. New York: HarperCollins.

Bill, J.A. and R. Springborg (2000) *Politics in the Middle East*. New York: Longman.

Binder, L. (1988) *Islamic Liberalism: A Critique of Development Ideologies*. Chicago, IL: University of Chicago Press.

Black, C.E. (1966) *The Dynamics of Modernization*. New York: Harper & Row.

Blanc, F. (2001) *Ben Laden et l'Amérique*. Paris: Bayard.

Bleuchot, H. (1982) "L'islam de M. el-Qadhafi", in Gellner, E. and J.-C. Vatin (eds) (1982) *Islam et politique au Maghreb*. Paris: CNRS.

Bleuchot, H. (1996) *Les institutions traditionnelles dans le monde arabe*. Paris: Khartala/IREMAM.

Blumenberg, H. (1999) *La légitimité des Temps Modernes*. Paris: Gallimard; First published 1966, *Die Ligitimität der Neuzeit*. Frankfurt am Main: Suhrkamp.

Bocco, R. and C. Velud (eds) (1995) "Tribus, tribalisme et États au Moyen-Orient", *Maghreb Machrek*, 147.

Bodansky, Y. (2001) *Bin Laden: The Man Who Declared War on America*. New York: Random House.

Bori, P.-C. (1991) *L'interprétation infinie*. Paris: Cerf.

Bosworth, E. (ed.) (1960) *Encyclopedia of Islam*. Leiden: Brill.

Bouamrane, C. (1978) *Le problème de la liberté humaine dans la pensée musulmane (solution mu'tazilite)*. Paris: Vrin.
Bouandel, Y. (2002) "Bouteflika's Reforms and the Question of Human Rigths in Algeria", *The Journal of North Africa Studies*, 7(2) Summer, 23–42.
Boubakeur, D. (2002) *Les défis de l'islam*. Paris: Flammarion.
Boudali, L.K. (2007) *The GSPC Newest Franchise in al-Qaeda's Global Jihad*. West Point, NY: The Combating Terrorism Center, United States Military Academy, http://ctc.usma.edu.
Boulares, S. (1995) "La Grande Muette livre ses secrets", *Les Cahiers de l'Orient*, troisième/quatrième trimestre, 39/40.
Bourdieu, P. (1972) *La distinction*. Paris: Minuit; Trans. by Richard Nice (1984) *Distinction*. London: Routledge & Kegan Paul.
Bourdieu, P. (1980) *Questions de Sociologie*. Paris: Minuit.
Bourdieu, P. (1982) *Ce que parler veut dire : L'économie des échanges linguistiques*. Paris: Fayard.
Bourdieu, P. (2001) *Langage et pouvoir symbolique*. Paris: Seuil; Version augmentée de (1991) *Language and Symbolic Power*. London: Polity Press (translation of (1982) *Ce que parler veut dire*. Paris: Fayard).
Braudel, F. (1979) *Civilisation, économie et capitalisme, XVe–XVIIIe siècles*. Paris: Armand Colin; Trans. (1981–1984) *Civilization and Capitalism, 15th–18th Centuries*. London: Collins.
Braudel, F. (1985) *La dynamique du capitalisme*. Paris: Arthaud.
Braudel, F. (1993) *Civilisation matérielle, économie et capitalisme*, 3 volumes, Paris: Edition Livre de poche.
Breynen, R., B. Korany and P. Noble (eds) (1995) *Political Liberalization and Democratization in the Arab World. Volume 1, Theoretical Perspectives*. Boulder, CO: Lynne Rienner.
Brière, C. and O. Carré (1983) *Islam, guerre à l'Occident?* Paris: Autrement.
Brooks, G. (1995) *Nine Parts of Desire: The Hidden World of Islamic Women*. New York: Doubleday.
Brown, C.L. (1973) "Islam's Role in North Africa", in W. Zartman (ed.) *State and Society in Contempary North Africa*. New York: Prager.
Brown, L.C. (1974) *The Tunisia of Ahmed Bey, 1837–1855*. Princeton, NJ: Studies on the Near East.
Brown, L.C. (2001) *Religion and State*. New York: Columbia University Press.
Brunschvig, R. (1976) *Etudes d'islamologie*, Vol. 1. Paris: Vrin.
Bugeat, F. and A. Lalande (1996) *La Libye*. Paris: PUF/Que sais-je?
Bull, H. (1977) *The Anarchical Society: A Study of Order in Politics*. New York: Columbia University Press.
Burgat, F. (1988) *L'islamisme au Maghreb*. Paris: Khartala.
Burgat, F. (1995) *L'islamisme en face*. Paris: La Découverte.
Burgat, F. (2003) *Face to Face with Political Islam*. London: I.B. Tauris.
Burgat, F. (2008) *Islamism in the Shadow of al-Qaeda*. London: I.B. Tauris.

Burr, M.J. and R.O. Collins (1999) *Africa's Thirty Year War: Libya, Chad and the Sudan, 1963–1993*. Boulder, CO: Westwiew Press.

Camau, M. (1979) "Caractère et rôle du constitutionnalisme dans les États maghrébins", in *Développements politiques au Maghreb*. Paris: CNRS.

Camau, M. (1984) "L'État tunisien: de la tutelle au désengagement", *Maghreb Machrek*, January–March, 103.

Caner, E.M. and E.F. Caner (2002) *Unveiling Islam: An Insider's Look at Muslim Life and Beliefs*. Grand Rapids, MI: Kregel.

Cantori, L.J. and R. Bianchi (1991) "Democratization in the Middle East", *American-Arab Affairs*, 36, 1–5.

Carlier, O. (1992) "De l'islahisme à l'islamisme: La thérapie politico-religieuse du FIS", *Cahiers d'études africaines*, 2.

Carré, O. (1984) *Mystique et politique: Lecture révolutionnaire du Coran par Sayyid Qutb*. Paris: Cerf.

Carré, O. (1986) "A propos de Weber et l'islam", *Archives de Sciences des Religions*, 61(1) 139–152.

Carré, O. (1988) "A propos de vues néo-khaldûnienne sur quelques systèmes politiques arabes", *Arabica*, XXXV(3) 368–387.

Cassirer, E. (1966) *La philosophie des Lumières*. Paris: Fayard/Agora; First published (1932) *Die Philosophie der Aufklärung*. Tübingen: Mohr.

Chalmers, D.A. (1991) "Corporatism and Compartive Politics", in H.J. Wiarda (ed.) *New Directions in Comparative Politics*. Boulder, CO: Westview Press.

Charfi, M. (1999) *Islam et liberté*. Paris: Albin Michel.

Chaudhuri, K.N. (1985) *Trade and Civilisation in the Indian Ocean*. Cambridge: Cambridge University Press.

Chaudhuri, K.N. (1991) *Asia before Europe: Economy and Civilisations of the Indian Ocean from the Rise of Islam to 1750*. Cambridge: Cambridge University Press.

Chebel, M. (2002) *Le sujet en islam*. Paris: Seuil.

Chekir, H. (2000) *Le statut de la femme entre les textes et les résistances. Le cas de la Tunisie*. Tunis: Chama.

Choudhury, M.A. (1997a) *Money in Islam*. London: Routledge.

Choudhury, M.A. (1997b) *Reforming the Muslim World*. London: Kegan Paul International.

Choudhury, M.A. (2003) *The Islamic World-System*. London: Routledge.

Cizakca, M. (1996) *A Comparative Evolution of Business Partnerships: The Islamic World and Europe, With Specific Reference to the Ottoman Archives*. Herndon, VA: Brill Academic Publishers.

Collective (2002) *L'autre Amérique. Les Américains contre la guerre*. Paris: Textuel.

Colliot-Thélène, C. (1990) "La place de l'islam dans la sociologie des religions de Weber", *MAUSS*, 10, 6–30.

Cook, M. (ed.) (1970) *Studies in the Economic History of the Middle East*. Oxford: Oxford University Press.

Corbin, J. (2002) *Al-Qaeda: In Search of the Terror Network that Threatens the World*. New York: Thunder's Mouth Press/Nation Books.

Coulson, N.J. (1964) *A History of Islamic Law*. Edinburgh: Edinburgh University Press; Trans. (1995) *Histoire du droit islamique*. Paris: PUF.

Coulson, N.J. (1969) *Conflicts and Tensions in Islamic Jurisprudence*. Chicago, IL: Chicago University Press.

Crone, P. (1980) *Slaves on Horses: The Evolution of the Islamic Polity*. Cambridge: Cambridge University Press.

Crone, P. (1987) *Meccan Trade and the Rise of Islam*. Princeton, NJ: Princeton University Press.

Crone, P. (1993) "Tribes and States in the Middle East", *Journal of the Royal Asiatic Society*, 3(2) July, 353–376.

Crone, P. (1994) "Even an Ethiopian Slave: The Transformation of a Sunni Tradition", *BSOAS*, LVII, Part I, 59–67.

Crone, P. (1999) "Weber, Islamic Law, and the Rise of Capitalism", in T.E. Huff and W. Schluchter (eds) *Max Weber and Islam*. New Brunswick, NY: Transaction, 247–272.

Crone, P. (2002) *Roman, Provincial and Islamic Law: The Origins of the Islamic Patronate*. Cambridge: Cambridge University Press.

Crone, P. (2003) *God's Caliph: Religious Authority in the First Centuries of Islam*. New York: Cambridge University Press.

Crone, P. and M. Cook (1977) *Hagarism: The Making of the Islamic World*. Cambridge: Cambridge University Press.

Darwish, A. (2001) "Gadaffi goes African", *Middle East*, 316, October.

Deeb, A.K. (1988) "Cultural Creation in a Fragmented Society", in H. Sharabi (ed.) *The Next Decade. Alternative Future*. Boulder, CO: Westview Press.

Deeb, M.-J. (1999) "Political and Economic Developments in Libya in the 1990s", in Y. Zoubir (ed.) *North Africa in Transition: State, Society, and Economic Transformation in the 1990s*. Gainesville, FL: University Press of Florida.

Deeb, M.-J. (2000) "Qadhafi Change Policy: Causes and Consequences", *Middle East Policy*, 7(2).

Deeb, M.K. (1978) "Islam and Arab Nationalism in Al-Qaddafi's Ideology", *Journal of South and Asian Middle Eastern Studies*, 2, Winter.

Deeb, M.K. (1996) "Militant Islam and its Critics: The Case of Libya", in J. Ruedy (ed.) *Islamism and Secularism in North Africa*. New York: St Martin Press.

Dekmejian, R.H. (1985) *Islam in Revolution: Fundamentalism in Arab World*. Syracuse, NY: Syracuse University Press.

Derrida, J. (1996) *Le monolinguisme de l'autre*. Paris: Galilée.

De Salies, B.C. (1997) "Les luttes de clan exacerbent la guerre civile", *Le Monde Diplomatique*, October.

Dialmy, A. (2000) "L'islamisme marocain: Entre révolution et intégration", *Archives des Sciences des Religions*, April–June, 110.

Diamond, L., J. Linz and S.M. Lipset (1990) *Politics in Developing Countries. Comparing Experiences with Democracy*. Boulder, CO: Lynne Rienner; Trans.

(1996) *Les pays en développement et l'expérience de la démocratie*. Paris: Nouveaux horizons.

Dictionnaire de l'Islam (religion et civilisation) (1997) Paris: Albin Michel.

Dieterici, F. (1900) *Der Musterstaat von Alfarâbî*. Leiden: E.J. Brill.

Dillman, B. (1998) "The Political Economy of Structural Adjustment", *The Journal of North Africa*, 3(3) Autumn, 1–24.

Dimashqî, A. (11th–12th centuries) (1994) *Eloge du Commerce*. Tunis: Arcanes.

Djaït, H. (1986) *Al-Kufa. Naissance de la ville islamique*. Paris: Maisonneuve & Larose.

Djaït, H. (1989) *La Grande Discorde*. Paris: Gallimard.

Djaziri, M. (1996) *État et société en Libye*. Paris: L'Harmattan.

Djaziri, M. (1998) "La crise de Lockerbie et le processus de réintégration de la Libye dans le système international", *Annuaire de l'Afrique du Nord*, XXXVII.

Dobb, M. and P. Sweesy (1977) *Du féodalisme au capitalisme: Problèmes de transition*. Paris: Maspéro.

Dunlop, D.M. (1945) "Ibn Bajjah's Tadbir'l Mutawahid (Rule of Solitary)", *Journal of Royal Asiatic Society*, 61–81.

Dunn, M. (1992) "Revitalist Islam and Democracy: Thinking about the Algerian Quandary", *Middle East Policy*, 1(2).

Dunn, M. (1998) "Usama Ben Laden the Nature of the Challenge", *Middle East Policy*, 6(2) 23–28.

Durkheim, É. (1975) *Textes*. Paris: Minuit.

Durkheim, É. (1994) *Les formes élémentaires de la vie religieuse*; First edn (1912) Paris: PUF/Quadrige.

Easton, D. (1965) *A System Analysis of Political Life*. New York: Wiley.

Eaton, R. (1993) "Islam History as a Global History", in M. Adas (ed.) *Islam and European Expansion: The Forging of a Global Order*. Philadelphia, PA: Temple University Press, 1–36.

Economic Trends in the MENA Region (Middle East and North Africa) (1998) Cairo: ERF Indicators.

Ehteshemay, A. (1999) "Is the Middle East Democratizing?", *British Journal of Middle Eastern Studies*, 26(2), 119–217.

Eickelman, D.E. (2000) "Islam and the Languages of Modernity", *Daedalus*, 129(1) 119–135.

Eickelman, D.E. and J.P. Piscatori (1996) *Muslim Politics*. Princeton, NJ: Princeton University Press.

Eisenstadt, S.N. (ed.) (1968) *Protestant Ethics and Modernization: A Comparative View*. New York: Basic Books.

Eisenstadt, S.N. (1973) *Tradition, Change and Modernity*. New York: John Wiley & Sons.

Eisenstadt, S.N. (1984) *Patrons, Clients and Friends: Interpersonal Relations and the Structure of Trust in Society*. Cambridge: Cambridge University Press.

Eisenstadt, S.N. (2000) "Multiple Modernities", *Daedalus*, 129(1) 1–29.

Eisenstadt, S.N., M. Hoexter and N. Levtzion (eds) (2002) *The Public Sphere in Muslim Societies*. New York: State University of New York Press.

Ellens, H. (ed.) (2004) *The Destructive Power of Religion. Violence in Judaism, Christianity and Islam*, 4 volumes. Westport, CT: Praeger.

Ellyas, A. (1997) "Eclaircie économique pour le pouvoir algérien", *Le Monde Diplomatique*, May.

Enayat, H. (1982) *Modern Islamic Political Thought*. London: Macmillan.

Entelis, J. (1982) "Algeria: Technocratic Rule, Military Power", in W. Zartman et al., *Political Elites in Arab North Africa*. New York: Longmans, pp. 92–143.

Entelis, J. (1992) "Introduction: State and Society in Transition", in J.P. Entelis and P.C. Naylor (eds) *State and Society in Algeria*. Boulder, CO: Westview Press, 1–30.

Entelis, J. (1994) "Islam, Democracy and the State: The Re-emergence of Authoritarian Politics in Algeria", in J. Ruedy (ed.) *Islamism and Secularism in North Africa*. New York: St Martin's Press.

Entelis, J.P. (1996) *Culture and Counterculture in Moroccan Politics*. Lanham, MD: University Press of America.

Entelis, J. (ed.) (1997) *Islam, Democracy, and the State in North Africa*. Bloomington, IN: Indiana University Press.

Entelis, J.P. and P.C. Naylor (1992) *State and Society in Algeria*. Boulder, CO: Westview Press.

Esposito, J.L. (1987) *Islam and Politics*. Syracuse, NY: Syracuse University Press.

Esposito, J.L. (1992) *The Islamic Threat, Myth or Reality*. Oxford: Oxford University Press.

Esposito, J.L. (2002) *Unholy War: Terror in the Name of Islam*. New York: Oxford University Press.

Esposito, J.L. and J. Piscatori (1991) "Democratization and Islam", *Middle East Journal*, 45, 427–440.

Esposito, J.L. and O. Voll (1996) *Islam and Democracy: Religion Identity and Conflict Resolution in the Muslim World*. New York: Oxford University Press.

Esposito, J.L. and O. Voll (2001) *Makers of Contemporary Islam*. New York: Oxford University Press.

Essid, Y. (1995) *A Critique of the Origins of Islamic Economic Thought*. Leiden: E.J. Brill; First published in French (1993) *Oikonomia/ tadbîr*. Tunis: Editions T.S.

Etienne, B. (1987) *L'islamisme radical*. Paris: Hachette.

Etienne, B. (2007) "Islam and Violence", *History and Anthropology*, 18(3) 237–248.

Fadhlallah, M.H. (1986) *Al-Islam wa mantiq al-quwa* (*Islam and Logic of the Mighty*). Beirut: Al-dar al-islamiya.

Fahim Kahn, M. (1995) *Essays in Islamic Economics*. Leicester: The Islamic Foundation.

Fahmy, M. (1954) *La révolution de l'industrie en Egypte et ses consequences sociales au XIXe siècle*. Leiden: Brill.

Fahmy, M. (2002) *La condition de la femme dans l'Islam*. Paris: Ed. Allia.

Falah, J.A. (ed.) (1997) *Post-Marxism and the Middle East*. London: Saqi Books.
Farabi (10th century) (1986) *Idées des habitants de la cité vertueuse*; Trans. Y. Karam, J. Chlacha and A. Jaussen. Beirut: Librairie orientale.
Fareed, M.G. (1995) *Legal Reform in the Muslim World: The Anatomy of a Scholarly Dispute in the 19th and the Early 20th Centuries over the Usage of Ijtihad as a Legal Tool*. London: Austin and Winfield Publishers.
Feldmann, N. (2003) *After Jihad: America and the Struggle for Islamic Democracy*. New York: Farrar, Straus and Giroux.
Ferjani, M.C. (1991) *Islamisme, laïcité et droits de l'homme*. Paris: L'Harmattan.
Ferry, L. (1990) *L'homo aesteticus*. Paris: Grasset.
Ferry, L. and A. Renaut (1985) *La pensée 68*. Paris: Gallimard.
Feyerabend, P. (1979) *Contre la méthode*. Paris: Seuil.
Filali-Ansary, A. (1996) "Islam and Liberal Democracy: The Challenge of Secularization", *Journal of Democracy*, 7(2) 76–80.
Filali-Ansary, A. (1997) *L'islam est-il hostile à la laïcité?* Casablanca: Le Fennec.
Filali-Ansary, A. (1999) "Muslims and Democracy", *Journal of Democracy*, 10(3) 18–32.
Fish, M.S. (2002) "Islam and Authoritarianism", *World Politics*, 55(1) 4–37.
Fletcher, R. (2003) *The Cross and the Crescent: Christianity and Islam from Muhammad to the Reformation*. London: Allen Lane History, The Penguin Press.
Fogel, R.W. and S.L. Engerman (1995) *Time on the Cross: The Economics of American Negro Slavery*. New York: W.W. Norton.
Fontaine, J. (1992) "Quartiers défavorisés et vote islamiste à Alger", *La Revue du monde musulman et méditérranén*, 65.
Fontaine, J. (1996) *La crise religieuse des écrivains syro-libanais chrétiens de 1825 à 1940*. Tunis: IBLA.
Ford, F.L. (1985) *Le meurtre politique. Du tyrannicide au terrorisme*. Paris: PUF.
Foucault, M. (1994) *Dits et Écrits*, Vol. 4. Paris: Gallimard.
Frakin, H., H. Haqqani and E. Brown (2006) *Current Trends in Islamist Ideology*, Vol. 3. Center on Islam, Democracy and the Future of Muslim World, Hudson Institute.
Frank, A.G. and B.K. Gills (eds) (1992) *The World System: Five Hundred Years or Five Thousand?* London: Routledge.
Frank, M. (1989) *Qu'est-ce que le néo-structuralisme?* Paris: Cerf; First edn (1984) *Was ist Neostructuralismus?* Frankfurt am Main: Suhrkamp.
Fregosi, F. (1997) "Les rapports entre l'islam et l'État en Tunisie et en Algérie: De leur revalorisation à leur contestation", in A. Mahiou (ed.) *L'État de droit dans le monde arabe*. Paris: CNRS.
Frère, B.-M. (2002) *L'Islam et la miséricorde*. Paris: Ed. Autrement.
Friedman, T.L. (2002) *Longitudes and Attitudes: Exploring the World After September 11*. New York: Farrar, Straus and Giroux.
Fukuyama, F. (1992) *The End of History and the Last Man*. New York: Free Press; Trans. (1992) *La fin de l'histoire et le dernier homme*. Paris: Flammarion.

Fuller, G. (1997) *Algérie l'intégrisme au pouvoir?* Paris: Editions Patrick Banon.

Fuller, G. (2003) *Islamist politics in Iraq after Saddam Hussein.* United States Institute of Peace, Special Report 108; www.usip.org.

Fyzee, A.A. (1964) *Outlines of Muhammaden Law.* Oxford: Oxford University Press.

Gabriel, M.A. (2002) *Islam and Terrorism.* Lake Mary, FL: Charisma House.

Galloux, M. (1997) *Finance islamique et pouvoir politique – le cas de l'Egypte moderne.* Paris: PUF.

Gambetta, D. and S. Hertog (2007) "Engineers of Jihad", *Sociological Working Papers,* Paper no. 2007–10, University of Oxford, www.sociology.ox.ac.uk/swp.htm.

Garcin, J.-C. (1988) "The Mamlûk Military System and the Blocking of Medieval Moslem Society", in J. Baechler, J. Hall and M. Mann (eds) *Europe and the Rise of Capitalism.* Oxford: Basil Blackwell, 113–130.

Gardet, L. (1967/2002) *L'Islam: Religion et communauté.* Paris: Desclée de Brouwer.

Gardet, L. (1969) *La cité musulmane: vie sociale et politique.* Paris: Vrin.

Gardet, L. (1977) *Les Hommes de l'Islam.* Paris: Hachette.

Gardet, L. and M. Anawati (1970) *Introduction à la théologie musulmane.* Paris: Vrin.

Gaudefroy-Demombynes, M. (1969) *Mahomet.* Paris: Albin Michel.

Gausse, F.G. III (2002) "Who Lost Middle Eastern Studies", *Foreign Affairs,* 81(2) 164–168.

Gellner, E. (1983) *Nation and Nationalism.* Ithaca, NY: Cornell University Press.

Gellner, E. (1989) *Plough, Sword and Book: The Structure of Human History.* Chicago, IL: University of Chicago Press.

Gellner, E. (1992) *Postmodernism, Reason and Religion.* London: Routledge.

Gellner, E. (1994) *Encounters with Nationalism.* Cambridge, MA: Blackwell.

Gellner, E. (1997) *Nationalism.* New York: New York University Press.

Gephart, W. (1993) *Gesellschaftstheorie und Recht.* Frankfurt am Main: Suhrkamp.

Gerber, H. (1987) *The Social Origins of Modern Middle East.* Boulder, CO: Lynne Rienner.

Gerges, F.A. (1999) *America and Political Islam: Clash of Cultures or Clash of Interests?* New York: Cambridge University Press.

Gerteiny, A.G. (1967) *Mauritania.* New York: Praeger Publishers.

Gerth, H. and C. Wright Mills (1991) *From Max Weber: Essays in Sociology.* London: Routledge.

Gibb, H. (1962) *Study in Civilisation of Islam.* Boston: Beacon Press.

Gibb, H. and J. Kramers (1995) *Concise Encyclopedia of Islam.* Leiden: E.J. Brill.

Giddens, A. (1990) *The Consequences of Modernity.* Stanford, CA: Stanford University Press.

Glasenapp, von H. (2003) *Die fünf Weltreligionen.* München: Heyne Verlag.

Goetein, S.D. (1968) *Studies in Islamic History and Institutions.* Leiden: E.J. Brill.

Gökalp, Z. (1959) *Turkish Nationalism and Western Civilization.* London: G. Allen and Unwin.

Gold, D. (2003) *Hatred's Kingdom: How Saudi Arabia Supports New Global Terrorism*. Washington, DC: Regnery.

Goldziher, I. (1967) *Muslim Studies*, Vol. 1, 22. London: G. Allen and Unwin.

Goldziher, I. (1981) *Introduction to Islamic Theology and Law*; trans. A. and R. Hamori. Princeton, NJ: Princeton University Press; First edn (1910) *Vorlesungen über den Islam*. Heidelberg: Winter.

Goodwin, J. (1995) *Price of Honour: Muslim Women Lift the Veil of Silence on the Islamic World*. New York: Dutton/Plume.

Gran, P. (1980) "Political Economy as Paradigm for Study of Islamic History", *Journal of Middle East Studies*, II, 511–526.

Green, A. (1978) *The Tunisian Ulama, 1873–1915: Social Structure and Response to Ideological Currents*. Leiden: E.J. Brill.

Gresh, A. and T. Ramadan (2002) *L'islam en questions*. Paris: Actes Sud.

Grunebaum, G.E. (1962) *Modern Islam. The Search for Cultural Identity*. Berkley, CA: University of California Press; Trans. (1973) *L'identité culturelle de l'islam*. Paris: Gallimard.

Guillard, P. (1995) "Le FIS parti de la démocratie", *La Cause*, 3(23) 21 July.

Habermas, J. (1986) *Morale et communication*. Paris: Cerf.

Habermas, J. (1987) *Théorie de l'agir communicationnel*, 2 volumes. Paris: Fayard; Trans. T. McCarthy (1984–1985) *The Theory of Communicative Action*, 2 volumes. Boston, MA: Beacon Press.

Habermas, J. (1988) *Le discours philosophique de la modernité*. Paris: Gallimard.

Habermas, J. (1996) *La paix perpétuelle*. Paris: Cerf.

Hacking, I. (1982) "Language, Truth and Reason", in M. Hollis and L. Steven, *Rationality and Relativism*, 48–66. Cambridge, MA: MIT Press.

Haddad, S. (2000) "La politique africaine de la Libye: De la tentation impériale à la stratégie unitaire", *Maghreb Machrek*, October–December, 170.

Haddad, Y. (1983) "The Qura'anic Justification for an Islamic Revolution: The View of Sayyid Qutb", *The Middle East Journal*, 37(1) Winter.

Hafez, M.M. (2003) *Why Muslims Rebel: Repression and Resistance in the Islamic World*. Boulder, CO: Lynne Rienner.

Haïm, S.G. (1962) *Arab Nationalism: An Anthology*. Berkeley, CA: University of California Press.

Hallaq, W.B. (1984) "Was the Gate of Ijtihad Closed?", *International Journal of Middle East Studies*, 16, 3–41.

Hallaq, W.B. (1984/1985) "The Logic of Legal Reasoning in Religious and Non-Religious Cultures", *Cleveland State Law Review*, 34, 79–96.

Halliday, F. (2002) *Two Hours that Shook the World*. London: I.B. Tauris.

Halpern, M. (1963) *The Politics of Social Change in the Middle East and North Africa*. Princeton, NJ: Princeton University Press.

Hambly, G. (1998) *Women in the Medieval Islamic World*. New York: St Martin's Press.

Hammoudi, A. (1997) *Master and Disciple. The Cultural Foundations of Moroccan Authoritarism*. Chicago, IL: University of Chicago Press.

Hamza, M. (1995) "Un Barbouze à Alger", *La Cause*, 3(25) 18 August.

Hamzawy, A. (2005) *The Key to Arab Reform: Moderate Islamists*. Carnegie Endowment for International Peace, Policy Brief, 40.

Hamzawy, A. et al. (2001) "Islamist Movements and the Democratic Process in the Arab World: Exploring the Gray Zones", Carnegie Papers, no. 27, March 2000.

Hamzawy, A. et al. (2007) *What Islamists Need to Be Clear About: The Case of the Egyptian Brotherhood*. Carnegie Endowment for International Peace, February 2007.

Hanafi, H., M.A. Jabri et al. (1990) *Hiwar al-Shraq wa al-Gharb* (*Dialogue Between East and West*). Cairo: Maktabat Madbouli.

Hasan, A.G. (2001) *American Muslims: The New Generation*. New York: Continuum.

Hefner, R.W. (2002) *Civil Islam: Muslims and Democratization in Indonesia*. Princeton, NJ: Princeton University Press.

Herb, M. (1999) *All in the Family: Absolutism, Revolution and Democracy in the Middle Eastern Monarchies*. Albany, NY: State University of New York Press.

Heydemann, S. (1991) "Can We Get There From Here? Lessons from the Syrian Case", in F.L. Cantori (ed.) "Democratization in the Middle East", *American-Arab Affairs*, 36, 27.

Hibou, B. (2000) "De la privatisation des économies à la privatisation des États", in B. Hibou (ed.) *La privatisation de l'État*. Paris: Khartala.

Hinnebusch, R. (2001) *Syria: Revolution from Above*. New York: Routledge.

Hodgson, M. (1974) *The Venture of Islam*, 3 volumes. Chicago, IL: University of Chicago Press.

Hollis, M. and L. Steven (1982) *Rationality and Relativism*. Cambridge MA: MIT Press.

Holt, P.M. (1958) *The Mahdist State in the Sudan, 1881–1898*, 2nd edn. Oxford: Clarendon Press.

Holten, D. and R. Jones (1981) *The House of Saud*. New York: Holt, Rinehart and Winston.

Hourani, A. (1983) *Arabic Thought in the Liberal Age, 1798–1939*; First edn (1962) New York: Cambridge University Press; French trans. (1991) *La pensée arabe et l'Occident*. Paris: Naufel.

Hourani, A. (1991) *A History of the Arab Peoples*. Cambridge, MA: Harvard University Press.

Hourani, A. (2005) A History of the Arab Peoples. London: Faber and Faber.

Hourani, G.F. (1995) *Arab Seafaring: In the Indian Ocean in Ancient and Early Medieval Times*. Princeton, NJ: Princeton University Press.

Hudson, M. (1977) *Arab Politics: The Search for Legitimacy*. New Haven, CT: Yale University Press.

Hudson, M. (1995) "The Political Cultural Approach to Arab Democratization: The Case for Bringing it Back in, Carefully", in R. Breynen, K. Bahgat and P.

Noble (eds) *Political Liberalization and Democratization in the Arab World. Volume 1, Theoretical Perspectives.* Boulder, CO: Lynne Rienner.

Huff, T.E. and W. Schluchter (eds) (1999) *Max Weber and Islam*. Edison, NY: Transaction.

Human Development Report (1996) *Economic Growth and Human Development*. New York: Human Development Report Office.

Hunter, S. (ed.) (1988) *Islamic Revitalism. Diversity and Unity*. Bloomington, IN: Indiana University Press.

Huntington, S.P. (1968) *Political Order in Changing Societies*. New Haven, CT: Yale University Press.

Huntington, S.P. (1984) "Will More Countries Become Democratic?" *Political Science Quarterly*, 99, 193–211.

Huntington, S.P. (1991) *The Third Wave: Democratization in the Late Twentieth Century*. Norman, OK: University of Oklahoma Press; Trans. (1991) *La troisième vague. Les démocratisations de la fin du XXe siècle*. Paris: Nouveaux horizons.

Huntington, S.P. (1997) *The Clash of Civilizations: Remaking of World Order*. New York: Touchstone.

Hussain, A. (1984) *Political Perspectives on the Muslim World*. New York: St. Martin's Press.

Husserl, E. (1976) *La crise des sciences européennes et la phenomenology transcendantale*. Paris: Gallimard.

Ibrahim, S.-E. (ed.) (1987) *Al-dawla wa al-mujtama'a fi al-watan al-arabî*. Beirut: Marqez dirâsset al-wihda al-arabiyya.

Inalcik, H. (1973) *The Ottoman Empire. The Classical Age: 1300–1600*. London: Longitude.

Ingelhart, R. (ed.) (1997) *Modernization and Postmodernization: Cultural, Economic and Political Change in 43 Societies*. Princeton, NJ: Princeton University Press.

International Crisis Group (ICG) (2005) *Understanding Islamism*. Middle East/North Africa Report no. 37, March 2.

International Crisis Group (2008) *Egypt's Muslim Brothers: Confrontation or Integration?* Middle East/North Africa Report, no. 76, June.

Iqbal, M. (1968) *The Reconstruction of Religious Thought in Islam*. Lahore: Muhammed Ashraf.

Iqbal, M. (1980) *La métaphysique en Perse*. Paris: Sindbad.

Issawi, C. (ed.) (1966) *The Economic History of the Middle East, 1800–1914*. Chicago. IL: University of Chicago Press.

Jackson, R.H. (1990) *Quasi-States: Sovereignty, International Relations and the Third World.* New York: Cambridge: Cambridge University Press.

Janin, H. and A. Kahlmeyer (2007) *Islamic Law: The Sharia from Muhammad's Time to the Present.* Jefferson, NC: McFarland.

Jansen, J. (1986) *The Neglected Duty: The Creed of Sadat's Assassins and Islamic Resurgence in the Middle East*. New York: Macmillan.

Jansen, P., A. Nef and C. Picard (2000) *Relations des pays d'islam avec le monde latin*. Paris: Sedes.

Jarvie, I.C. (1983) "Rationality and Relativism", *The British Journal of Sociology*, 34(1) 44–60.

Joffé, G. (1988) "Islamic Opposition in Libya", *Third World Quarterly*, 10(2) 615–631.

Jomier, O.P. (1954) *Le commentaire coranique du manâr*. Paris: Maisonneuve.

Jones, E.L. (1981) *The European Miracle: Environment; Economies and Geopolitics in the History of Europe and Asia*. Cambridge: Cambridge University Press.

Juergensmeyer, M. (1993) *The New Cold War? Religious Nationalism Confronts the Secular State*. Berkeley, CA: University of California Press.

Juergensmeyer, M. (2000) *Terror in the Mind of God: The Global Rise of Religious Violence*. Berkeley, CA: University of California Press.

Kahf, M. (1993) *Islamic Economy*. Washington, DC: American Trust Publications.

Kakar, S. (1996) *The Colors of Violence: Cultural Identities, Religion, and Conflict*. Chicago, IL: University of Chicago Press.

Kamali, M.H. (2005) *Principles of Islamic Jurisprudence*. Islamic Texts Society.

Kamali, S.A. (1959) "Abu Kalam Azad's Commentary of the Qu'ran", *Muslim World*, XXIX(1) 5–18.

Karagiannis, E. and C. McCauley (2006) "Hizb ut-Tahrir al-Islami: Evaluating the Threat Posed by a Radical Islamic Group that Remains Nonviolent", *Terrorism and Political Violence*, 18, 315–334.

Katznelson, I. (1997) "Culture and Identity in Comparative Political Analysis", in M.I. Lichbach and A.S. Zuckerman (eds) *Comparative Politics. Rationality, Culture and Structure*. Cambridge: Cambridge University Press.

Keck, M. and K. Sikkink (1998) *Activist Beyond Borders. Advocacy Neworks in Inernational Politics*. Ithaca, NY: Cornell University Press.

Keddie, N. (1972) *Sayyid Jamal al-Din "al-Afghani": A Political Biography*. Berkeley, CA: University of California Press.

Keddie, N. (1981) *Roots of Revolution: An Interpretative History of Modern Iran*. New Haven, CT: Yale University Press.

Keddie, N. (1995) *Iran in the Muslim World: Resistance and Revolution*. London: Macmillan.

Kedourie, E. (1963) "Egypt and the Caliphate 1915–1946", *Journal of Royal Asiatic Society*, 3, 208–248.

Kedourie, E. (1994) *Democracy and Arab Political Culture*. London: Frank Cass.

Kedourie, E. (1997) *Afghani and 'Abduh. An Essay on Religious Unbelief and Political Activism in Modern Islam*; First published 1966. London: Frank Cass.

Kedourie, E. (ed.) (1998) *Turkey. Identity, Democracy, Politics*. London: Frank Cass.

Kepel, G. (1986) *Muslim Extermism in Egypt: The Prophet and the Pharaon*. Berkeley, CA: University of California Press.

Kepel, G. (1991) *La revanche de Dieu.* Paris: Seuil.

Kepel, G. (2000) *Jihad.* Paris: Gallimard; Trans. (2003) *Jihad: The Trail of Political Islam.* London: I.B. Tauris.

Kepel, G. (2004) *The War for Muslim Minds: Islam and the West.* Cambridge, MA: The Belknap Press.

Kepel, G. (2005) *The Roots of Radical Islam.* London: Saqi Books.

Kepel, G. (2008) *Beyond Terror and Martyrdom: The Future of the Middle East.* Cambridge, MA: Harvard University Press.

Kerr, M. (1966) *Islamic Reform: The Legal and Political Theories of Muhammad Abduh and Rashid Rida.* Berkeley, CA: University of California Press.

Kerrou, M. (1996) "Blasphème et apostasie en islam", in *Monothéismes et Modernités.* Tunis: OROC/Friedrich-Naumann Stiftung, 117–204.

Kerrou, M. (1998) "Politiques de l'islam en Tunisie", in M. Kilani (ed.) *Islam et changement social.* Lausanne: Payot, 81–102.

Khadduri, M. (trans.) (1961) *Islamic Jurisprudence. Shafi'i's Risala.* Baltimore, MD: The Johns Hopkins University Press.

Khatibi, A. (1977) "Le Maghreb comme horizon de pensée", *Les Temps Modernes: Du Maghreb*, October, 375.

Khawaja, M.A. (2000) *Muslims and the West: Quest for Change and Conflict Resolution.* Lanham, MD: University Press of America.

Khayr Eddin (1987) *Essai sur les réformes nécessaires aux États musulmans*; First published 1867. Paris: Edisud.

Khelladi, A. (1995) "Esquisse d'une géographie des groupes islamistes en Algérie", *Hérodote*, 77.

Khomeiny, l'Ayatollah (1979) *Pour un gouvernement islamique.* Paris: Fayole.

Khosrokavar, F. (1993) "Iran: de la révolution à l'islamisme hezbollah", in F. Khosrokavar (1995) *L'islamisme et la mort.* Paris: L'Harmattan.

Khosrokhavar, F. (2006) *Quand al-Qäida parle: Témoignages derrière les barreaux.* Paris: Grasset.

King, S. (1998) "Economic Reform and Tunisi'a Hegemonic Party: The End of Administrative Elite", *Arab Study Quarterly*, Spring, 59–86.

Kissling, H.J. (1996) *The Last Great Muslim Empires: History of the Muslim World.* Princeton, NJ: Marcus Wiener.

Kohler, J. (1889) "Über das vorislamische Recht der Araber", *Zeitschrift für vergleichende Rechtswissenschaft*, 8, 238–261.

Kohler, J. (1905) "Zum Islamrecht", *Zeitschrift für vergleichende Rechtswissenschaft*, 17, 194–216.

Kohler, J. (1906) "Die Wirklichkeit und Unwirklichkeit des islamischen Rechts", *Zeitschrift für vergleichende Rechtswissenschaft*, 19, 37–40.

Koran (1994) A. Jones (ed.). London: Everyman.

Korany, B. (1994) "Arab Democratization: a Poor Cousin", *Political Science and Politics*, XVII(3).

Kraim, M. (1973) *La Tunisie précoloniale.* Tunis: STD.

Kramer, G. (1993) "Islamic Notions of Democracy", *Middle East Report*, 23(4) 1–8.

Kramer, M. (2001) *Ivory Towers on Sand: The Failure of Middle Eastern Studies in America*. Washington, DC: Washington Institute for Near East Policy.

Kruglanski, A.W. and S. Fishman (2006) "The Psychology of Terrorism: 'Syndrome' versus 'Tool' Perspectives", *Terrorism and Political Violence*, 18, 193–215.

Kuran, T. (1997) "The Genesis of Islamic Economics: A Chapter in the Politics of Muslim Identity", *Social Research*, 64(2) 301–338.

Kuran, T. (2001) "The Islamic Commercial Crisis: Institutional Roots of the Delay in the Middle East's Economic Modernization", USC CLEO Research Paper no. C01–12, University of Southern California.

Kuran, T. (2004) *Islam and Mammon: The Economic Predicaments of Islamism*. Princeton, NJ: Princeton University Press.

Kuran, T. (2007) "Islamism and Economics: Policy Prescriptions for a Free Society", in S. Behdad and F. Nomani (eds) *Islam and the Everyday World*. London: Routledge.

Kurzman, C. (2002) *Modernist Islam: 1840–1940*. Oxford: Oxford University Press.

Lacoste, Y. (1995) "Les causes spécifiques du drame algérien ou le slogan de la guerre d'indépendance incomplète", *Hérodote*, 77.

Lahouari, A. (1994) *L'Algérie et la démocratie*. Paris: La Découverte.

Lambton, A. (1971) "Islamic Mirrors of Princes", in *La Persia nel Medievo: Atti de Convegno Internazionale*, Quaderno 160, 419–442. Roma: Academia Nazionale dei Lincei.

Laoust, H. (1965) *Les schismes en islam*. Paris: Payothèque.

Lapidus, I.M. (ed.) (1969) *Middle Eastern Cities*. Berkeley, CA: University of California Press.

Lapidus, I.M. (1988) *A History of Islamic Societies*. New York: Cambridge University Press.

Laqueur, W. (1977) *Terrorism*. London: Weidenfeld and Nicolson.

Laroui, A. (1977) *L'Idéologie arabe contemporaine*. Paris: Maspéro.

Laroui, A. (1997a) "Western Orientalism and Liberal Islam: Mutual Distrust?", *MESA Bulletin*, 1, 3–10.

Laroui, A. (1997b) *Islamisme, modernisme, libéralisme*. Casablanca: Centre Culturel Marocain.

Laurance, R. (2002) *Portrait of Islam: A Journey through the Muslim World*. London: Thames and Hudson.

Layachi, E. (2000) "Reform and Politics of Inclusion in the Maghrib", *The Journal of North Africa*, 5(3) Autumn, 15–42.

Leca, J., M. Verges and M. Bennani-Chraibi (2001) "Daniel Lerner Revisited, the Audio-visual Media and its Reception: Two North African Cases", in C.E. Butterworth (ed.) *In Between the State and Islam*. Cambridge: Cambridge University Press.

Lee, R. (1997) *Overcoming Tradition and Modernity*. Boulder, CO: Westview Press.
Legoff, J. (1988) *Histoire et mémoire*. Paris: Gallimard/Poche.
Leiken, R.S. and S. Brooke (2007) "The Moderate Brotherhood", *Foreign Affairs*, 86(2) 107–121.
Lelyveld, D. (1978) *Aligarh's First Generation: Muslim Solidarity in British India*. Princeton, NJ: Princeton University Press.
Lerner, D. (1958) *The Passing of Traditional Society. Modernization in the Middle East*. London: The Free Press of Glencoe/Collier-Macmillan.
Leveau, R. (1993) *Le sabre et le turban*. Paris: François Bourin.
Leverrier, I. (1993) "Le FIS entre la hâte et la patience", in G. Kepel, *Les politiques de Dieu*. Paris: Seuil, 45–46.
Lévi-Strauss, C. (1955) *Tristes Tropiques*. Paris: Plon/Pocket.
Lévi-Strauss, C. (1974) *Anthropologie structurale*. Paris: Plon/Agora.
Levy, M.J. Jr (1966) *Modernization and the Structure of Societies*. Princeton, NJ: Princeton University Press.
Lewis, B. (1964) *The Middle East and the West*. New York: Harper Torchbooks.
Lewis, B. (1961/1968) *The Emergence of Modern Turkey*. New York: Oxford University Press.
Lewis, B. (1984) *Comment l'islam a découvert l'Europe?* Paris: La découverte; First published (1982) *The Muslim Discovery of Europe*. New York: W.W. Norton.
Lewis, B. (1988) *The Political Language of Islam*. Chicago, IL: University of Chicago Press; Trans. (1988) *Le langage politique de l'Islam*. Paris: Gallimard.
Lewis, B. (1991) *Islam and the West*. Oxford: Oxford University Press.
Lewis, B. (1994) "La foi et les croyants", in B. Lewis (ed.) *L'Islam d'hier à aujourd'hui*. Paris: Petite Bibliothèque Payot.
Lewis, B. (1996) "Islam and Liberal Democracy. A Historical Overview", *Journal of Democracy*, 7(2) 52–63.
Lewis, B. (1997a) *The Middle East: A Brief History of the Last 2,000 Years*. New York: Pocket Books.
Lewis, B. (1997b) "The West and the Middle East", *Foreign Affairs*, 76(1) January–February.
Lewis, B. (1998a) "License to Kill. Usama Ben Laden's Declaration of Jihad", *Foreign Affairs*, 77(6) 14–19.
Lewis, B. (1998b) *The Multiple Identities of the Middle East*. New York: Schocken Books.
Lewis, B. (2002a) *Arabs in History*. New York: Oxford Paperbacks.
Lewis, B. (2002b) *What Went Wrong? Western Impact and Middle Eastern Response*. New York: Oxford University Press; Trans. (2002) *Que s'est-il passé? L'islam, l'Occident et la modernité*. Paris: Gallimard.
Lewis, B. (2003a) *Assassins: A Radical Sect in Islam*. London: Weidenfeld and Nicolson.

Lewis, B. (2003b) *The Crisis of Islam: Holy War and Unholy Terror*. London: Weidenfeld and Nicolson.

Liebman, C.S. and D.-Y. Eliezer (1984) *Religions and Politics in Israel*. Bloomington, IN: Indiana University Press.

Lippman, T.W. (1982) *Understanding Islam: An Introduction to the Moslem World*. New York: A Mentor Book, New American Library.

Lipset, S.M. (1959) "Some Social Requisites of Democracy: Economic Development and Political Legitimacy", *American Political Science Review*, 53, 69–105.

Locke, J. (1992) *Lettre sur la tolérance et autres essais: Essai sur la tolérance; Sur la différence entre pouvoir ecclésiastique et pouvoir civil*, trans. J. Le Clerc. Paris: Garnier-Flammarion.

Lopez, G.B. (1992) "Le Makhzen, la 'amma et l'arbitre au Maroc: Administration et société civile aux élections locales et législatives 1992–93", *Annuaire de l'Afrique du Nord*, XXXI, 415–435.

Luciano, G. (1990a) "Allocation vs Production States: A Theorethical Framework", in G. Luciano (ed.) *The Arab State*. Berkeley, CA: University of California Press.

Luciano, G. (1990b) *The Arab State*. London: Routledge.

Luciano, G. (1994) "The Oil Rent and the Fiscal Crisis of the Arab State", in G. Salamé (ed.) *Democracy without Democrats? The Renewal of Politics in the Muslim World*. London: I.B. Tauris.

Madani, A. (1989) *Azmat al-fikr al-hadith wa mubarrirât al-hall al-islami* (*La crise de la pensée moderne et les justifications de la solution islamique*) first edn. Alger: Imp. Ameziane.

Mahdawy, H. (1970) "The Pattern and Problems of Economic Development in Rentier State", in M. Cook (ed.) *Studies in the Economic History of the Middle East*. London: Oxford University Press, 428–467.

Malik, H. (1963) *Moslem Modernism in India and Pakistan*. Washington, DC: Public Affairs Press.

Mansfield, L. (2006) *His Own Words: A Translation of the Writings of Dr Ayman Al Zawahiri*. LULU.

Mansfield, P. (1992) *The Arabs*. Harmondsworth: Penguin.

Mansour, F. (1992) *Arab World: Nation, State and Democracy*. New York: St Martin's Press.

Mantran, R. (1969) *L'expansion musulmane (VII–IXe siècles)*. Paris: PUF.

Mardin, S. (1962) *The Genesis of Ottoman Thought: A Study in the Modernization of Turkish Political Ideas*. Princeton, NJ: Princeton University Press.

Markov, N. (1986) *Action collective et mobilisation. De l'analyse historique aux modèles sociologique: Le chemin de Charles Tilly*. Etudes et recherches, no. 20. Geneva: Département de science politique, Faculté SES.

Marshall, P. (2005) "The Islamists' Other Weapon", *Commentary*, 119(4) 60–63.

Martinez, L. (2000) "L'après-embargo en Libye", *Maghreb Machrek*, 170, October–December.

Martinez, L. (2000) *The Algerian Civil War, 1990–1998*. London: Hurst.
Massignon, L. (1975) *La passion d'al-Hallaj*. Paris: Gallimard.
Mâturidi (9th–10th centuries) Abu Mansûr M. Ibn Mahmûd (1986) *Kitab al-Tawhïd*. Beirut: dâr-el-Machreq.
Mayer, A.E. (1991) *Islam and Human Rights*. Boulder, CO: Westview Press/San Francisco, CA: Pinter.
Mayer, A.E. (2005) "Clashing Human Rights Priorities: How the United States and Muslim Countries Selectively use Provisions of International Human Rights Law", *Forum for Intercultural Philosophy*, 6.
McAmis, R.D. (2002) *Malay Muslims: The History and Challenge of Resurgent Islam in Southeast Asia*. Grand Rapids, MI: William B. Eerdmans.
McCants, W. (ed.) (2006) *Militant Ideology Atlas*. West Point, NY: Combating Terrorism Center, US Military Academy.
McGown, R.B. (1999) *Muslims in the Diaspora: The Somali Communities of London and Toronto*. Toronto: University of Toronto Press.
Meisels, T. (2006) "The Trouble with Terror: The Apologetics of Terrorism – A Refutation", *Terrorism and Political Violence*, 18, 465–483.
Mendes-France, M.-C. (1995) "Préface", in *Le livre noir de l'Algérie*. Paris: Reporters sans Frontières.
Merad, A. (1974) "Islam et violence", in *Rencontre islamo-chrétienne*. Tunis: CERES, 159–166.
Merad, A. (1987) *L'Islam contemporain*. Paris: PUF.
Mernissi, F. (2002) *Islam and Democracy: Fear of the Modern World*. Cambridge, MA: Perseus Publishing.
Merr, P. (2006) *Who are the Iraq's New Leaders? What do They Want?* United States Institute of Peace, Special Report 134, www.usip.org.
Metcalf, B. (1982) *Islamic Revival in British India: Deoband, 1860–1900*. Princeton, NJ: Princeton University Press.
Metcalf, B. (1999) "Weber and Islamic Reform", in T.E. Huff and W. Schluchter (eds) *Max Weber and Islam*. London: Transaction, 217–230.
Migdal, J.S. (1988) *Strong Societies and Weak States: State-Society Relations and State Capabilities in the Third World*. Princeton, NJ: Princeton University Press.
Miller, J. and A. Kenedi (eds) (2002) *Inside Islam: The Faith, the People and the Conflicts of the World's Fastest-Growing Religion*. New York: Avalon.
Milton-Edwards, B. and P. Hinchcliffe (2001) *Jordan: A Heshemite Legacy*. London: Routledge.
Moaddel, M. and K. Talattof (eds) (2000) *Contemporary Debates in Islam: An Anthology of Modernist and Fundamentalist Thought*. Basingstoke: Palgrave Macmillan.
Moghadem, A. (2007) "Mayhem, Myths, and Martyrdom: The Shia Conception of Jihad", *Terrorism and Political Violence*, 19, 125–143.
Mohammadi, A. and M. Ahsan (2002) *Globalisation or Recolonisation?* London: Ta-Ha Publishers.

Monroe, K.R. (ed.) (1997) *Contemporary Empirical Political Theory.* Berkeley, CA: University of California Press.

Moore, B. Jr (1966) *Social Origins of Dictatorship and Democracy*. Boston, MA: Beacon Press.

Morabia (1993) *Le Gihad dans l'Islam médiéval*. Paris: Albin Michel.

Mortimer, R. (1993) "Algeria. The Clash Between Islam, Democracy and Military", *Current History*, 92(570).

Mos'ad, N. (1994) "Violence politique et mouvements socio-religieux: Le Front islamique du salut en Algérie", in *Le phénomène de la violence politique: Perspectives comparatives et paradigme égyptien*. Cairo: Dossier du CEDEJ.

Moutadayenne, A. (2001) "Economic Crises and Democratisation in Morroco", *The Journal of North Africa*, 6(3) 70–82.

Mumisa, M. (2002) *Islamic Law: Theory & Interpretation*. Willowbrook, IL: Amana.

Murphy, E.C. (1998) "Legitmacy and Economic Reform in the Arab World", *The Journal of North Africa*, 3(3) Autumn, 71–92.

Murphy, E.C. (1999) *Economic and Political Change in Tunisia: From Bourguiba to Ben Ali*. New York: St Martin's Press.

Mussallam, A.A. (2005) *From Secularism to Jihad: Sayyd Qutb and the Foundations of Radical Islamism*. New York: Praeger.

Najjar, F. (1980) "Democracy in Islamic Political Philosophy", *Arabica*, LI, 107–122.

Naqeeb, K. (1990) *Society and State in the Gulf and Arab Peninsula: A Different Perspective*. London: Routledge.

Nienhaus, V. (2007) "Zakat, taxes, and public finance in Islam", in S. Behdad and F. Nomani (eds) *Islam and the Everyday World*. London: Routledge.

Nomani, F. (2007) "The Dilemma of Riba-free Banking in Islamic Public Policy", in S. Behdad and F. Nomani (eds) *Islam and the Everyday World*, 193–223. London: Routledge.

Norris, H. (1993) *Islam in the Balkans: Religion and Society between Europe and the Arab World*. Columbia, SC: University of South Carolina Press.

Norton, A.R. (ed.) (1994 and 1995) *Civil Society in the Middle East*. Leiden: E.J. Brill.

Nouira Ben Daiya, A. (2001) *Le Mufti de la République en Tunisie. L'Institution et la fonction* [in Arabic]. Tunis: CÉRÈS.

O'Donnel, G. (1996) "Illusions about Consolidation", *Journal of Democracy*, 7(2) 34–51.

O'Donnel, G. and P.C. Schmitter (1993) *Transitions from Authoritarian Rule. Tentative Conclusions about Uncertain Democracies*. Baltimore, MD: The Johns Hopkins University Press.

Omaya, A. and M. Ottaway (2007) *Women in Islamist Movements: Toward an Islamist Model of Women's Activism*. Carnegie Papers, Carnegie Middle East Center, no. 2, June.

Otayek, R. (1986) *La politique africaine de la Libye*. Paris: Khartala.

Otto, R. (1996) *Rudolf Otto: Autobiographical and Social Essays*. Berlin: Walter de Gruyter.

Ouaziani, C. (1998) "Kaddafi contre les "Afghans", *Jeune Afrique*, 1954, 23 June.

Ounaès, M. (1994) "Les comités révolutionnaires: Mouvement social ou expression clientéliste", *Revue Tunisienne de Sciences Sociales*, 116.

Owen, R. (1981) *The Middle East in the World Economy, 1800–1914*. London: Methuen.

Özbudun, E. (1996) "Turkey, How Far from Consolidation?" *Journal of Democracy*, 7(3) 123–138.

Parmentier, M.J.C. (1999) "Secularisation and Islamisation in Morroco", *The Journal of North Africa*, 4(4) Winter, 27–50.

Pazzanita, A.G. (1999) "Political Transition in Mauritania: Problems and Prospects", *The Middle East Journal*, 58(1) 53–56.

Peters, R. (1980) "Ijtihad and Taqlid in 18th and 19th Century Islam", *Die Welt des Islams*, 132–145.

Peters, R. (1996) *Jihad in Classic and Modern Islam: A Reader*. Princeton, NJ: Marcus Wiener.

Peters, R. (1999) "Paradise or Hell? The Religious Doctrine of Election in 18th and 19th Century Islamic Fundamentalism and Protestant Calvinism", in T.E. Huff and W. Schluchter (eds) *Max Weber and Islam*. New Brunswick, NJ: Transaction, 205–216.

Piazza, J.A. (2006) "Rooted in Poverty?: Terrorism, Poor Economic Development, and Social Cleavages", *Terrorism and Political Violence*, 18, 159–177.

Pipes, D. (1981) *Slaves Soldiers and Islam: The Genesis of a Military System*. New Haven, CT: Yale University Press.

Pipes, D. (1983) *In the Path of God: Islam and Political Power*. New York: Basic Books.

Pipes, D. (1992) "Dealing with Middle Eastern Conspiracy Theories", *Orbis*, 36(1) Winter.

Pipes, D. (1995) "The Western Mind of Radical Islam", *First Things*, 58, 18–23.

Pipes, D. (1996) *The Hidden Hands. Middle East Conspiracy*. New York: St Martin's Griffen.

Powers, D. (2002) *Law, Society and Culture in the Maghrib, 1300–1500*. Cambridge: Cambridge University Press.

Provost, L. (1996) "Paris et Alger entre brouilles et complicités", *Le Monde Diplomatique*, September.

Pryce-Jones, D. (2002) *The Closed Circle: An Interpretation of the Arabs*. New York: Ivan R Dee.

Przeworski, Adam and F. Limongi (1996) "Modernization. Theories and Facts", *World Politics*, 49(2) 155–183.

Quataert, D. (2005) *The Ottoman Empire, 1700–1922*. Cambridge: Cambridge University Press.

Qureshi, I.H. (1962) *The Muslim Community in the Indo-Pakistani Sub-Continent*. The Hague: Mouton.

Qureshi, I.H. (1980) *Milestones*. Beirut: The Holy Koran Publishing House.

Qutb, S. (1990) *Milestones*. Indianapolis, IN: American Trust Publications.

Qutb, S. (2000) *Social Justice in Islam*, trans. J.B. Hardie. New York: Octagon Books.

Qutb, S. (2005) *Basic Principles of Islamic Worldview*. North Haledon, NJ: Islamic Publications International.

Rahbar, D. (1956) "Sir Sayyid Ahmed Khan's Principles of Exegesis", trans. from "Tahrîr fî usûls al-tafsîr", *Muslim World*, XLVI(2) 104–112.

Rahman, F. (1982) *Islam and Modernity. Transformation of an Intellectual Tradition*. Chicago, IL: The University of Chicago Press.

Rahman, M. (ed.) (1987) *Muslim World*. Lanham, MD: University Press of America.

Rapaport, D. (2001) "The Fourth Wave: September 11 in the History of Terrorism", *Current History*, December, 419–424.

Rawls, J. (1971) *A Theory of Justice*, trans. C. Audard from (1987) *Théorie de la justice*. Paris: Seuil/Empruntes.

Raymer, S. (2001) *Living Faith: Inside the Muslim World of Southeast Asia*. Boston, MA: Charles E. Tuttle.

Redissi, H. (1991) "Le discours musulman sur la modernité: La totalité désunie", *Carrefour (Ottawa)* 13(1) 86–103.

Redissi, H. (1992) La modernité dans la pensée arabo-musulmane. Thèse de doctorat d'Etat en Sciences Politiques. Tunis: Faculté de Droit.

Redissi, H. (1994) "Lectures musulmanes modernes du Coran", *Annali di Storia dell'egesi*, 11(1).

Redissi, H. (1998) *Les politiques en islam: Le prophète, le roi et le savant*. Paris: L'Harmattan.

Redissi, H. (2007) "Islam und *Sharia*", in J. Pattillo-Hess and A.R. Smole (eds) *Islam, Dialog und Kontroverse*, 15–26. Wien: Löcker.

Redissi, H. (2008) *Le Pacte de Nadjd. Ou Comment l'islam sectaire est devenu l'islam*. Paris: Seuil.

Ridha, R. (1988) *Al Khilafa* (*the Caliphate*). Cairo: Az-zahra li-l i'lam alarabi; First published 1929, trans. H. Laoust (1986) *Le Califat dans la doctrine de Rashid Ridha*; First published 1938. Paris: Maisonneuve.

Risse, T., S.C. Ropp and K. Sikkinink (eds) (1999) *The Power of Human Rights, International Norm and Domestic Change*. Cambridge: Cambridge University Press.

Rizvi, S. (1982) "Shah Abd al-Aziz: Puritanism, Sectarism Polemics, and Jihad", *Journal of Asian Studies*, 43, 586–587.

Robinson, A. (2002) *Bin Laden: Behind the Mask of the Terrorist*. New York: Arcade.

Robinson, F. (1999) “Secularisation, Weber and Islam”, in T.E. Huff and W. Schluchter (eds) *Max Weber and Islam*, 231–245. New Brunswick, NJ: Transaction.
Rodinson, M. (1961) *Mahomet*. Paris: Seuil; Trans. (1971) *Mohammed*. London: Allen Lane, and (2002) *Muhammad*. New York: New Press.
Rodinson, M. (1966) *Islam et capitalisme*. Paris: Seuil; Trans. B. Peace (1978) *Islam and Capitalism*. Austin: University of Texas Press.
Rodinson, M. (1972) *Marxisme et monde musulman*. Paris: Seuil.
Rodinson, M. (1993) *L'Islam politique et croyance*. Paris: Fayard.
Rogerson, B. (2003) *The Prophet Muhammad*. Boston, MA: Little, Brown.
Ro'I, Y. (ed.) (1995) *Muslim Eurasia: Conflicting Legacies*. London: Frank Cass.
Rosanvallon, P. (1984) *La crise de l'État providence*. Paris: Seuil.
Rosenthal, E. (1956) *Averroes' Commentary on Plato's Republic*. Cambridge: Cambridge University Press.
Rosenthal, E. (1958) *Political Thought in Medieval Islam*. Cambridge: Cambridge University Press.
Ross, H.M. (1997) “Structure and Configuration in Comparative Politics”, in M.I. Lichbach and A.S. Zuckerman (eds) *Comparative Politics. Rationality, Culture and Structure*. Cambridge: Cambridge University Press.
Rostovtzeff, M. (1986) *Social and Economic History of the Hellenistic World*. Oxford: Oxford University Press.
Rostovtzeff, M (1988) *Histoire économique de l'Empire romain*, Paris: Laffont.
Rouadjia, A. (1990) *Les Frères et la mosque*. Paris: Khartala.
Roussillon, A. (1994) “Changer la société par le jihad”, in *Le phénomène de la violence*. Cairo: Dossier CEDEJ, 295–319.
Roy, O. (1994) *The Failure of Political Islam*. Cambridge, MA: Harvard University Press.
Roy, O. (2000) *The New Central Asia: Creation of Nations* London: I.B. Tauris.
Roy, O. (2004) *Globalised Islam: The Search for a New Ummah*. London: Hurst.
Roy, O. (2007) *Secularism Confronts Islam*. New York: Columbia University Press.
Roy, O. (2008) *The Politics of Chaos in the Middle East*. London: Hurst.
Safadi, M. (1990) *Al-hadâtha Mâ ba'ada al-hadâtha* (*Modernity, Postmodernity*). Beirut: Markez al-inma al-arabi.
Said, E.W. (1979) *Orientalism*. NewYork: Random House.
Said, E.W. (1993) *Culture and Imperialism*. New York: Knopf.
Said, E.W. (1994) *Des intellectuels et du pouvoir*. Paris: Seuil.
Said, E.W. (1997) *Covering Islam: How the Media and the Experts Determine How We See the Rest of the World*. London: Vintage.
Said, E.W. (2003) *Orientalism: Western Conceptions of the Orient*. Harmondsworth: Penguin Classics.
Saikal, A. (2003) *Islam and the West. Conflict or Cooperation?* Basingstoke: Palgrave Macmillan.
Sajoo, A. (ed.) (2002) *Civil Society in the Muslim World: Contemporary Perspectives*. London: I.B. Tauris.

Salamé, G. (1991) "Sur la causalité d'un manque: pourquoi le monde arabe n'est-il donc pas démocratique?" *Revue Française de Science politique*, 41(3) 307–341.

Salamé, G. (1992) *Démocratie sans démocrates*. Paris: Fayard; Trans. (1995) *Democracy without Democrats? The Renewal of Politics in the Muslim World*. New York: St Martin's Press.

Salvatore, A. (1996) "Beyond Orientalism? Max Weber and the Displacement of 'Essentialism' in the Study of Islam", *Arabica*, XLIII, 457–485.

Samuelson, K. (1993) *Religion and Economic Action: The Protestant Ethic, the Rise of Capitalism and the Abuses of Scholarship*. Toronto: University of Toronto Press.

Sanderson, S. (ed.) (1995) *Civilizations and World Systems*. Walnut Creek, CA: Altamira Press.

Sanson, H. (1983) *Laïcité islamique en Algérie*. Paris: CNRS.

Sayer, D. (1990) *Capitalism and Modernity: Excursus on Marx and Weber*. London: Routledge.

Schacht, J. (1926) "Die Arabishe hiyal Literatur", *Der Islam*, 15, 211–232.

Schacht, J. (1964) *An Introduction to Islamic Law*. Oxford: Oxford University Press.

Schacht, J. (1983) *An Introduction to Islamic Law*. Oxford: Oxford University Press; Trans. (1983) *Introduction au droit musulman*. Paris: Maisonneuve & Larose.

Schluchter, W. (1987) *Max Webers Sicht des Islams. Interpretation und Kritik*. Frankfurt: Suhrkamp.

Schluchter, W. (1989) *Rationalism, Religion and Domination*. Berkeley, CA: University of California Press.

Schumpeter, J.A. (1989) *Essays: On Entrepreneurs, Innovations, Business Cycles and the Evolution of Capitalism*. New Brunswick, NJ: Transaction.

Schwarz, R. (2002) "Human Rights Discource and Practice as Crisis Menagement: Insights from Algerai Case", *The Journal of North Africa*, 7(2) Summer, 57–85.

Schwedler, J. (1995) *Toward Civil Society in the Middle East*. London: Lynne Rienner.

Scruton, R. (2002) *The West and the Rest: Globalisation and the Terrorist Threat*. New York: Continuum.

Shadid, A. (2002) *Legacy of the Prophet: Despots, Democrats and the New Politics of Islam*. Boulder, CO: Westview Press.

Sharabi, H. (1988a) *Neopatriarchy: A Theory of Distorted Change in Arab Society*. New York: Oxford University Press; Trans. (1996) *Le néopatriarcat*. Paris: Mercure de France.

Sharabi, H. (ed.) (1988b) *The Next Decade. Alternative Future*. Boulder, CO: Westview Press.

Shariati, A. (1979) *On the Sociology of Islam*. Berkley, CA: Mizan Press.

Shariati, A. (1982) *Histoire et destinée*. Paris: Sindbad.

Shatzmiller, M. (2001) "Islamic Institutions and Property Rights: The Case of the 'Public Good' Waqf", *Journal of the Economic and Social History of the Orient*, 44(1) 44–74.

Shayegan, D. (1992) *Les illusions de l'identité*. Paris: Editions du Félin.

Shidyak, A.F. (1995) *The Unknown Works of Ahmed Faris Ash-Shidyak* [in Arabic]. London: Riad El-Rayyes.

Sivan, E. (1985) *Radical Islam. Medieval Theology and Modern Politics*. New Haven, CT: Yale University Press.

Sivan E. (1995) *Mythes politiques arabes*. Paris: Fayard/Esprit de la cité.

Sivan, E. (1997.) "Constraints & Opportunities in the Arab World ", *The Journal of Democracy*, 8(2) 102–113.

Skocpol, T. (1982) "Rentier State and Shi'a Islam in the Iranian Revolution", *Theory and Society*, 11(3) 265–283.

Snouck, H. (1888) *Mekka*, Vol. 1. The Hague: Nijhoff.

Sombart, W. (1932) *L'apogée du capitalisme*. Paris: Payot.

Sourdel, D. and J. Sourdel (1983) *La civilisation de l'Islam classique*. Paris: Arthaud.

Spencer, R. (2002) *Islam Unveiled: Disturbing Questions about the World's Fastest-Growing Faith*. San Francisco, CA: Encounter Books.

Spinoza, Ch. and H. Dreyfus (1996) "Two Kinds of Essentialism and their Consequences", *Critical Inquiry*, 22(4) 735–763 and (1997) 23(4) 910–932.

Springborg, P. (1986) "Politics, Primordialism and Orientalism: Marx, Aristotle, and the Myth of Gemeinschaft", *American Political Science Review*, 80(1) March.

Spuler, B. (1994a) *The Age of the Caliphs, History of the Muslim World*, Vol. 1. Princeton, NJ: Marcus Wiener.

Spuler, B. (1994b) *The Mongol Period, History of the Muslim World*, Vol. 2. Princeton, NJ: Marcus Wiener.

Stahnke, T. and R.C. Blitt (2005) *The Religion–State Relationship and the Right to Freedom of Religion or Belief: A Comparative Textual Analysis of the Constitutions of Predominantly Muslim Countries*. United States Commission on International Religious Freedom.

Stepan, A. (2000) "Religion, Democracy, and the 'Twin Tolerations'", *Journal of Democracy*, 11(4) 37–57.

St John, P. (1996) "Insurrection, légitimité et intervention en Algérie", Commentaire no. 65. Publications du Service Canadien du renseignement et de la sécurité, January.

Tabari (1958) *Chronique* [in Arabic], Vol. 1; In French, *Chronique de Tabari*, trans. Zotenberg, Vol. 3. Paris: G.-P. Maisonneuve.

Tahtawi, R. (1988) *L'Or de Paris*. Paris: Sindbad.

Takeyh, R. (2000) "Qadhafi's Libya and the Prospect of Islamic Succession", *Middle East Policy*, 7(2).

Takeyh, R. (2001) "The Rogue who Came in from the Cold", *Foreign Affairs*, 80(3) 62–72.

Talbi, M. and G. Jarczyk (2002) *Penseur libre en Islam*. Paris: Albin Michel.

Tawney, R.H. (1990) *Religion and the Rise of Capitalism*. Harmondsworth: Penguin Books.

Taylor, C. (1995) "Two Theories of Modernity ", *Hastings Center Report*, 25(2) March–April.

Taymi'yah, A.A.Ḥ.I. (1966) *Ibn Taimiyya on Public and Private Law in Islam: Or Public Policy in Islamic Jurisprudence*. Beirut: Khayats.

Temimi, A. (ed.) (2000) *Habib Bourguiba et l'établissement de l'État national: approches scientifiques du bourguibisme*. Zaghouan (Tunisie): Publication Fondation Temimi.

Tibi, B. (1998) *The Challenge of Fundamentalism. Political Islam and New World Disorder*. Berkeley, CA: University of California Press.

Tibi, B. (2000) *The Challenge of Fundamentalism: Political Islam and the New World Order.* Berkeley: University of California Press.

Tibi, B. (2009) *Islam's Predicament with Modernity.* London: Routledge.

Torres, M.R., J. Jordan and N. Horsburgh (2006) "Analysis and Evolution of the Global Jihadist Movement Propaganda", *Terrorism and Political Violence*, 18, 399–421.

Touraine, A. (1992) *Critique de la modernité*. Paris: Fayard.

Touraine, A. (1994) *Qu'est-ce que la démocratie?* Paris: Fayard.

Trifkovic, S. (2002) *The Sword of the Prophet: The Politically Incorrect Guide to Islam: History, Theology, Impact on the World*. Bend, OR: Regina Orthodox Press.

Trimingham, S. (1971) *The Sufi Orders in Islam*. London: Oxford University Press.

Troll, C. (1980) "Sayyid Ahmed Khan: A Reinterpretation of Muslim Theology", *Journal of Asian Studies*, 39, 394–396.

Turner, B.S. (1974) *Max Weber and Islam: A Critical Study*. London: Routledge & Kegan Paul.

Turner, B.S. (1978) *Marx and the End of Orientalism*. London: Allen and Unwin.

Turner, B.S. (1987) "Marx, Weber, and the Coherence of Ideology", in N. Wiley, *The Marx-Weber Debate*, 169–204. Beverly Hills, CA: Sage.

Turner, C. (2000) *The Muslim World.* Stroud: Sutton.

Turner, S. (2000) *The Cambridge Companion to Weber*. Cambridge: Cambridge University Press.

Ulrich, F. (1912) *Die Vorherbestimmungslehre im Islam und Christentum. Eine religionsgschichtliche Parallele*. Gütersloh: Bertelsmann.

Ursinus, M. (1989) "Zur Diskussion um 'millet' im Osmanischen Reich", *Südost–Forschungen*, 48, 195–207.

Urvoy, D. (1998) *Averroès*. Paris: Flammarion.

Vandewalle, D. (1998) *Libya Since Independence: Oil and State-building.* Ithaca, NY: Cornell University Press.

Van Krieken, G.S. (1976) *Khayr al-dîn et la Tunisie (1850–1881)*. Leiden: E.J. Brill.

Van Schendel W. and E.J. Zurcher (eds) (2000) *Identity Politics in Central Asia and the Muslim World*. London: I.B. Tauris.

Varshney, A. (2002) *Ethic Conflict and Civic Life: Hindus and Muslims in India*. London: Yale University Press.

Vattimo, G. (1987) *La fin de la modernité*. Paris: Seuil.

Verba, S. (1965) "Comparative Political Culture", in L.W. Pye and S. Verba (eds) *Culture and Political Development*. Princeton, NJ: Princeton University Press.

Vikor, K.S. (2005) *Between God and the Sultan. A History of Islamic Law*. London: Hurst.

Vogel, F.E. and S. L. Hayes (1998) *Islamic Law and Finance: Religion, Risk and Return*. Washington, DC: CQ Press.

Voll, J.O. (1994) "Islam as Special World System", *Journal of World History*, 5(2) 213–226.

Von Grunebaum, G.E. (1953) *Medieval Islam. A Study in Cultural Orientation*. Chicago, IL: University of Chicago Press.

Von Grunebaum, G.E. (1962) *L'Islam médiéval. Histoire et civilisation*. Paris: Payot.

Von Grunebaum, G.E. and K. Watson (1996) *Classical Islam, A History 600 AD–1258 AD*. New York: Barnes and Noble.

Wael, B.H. (2005) *The Origins and Evolution of Islamic Law*. Montreal: McGill University.

Wael, B.H. (1999) *A History of Islamic Legal Theories: An Introduction to Sunni usul al-fiqh*. Cambridge: Cambridge University Press.

Wahid, A. (2006) "Right Islam versus Wrong Islam", reprinted in H. Fradkin, H. Husain and E. Brown, *Current Trends in Islamic Ideology*, Vol. 3. Hudson Institute.

Wallerstein, I. (1974, 1980 and 1989) *The Modern World System*. Academic Press, 3 Volumes.

Wallerstein, I. (1979) *The Capitalist World Economy*. Cambridge University Press.

Wallerstein, I. (1983) *Historical Capitalism*. London: Verso; Trans. (1985) *Le capitalisme historique*. Paris: La découverte.

Walzer, R. (1970) *L'éveil de la philosohie islamique*. Paris: Geuthner, REI, 1.

Walzer, R. (1985) *Alfarabi On the Perfect State: Abû Nasr al-Farâbî's Mabâdi arâ ahl al-madîna al-fâdila*. Oxford: Oxford University Press.

Wasserman, J. (2001) *The Templars and the Assassins; The Militia of Heaven*. Rochester, VT: Inner Traditions.

Waterbury, J. (1979) "La légitimité du pouvoir au Maghreb: Tradition, protestation et répression", in *Développements politiques au Maghreb*. Paris: CNRS.

Watt, M. (1946) "Free Will and Predestination in Early Islam", *Moslem World*, 36, 131–132.

Watt, M. (1962) *Muhammad at Medina*. Oxford: Oxford University Press.

Watt, M. (1964) *Muhammad: Prophet and Statesman*. Oxford: Oxford University Press.

Watt, M. (1965) *Muhammad at Mecca*. Oxford: Oxford University Press.

Watt, M. (1985) "Islamic Alternatives to the Concept of Free Will", *La notion de liberté au Moyen Age: Islam, Byzance, Occident*, 15–24. Paris: Société d'édition.

Watt, M. (1995) *La pensée politique en Islam*. Paris: PUF.

Weber, M. (1913) "The Social Psychology of the World Religions" ("Die Wirtschaftsethik der Weltreligionen", 1913), in *From Max Weber: Essays in Sociology*. Gerth & Mills.

Weber, M. (1920) *Gesammelte Aufsätze zur Religionssoziologie I–III*. Tübingen: JCB Mohr.

Weber, M. (1922) *Gesammelte Aufsätze zur Wissenschaftslehre*. Tubingen: JCB Mohr.

Weber, M. (1949) *The Methodology of Social Sciences*. New York: The Free Press.

Weber, M. (1967) *Ancient Judaism*. New York: The Free Press.

Weber, M. (1968) *The Religion of China*. New York: The Free Press.

Weber, M. (1978) *Economy and Society*, Volumes I–II. Berkeley, CA: University of California Press.

Weber, M. (1981) *General Economic History*. New Brunswick, NJ: Transaction.

Weber, M. (1985) *The Protestant ethics and the Spirit of Capitalism*. London: Unwin Paperbacks.

Weber, M. (1988) *Max Weber: A Biography*. New Brunswick, NJ: Transaction.

Weber, M. (1988a) *Gesammelte Aufsätze zur Religionssoziologie I*. Stuttgart: UTB (Auflage: Nachdruck der Erstauflage, 1920).

Weber, M (1988b) *Gesammelte Aufsätze zur Religionssoziologie II*. Stuttgart: UTB.

Weber, M (1988c) *Gesammelte Aufsätze zur Religionssoziologie III*. Stuttgart: UTB.

Weber, M. (1988d) *Gesammelte Aufsätze: Zur Religionssoziologie I/III, Sozial- und Wirtschaftsgeschichte, Soziologie und Sozialpolitik, Wissenschaftslehre, Gesammelte Politische Schriften*: 7 Bände. Herausgeber: Marianne Weber, Johannes Winckelmann. Stuttgart: UTB.

Weber, M. (1991a) *Économie et société*, 1, Paris: Plon/Pocket.

Weber, M. (1991b) *Histoire économique*. Paris: Gallimard.

Weber, M. (1993) *The Sociology of Religion*. Boston, MA: Beacon Press.

Weber, M. (1995) *Économie et société*, Vol. 1. Paris: Plon.

Weber, M. (1996a) *The Religion of India*, trans. H. Gerth and ed. D. Martindale; First edn (1958) New Delhi: Munshiran Manoharlal.

Weber, M. (1996b) *Sociologie de la religion*. Paris: Gallimard.

Weber, M. (1996c) *Sociologie des religions*. Paris: Gallimard.

Weber, M. (1997) *Schriften zur Sozialgeschichte und Politik*. Reclam, Ditzingen.

Weber, M. (1998) *The Agrarian Sociology of Ancient Civilizations*. London: Verso.

Weber, M. (2001) *The Protestant Ethic and the Spirit of Capitalism*. London: Routledge.

Weber, M. and W.G. Runciman (eds) (1978) *Selections in Translation*. New York: Cambridge University Press.
Wedeen, L. (2003) "Beyond the Crusades: Why Huntington, and Bin Laden, are Wrong", *Middle East Policy*, X(2) 54–61.
Weiner, M. and S. Huntington (eds) (1987) *Understanding Political Development*. Boston, MA: Little, Brown.
Wellhausen J. (1909/1960) *Das Arabische Reich und sein Sturz*. Berlin: Walter de Gruyter.
Wellmer, A. (1988) "Dialectique de la modernité et de la postmodernité", *Cahiers de philosophie*, 5, Spring.
Wensinck, A.J. (1992) *Concordance et indices de la tradition musulmane*, 3 volumes. Leiden: Brill; First edn (1926).
Werenfels, I. (2002) "Obstacles to Privatization of State-owned Industries in Algeria: The Political Economy of an Distributive Conflict", *The Journal of North Africa*, 7(1) 1–28.
Whimster, S. (ed.) (2004) *The Essential Weber*. London: Routledge.
Wiktorowics, Q. and J. Kaltner (2003) "Killing in the Name of Islam: Al-Qaeda's Justification for September 11", *Middle East Policy*, X(2) 76–92.
Wiley, N. (ed.) (1987) *The Marx-Weber Debate*. Beverly Hills, CA: SAGE.
Willis, M. (1998) "Algeria's Other Islamists: Abdallah Jaballah and the Ennahdha Movement", *The Journal of North Africa*, 3(3) 46–70.
Wintle, J. (2003) *History of Islam*. London: Rough Guides.
Wittfogel, K.A. (1964) *Oriental Despotism: A Comparative Study of Total Power*. New Haven, CT: Yale University Press.
Wright, R. (1985) *The Sacred Rage*. New York: Linden Press.
Yacoubian, M. (2007) *Engaging Islamists and Promoting Democracy*. United States Institute of Peace, Special Report 190, www.usip.org
Yeor, B. (2002) *Minorities in the Middle East: A History of Struggle and Self-Expression*. Jefferson, NC: McFarland.
Zakariya, F. (1991) *Laïcité ou islamisme*. Paris: La Découverte.
Zartman, W.I. (1992) "Democracy and Islam: The Cultural Dialectic", *Annals of Academy of Political and Social Science*, 524, November, 181–191.
Zartman, W. (1995) *Collapsed States. The Disintegration and Restauration of Legitimate Authority*. Boulder, CO: Lynne Rienner; Trans. (1997) *L'effondrement de l'État*. Paris: Nouveaux horizons.
Zeiden, D. (2003) *The Resurgence of Religion, a Comparative Study of Selected Themes in Christian and Islamic Dscourses*. Leiden: Brill.
Zghal, A. (1991) "Le concept de société civile et la transition vers le multipartisme", in M. Camau (ed.) (1991) *Changements politiques au Maghreb*. Paris: CNRS.
Ziad, A.A. (1994) *Islamic Fundamentalism in the West Bank and Gaza: Muslim Brotherhood and Islamic Jihad*. Bloomington, IN: Indiana University Press.
Zimmerman, J.C. (2004) "Sayyid Qotb's Influence on the September 11 Attacks", *Terrorism and Political Violence*, 16(2) 222–252.

Zubaida, S. (1989) *Islam, the People and the State: Essay on Political Ideas and Movements in the Middle East*. New York: Routledge.
Zoubir, Y. (ed.) (1999) *North Africa in Transition: State, Society, and Economic Transformation in the 1990s*. Gainesville, FL: University Press of Florida.
Zoubir, Y. (2000) "Algerian Democratic Transition under Bouteflika's Rule: One Step Forward or Two Steps Back?", *Civil Society*, 9(101).

Press of the FIS

La Cause, official foreign publication of the FIS.

Press of independent Algeria

El Watan, daily Algerian independent in French language.
Le Matin, daily Algerian independent in French language.

Arab Press

Al Hayat, Arab daily published in London.

Sources for Tables and Appendix

World Bank (2000) World Development Indicators 2000, Washington, DC: World Bank (CD-ROM).
Barrett, D.B. et al. (2001) World Christian Encyclopedia: A Comparative Study of Churches and Religions in the Modern World, 2nd ed., Oxford: Oxford University Press.
Freedom House (annually) Annual Survey of Freedom House Country Scores; available from <http://www.freedomhouse.org>.
Encyclopaedia Britannica (annually), Britannica World Data, Chicago, IL: Encyclopaedia Britannica.

Index

Page numbers in **bold** refer to main discussion; *a* indicates appendices; *passim* denotes numerous scattered references within page range.